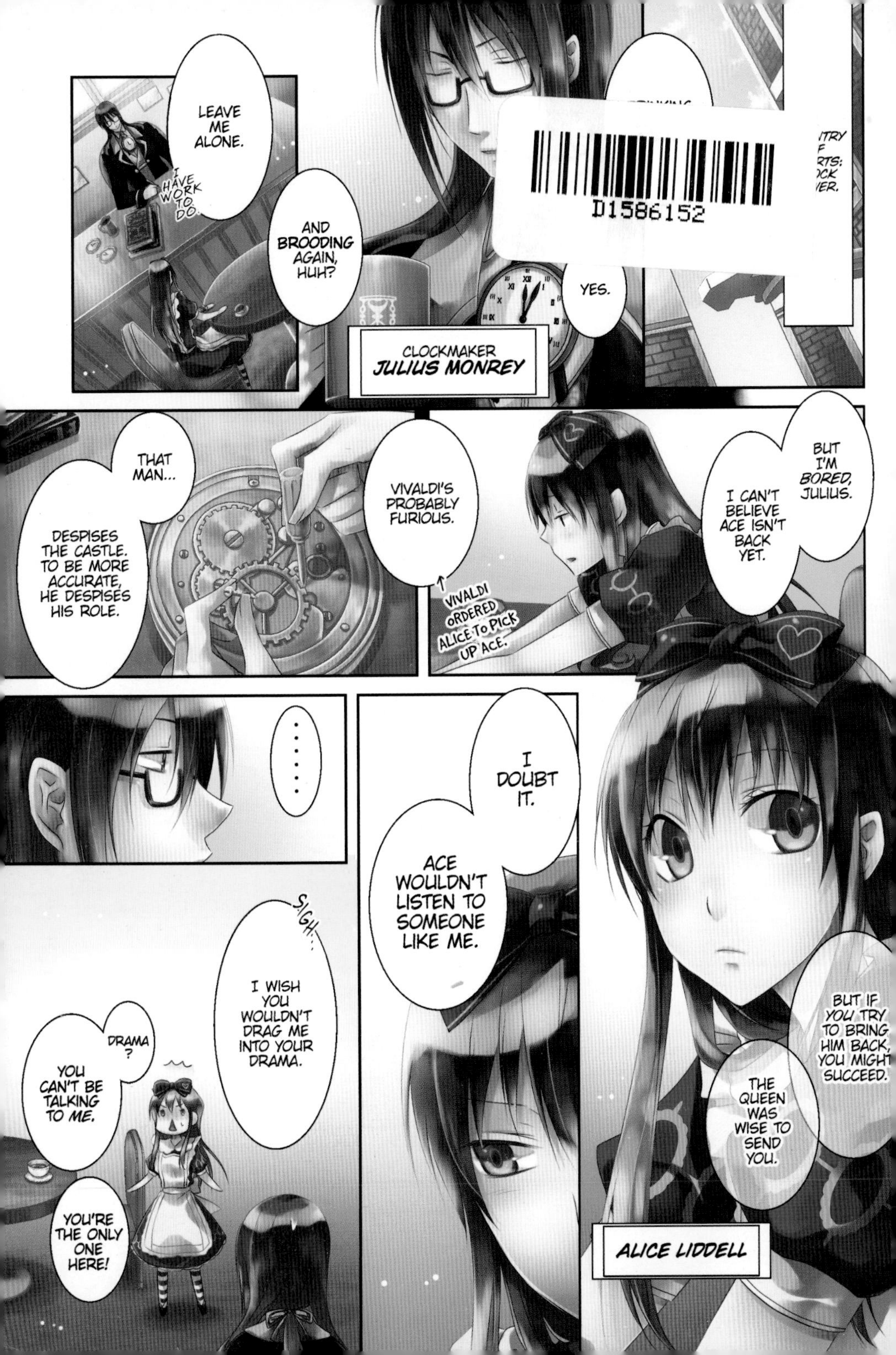
D1586152
AND BROODING AGAIN, HUH?
YES.
CLOCKMAKER JULIUS MONREY
LEAVE ME ALONE.
I HAVE WORK TO DO.
BUT I'M *BORED*, JULIUS.
I CAN'T BELIEVE ACE ISN'T BACK YET.
VIVALDI'S PROBABLY FURIOUS.
VIVALDI ORDERED ALICE TO PICK UP ACE.
THAT MAN...
DESPISES THE CASTLE. TO BE MORE ACCURATE, HE DESPISES HIS ROLE.
I DOUBT IT.
ACE WOULDN'T LISTEN TO SOMEONE LIKE ME.
BUT IF *YOU* TRY TO BRING HIM BACK, YOU MIGHT SUCCEED.
THE QUEEN WAS WISE TO SEND YOU.
ALICE LIDDELL
......
SIGH...
I WISH YOU WOULDN'T DRAG ME INTO YOUR DRAMA.
DRAMA?
YOU CAN'T BE TALKING TO *ME*.
YOU'RE THE ONLY ONE HERE!

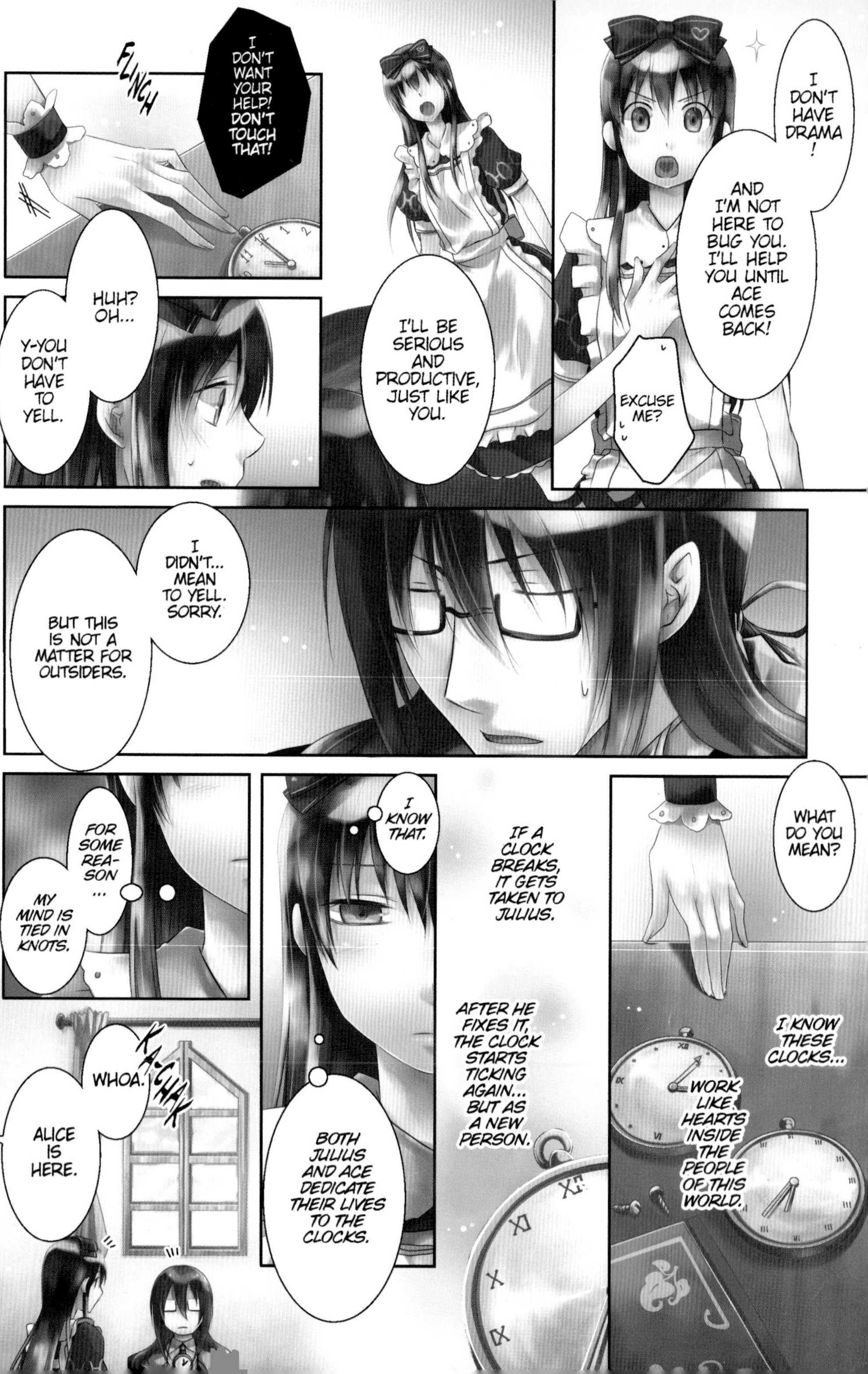

I DON'T HAVE DRAMA!
AND I'M NOT HERE TO BUG YOU. I'LL HELP YOU UNTIL ACE COMES BACK!
EXCUSE ME?
I'LL BE SERIOUS AND PRODUCTIVE, JUST LIKE YOU.
I DON'T WANT YOUR HELP! DON'T TOUCH THAT!
FLINCH
HUH? OH...
Y-YOU DON'T HAVE TO YELL.
I DIDN'T... MEAN TO YELL. SORRY.
BUT THIS IS NOT A MATTER FOR OUTSIDERS.
WHAT DO YOU MEAN?
I KNOW THESE CLOCKS...
WORK LIKE HEARTS INSIDE THE PEOPLE OF THIS WORLD.
IF A CLOCK BREAKS, IT GETS TAKEN TO JULIUS.
AFTER HE FIXES IT, THE CLOCK STARTS TICKING AGAIN... BUT AS A NEW PERSON.
I KNOW THAT.
BOTH JULIUS AND ACE DEDICATE THEIR LIVES TO THE CLOCKS.
FOR SOME REASON...
MY MIND IS TIED IN KNOTS.
KA-CHAK
WHOA.
ALICE IS HERE.

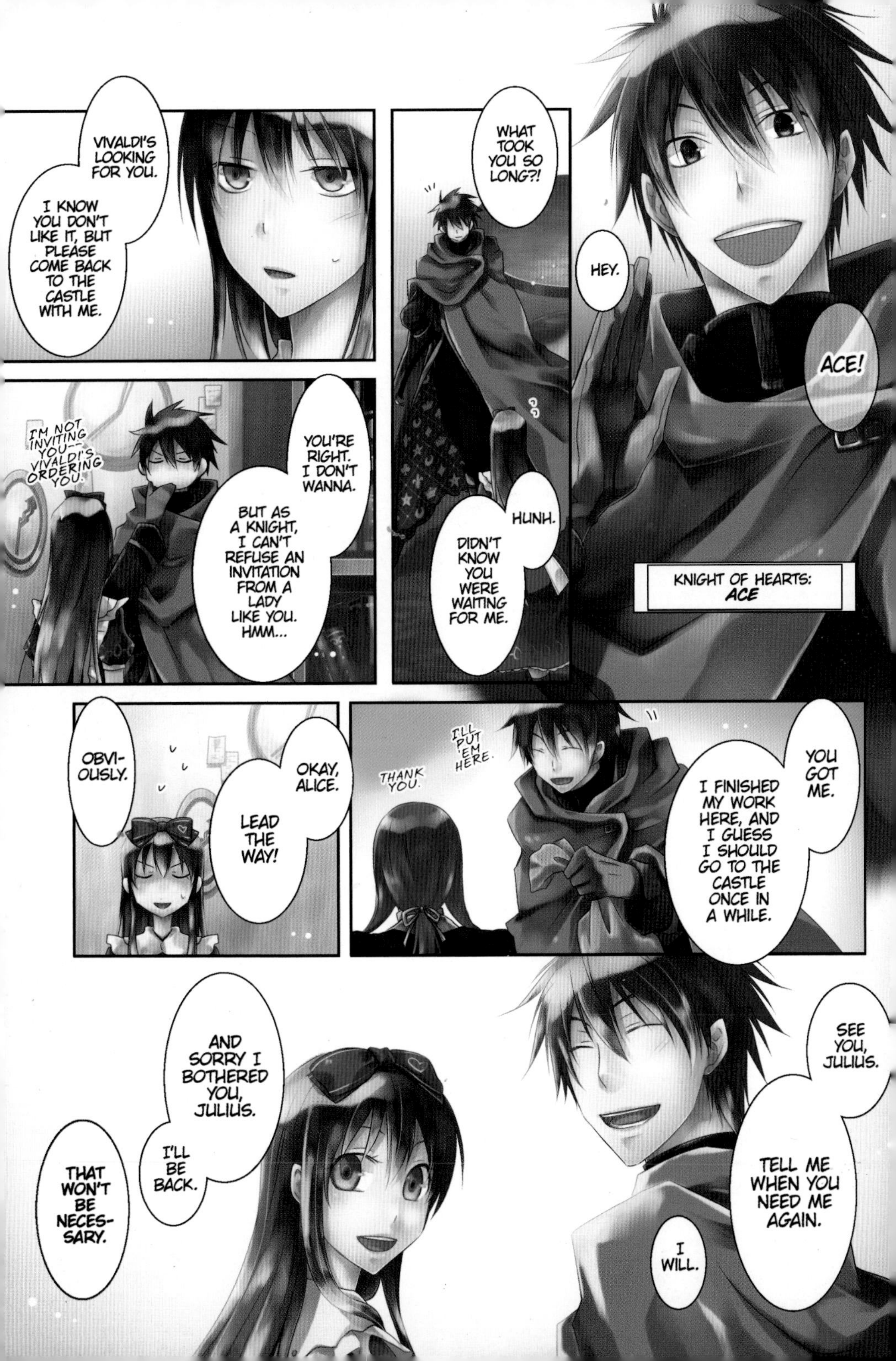
HEY.
ACE!
KNIGHT OF HEARTS: ACE
WHAT TOOK YOU SO LONG?!
HUNH.
DIDN'T KNOW YOU WERE WAITING FOR ME.
VIVALDI'S LOOKING FOR YOU.
I KNOW YOU DON'T LIKE IT, BUT PLEASE COME BACK TO THE CASTLE WITH ME.
YOU'RE RIGHT. I DON'T WANNA.
BUT AS A KNIGHT, I CAN'T REFUSE AN INVITATION FROM A LADY LIKE YOU. HMM...
I'M NOT INVITING YOU-- VIVALDI'S ORDERING YOU.
YOU GOT ME.
I FINISHED MY WORK HERE, AND I GUESS I SHOULD GO TO THE CASTLE ONCE IN A WHILE.
I'LL PUT 'EM HERE.
THANK YOU.
OKAY, ALICE.
LEAD THE WAY!
OBVI-OUSLY.
SEE YOU, JULIUS.
TELL ME WHEN YOU NEED ME AGAIN.
I WILL.
AND SORRY I BOTHERED YOU, JULIUS.
I'LL BE BACK.
THAT WON'T BE NECES-SARY.

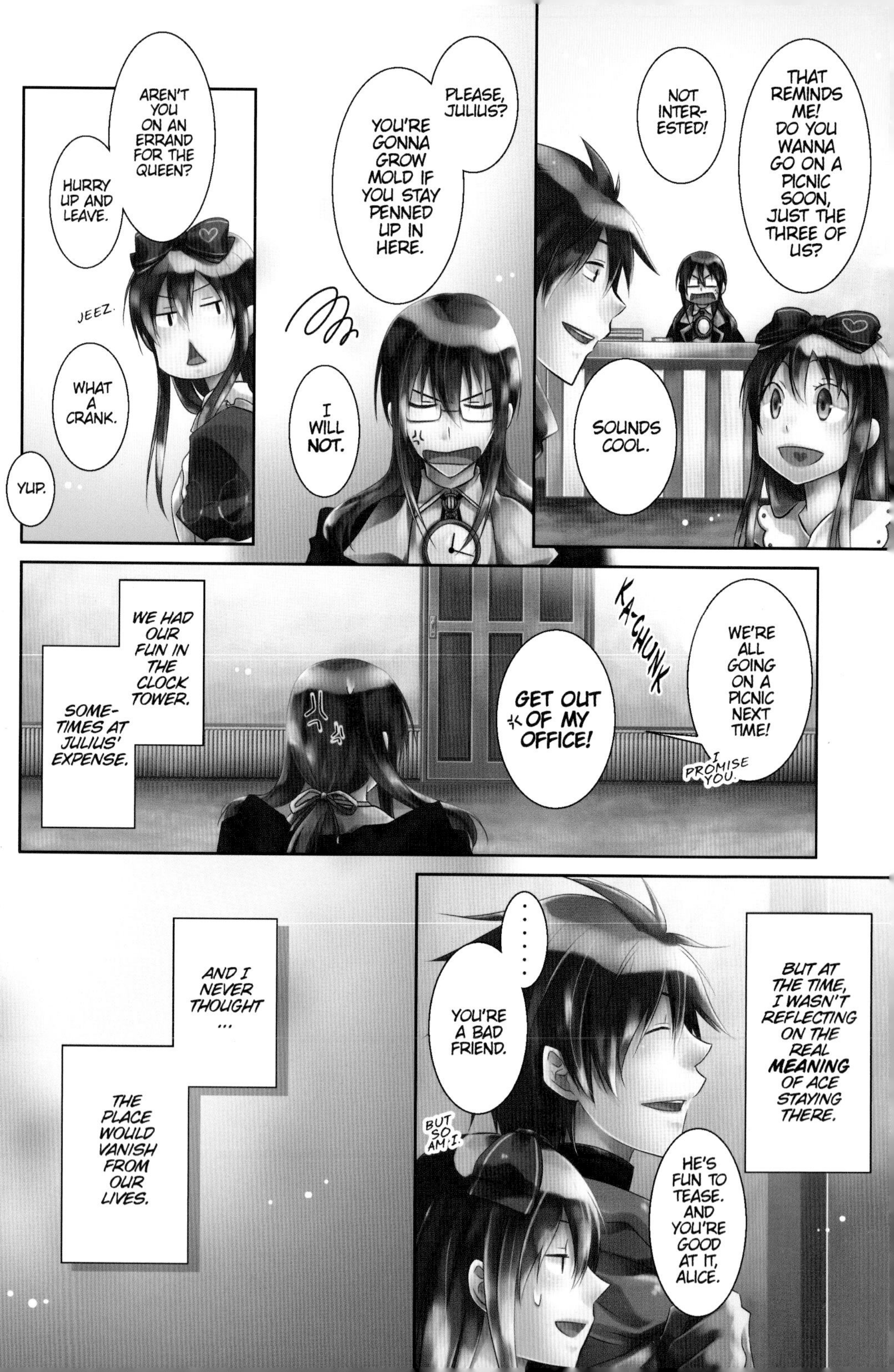
THAT REMINDS ME! DO YOU WANNA GO ON A PICNIC SOON, JUST THE THREE OF US?
NOT INTER-ESTED!
SOUNDS COOL.
PLEASE, JULIUS?
YOU'RE GONNA GROW MOLD IF YOU STAY PENNED UP IN HERE.
I WILL NOT.
AREN'T YOU ON AN ERRAND FOR THE QUEEN?
HURRY UP AND LEAVE.
JEEZ.
WHAT A CRANK.
YUP.
KA-CHUNK
WE'RE ALL GOING ON A PICNIC NEXT TIME!
I PROMISE YOU.
GET OUT OF MY OFFICE!
WE HAD OUR FUN IN THE CLOCK TOWER.
SOME-TIMES AT JULIUS' EXPENSE.
BUT AT THE TIME, I WASN'T REFLECTING ON THE REAL MEANING OF ACE STAYING THERE.
......
HE'S FUN TO TEASE. AND YOU'RE GOOD AT IT, ALICE.
YOU'RE A BAD FRIEND.
BUT SO AM I.
AND I NEVER THOUGHT ...
THE PLACE WOULD VANISH FROM OUR LIVES.

Alice in the Country of Clover
~Ace of Hearts~

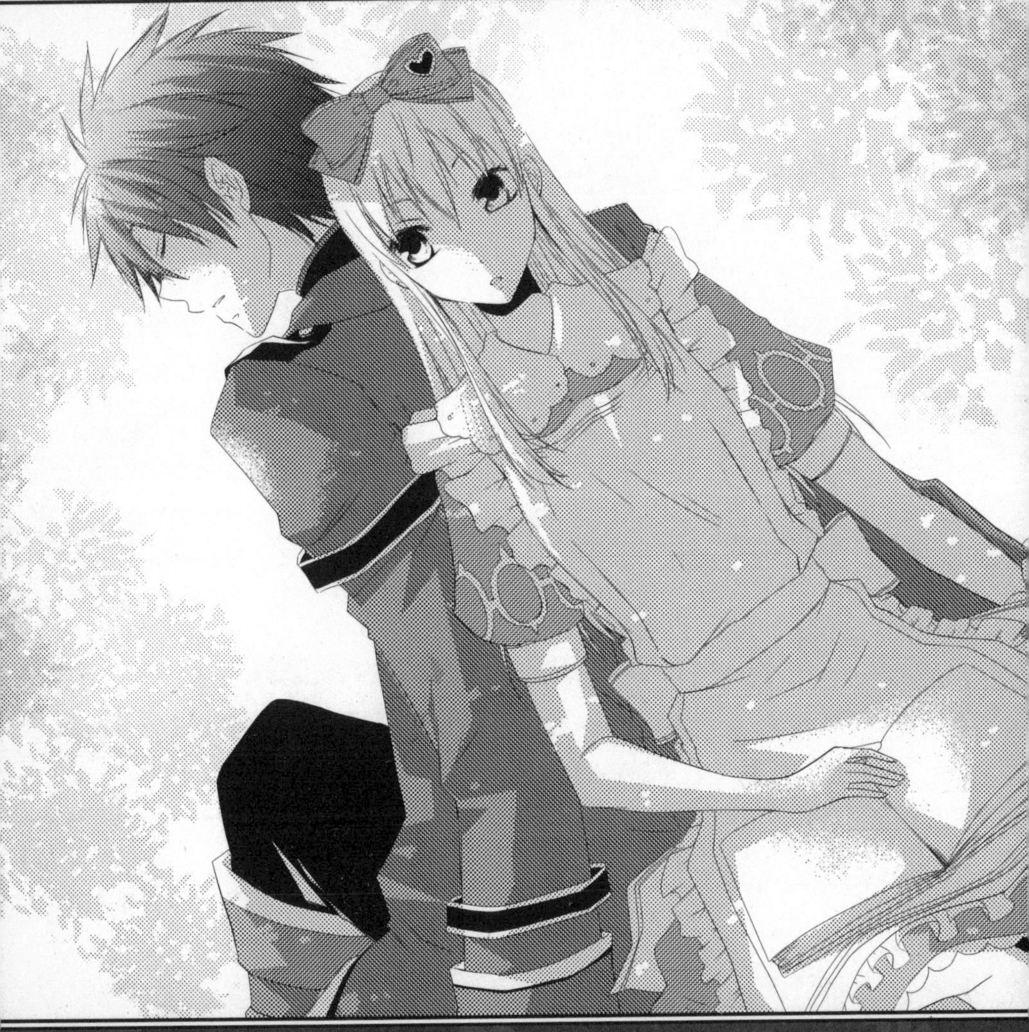

Mamenosuke Fujimaru
藤丸 豆ノ介

Alice IN THE COUNTRY OF Clover
ACE OF HEARTS

story by **QuinRose**
art by **Mamenosuke Fujimaru**

STAFF CREDITS

translation	**Angela Liu**
adaptation	**Lianne Sentar**
lettering	**Roland Amago**
layout	**Bambi Eloriaga-Amago**
cover design	**Nicky Lim**
proofreader	**Shanti Whitesides**
editor	**Adam Arnold**
publisher	**Jason DeAngelis** **Seven Seas Entertainment**

ALICE IN THE COUNTRY OF CLOVER: ACE OF HEARTS
Copyright © Mamenosuke Fujimaru / QuinRose 2010
First published in Japan in 2010 by ICHIJINSHA Inc., Tokyo.
English translation rights arranged with ICHIJINSHA Inc., Tokyo, Japan.

ISBN: 978-1-937867-40-9

Printed in Canada

First Printing: June 2013

10 9 8 7 6 5 4 3 2

FOLLOW US ONLINE: www.gomanga.com

READING DIRECTIONS

This book reads from *right to left*, Japanese style.
If this is your first time reading manga, you start
reading from the top right panel on each page and
take it from there. If you get lost, just follow the
numbered diagram here. It may seem backwards
at first, but you'll get the hang of it! Have fun!!

QuinRoseBox

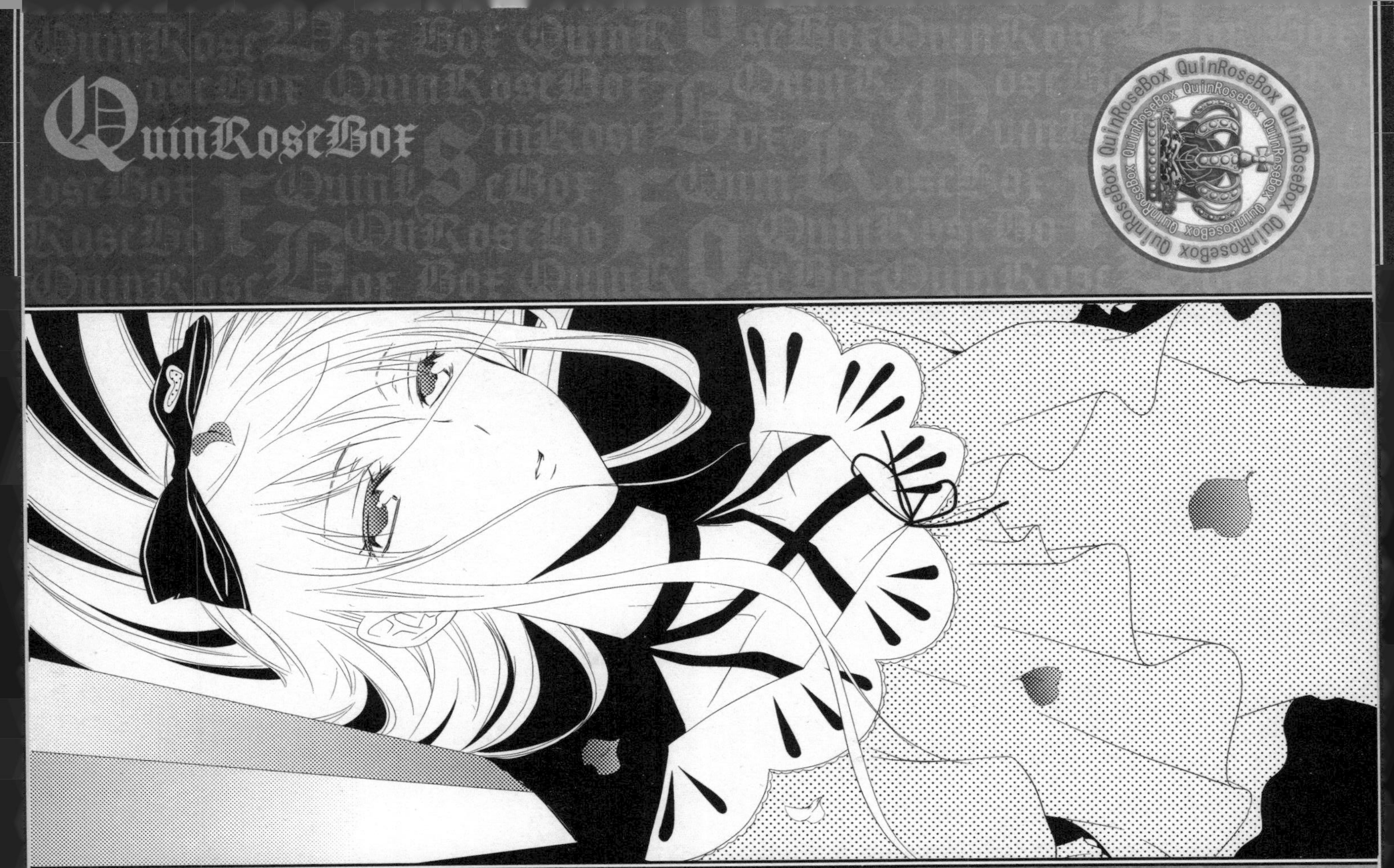

Alice in the Country of Hearts

ハートの国の
アリス

~ Wonderful Wonder World ~

- STORY -

This is a love adventure game. It is based on *Alice in Wonderland,* but evolves into a completely different story.

The main character is far from a romantic. In fact, she's especially sick of love relationships.

She's pulled (against her will) into the dangerous Country of Hearts, which is not as peaceful as the name makes it sound. The Hatters are a mafia family and even the employees of the Amusement Park carry weapons.

The leaders of the three domains are constantly trying to kill each other. Many of the skirmishes are the result of territory grabs by three major powers trying to control more land: the Hatter, the Queen of Hearts, and Gowland.

After drinking some strange medicine (again, against her will), the main character is unable to return to her world. She quickly decides that she's trapped in a dream and allows herself to enjoy(?) the extraordinary experience she's been thrown into.

What territory will she stay with and who will she interact with to get herself home? And will this girl, so jaded about love, fall into a relationship she doesn't expect?

Alice in Country of Hearts Character Information

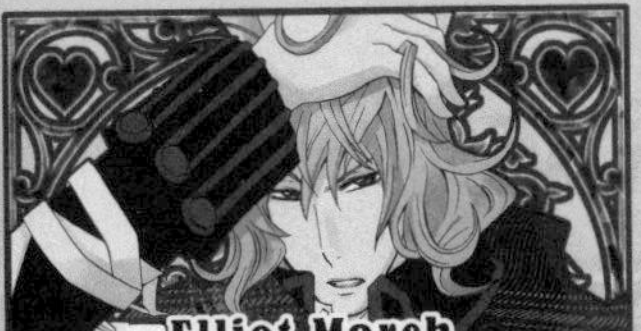

Elliot March
VA: Tsuguo Mogami

The No. 2 of the Hatter Family and Blood's right-hand man, Elliot is an ex-criminal and an escaped convict. Very short-tempered, he used to be a "very bad guy" who shot before asking questions. After partnering up with Blood, he rounded out and changed to a "slightly bad guy" who thinks for about three seconds before shooting. In his mind, this is a vast improvement.

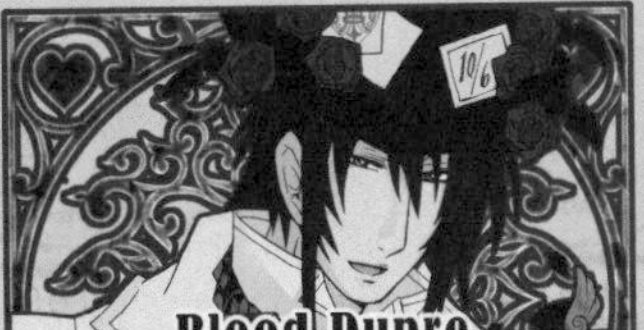

Blood Dupre
VA: Katsuyuki Konishi

The dangerous leader of the crime syndicate known as the Hatter Family. Since he enjoys plotting more than working directly, he controls everything from the shadows. He's incredibly smart, but due to his temperamental moods and his desire to keep things "interesting," he often digs his own grave in his secret plans.

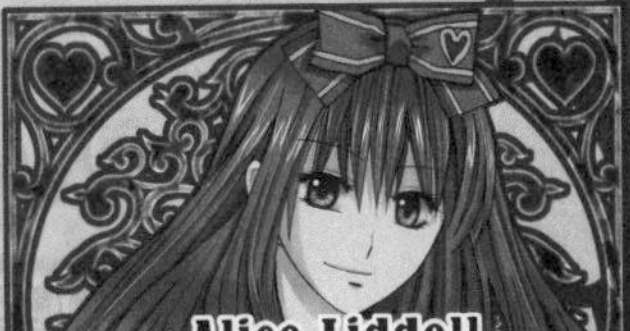

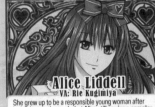

Alice Liddell
VA: Rie Kugimiya

She grew up to be a responsible young woman after losing her mother early, but Alice still carries a complex toward her older sister. She respects her older sister very much, but is frustrated about always being compared to her. Since her first love fell for her older sister, she has no confidence in herself when it comes to romance.

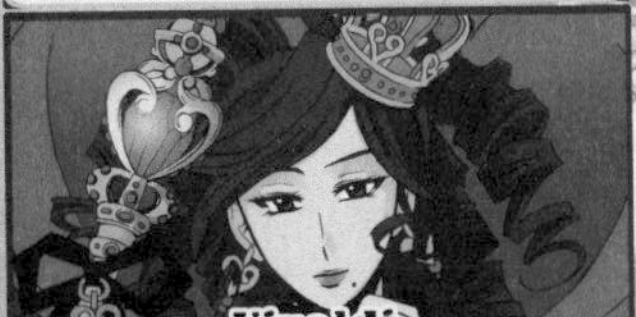

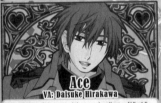

Vivaldi
VA: Yuuko Kaida

Ruthless and cruel, the Queen of Hearts is an arrogant beauty with a wild temper. She's enemies with the Hatter and Gowland. Impatient at heart, Vivaldi takes her fury out on everyone around her including her subordinates, whom she considers pawns. Anyone **not** working for her doesn't even register as existing.

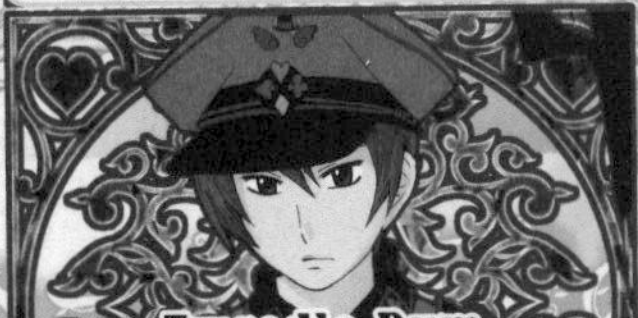

Tweedle Dum
VA: Jun Fukuyama

The second "Bloody Twin" and a dead ringer for his brother—in both appearance and personality. As they often change places, it's uncertain which one is the older twin.

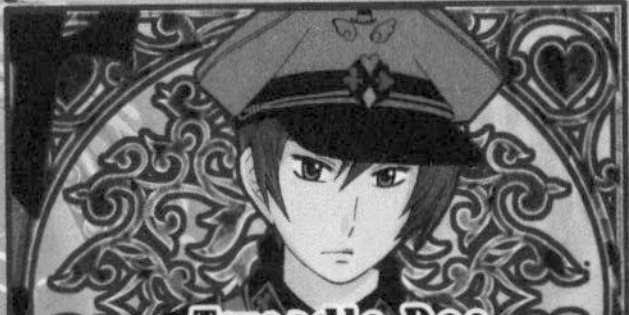

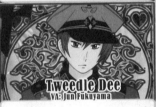

Tweedle Dee
VA: Jun Fukuyama

Gatekeeper of the Hatter territory, and one of the dark, sneaky twins. They sometimes show an innocent side, but they usually have a malicious agenda. Also known as the "Bloody Twins" due to their unsavory activities.

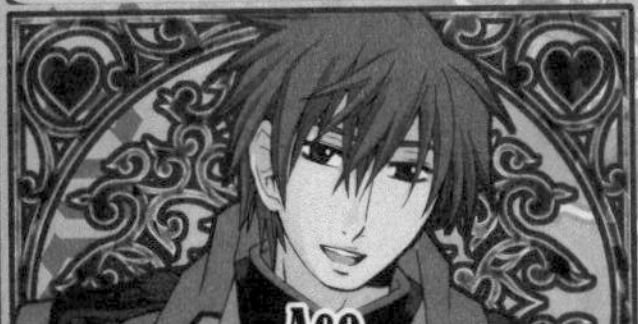

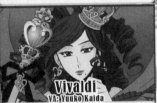

Ace
VA: Daisuke Hirakawa

The knight of Hearts and the ex-subordinate of Vivaldi. He's left the castle and is currently wandering. He's a very unlucky and unfortunate man, yet remains strangely positive, thus he tends to plow forward and make mistakes that only worsen his situation. He's one of the few friends of the clockmaker, Julius.

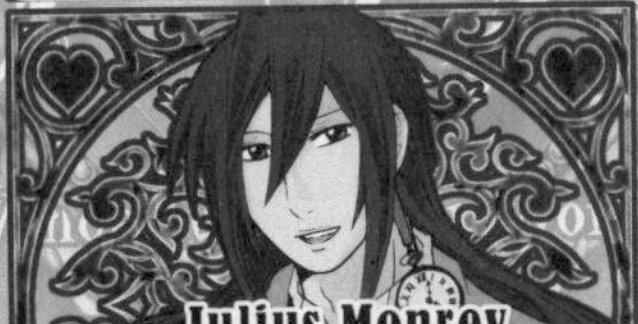

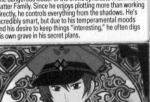

Julius Monrey
VA: Takehito Koyasu

The clockmaker, a gloomy machine expert who easily falls into depression. He lives in the Clock Tower and doesn't get out much. He always thinks of everything in the most negative way and tends to distrust people, but he gets along with Ace.
He had some part in the imprisonment of the March Hare, Elliot, and is thus the target of Elliot's hatred.

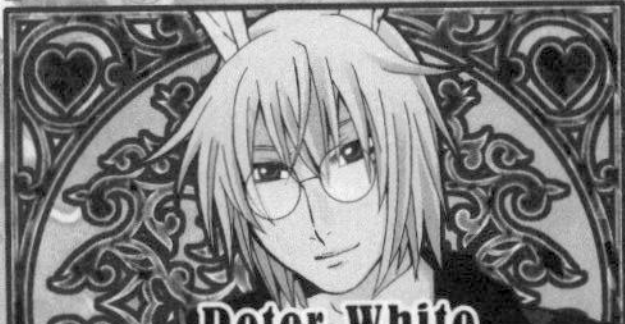

Peter White
VA: Kouki Miyata

Don't be fooled by the cute ears—Peter is the dangerous guide who dragged Alice to Wonderland in the first place. He claims to always be worried about the time, despite having a strange grasp on it. Rumors say his heart is as black as his hair is white.

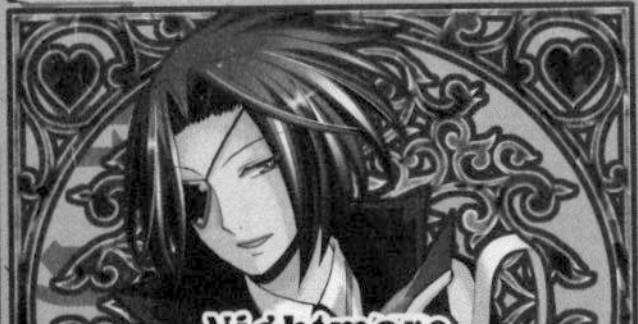

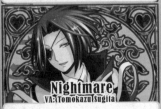

Nightmare
VA: Tomokazu Sugita

A sickly nightmare. He appears in Alice's dream, sometimes to guide her—and other times, to **misguide** her.

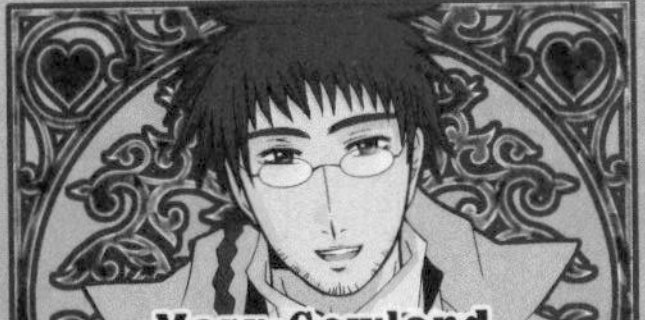

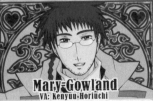

Mary Gowland
VA: Kenyuu Horiuchi

The owner of the Amusement Park. He hides his hated first name, Mary, but pretty much everyone already knows it. His full name is a play on words that sounds like "Merry Go Round" when said quickly. If his musical talent was given a numerical value, it would be closer to negatives than zero.

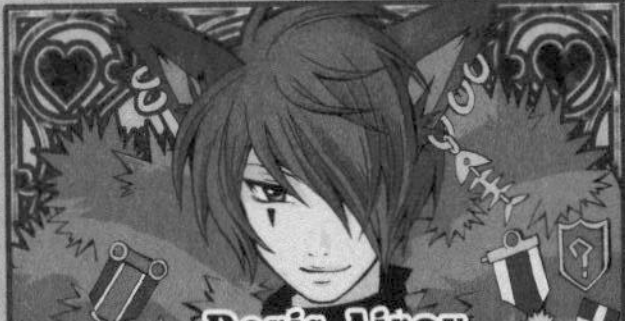

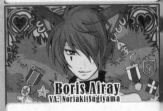

Boris Airay
VA: Noriaki Sugiyama

A riddle-loving cat with a signature smirk. He sometimes gives hints to his riddles, but the hints usually just cause more confusion. He also has a tendency to pose questions and never answer them.

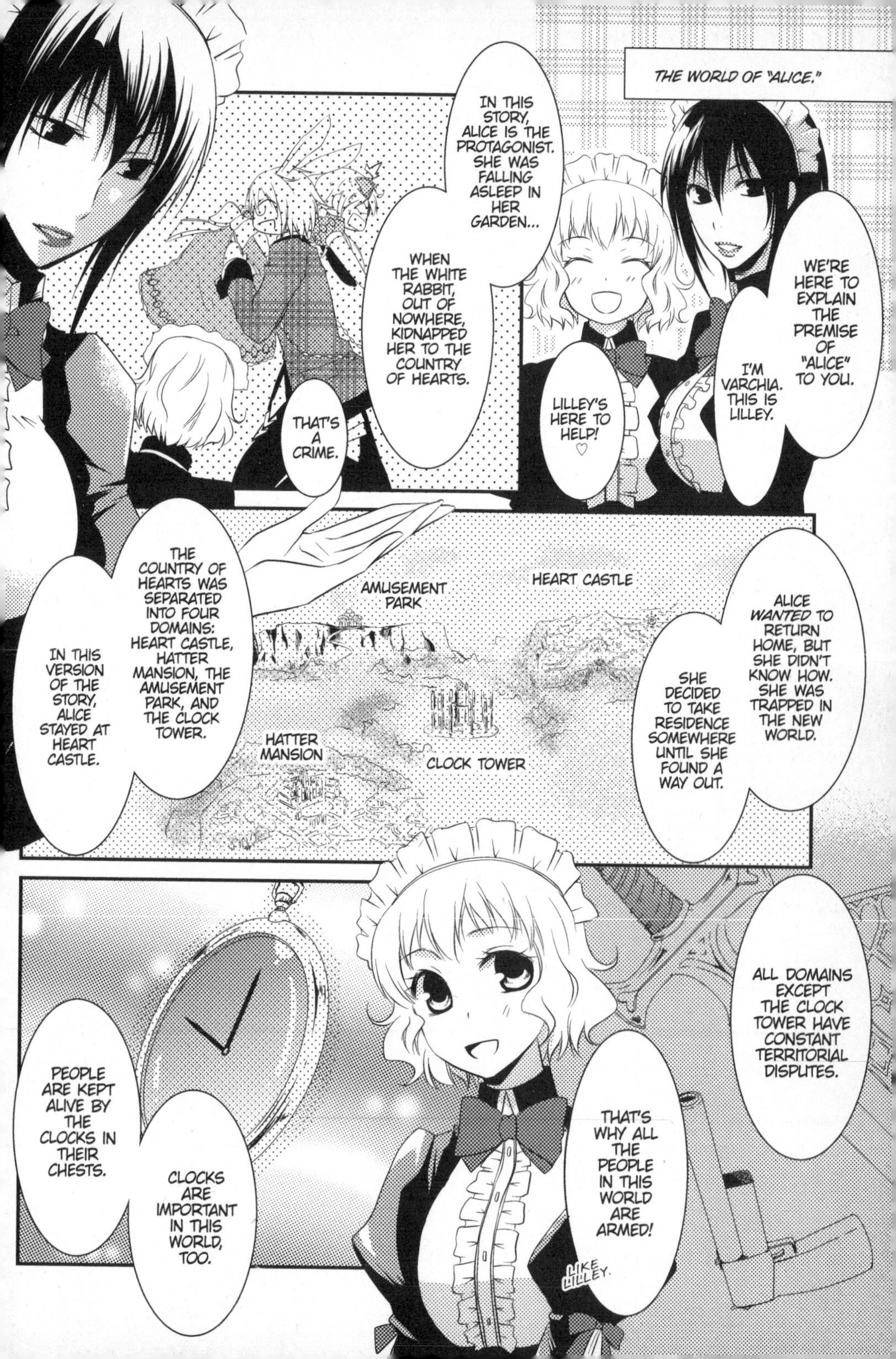
THE WORLD OF "ALICE."
WE'RE HERE TO EXPLAIN THE PREMISE OF "ALICE" TO YOU.
I'M VARCHIA. THIS IS LILLEY.
LILLEY'S HERE TO HELP! ♡
IN THIS STORY, ALICE IS THE PROTAGONIST. SHE WAS FALLING ASLEEP IN HER GARDEN...
WHEN THE WHITE RABBIT, OUT OF NOWHERE, KIDNAPPED HER TO THE COUNTRY OF HEARTS.
THAT'S A CRIME.
ALICE *WANTED* TO RETURN HOME, BUT SHE DIDN'T KNOW HOW. SHE WAS TRAPPED IN THE NEW WORLD.
SHE DECIDED TO TAKE RESIDENCE SOMEWHERE UNTIL SHE FOUND A WAY OUT.
HEART CASTLE
AMUSEMENT PARK
CLOCK TOWER
HATTER MANSION
THE COUNTRY OF HEARTS WAS SEPARATED INTO FOUR DOMAINS: HEART CASTLE, HATTER MANSION, THE AMUSEMENT PARK, AND THE CLOCK TOWER.
IN THIS VERSION OF THE STORY, ALICE STAYED AT HEART CASTLE.
ALL DOMAINS EXCEPT THE CLOCK TOWER HAVE CONSTANT TERRITORIAL DISPUTES.
THAT'S WHY ALL THE PEOPLE IN THIS WORLD ARE ARMED!
LIKE LILLEY.
PEOPLE ARE KEPT ALIVE BY THE CLOCKS IN THEIR CHESTS.
CLOCKS ARE IMPORTANT IN THIS WORLD, TOO.

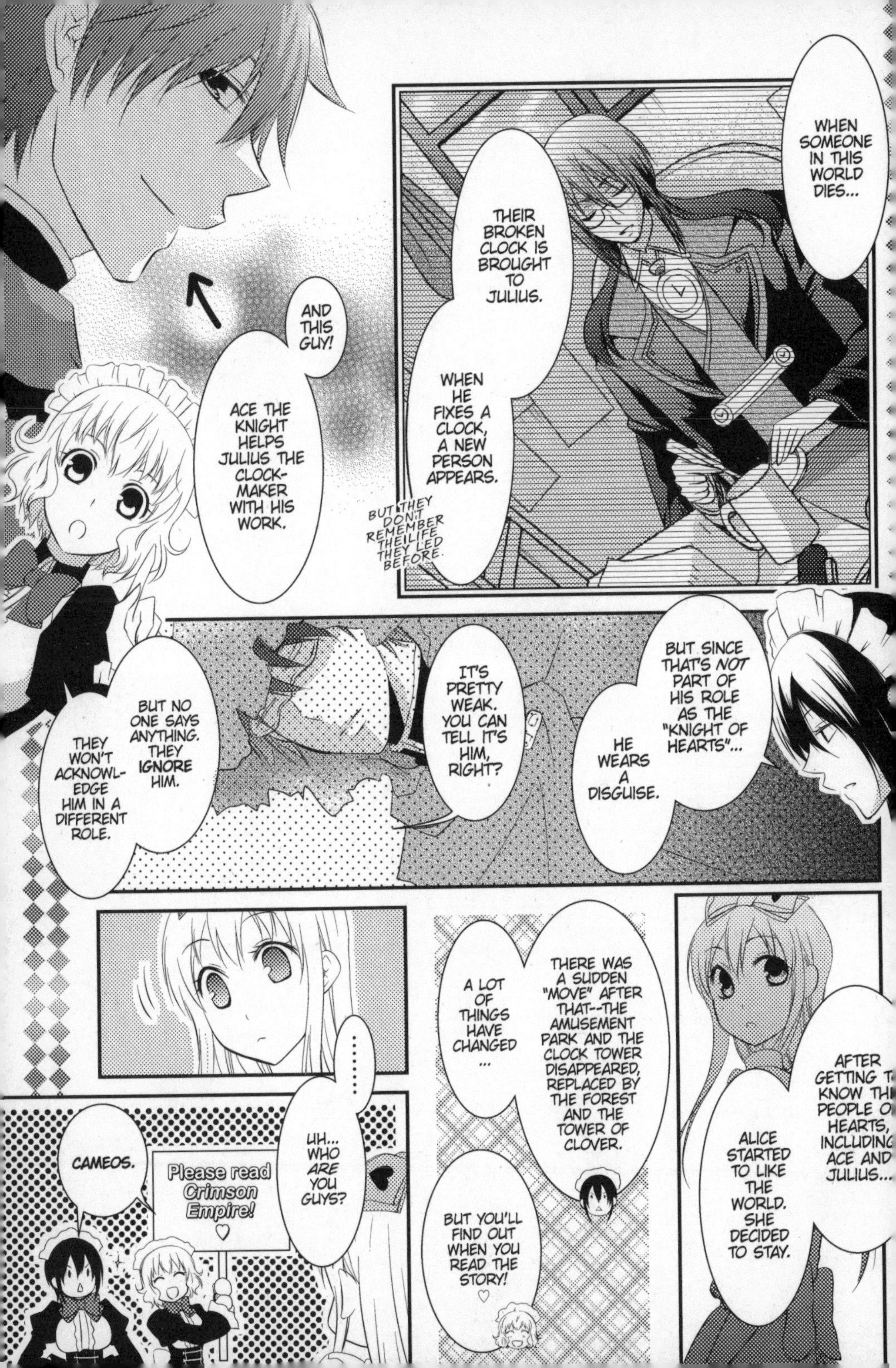
WHEN SOMEONE IN THIS WORLD DIES...
THEIR BROKEN CLOCK IS BROUGHT TO JULIUS.
WHEN HE FIXES A CLOCK, A NEW PERSON APPEARS.
BUT THEY DON'T REMEMBER THEILIFE THEY LED BEFORE.
AND THIS GUY!
ACE THE KNIGHT HELPS JULIUS THE CLOCK-MAKER WITH HIS WORK.
BUT SINCE THAT'S *NOT* PART OF HIS ROLE AS THE "KNIGHT OF HEARTS"...
HE WEARS A DISGUISE.
IT'S PRETTY WEAK. YOU CAN TELL IT'S HIM, RIGHT?
BUT NO ONE SAYS ANYTHING. THEY **IGNORE** HIM.
THEY WON'T ACKNOWL-EDGE HIM IN A DIFFERENT ROLE.
AFTER GETTING T KNOW TH PEOPLE O HEARTS, INCLUDING ACE AND JULIUS...
ALICE STARTED TO LIKE THE WORLD. SHE DECIDED TO STAY.
THERE WAS A SUDDEN "MOVE" AFTER THAT--THE AMUSEMENT PARK AND THE CLOCK TOWER DISAPPEARED, REPLACED BY THE FOREST AND THE TOWER OF CLOVER.
A LOT OF THINGS HAVE CHANGED ...
BUT YOU'LL FIND OUT WHEN YOU READ THE STORY! ♡
......
UH... WHO *ARE* YOU GUYS?
Please read *Crimson Empire!* ♡
CAMEOS.

Alice in the Country of Clover

クローバーの国の
アリス

~Wonderful Wonder World~

- STORY -

In *Alice in the Country of Clover*, the game starts with Alice having not fallen in love, but still deciding to stay in Wonderland.

She's acquainted with all the characters from the previous game, *Alice in the Country of Hearts.*

Since love would now start from a place of friendship rather than passion with a new stranger, she can experience a different type of romance from that in the previous game. Her dynamic with the characters is different because of this friendship—characters can't always be forceful with her, and in many ways it's more comfortable to grow intimate. The relationships *between* the Ones With Duties have also become more of a factor.

In this game, the story focuses on Heart Castle. Alice attends the suited meetings (forcefully) and gets involved in various gunfights (forcefully), among other things.

Land fluctuations, sea creatures in the forest, and whispering doors—it's a game more fantastic and more eerie than the first.

Will our everywoman Alice be able to have a romantic relationship in a world devoid of common sense?

Alice in the Country of Clover
Character Information

Elliot March
VA: Tsuguo Mogami

Blood's right-hand man has a criminal past... and a temperamental present. But he's not as bad as he used to be, so that's something. Joining Blood has been good(?) for him.

Blood Dupre
VA: Katsuyuki Konishi

The head of the mafia Hatter Family, Blood is a cunning yet moody puppet-master. Alice now has the pleasure of having him for a landlord.

Alice Liddell
VA: Rie Kugimiya

A normal girl with a bit of a chip on her shoulder. Deciding to stay in the Wonderland she was carried to, she's adapted to her strange new lifestyle.

Vivaldi
VA: Yuuko Kaida

The beautiful Queen of Hearts has an unrivaled temper—which is really saying something in Wonderland. Although a picture-perfect Mad Queen, she cares for Alice as if Alice were her little sister...or a very interesting plaything.

Tweedle Dum
VA: Jun Fukuyama

The second "Bloody Twin" is equally cute and equally scary. In Clover, Dum can also turn into an adult.

Tweedle Dee
VA: Jun Fukuyama

One of the "Bloody Twin" gatekeepers of the Hatter territory, Dee can be cute when he's not being terrifying. In Clover, he sometimes turns into an adult.

Boris Airay
VA: Noriaki Sugiyama

This riddle-loving cat has a signature smirk—and in Clover, a new toy. One of his favorite pastimes is giving the Sleepy Mouse a hard time.

Ace
VA: Daisuke Hirakawa

The unlucky knight of Hearts was a former subordinate of Vivaldi and is perpetually lost. Even though he's depressed to be separated from his friend and boss Julius, he stays positive and tries to overcome it with a smile. He seems like a classic nice guy... or is he?

Peter White
VA: Kouki Miyata

The Prime Minister of Heart Castle—who has rabbit ears growing out of his head—invited (kidnapped) Alice to Wonderland. He loves Alice and hates everything else. His cruel, irrational actions are disturbing, but he acts like a completely different person (rabbit?) when in the throes of his love for Alice.

Gray Ringmarc
VA: Kazuya Nakai

Nightmare's subordinate in Clover. He used to have strong social ambition and considered assassinating Nightmare... but since Nightmare was such a useless boss, Gray couldn't help but feel sorry for him and ended up a dedicated assistant. He's a sound thinker with a strong work ethic. He's also highly skilled with his blades, rivaling even Ace.

Nightmare Gottschalk
VA: Tomokazu Sugita

A sickly nightmare who hates the hospital and needles. He has the power to read people's thoughts and enter dreams. Even though he likes to shut himself away in dreams, Gray drags him out to sulk from time to time. He technically holds a high position and has many subordinates, but since he can't even take care of his own health, he leaves most things to Gray.

Pierce Villiers
VA: Souichirou Hoshi

New to Clover, Pierce is an insomniac mouse who drinks too much coffee. He loves Nightmare (who can help him sleep) and hates Boris (who terrifies him). He dislikes Blood and Vivaldi for discarding coffee in favor of tea. He likes Elliot and Peter well enough, since rabbits aren't natural predators of mice.

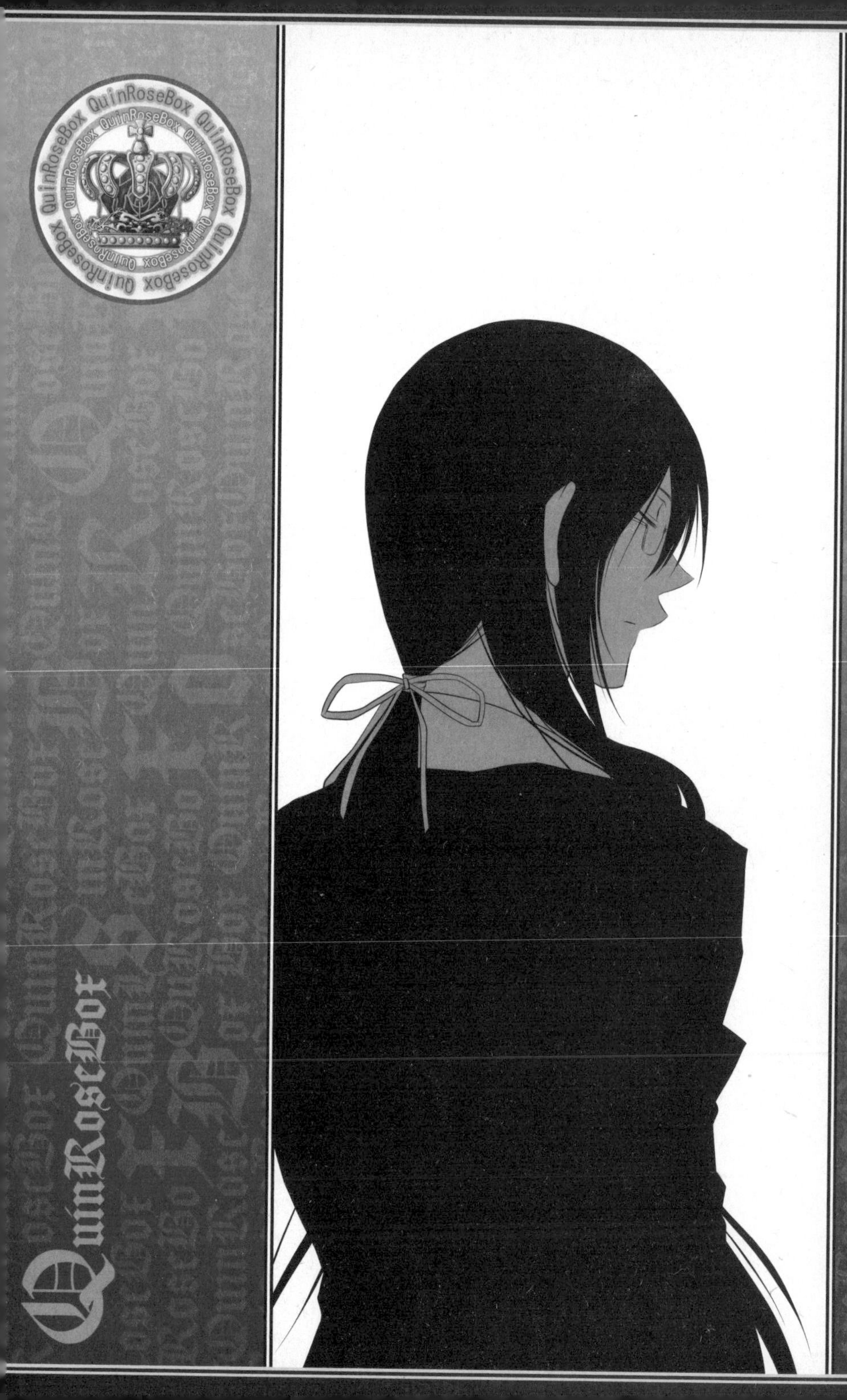

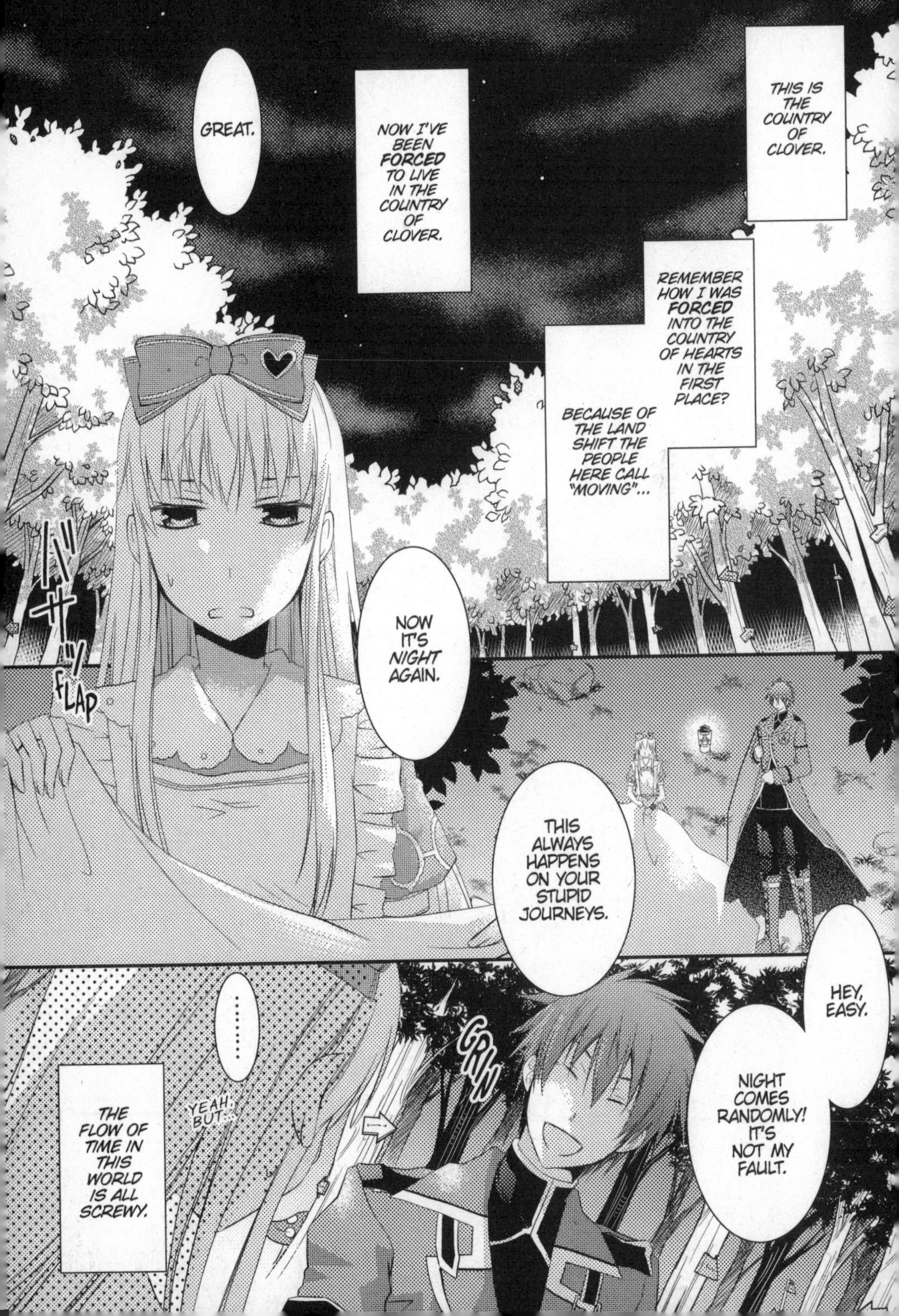
THIS IS THE COUNTRY OF CLOVER.
REMEMBER HOW I WAS FORCED INTO THE COUNTRY OF HEARTS IN THE FIRST PLACE?
BECAUSE OF THE LAND SHIFT THE PEOPLE HERE CALL "MOVING"...
NOW I'VE BEEN FORCED TO LIVE IN THE COUNTRY OF CLOVER.
GREAT.
NOW IT'S NIGHT AGAIN.
バサッ
FLAP
THIS ALWAYS HAPPENS ON YOUR STUPID JOURNEYS.
HEY, EASY.
NIGHT COMES RANDOMLY! IT'S NOT MY FAULT.
GRIN
......
YEAH, BUT...
THE FLOW OF TIME IN THIS WORLD IS ALL SCREWY.

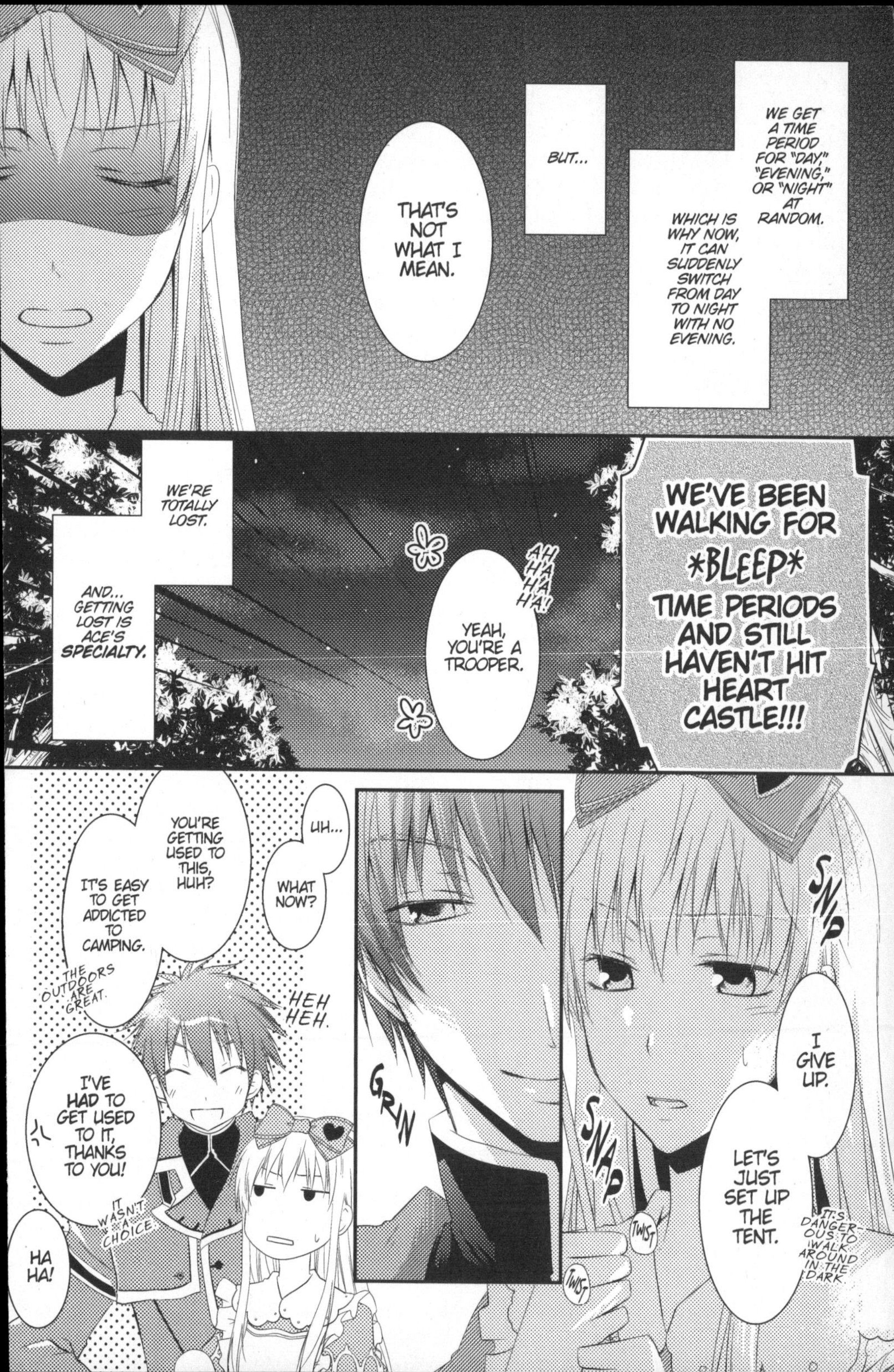
WE GET A TIME PERIOD FOR "DAY," "EVENING," OR "NIGHT" AT RANDOM.
WHICH IS WHY NOW, IT CAN SUDDENLY SWITCH FROM DAY TO NIGHT WITH NO EVENING.
BUT...
THAT'S NOT WHAT I MEAN.
WE'VE BEEN WALKING FOR *BLEEP* TIME PERIODS AND STILL HAVEN'T HIT HEART CASTLE!!!
AH HA HA HA!
YEAH, YOU'RE A TROOPER.
WE'RE TOTALLY LOST.
AND... GETTING LOST IS ACE'S SPECIALTY.
SNIP
I GIVE UP.
SNAP
LET'S JUST SET UP THE TENT.
IT'S DANGER-OUS TO WALK AROUND IN THE DARK.
TWIST
TWIST
GRIN
UH... WHAT NOW?
YOU'RE GETTING USED TO THIS, HUH?
IT'S EASY TO GET ADDICTED TO CAMPING.
THE OUTDOORS ARE GREAT.
HEH HEH.
I'VE HAD TO GET USED TO IT, THANKS TO YOU!
IT WASN'T A CHOICE.
HA HA!

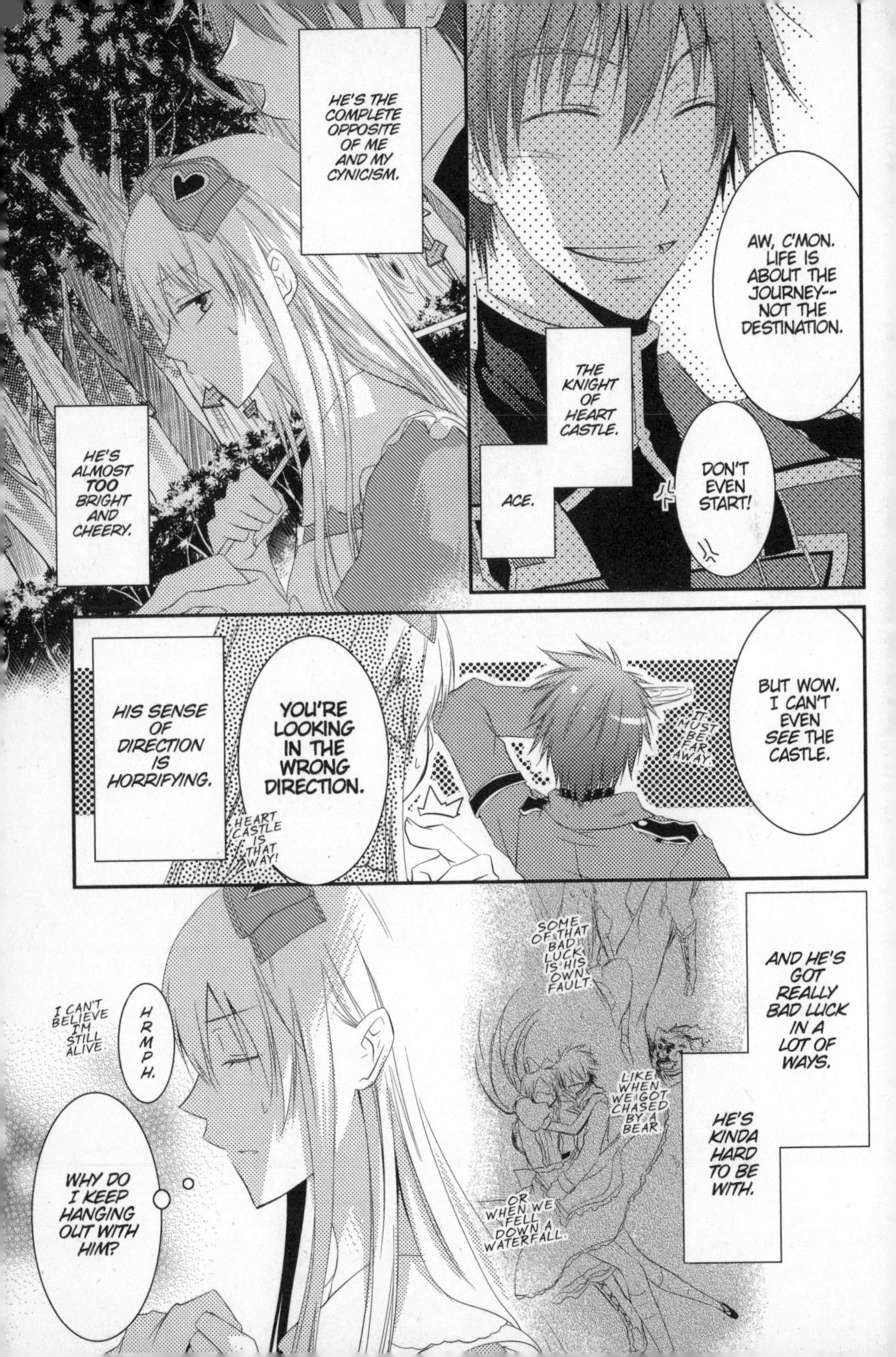
AW, C'MON. LIFE IS ABOUT THE JOURNEY-- NOT THE DESTINATION.
THE KNIGHT OF HEART CASTLE.
DON'T EVEN START!
ACE.
HE'S THE COMPLETE OPPOSITE OF ME AND MY CYNICISM.
HE'S ALMOST TOO BRIGHT AND CHEERY.
BUT WOW. I CAN'T EVEN SEE THE CASTLE.
IT MUST BE FAR AWAY.
YOU'RE LOOKING IN THE WRONG DIRECTION.
HEART CASTLE IS THAT WAY!
HIS SENSE OF DIRECTION IS HORRIFYING.
AND HE'S GOT REALLY BAD LUCK IN A LOT OF WAYS.
SOME OF THAT BAD LUCK IS HIS OWN FAULT.
LIKE WHEN WE GOT CHASED BY A BEAR.
HE'S KINDA HARD TO BE WITH.
OR WHEN WE FELL DOWN A WATERFALL.
HRMPH.
I CAN'T BELIEVE I'M STILL ALIVE.
WHY DO I KEEP HANGING OUT WITH HIM?

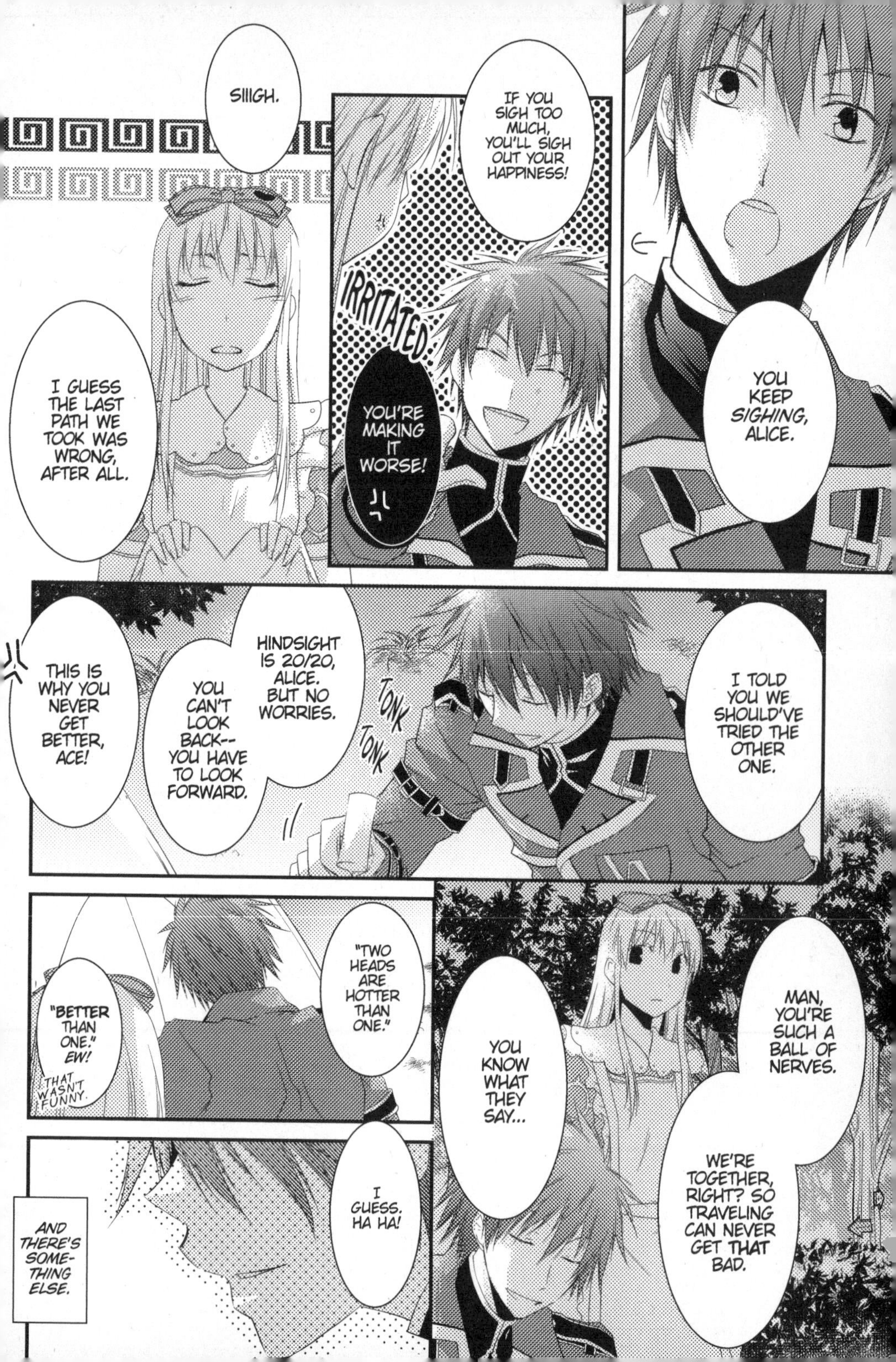

YOU KEEP SIGHING, ALICE.
IF YOU SIGH TOO MUCH, YOU'LL SIGH OUT YOUR HAPPINESS!
IRRITATED
YOU'RE MAKING IT WORSE!
SIIIGH.
I GUESS THE LAST PATH WE TOOK WAS WRONG, AFTER ALL.
I TOLD YOU WE SHOULD'VE TRIED THE OTHER ONE.
HINDSIGHT IS 20/20, ALICE. BUT NO WORRIES.
TONK TONK
YOU CAN'T LOOK BACK-- YOU HAVE TO LOOK FORWARD.
THIS IS WHY YOU NEVER GET BETTER, ACE!
MAN, YOU'RE SUCH A BALL OF NERVES.
WE'RE TOGETHER, RIGHT? SO TRAVELING CAN NEVER GET THAT BAD.
YOU KNOW WHAT THEY SAY...
"TWO HEADS ARE HOTTER THAN ONE."
"BETTER THAN ONE." EW!
THAT WASN'T FUNNY.
I GUESS. HA HA!
AND THERE'S SOMETHING ELSE.

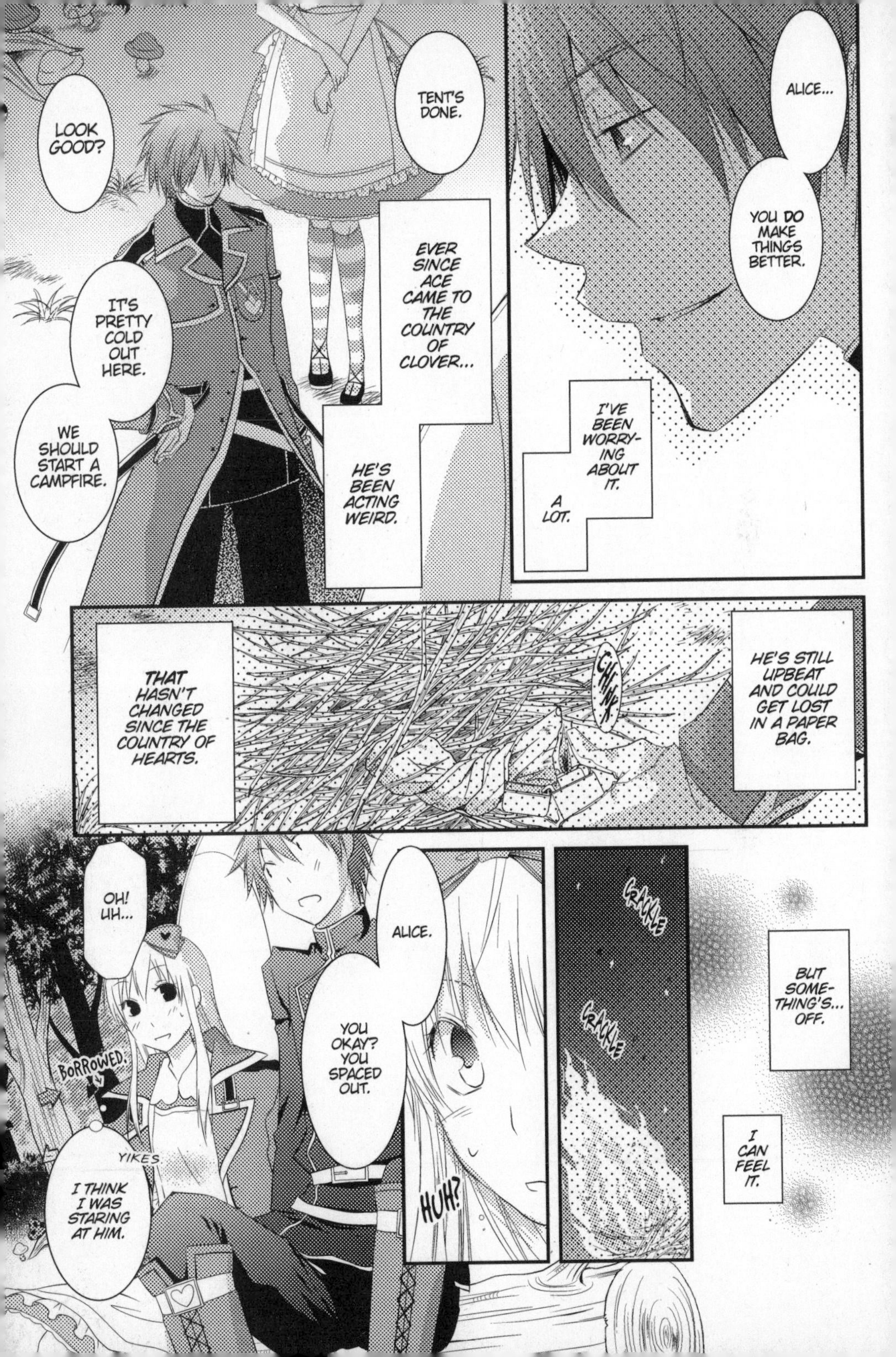
ALICE...
YOU DO MAKE THINGS BETTER.
I'VE BEEN WORRYING ABOUT IT.
A LOT.
TENT'S DONE.
LOOK GOOD?
EVER SINCE ACE CAME TO THE COUNTRY OF CLOVER...
HE'S BEEN ACTING WEIRD.
IT'S PRETTY COLD OUT HERE.
WE SHOULD START A CAMPFIRE.
HE'S STILL UPBEAT AND COULD GET LOST IN A PAPER BAG.
CHINK
THAT HASN'T CHANGED SINCE THE COUNTRY OF HEARTS.
BUT SOMETHING'S... OFF.
I CAN FEEL IT.
CRACKLE
CRACKLE
HUH?
ALICE.
YOU OKAY? YOU SPACED OUT.
OH! UH...
BORROWED.
YIKES
I THINK I WAS STARING AT HIM.

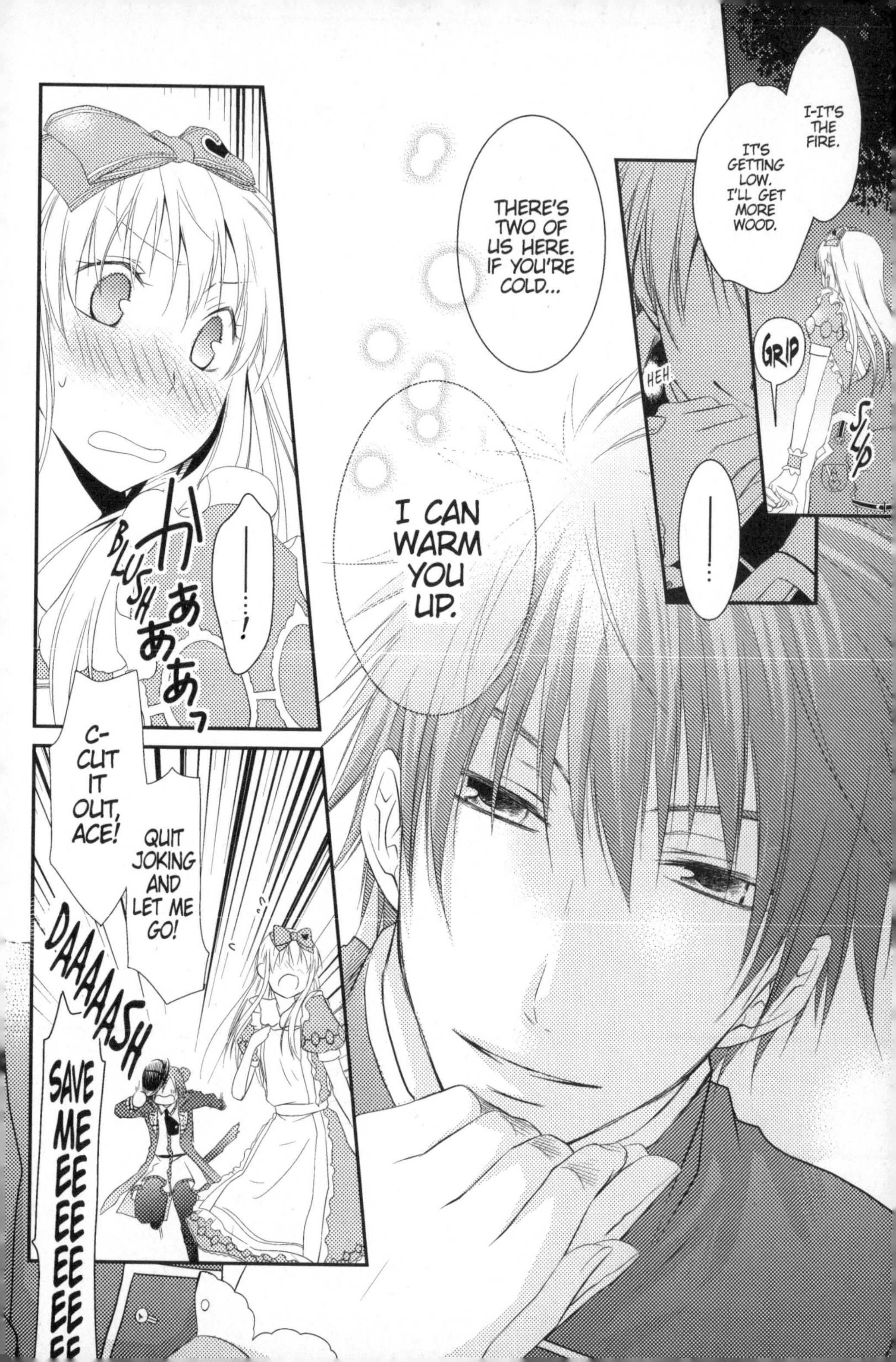
I-IT'S THE FIRE.
IT'S GETTING LOW. I'LL GET MORE WOOD.
GRIP
SLIP
HEH
!...
THERE'S TWO OF US HERE. IF YOU'RE COLD...
I CAN WARM YOU UP.
!...!
BLUSH
かあああっ
C-CUT IT OUT, ACE!
QUIT JOKING AND LET ME GO!
DAAAAASH
SAVE MEEEEEEEEEEEEE

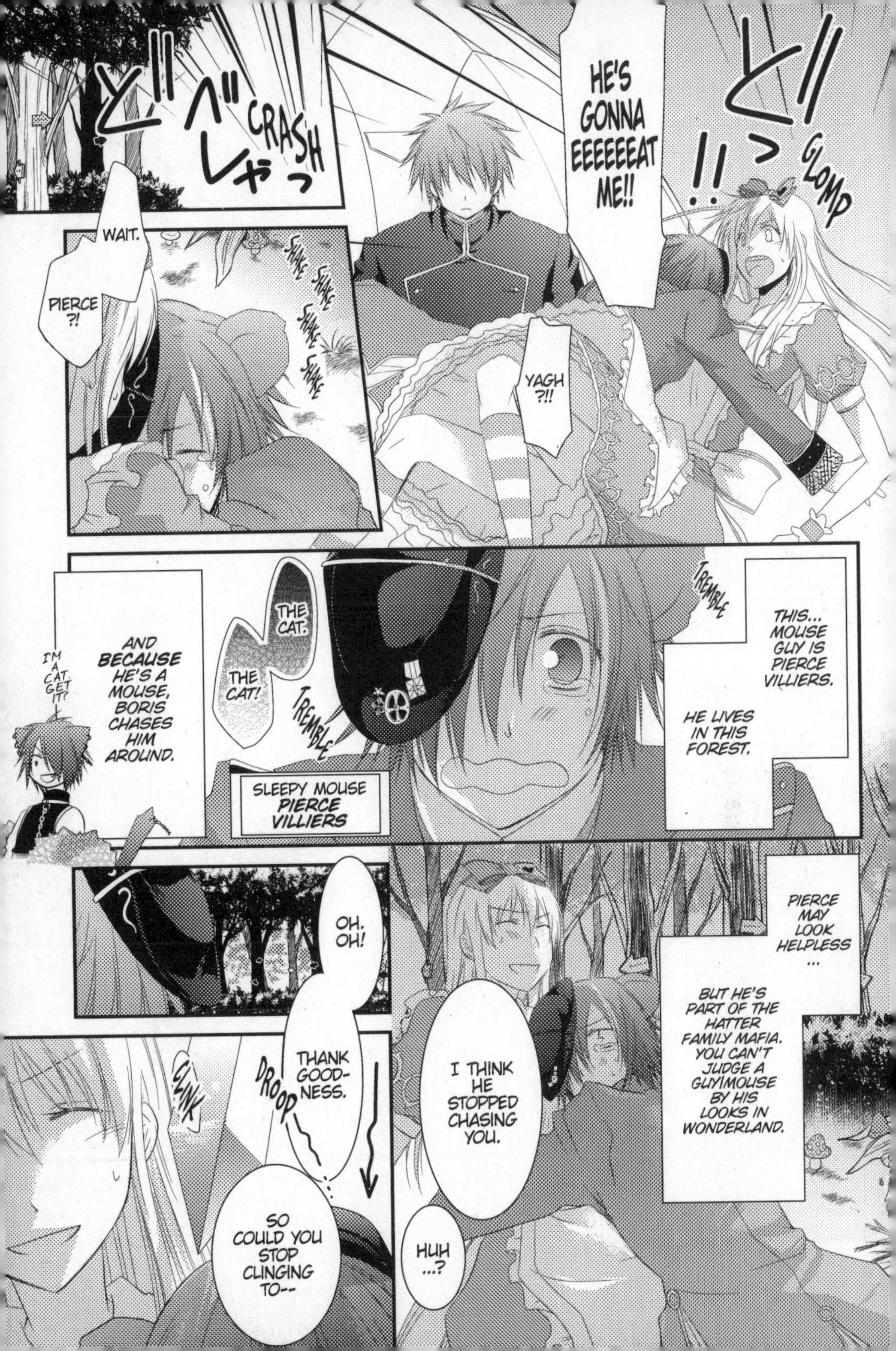
どっ!!
GLOMP
HE'S GONNA EEEEEEAT ME!!
YAGH?!!
どべしゃっ
CRASH
WAIT.
PIERCE?!
SHAKE SHAKE SHAKE SHAKE
THIS... MOUSE GUY IS PIERCE VILLIERS.
HE LIVES IN THIS FOREST.
TREMBLE
THE CAT.
THE CAT!
TREMBLE
SLEEPY MOUSE PIERCE VILLIERS
AND BECAUSE HE'S A MOUSE, BORIS CHASES HIM AROUND.
I'M A CAT. GET IT?
PIERCE MAY LOOK HELPLESS...
BUT HE'S PART OF THE HATTER FAMILY MAFIA. YOU CAN'T JUDGE A GUY/MOUSE BY HIS LOOKS IN WONDERLAND.
I THINK HE STOPPED CHASING YOU.
HUH...?
OH. OH!
THANK GOODNESS.
DROOP
CLINK
SO COULD YOU STOP CLINGING TO--

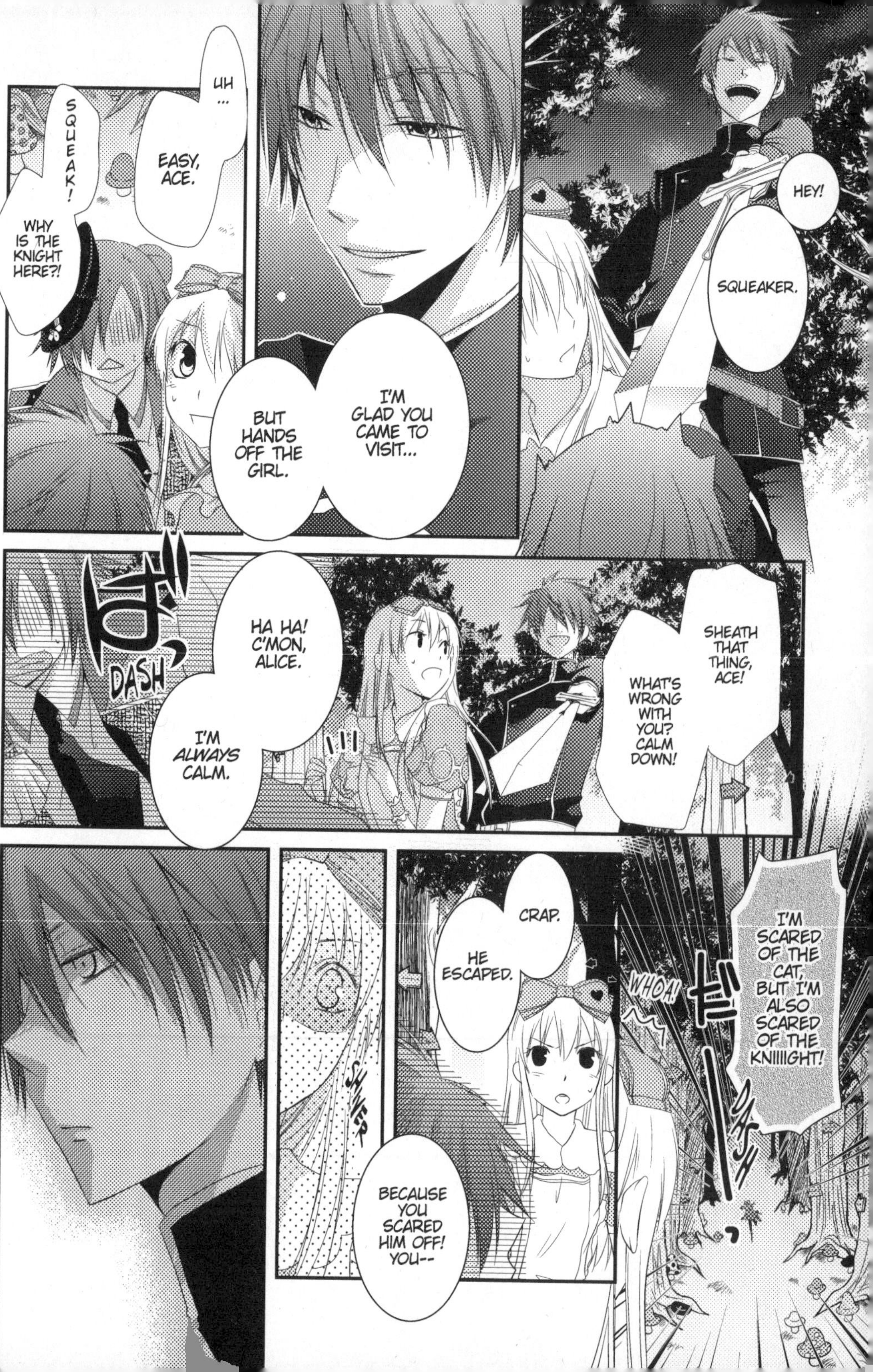
HEY!
SQUEAKER.
I'M GLAD YOU CAME TO VISIT...
BUT HANDS OFF THE GIRL.
UH...
EASY, ACE.
SQUEAK!
WHY IS THE KNIGHT HERE?!
SHEATH THAT THING, ACE!
WHAT'S WRONG WITH YOU? CALM DOWN!
HA HA! C'MON, ALICE.
I'M ALWAYS CALM.
DASH
I'M SCARED OF THE CAT, BUT I'M ALSO SCARED OF THE KNIIIIGHT!
WHOA!
DASH
CRAP.
HE ESCAPED.
BECAUSE YOU SCARED HIM OFF! YOU--
SHIVER

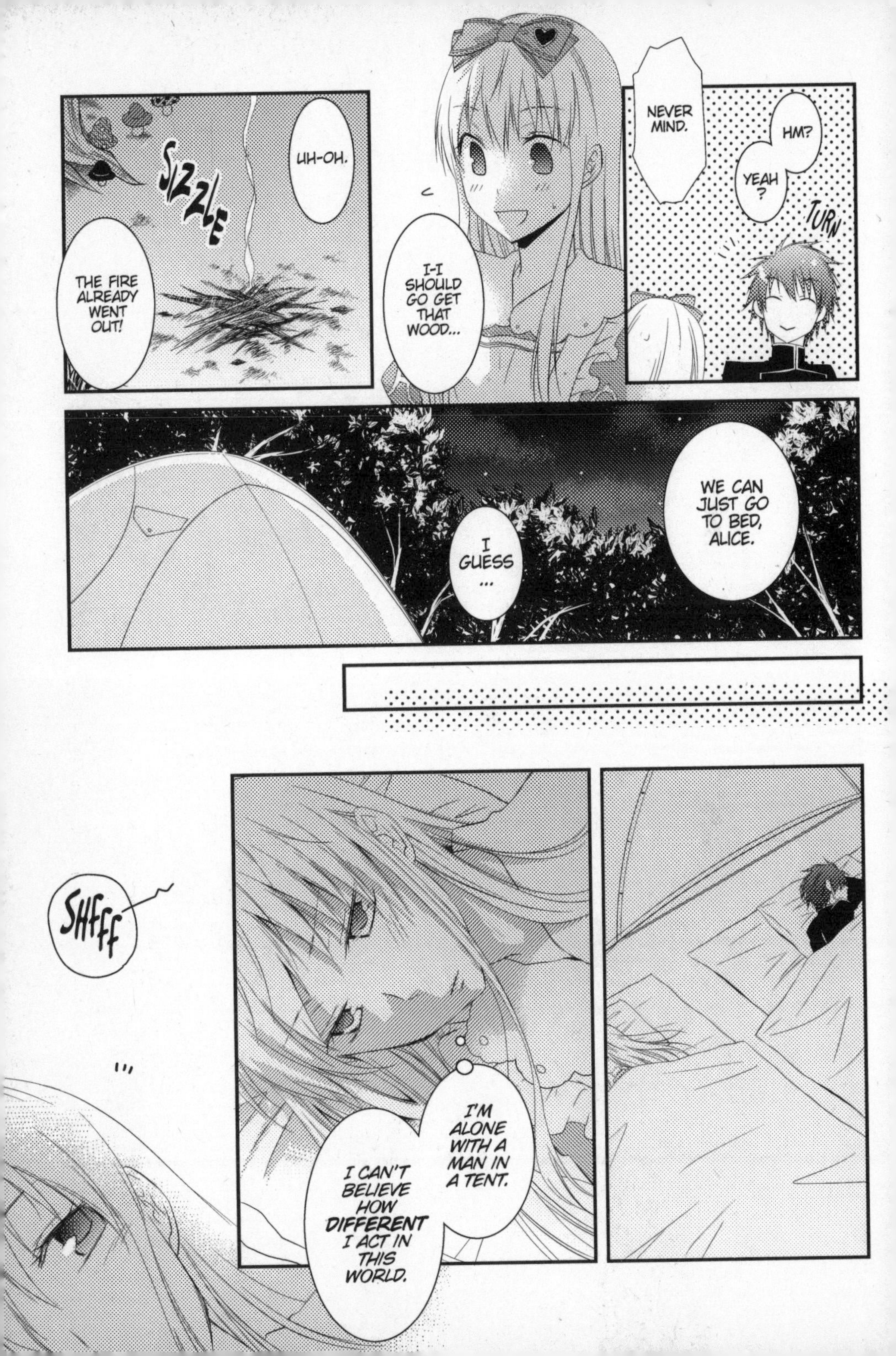
HM?
YEAH?
TURN
NEVER MIND.
I-I SHOULD GO GET THAT WOOD...
UH-OH.
SIZZLE
THE FIRE ALREADY WENT OUT!
WE CAN JUST GO TO BED, ALICE.
I GUESS...
I'M ALONE WITH A MAN IN A TENT.
I CAN'T BELIEVE HOW DIFFERENT I ACT IN THIS WORLD.
SHFFF

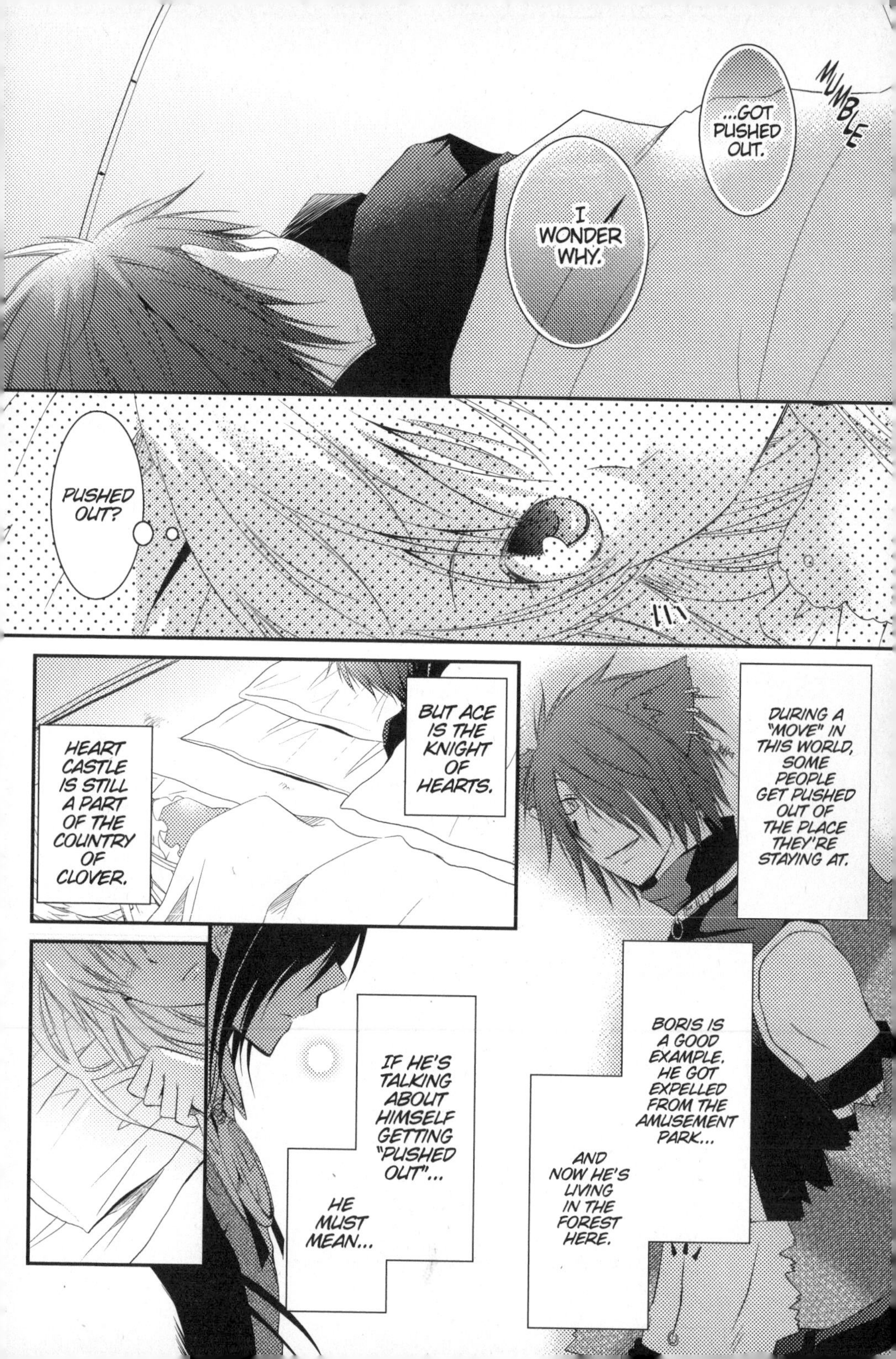
MUMBLE
...GOT PUSHED OUT.
I WONDER WHY.
PUSHED OUT?
DURING A "MOVE" IN THIS WORLD, SOME PEOPLE GET PUSHED OUT OF THE PLACE THEY'RE STAYING AT.
BUT ACE IS THE KNIGHT OF HEARTS.
HEART CASTLE IS STILL A PART OF THE COUNTRY OF CLOVER.
BORIS IS A GOOD EXAMPLE. HE GOT EXPELLED FROM THE AMUSEMENT PARK...
AND NOW HE'S LIVING IN THE FOREST HERE.
IF HE'S TALKING ABOUT HIMSELF GETTING "PUSHED OUT"...
HE MUST MEAN...

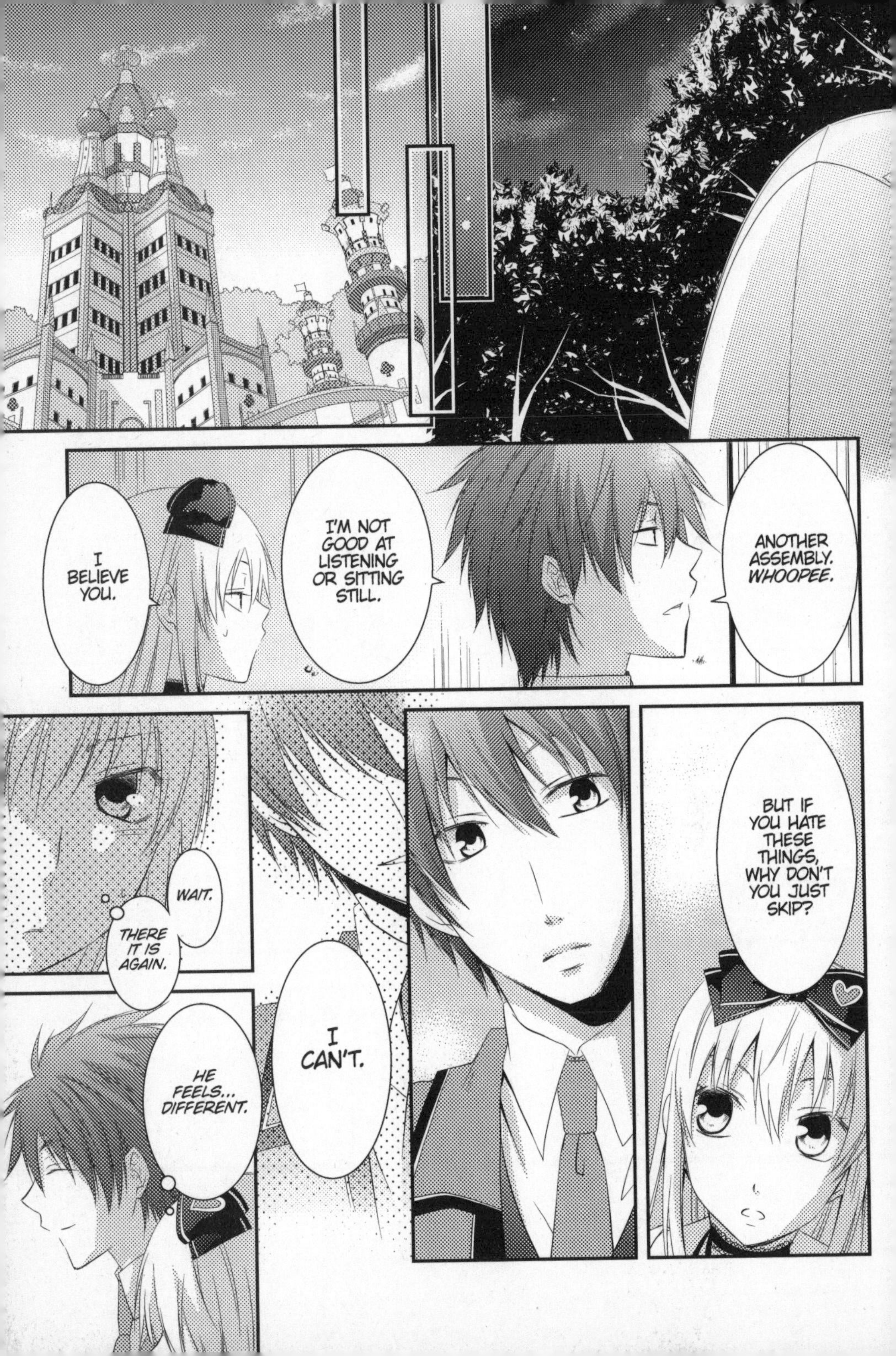
ANOTHER ASSEMBLY. WHOOPEE.
I'M NOT GOOD AT LISTENING OR SITTING STILL.
I BELIEVE YOU.
BUT IF YOU HATE THESE THINGS, WHY DON'T YOU JUST SKIP?
I CAN'T.
WAIT.
THERE IT IS AGAIN.
HE FEELS... DIFFERENT.

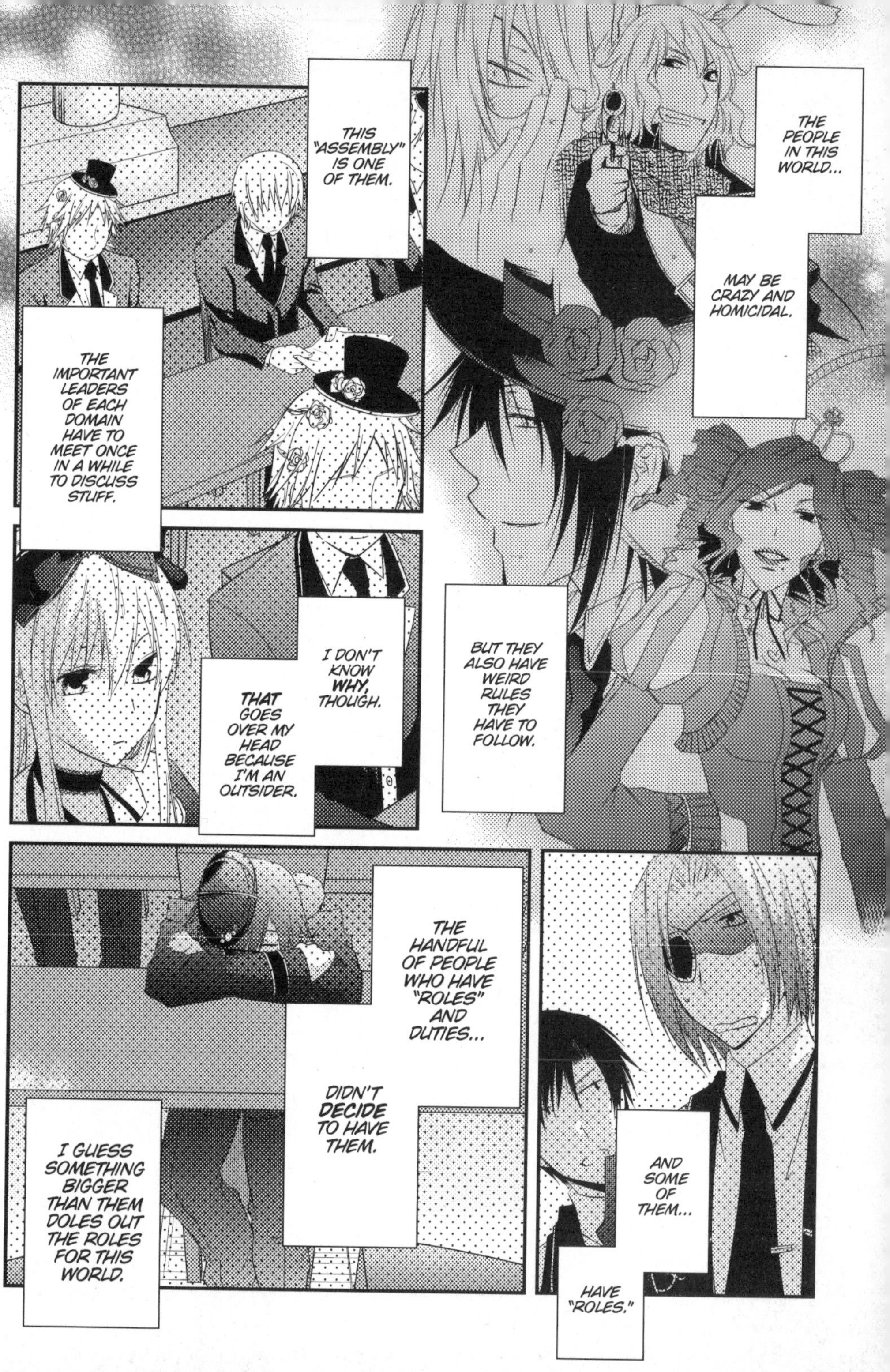

THE PEOPLE IN THIS WORLD...
MAY BE CRAZY AND HOMICIDAL.
BUT THEY ALSO HAVE WEIRD RULES THEY HAVE TO FOLLOW.
THIS "ASSEMBLY" IS ONE OF THEM.
THE IMPORTANT LEADERS OF EACH DOMAIN HAVE TO MEET ONCE IN A WHILE TO DISCUSS STUFF.
I DON'T KNOW WHY, THOUGH.
THAT GOES OVER MY HEAD BECAUSE I'M AN OUTSIDER.
AND SOME OF THEM...
HAVE "ROLES."
THE HANDFUL OF PEOPLE WHO HAVE "ROLES" AND DUTIES...
DIDN'T DECIDE TO HAVE THEM.
I GUESS SOMETHING BIGGER THAN THEM DOLES OUT THE ROLES FOR THIS WORLD.

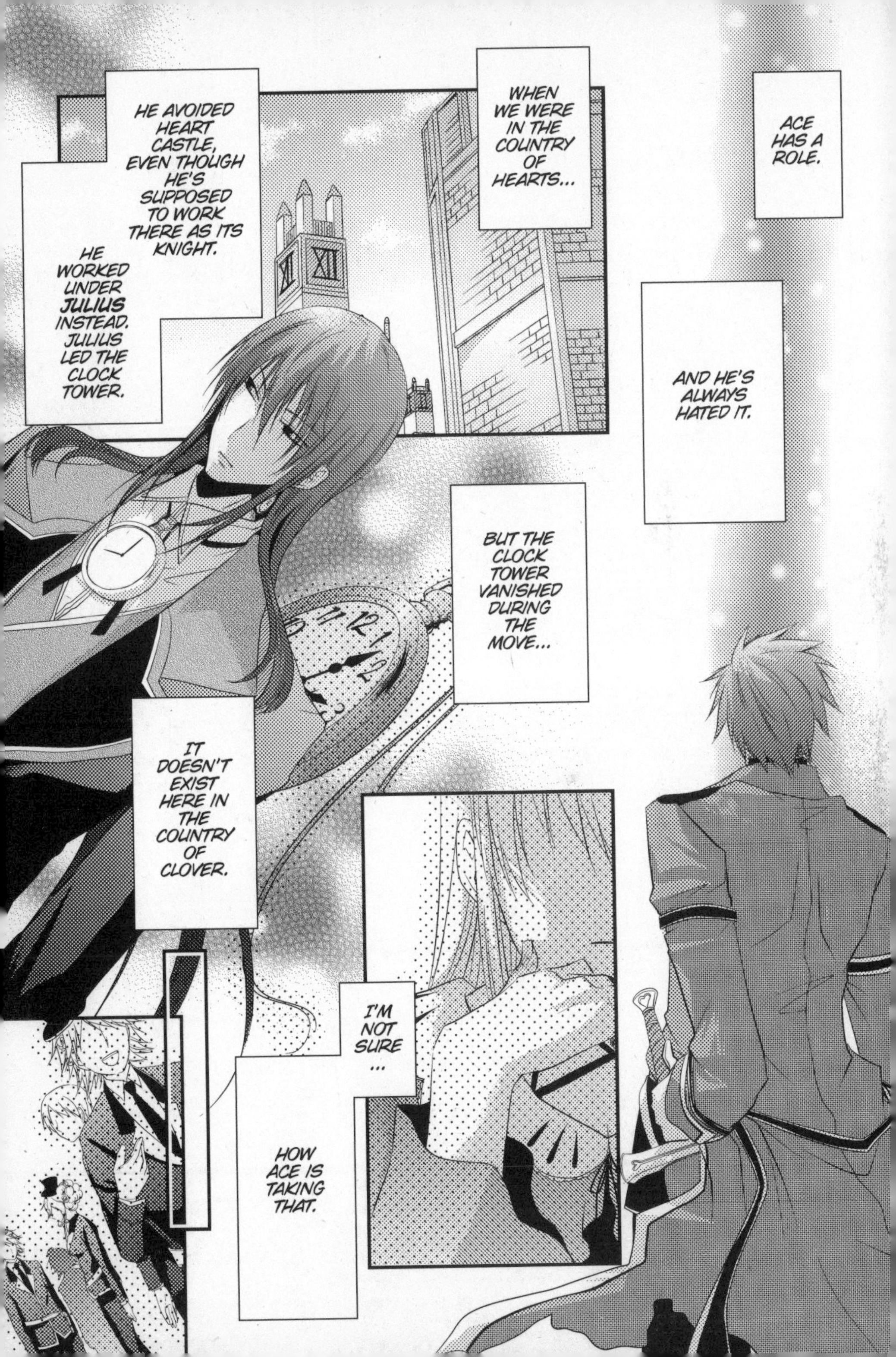
ACE HAS A ROLE.
AND HE'S ALWAYS HATED IT.
WHEN WE WERE IN THE COUNTRY OF HEARTS...
HE AVOIDED HEART CASTLE, EVEN THOUGH HE'S SUPPOSED TO WORK THERE AS ITS KNIGHT.
HE WORKED UNDER **JULIUS** INSTEAD. JULIUS LED THE CLOCK TOWER.
BUT THE CLOCK TOWER VANISHED DURING THE MOVE...
IT DOESN'T EXIST HERE IN THE COUNTRY OF CLOVER.
I'M NOT SURE ...
HOW ACE IS TAKING THAT.

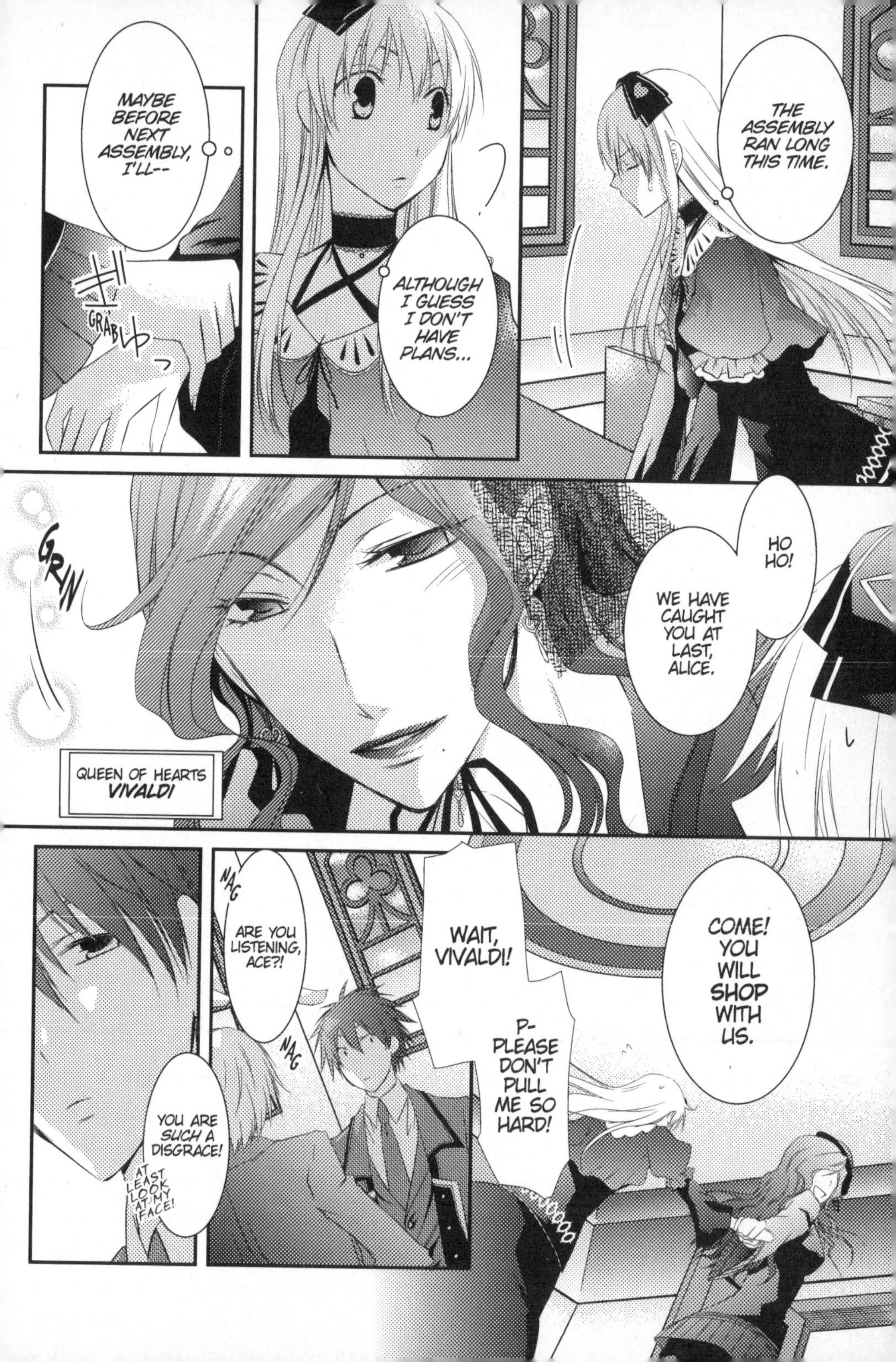
THE ASSEMBLY RAN LONG THIS TIME.
ALTHOUGH I GUESS I DON'T HAVE PLANS...
MAYBE BEFORE NEXT ASSEMBLY, I'LL--
GRAB
HO HO!
WE HAVE CAUGHT YOU AT LAST, ALICE.
GRIN
QUEEN OF HEARTS VIVALDI
COME! YOU WILL SHOP WITH US.
WAIT, VIVALDI!
P-PLEASE DON'T PULL ME SO HARD!
NAG
ARE YOU LISTENING, ACE?!
NAG
YOU ARE SUCH A DISGRACE!
AT LEAST LOOK AT MY FACE!

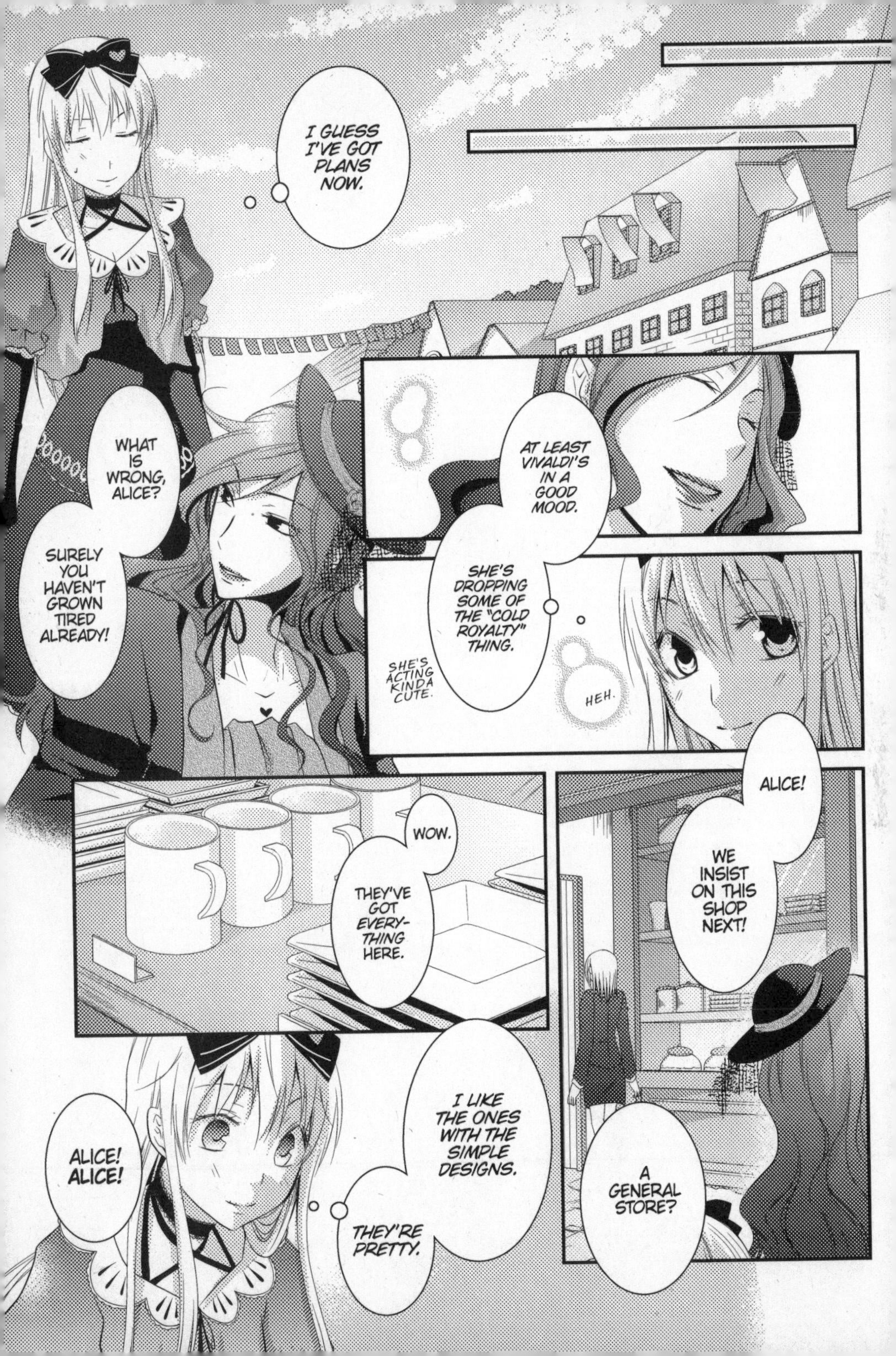
I GUESS I'VE GOT PLANS NOW.
WHAT IS WRONG, ALICE?
SURELY YOU HAVEN'T GROWN TIRED ALREADY!
AT LEAST VIVALDI'S IN A GOOD MOOD.
SHE'S DROPPING SOME OF THE "COLD ROYALTY" THING.
SHE'S ACTING KINDA CUTE.
HEH.
ALICE!
WE INSIST ON THIS SHOP NEXT!
A GENERAL STORE?
WOW.
THEY'VE GOT EVERYTHING HERE.
I LIKE THE ONES WITH THE SIMPLE DESIGNS.
THEY'RE PRETTY.
ALICE! ALICE!

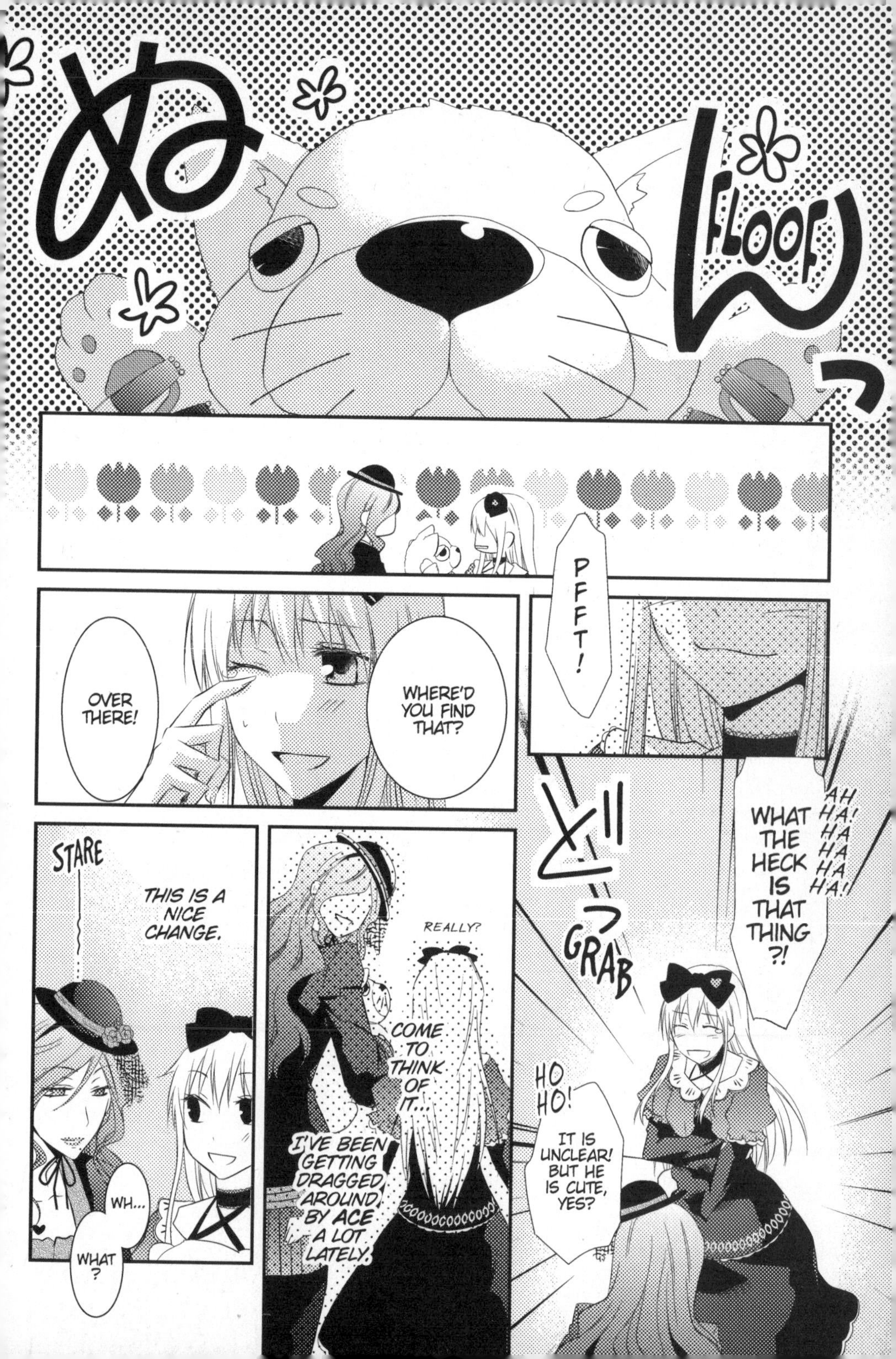

ぬいっ
FLOOF
PFFT!
WHERE'D YOU FIND THAT?
OVER THERE!
WHAT THE HECK IS THAT THING?!
AH HA! HA HA HA HA!
GRAB
HO HO!
IT IS UNCLEAR! BUT HE IS CUTE, YES?
REALLY?
COME TO THINK OF IT...
I'VE BEEN GETTING DRAGGED AROUND BY ACE A LOT LATELY.
STARE
THIS IS A NICE CHANGE.
WH...
WHAT?

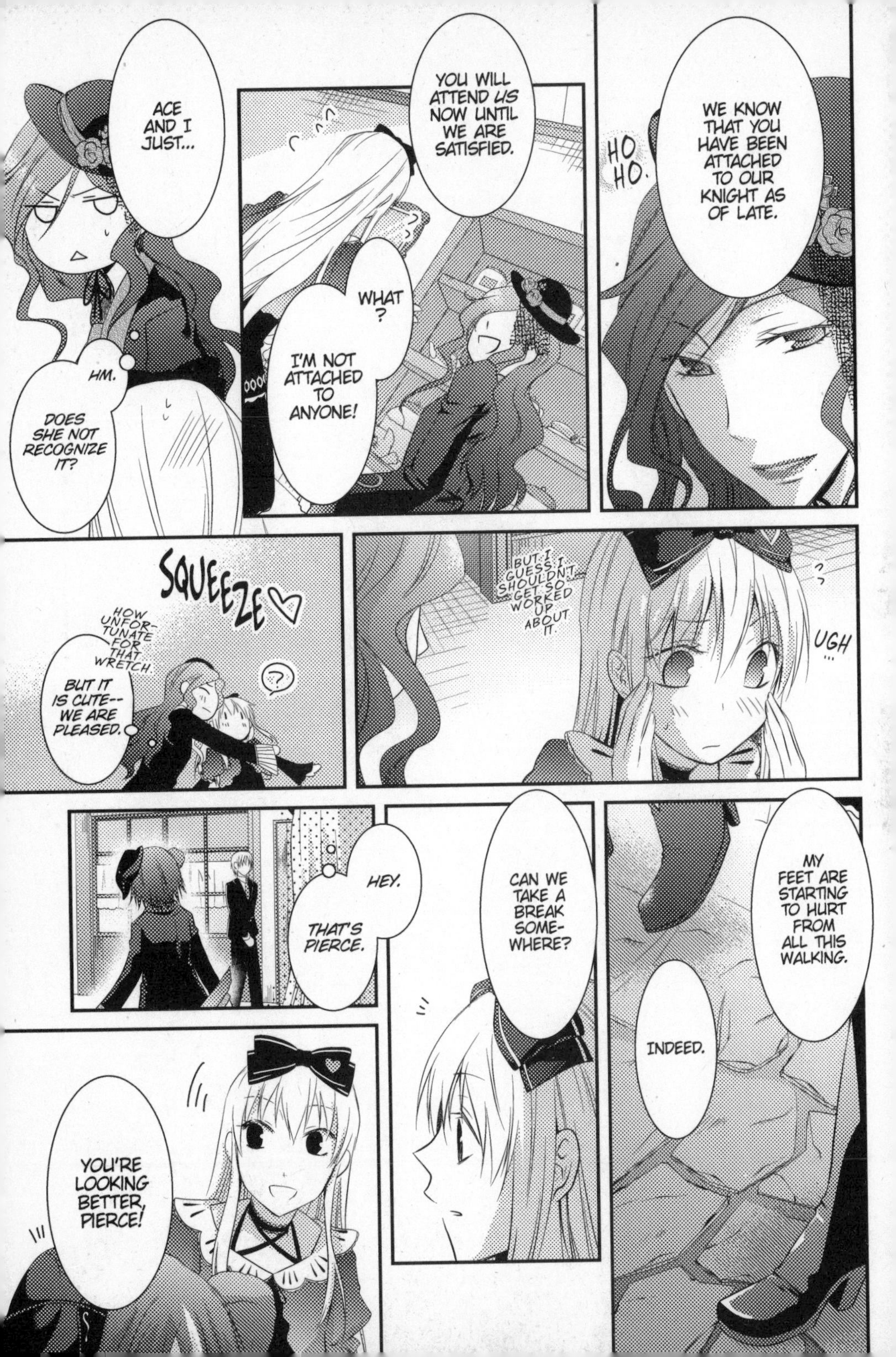
HO HO.
WE KNOW THAT YOU HAVE BEEN ATTACHED TO OUR KNIGHT AS OF LATE.
YOU WILL ATTEND US NOW UNTIL WE ARE SATISFIED.
WHAT?
I'M NOT ATTACHED TO ANYONE!
ACE AND I JUST...
HM.
DOES SHE NOT RECOGNIZE IT?
UGH...
BUT I GUESS I SHOULDN'T GET SO WORKED UP ABOUT IT.
SQUEEZE
HOW UNFORTUNATE FOR THAT WRETCH.
BUT IT IS CUTE-- WE ARE PLEASED.
?
MY FEET ARE STARTING TO HURT FROM ALL THIS WALKING.
INDEED.
CAN WE TAKE A BREAK SOMEWHERE?
HEY.
THAT'S PIERCE.
YOU'RE LOOKING BETTER, PIERCE!

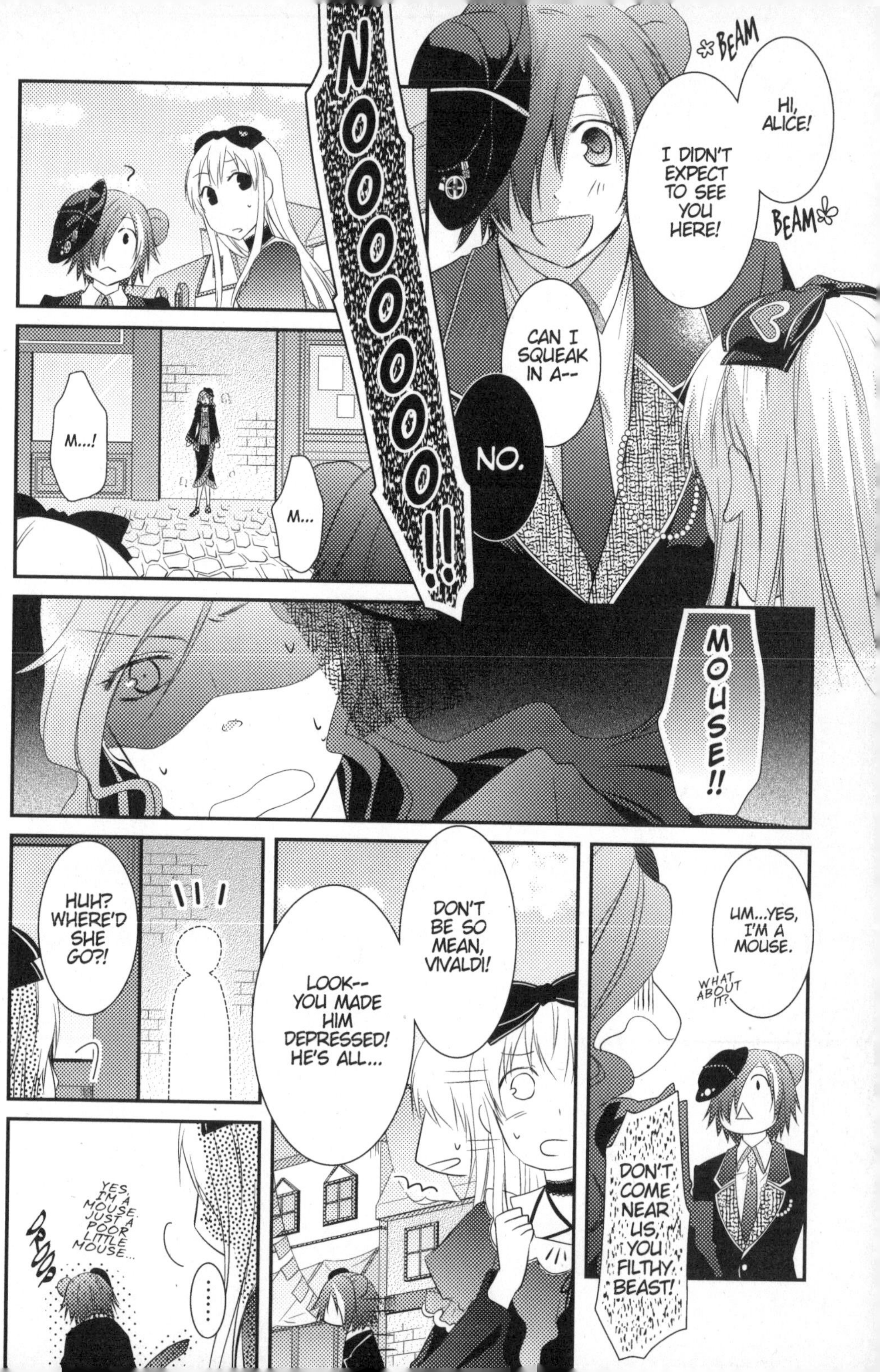
BEAM
HI, ALICE!
I DIDN'T EXPECT TO SEE YOU HERE!
BEAM
CAN I SQUEAK IN A--
NO.
NOOOOOOO!!
?
M...!
M...
MOUSE!!
UM...YES, I'M A MOUSE.
WHAT ABOUT IT?
DON'T COME NEAR US, YOU FILTHY BEAST!
DON'T BE SO MEAN, VIVALDI!
LOOK-- YOU MADE HIM DEPRESSED! HE'S ALL...
HUH? WHERE'D SHE GO?!
YES, I'M A MOUSE. JUST A POOR LITTLE MOUSE...
DROOP
......

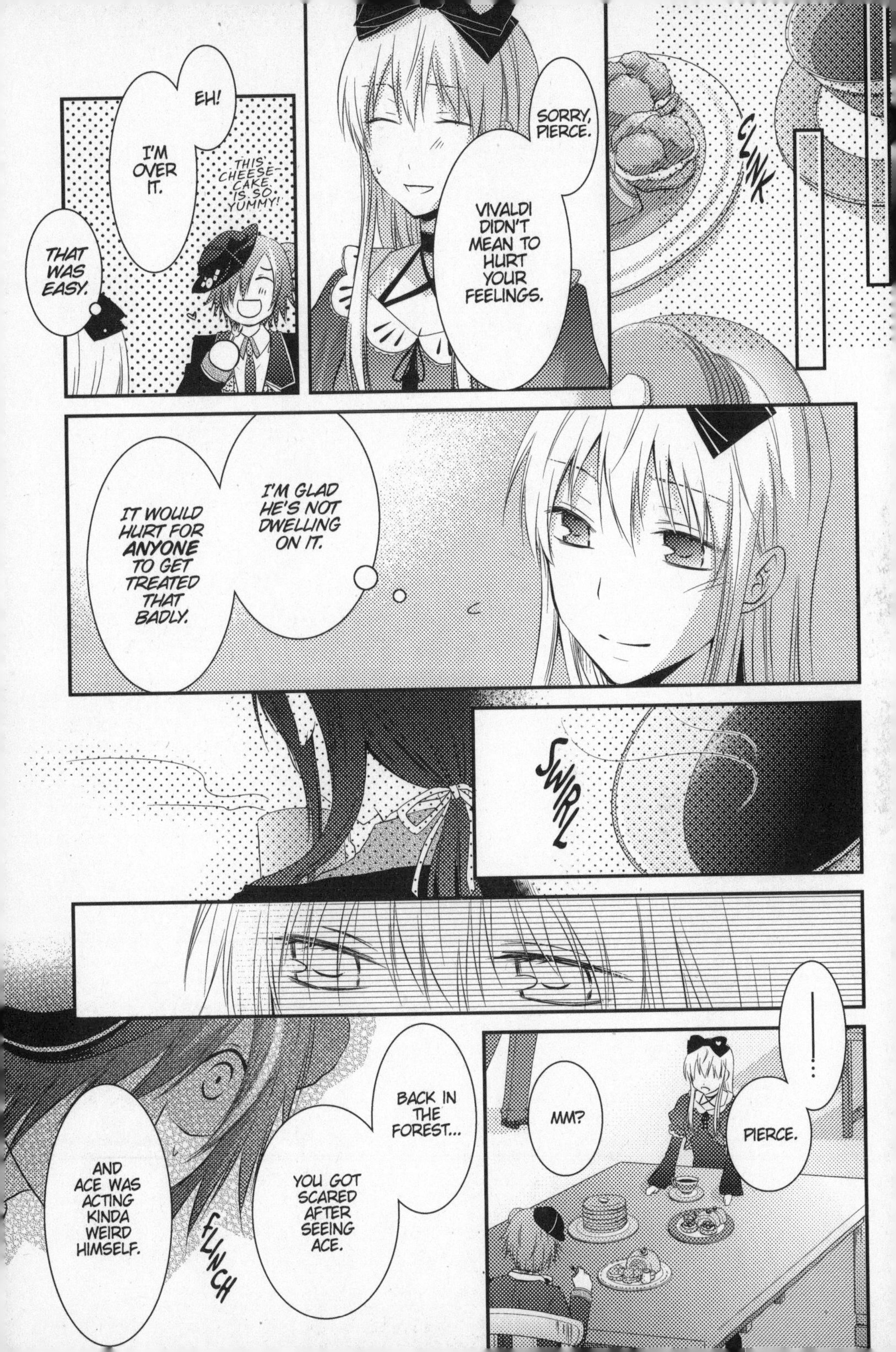
CLINK
SORRY, PIERCE.
VIVALDI DIDN'T MEAN TO HURT YOUR FEELINGS.
EH!
I'M OVER IT.
THIS CHEESECAKE IS SO YUMMY!
THAT WAS EASY.
I'M GLAD HE'S NOT DWELLING ON IT.
IT WOULD HURT FOR **ANYONE** TO GET TREATED THAT BADLY.
SWIRL
!......
PIERCE.
MM?
BACK IN THE FOREST...
YOU GOT SCARED AFTER SEEING ACE.
AND ACE WAS ACTING KINDA WEIRD HIMSELF.
FLINCH

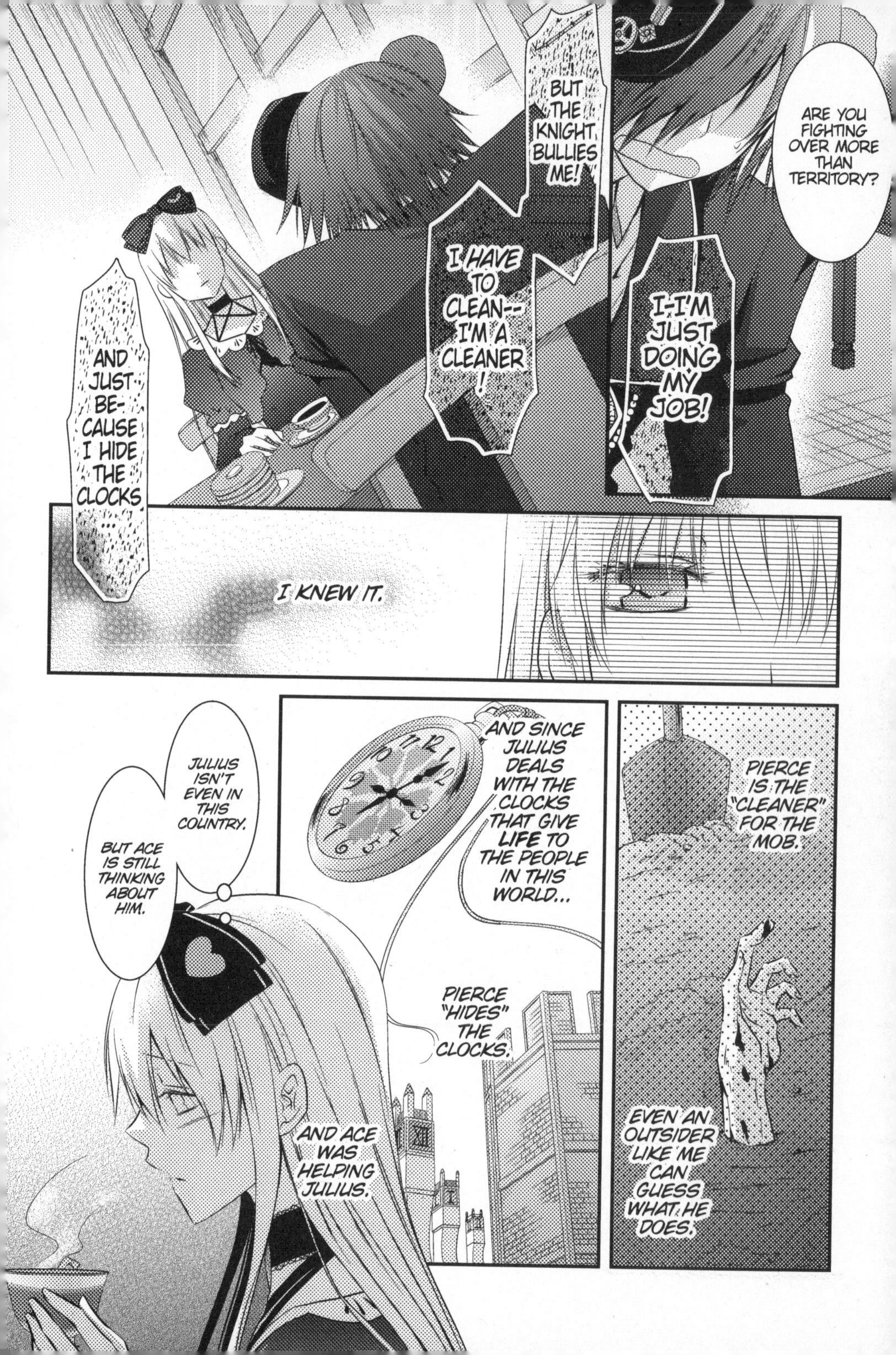
ARE YOU FIGHTING OVER MORE THAN TERRITORY?
I-I'M JUST DOING MY JOB!
BUT THE KNIGHT BULLIES ME!
I HAVE TO CLEAN-- I'M A CLEANER!
AND JUST BE-CAUSE I HIDE THE CLOCKS...
I KNEW IT.
PIERCE IS THE "CLEANER" FOR THE MOB.
EVEN AN OUTSIDER LIKE ME CAN GUESS WHAT HE DOES.
AND SINCE JULIUS DEALS WITH THE CLOCKS THAT GIVE **LIFE** TO THE PEOPLE IN THIS WORLD...
PIERCE "HIDES" THE CLOCKS.
AND ACE WAS HELPING JULIUS.
JULIUS ISN'T EVEN IN THIS COUNTRY.
BUT ACE IS STILL THINKING ABOUT HIM.

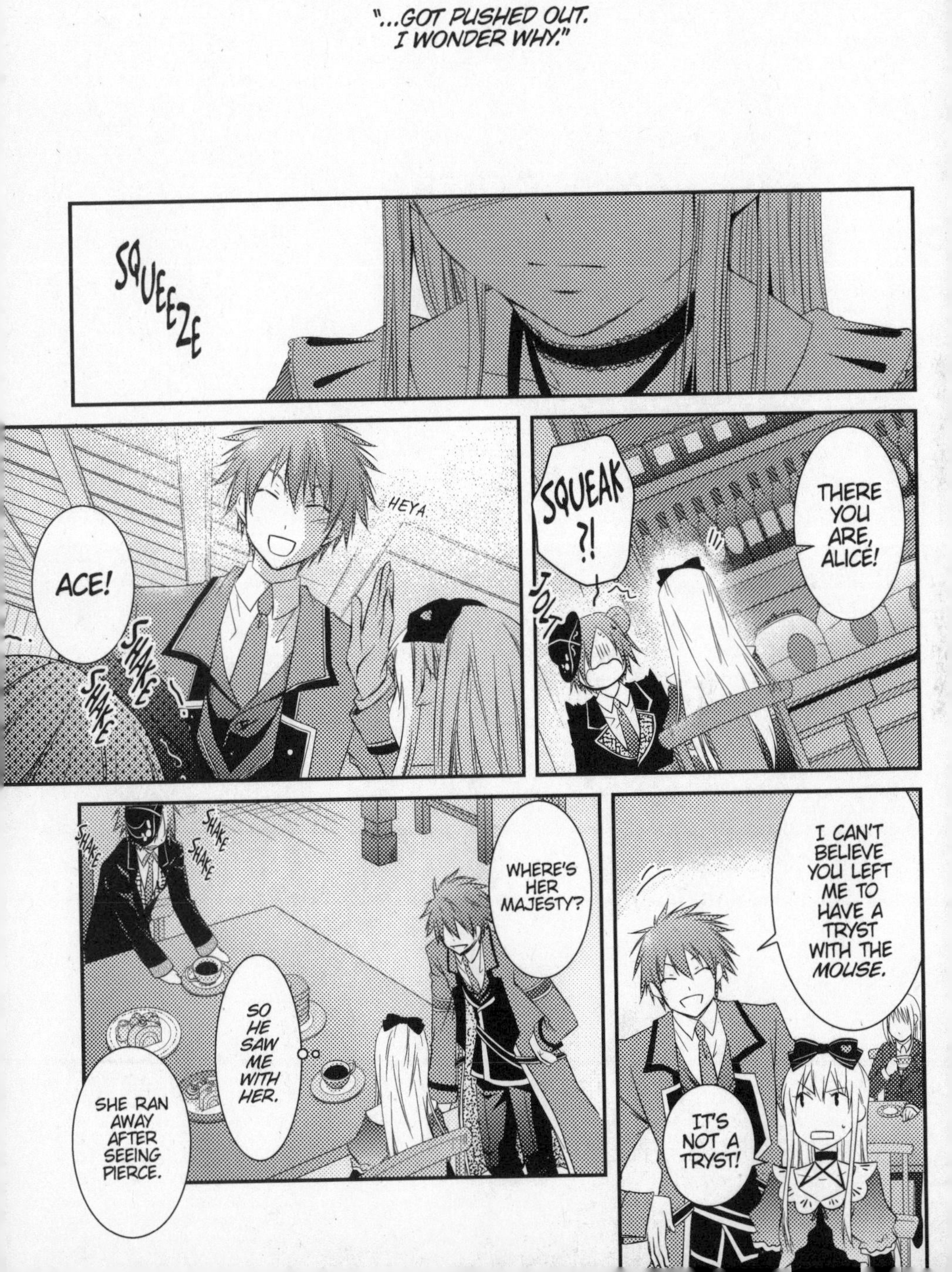
"...GOT PUSHED OUT. I WONDER WHY."
SQUEEZE
THERE YOU ARE, ALICE!
SQUEAK ?!
JOLT
HEYA.
ACE!
SHAKE
SHAKE
I CAN'T BELIEVE YOU LEFT ME TO HAVE A TRYST WITH THE *MOUSE*.
IT'S NOT A TRYST!
WHERE'S HER MAJESTY?
SO HE SAW ME WITH HER.
SHE RAN AWAY AFTER SEEING PIERCE.
SHAKE
SHAKE
SHAKE

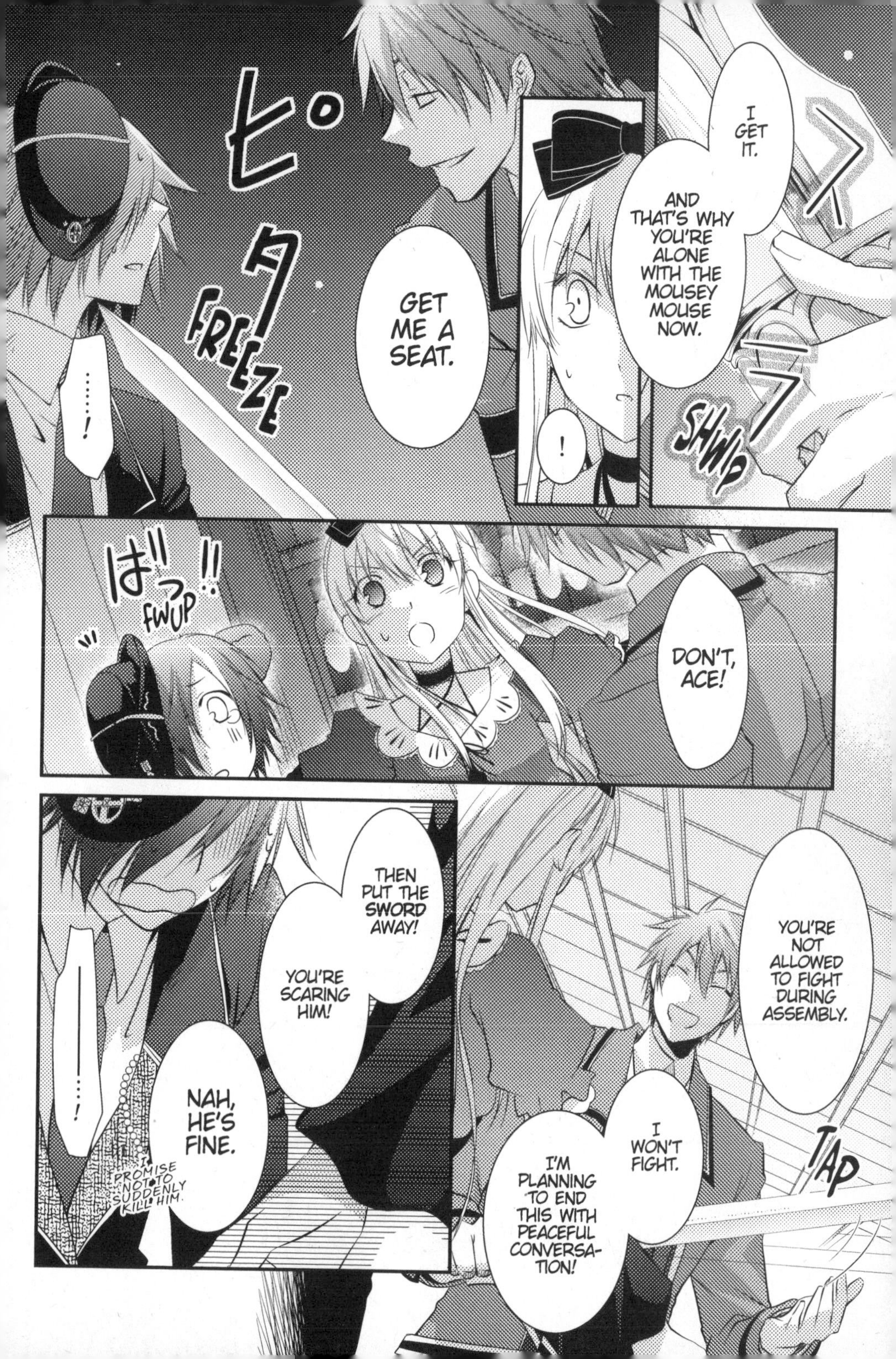
I GET IT.
AND THAT'S WHY YOU'RE ALONE WITH THE MOUSEY MOUSE NOW.
SHWIP
!
GET ME A SEAT.
FREEZE
......!
DON'T, ACE!
FWUP
YOU'RE NOT ALLOWED TO FIGHT DURING ASSEMBLY.
TAP
I WON'T FIGHT.
I'M PLANNING TO END THIS WITH PEACEFUL CONVERSA-TION!
THEN PUT THE SWORD AWAY!
YOU'RE SCARING HIM!
NAH, HE'S FINE.
I PROMISE NOT TO SUDDENLY KILL HIM.
......!

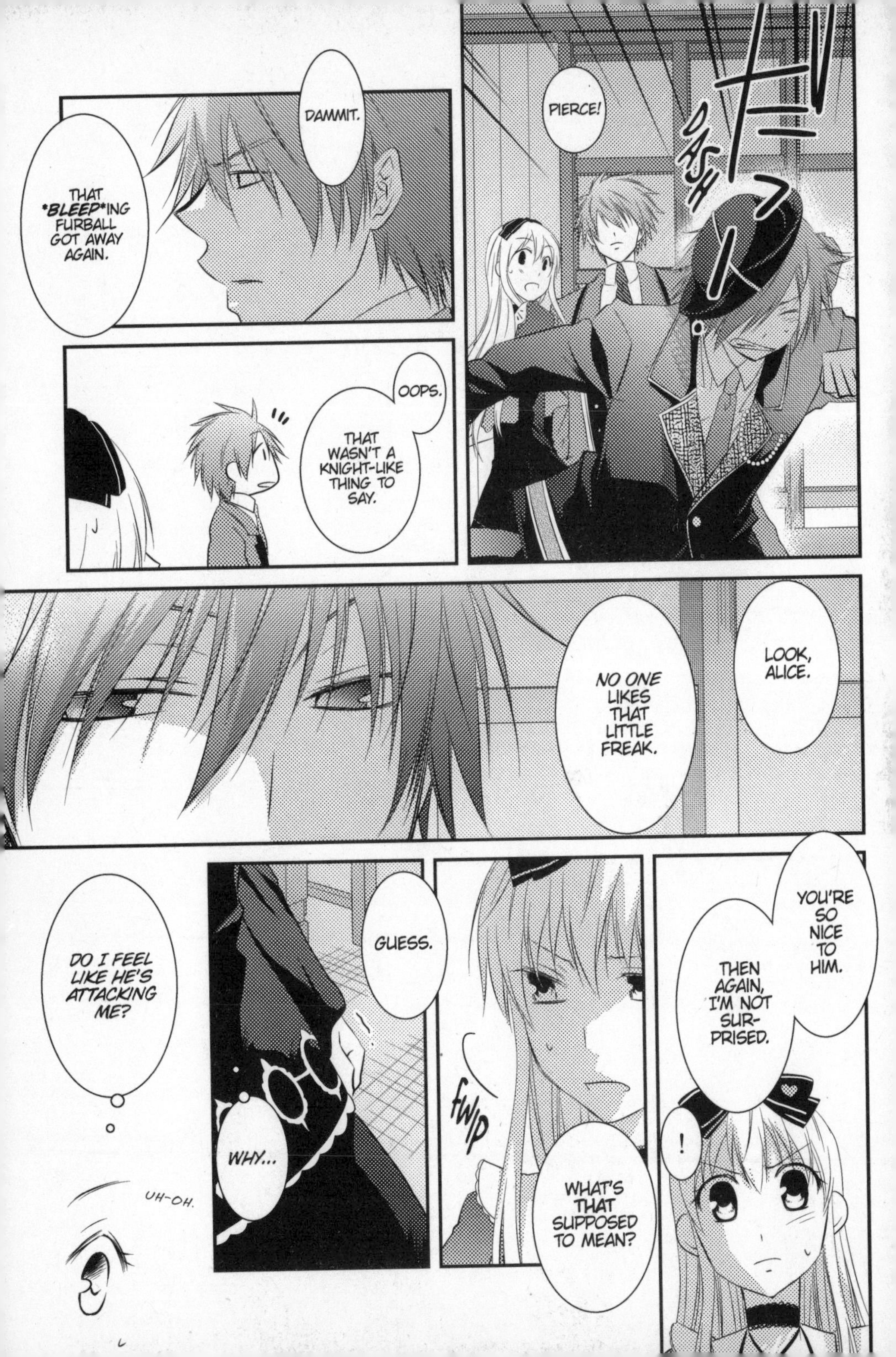
DASH
PIERCE!
DAMMIT.
THAT *BLEEP*ING FURBALL GOT AWAY AGAIN.
OOPS.
THAT WASN'T A KNIGHT-LIKE THING TO SAY.
LOOK, ALICE.
NO ONE LIKES THAT LITTLE FREAK.
YOU'RE SO NICE TO HIM.
THEN AGAIN, I'M NOT SUR-PRISED.
!
FWIP
WHAT'S THAT SUPPOSED TO MEAN?
GUESS.
WHY...
DO I FEEL LIKE HE'S ATTACKING ME?
UH-OH.

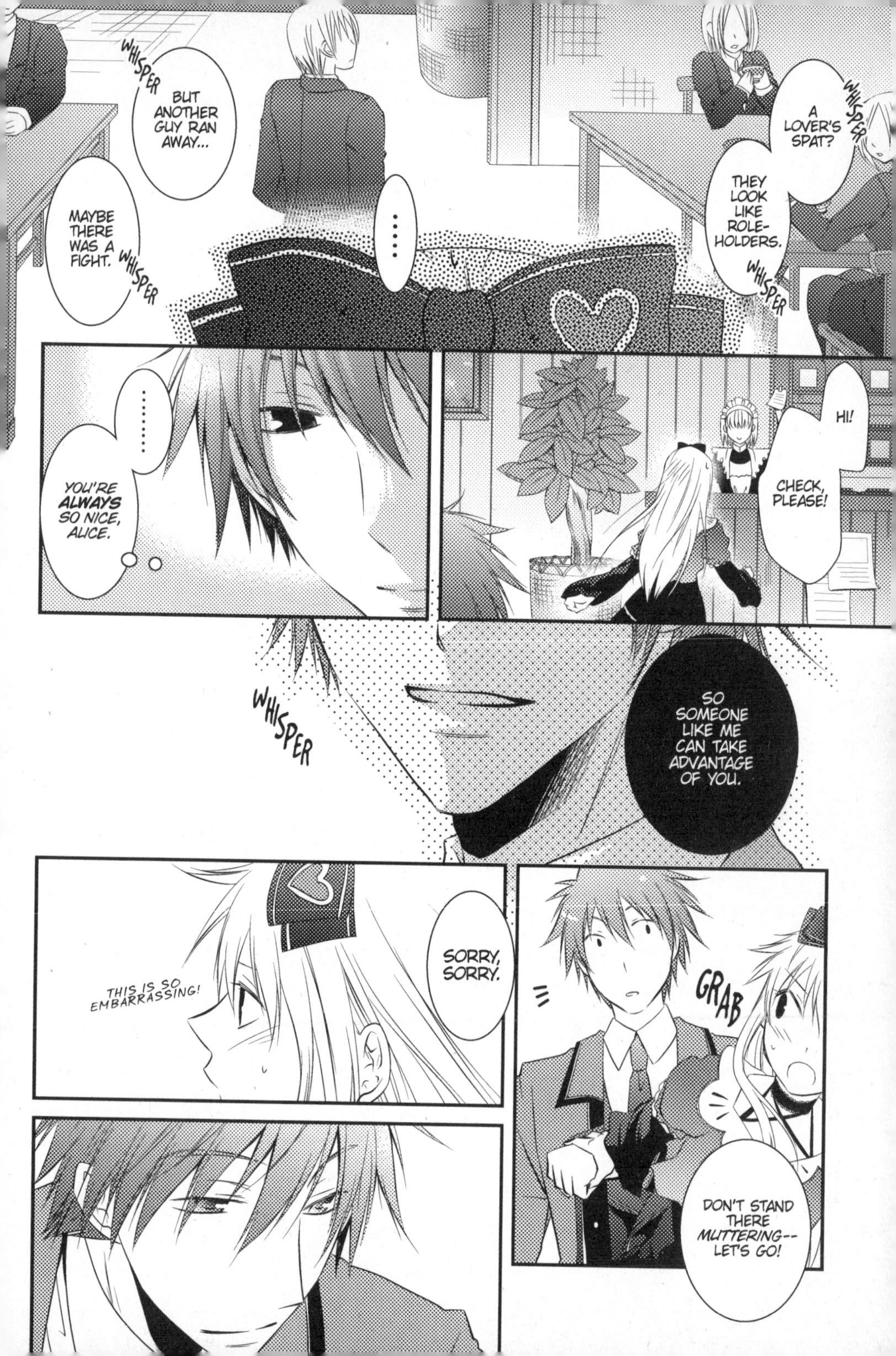
WHISPER
A LOVER'S SPAT?
THEY LOOK LIKE ROLE-HOLDERS.
WHISPER
......
WHISPER
BUT ANOTHER GUY RAN AWAY...
MAYBE THERE WAS A FIGHT.
WHISPER
HI!
CHECK, PLEASE!
......
YOU'RE **ALWAYS** SO NICE, ALICE.
SO SOMEONE LIKE ME CAN TAKE ADVANTAGE OF YOU.
WHISPER
GRAB
DON'T STAND THERE *MUTTERING*-- LET'S GO!
SORRY, SORRY.
THIS IS SO EMBARRASSING!

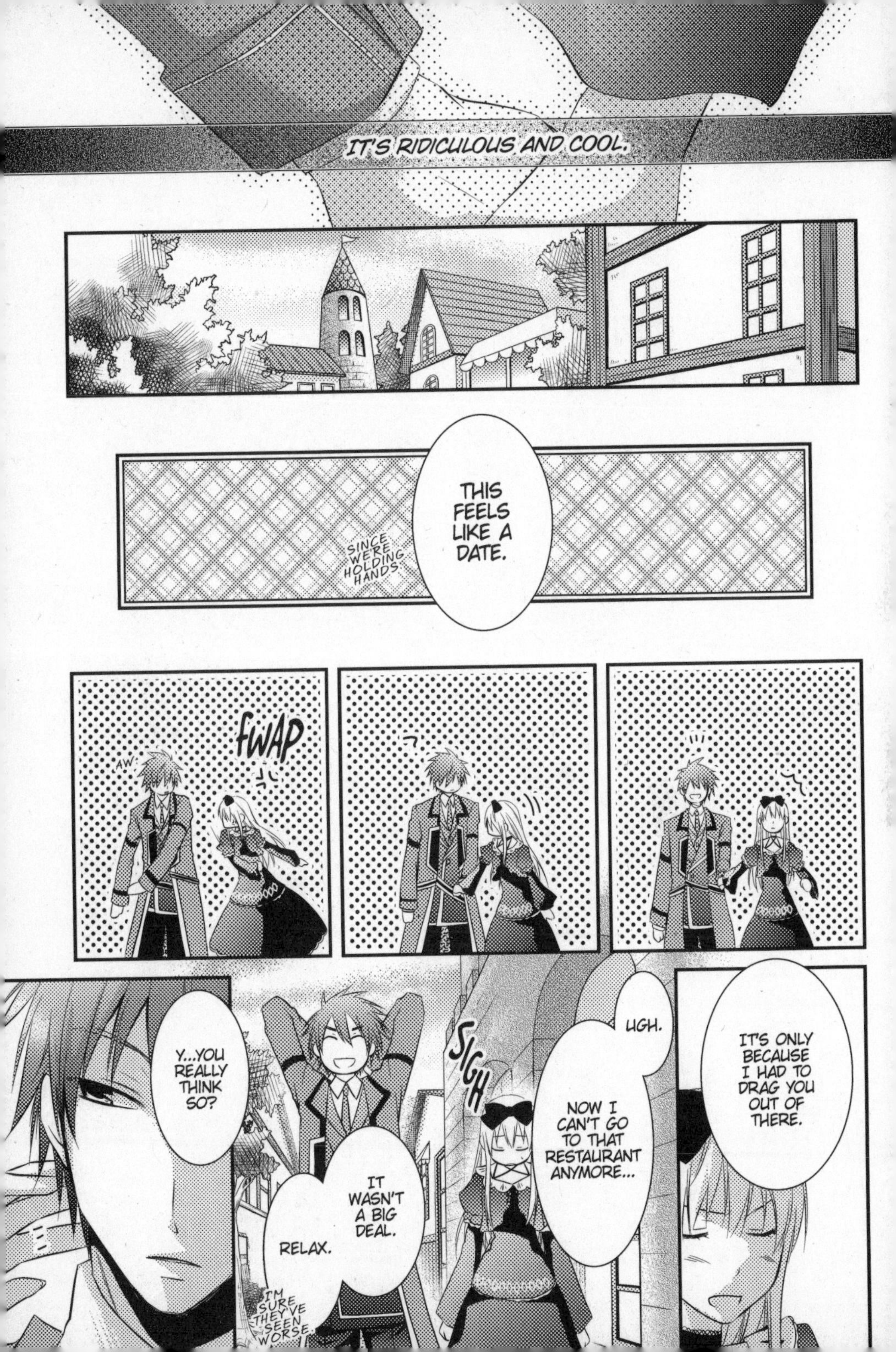
IT'S RIDICULOUS AND COOL.
THIS FEELS LIKE A DATE.
SINCE WE'RE HOLDING HANDS.
FWAP
AW.
IT'S ONLY BECAUSE I HAD TO DRAG YOU OUT OF THERE.
UGH.
NOW I CAN'T GO TO THAT RESTAURANT ANYMORE...
SIGH
IT WASN'T A BIG DEAL.
RELAX.
I'M SURE THEY'VE SEEN WORSE.
Y...YOU REALLY THINK SO?

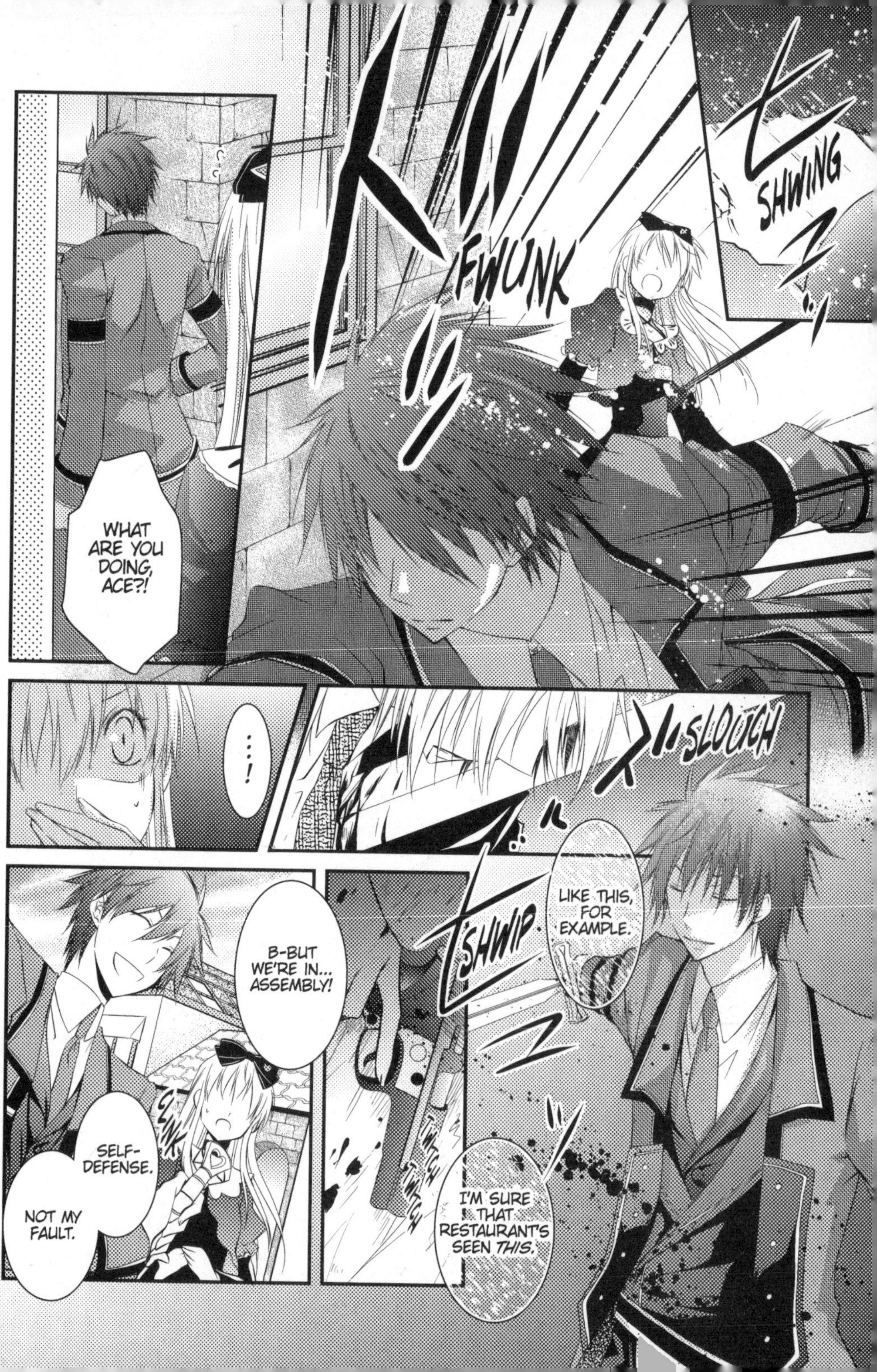
SHWING
FWUNK
WHAT ARE YOU DOING, ACE?!
SLOUCH
...!
SHWIP
LIKE THIS, FOR EXAMPLE.
I'M SURE THAT RESTAURANT'S SEEN *THIS.*
B-BUT WE'RE IN... ASSEMBLY!
TWITCH TWITCH
SELF-DEFENSE.
NOT MY FAULT.
CLINK

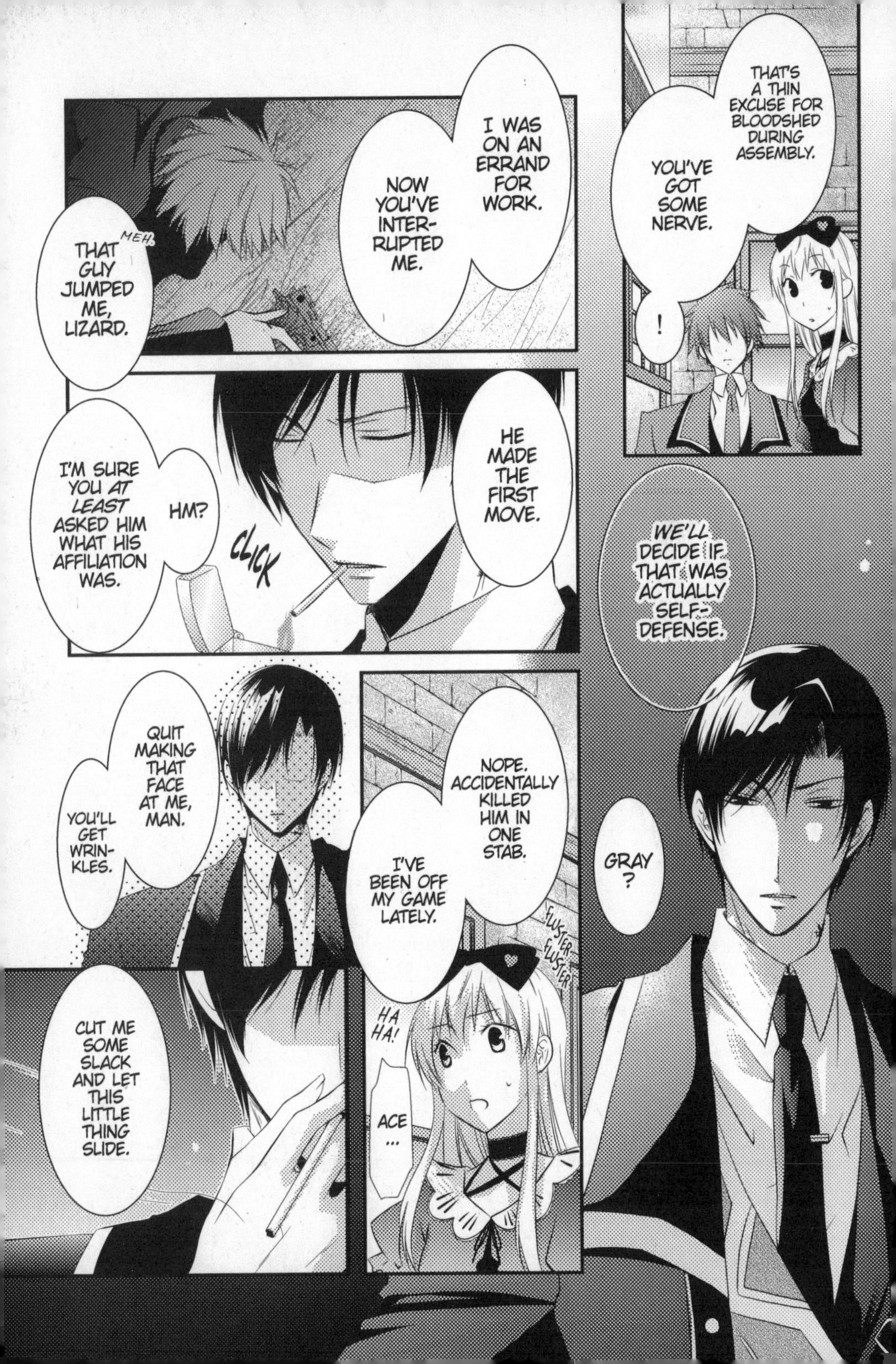
THAT'S A THIN EXCUSE FOR BLOODSHED DURING ASSEMBLY.
YOU'VE GOT SOME NERVE.
!
I WAS ON AN ERRAND FOR WORK.
NOW YOU'VE INTER-RUPTED ME.
MEH.
THAT GUY JUMPED ME, LIZARD.
HE MADE THE FIRST MOVE.
HM?
I'M SURE YOU *AT LEAST* ASKED HIM WHAT HIS AFFILIATION WAS.
CLICK
WE'LL DECIDE IF THAT WAS ACTUALLY SELF-DEFENSE.
GRAY?
NOPE. ACCIDENTALLY KILLED HIM IN ONE STAB.
I'VE BEEN OFF MY GAME LATELY.
QUIT MAKING THAT FACE AT ME, MAN.
YOU'LL GET WRIN-KLES.
FLUSTER FLUSTER
HA HA!
ACE...
CUT ME SOME SLACK AND LET THIS LITTLE THING SLIDE.

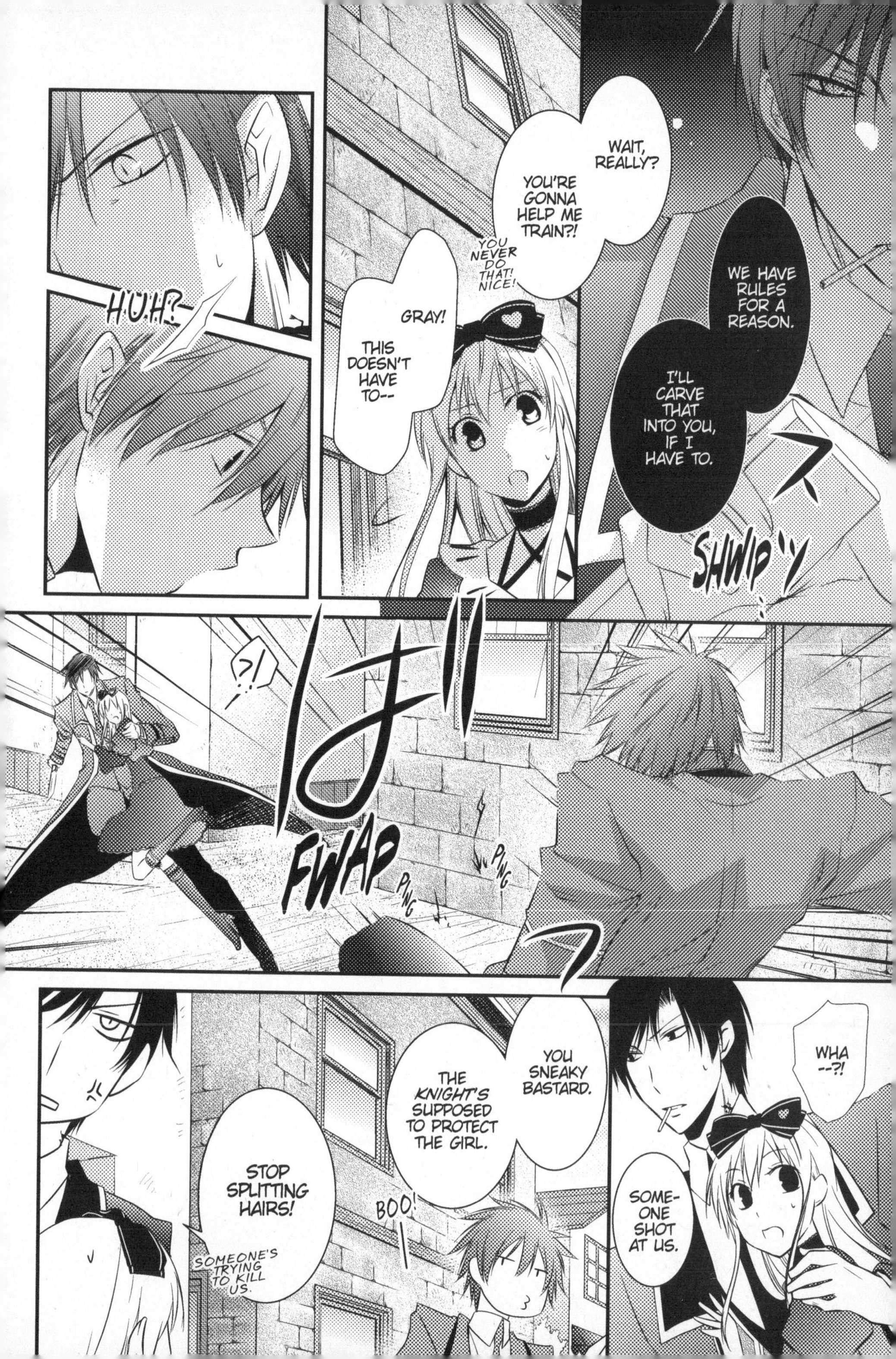
WE HAVE RULES FOR A REASON.
I'LL CARVE THAT INTO YOU, IF I HAVE TO.
SHWIP
WAIT, REALLY?
YOU'RE GONNA HELP ME TRAIN?!
YOU NEVER DO THAT! NICE!
GRAY!
THIS DOESN'T HAVE TO--
HUH?
?!
FWAP
PING
PING
WHA --?!
SOME-ONE SHOT AT US.
YOU SNEAKY BASTARD.
THE *KNIGHT'S* SUPPOSED TO PROTECT THE GIRL.
BOO!
STOP SPLITTING HAIRS!
SOMEONE'S TRYING TO KILL US.

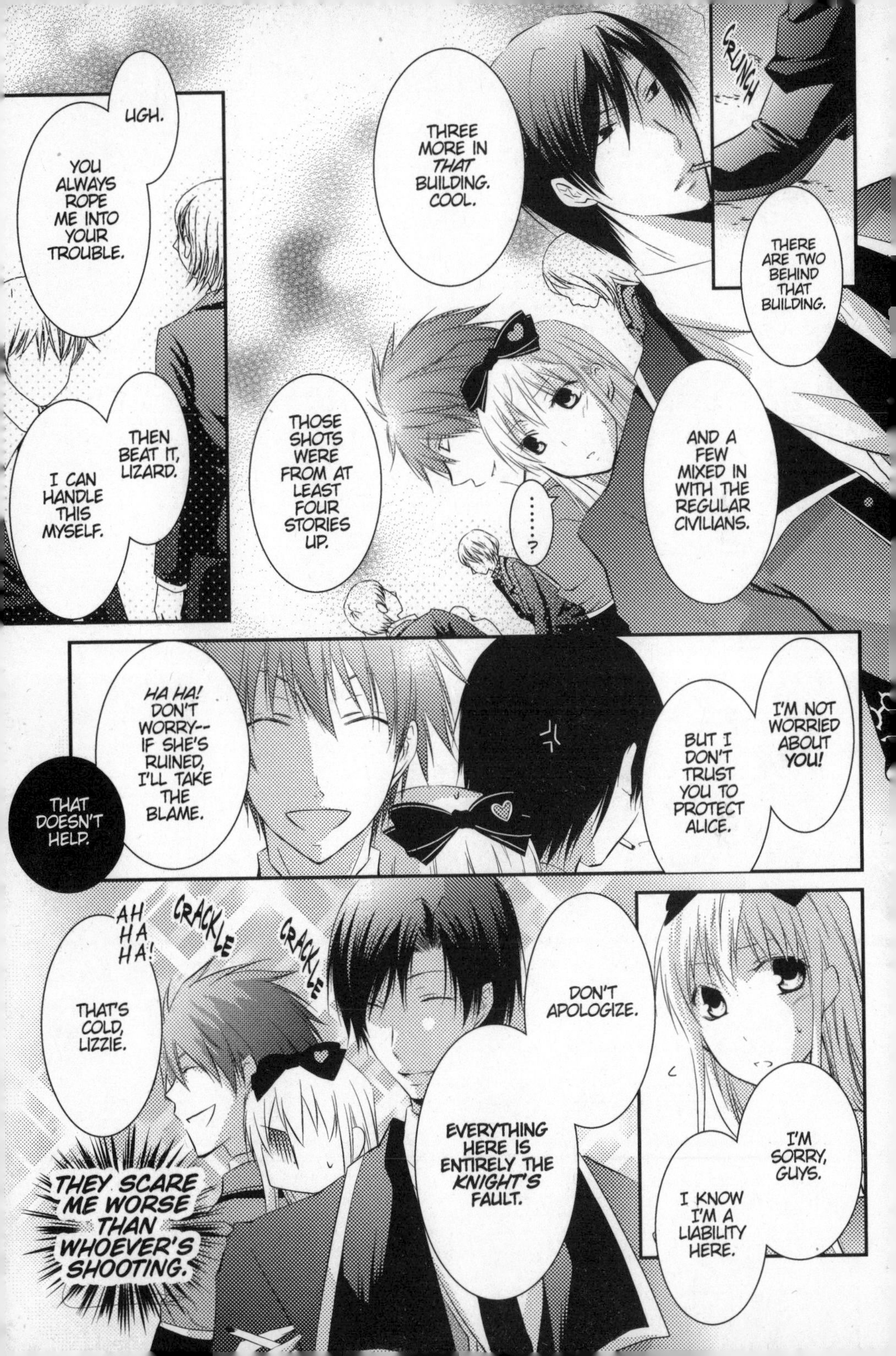
CRUNCH
THERE ARE TWO BEHIND THAT BUILDING.
THREE MORE IN *THAT* BUILDING. COOL.
AND A FEW MIXED IN WITH THE REGULAR CIVILIANS.
THOSE SHOTS WERE FROM AT LEAST FOUR STORIES UP.
......?
UGH.
YOU ALWAYS ROPE ME INTO YOUR TROUBLE.
THEN BEAT IT, LIZARD.
I CAN HANDLE THIS MYSELF.
I'M NOT WORRIED ABOUT **YOU!**
BUT I DON'T TRUST YOU TO PROTECT ALICE.
HA HA! DON'T WORRY-- IF SHE'S RUINED, I'LL TAKE THE BLAME.
THAT DOESN'T HELP.
I'M SORRY, GUYS.
I KNOW I'M A LIABILITY HERE.
DON'T APOLOGIZE.
EVERYTHING HERE IS ENTIRELY THE *KNIGHT'S* FAULT.
CRACKLE
CRACKLE
AH HA HA!
THAT'S COLD, LIZZIE.
THEY SCARE ME WORSE THAN WHOEVER'S SHOOTING.

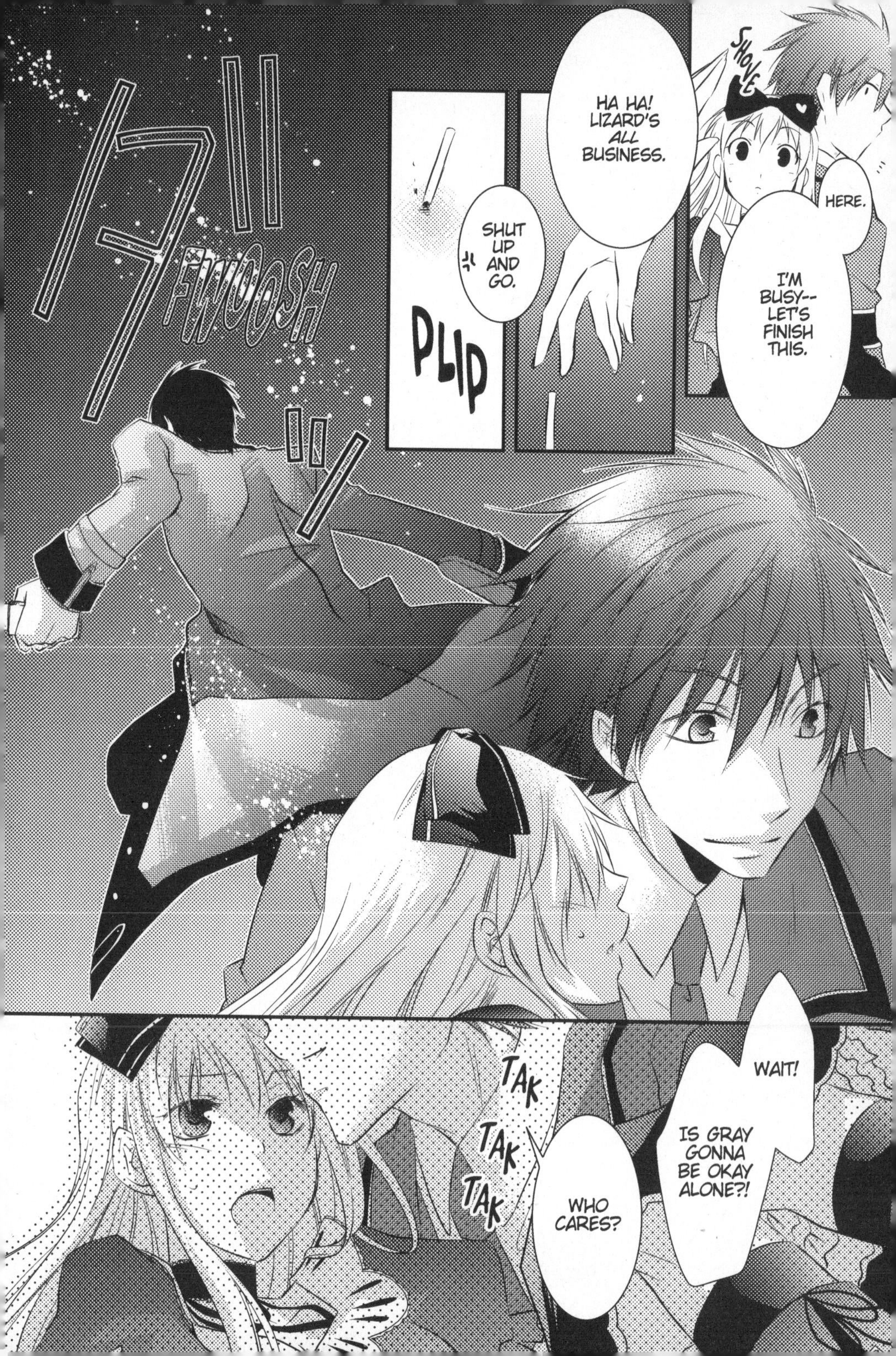
SHOVE
HERE.
I'M BUSY-- LET'S FINISH THIS.
HA HA! LIZARD'S ALL BUSINESS.
SHUT UP AND GO.
PLIP
FWOOSH
WAIT!
IS GRAY GONNA BE OKAY ALONE?!
TAK
TAK
TAK
WHO CARES?

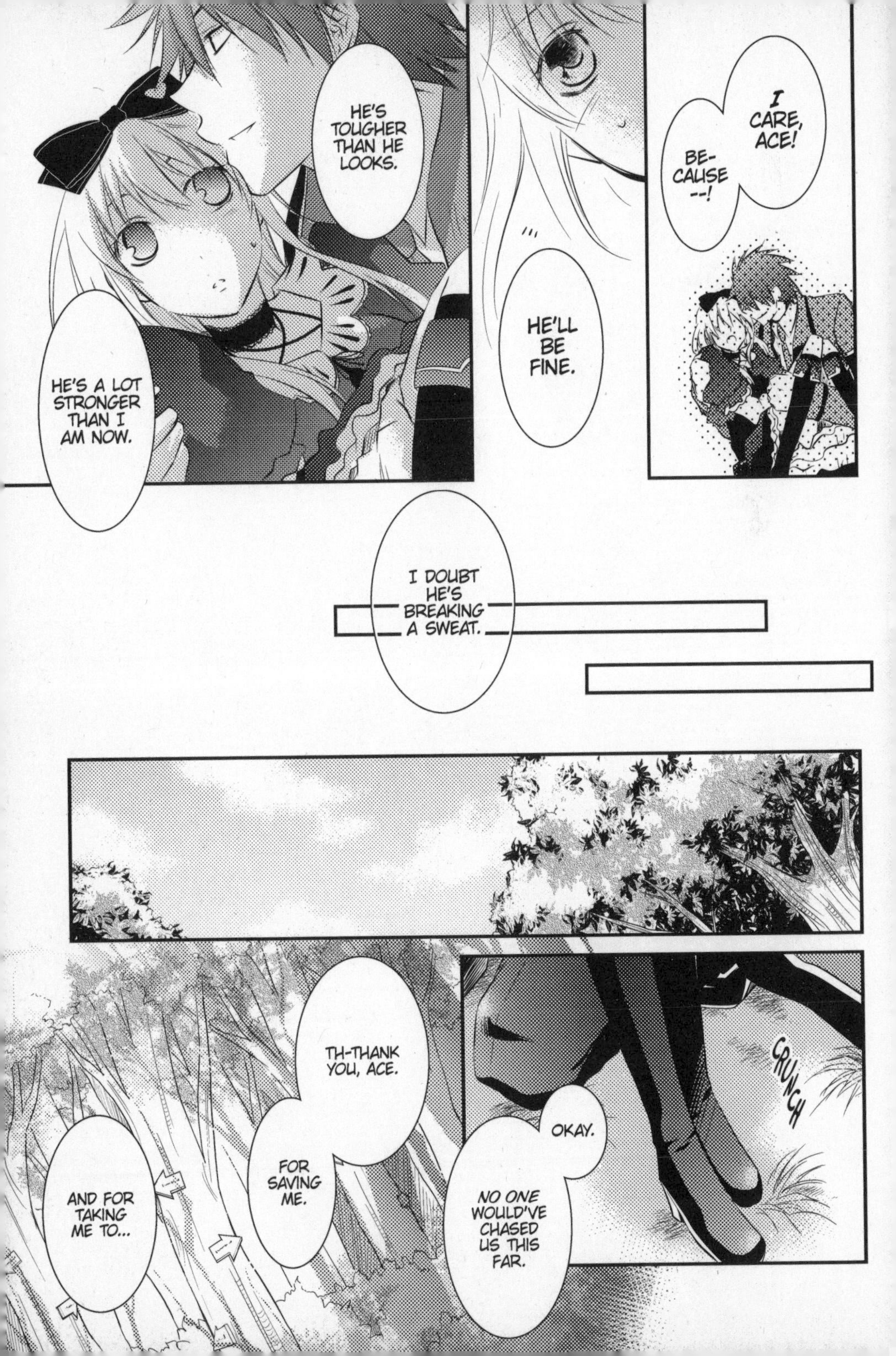
I CARE, ACE!
BE-CAUSE --!
HE'LL BE FINE.
HE'S TOUGHER THAN HE LOOKS.
HE'S A LOT STRONGER THAN I AM NOW.
I DOUBT HE'S BREAKING A SWEAT.
CRUNCH
OKAY.
NO ONE WOULD'VE CHASED US THIS FAR.
TH-THANK YOU, ACE.
FOR SAVING ME.
AND FOR TAKING ME TO...

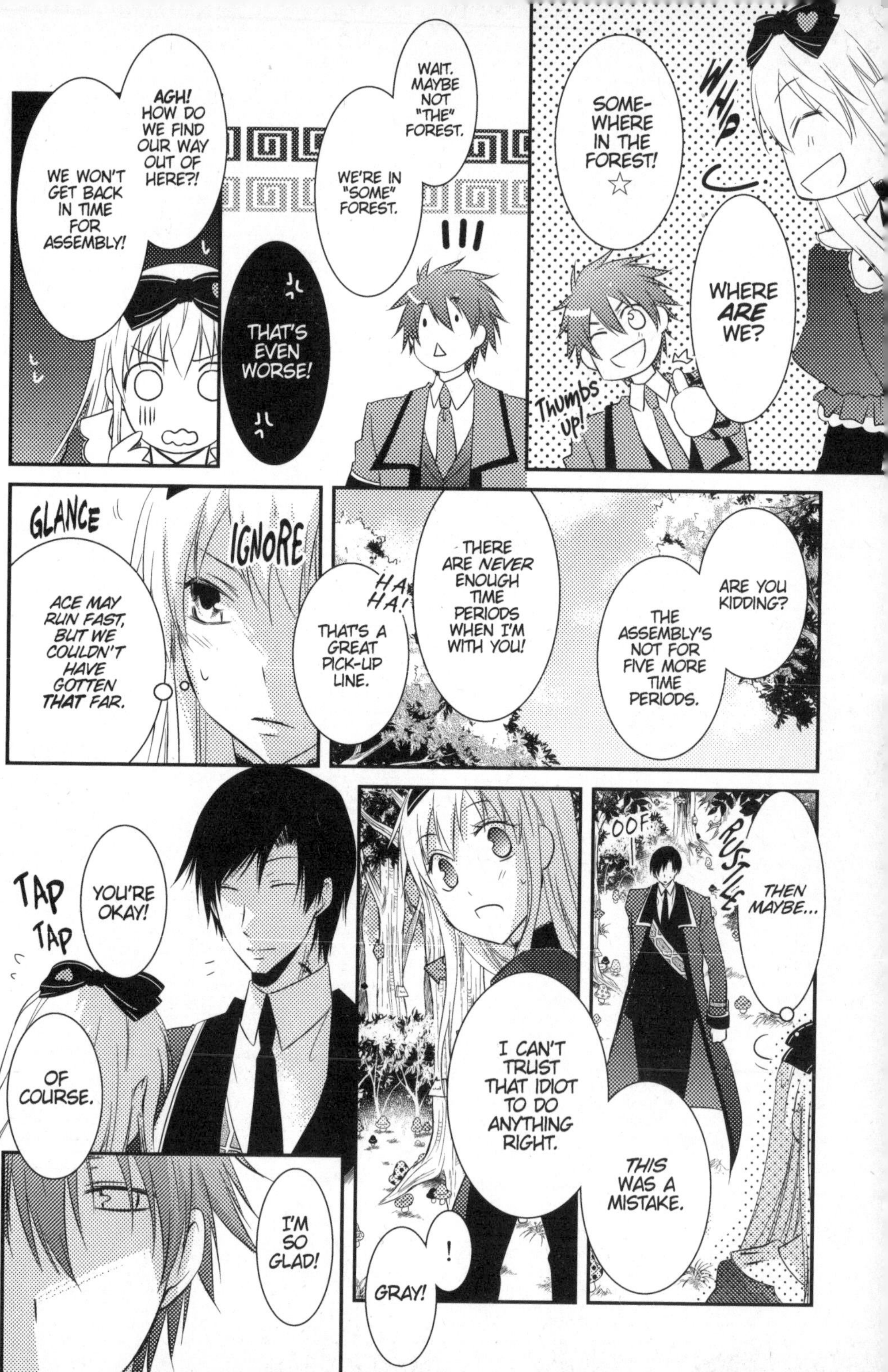
WHIP
WHERE ARE WE?
SOME-WHERE IN THE FOREST! ☆
Thumbs up!
WAIT. MAYBE NOT "THE" FOREST.
WE'RE IN "SOME" FOREST.
THAT'S EVEN WORSE!
AGH! HOW DO WE FIND OUR WAY OUT OF HERE?!
WE WON'T GET BACK IN TIME FOR ASSEMBLY!
ARE YOU KIDDING?
THE ASSEMBLY'S NOT FOR FIVE MORE TIME PERIODS.
THERE ARE NEVER ENOUGH TIME PERIODS WHEN I'M WITH YOU!
HA HA!
THAT'S A GREAT PICK-UP LINE.
GLANCE
IGNORE
ACE MAY RUN FAST, BUT WE COULDN'T HAVE GOTTEN THAT FAR.
RUSTLE
OOF
THEN MAYBE...
THIS WAS A MISTAKE.
I CAN'T TRUST THAT IDIOT TO DO ANYTHING RIGHT.
!
GRAY!
TAP TAP
YOU'RE OKAY!
OF COURSE.
I'M SO GLAD!

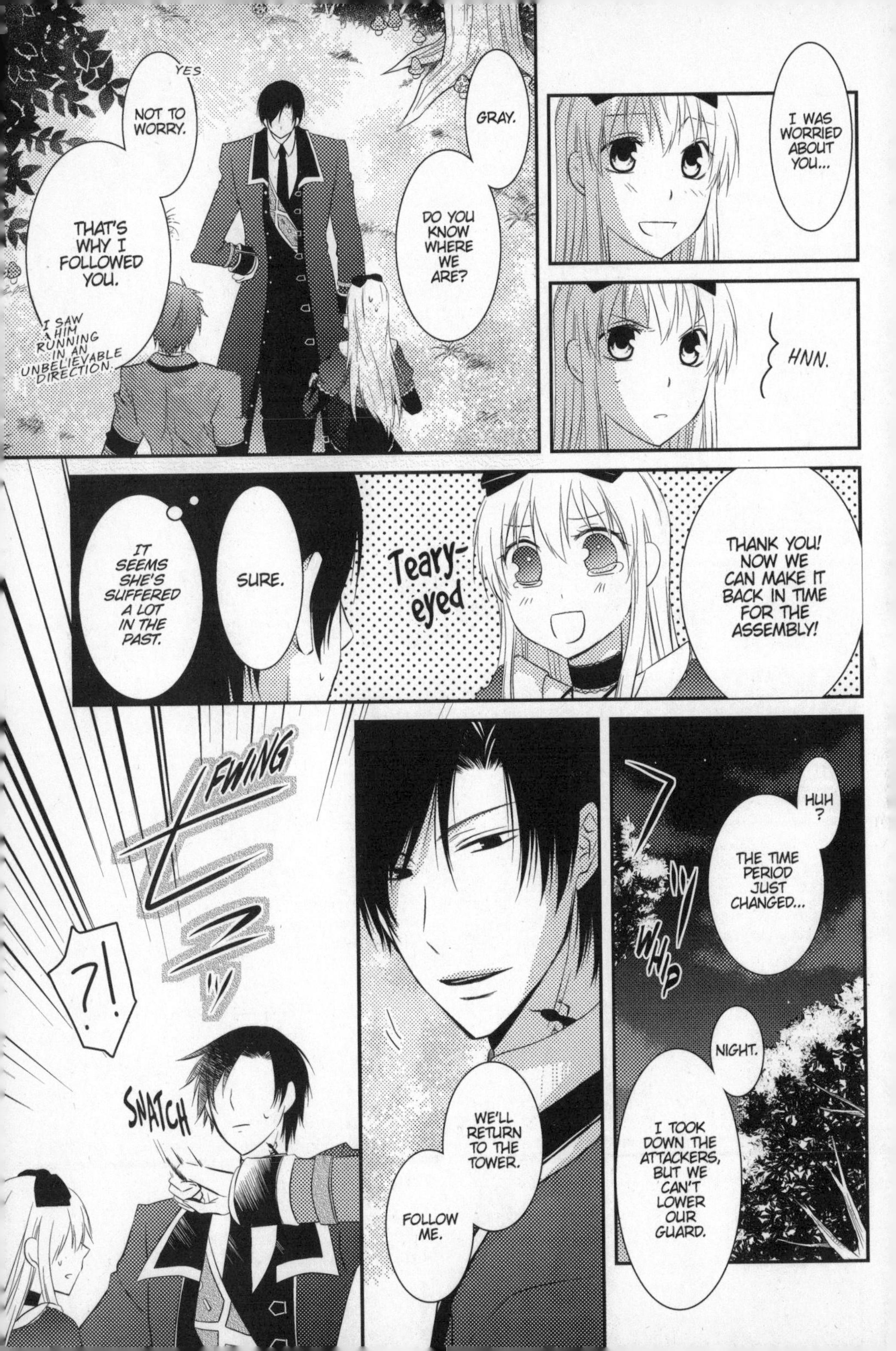
I WAS WORRIED ABOUT YOU...
HNN.
GRAY.
DO YOU KNOW WHERE WE ARE?
YES.
NOT TO WORRY.
THAT'S WHY I FOLLOWED YOU.
I SAW HIM RUNNING IN AN UNBELIEVABLE DIRECTION.
THANK YOU! NOW WE CAN MAKE IT BACK IN TIME FOR THE ASSEMBLY!
Teary-eyed
SURE.
IT SEEMS SHE'S SUFFERED A LOT IN THE PAST.
HUH?
THE TIME PERIOD JUST CHANGED...
WHIP
NIGHT.
I TOOK DOWN THE ATTACKERS, BUT WE CAN'T LOWER OUR GUARD.
WE'LL RETURN TO THE TOWER.
FOLLOW ME.
FWING
?!
SNATCH

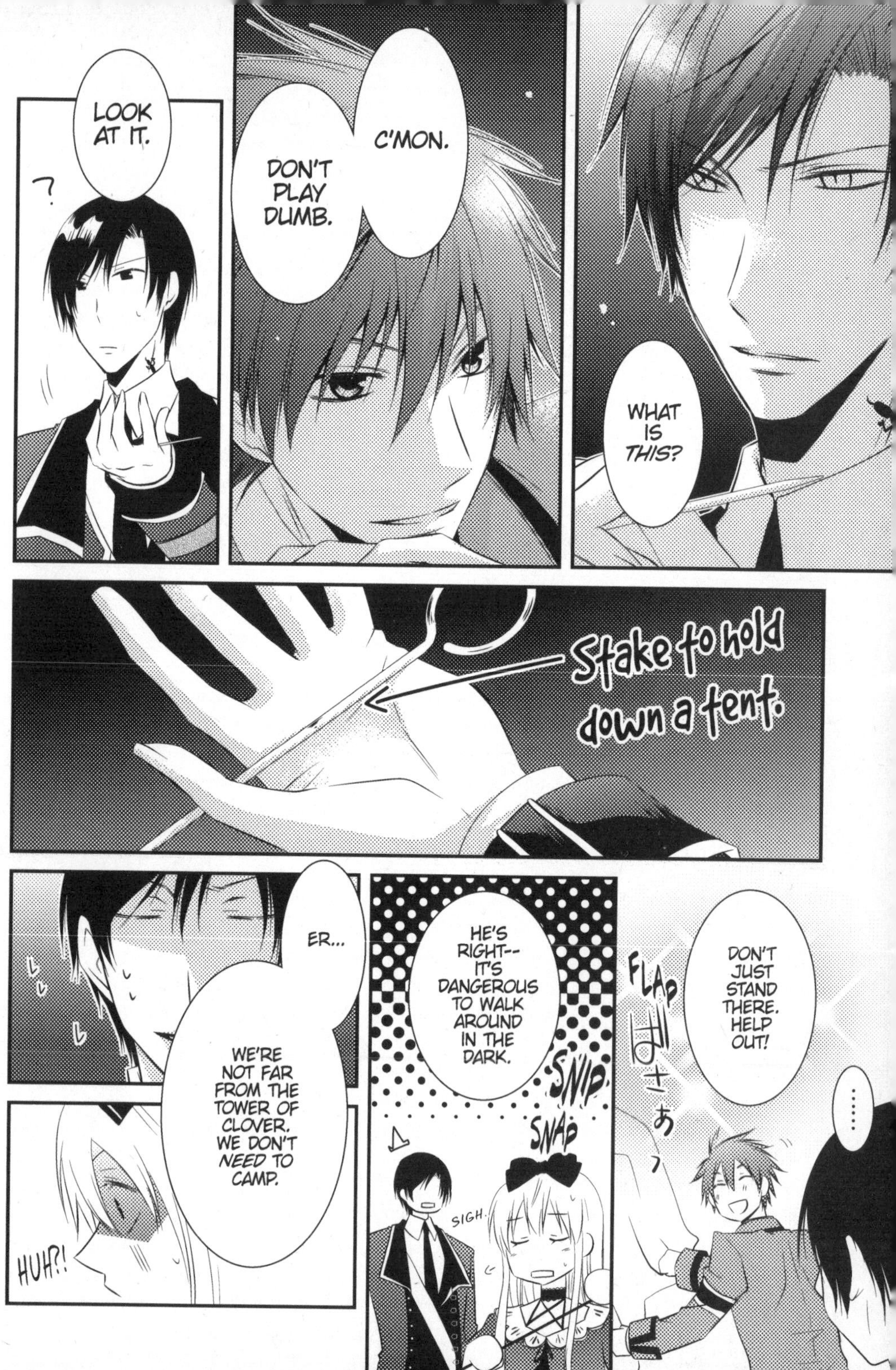
WHAT IS THIS?
C'MON.
DON'T PLAY DUMB.
LOOK AT IT.
?
Stake to hold down a tent.
DON'T JUST STAND THERE. HELP OUT!
FLAP
......
HE'S RIGHT-- IT'S DANGEROUS TO WALK AROUND IN THE DARK.
SNIP
SNAP
SIGH.
ER...
WE'RE NOT FAR FROM THE TOWER OF CLOVER. WE DON'T NEED TO CAMP.
HUH?!

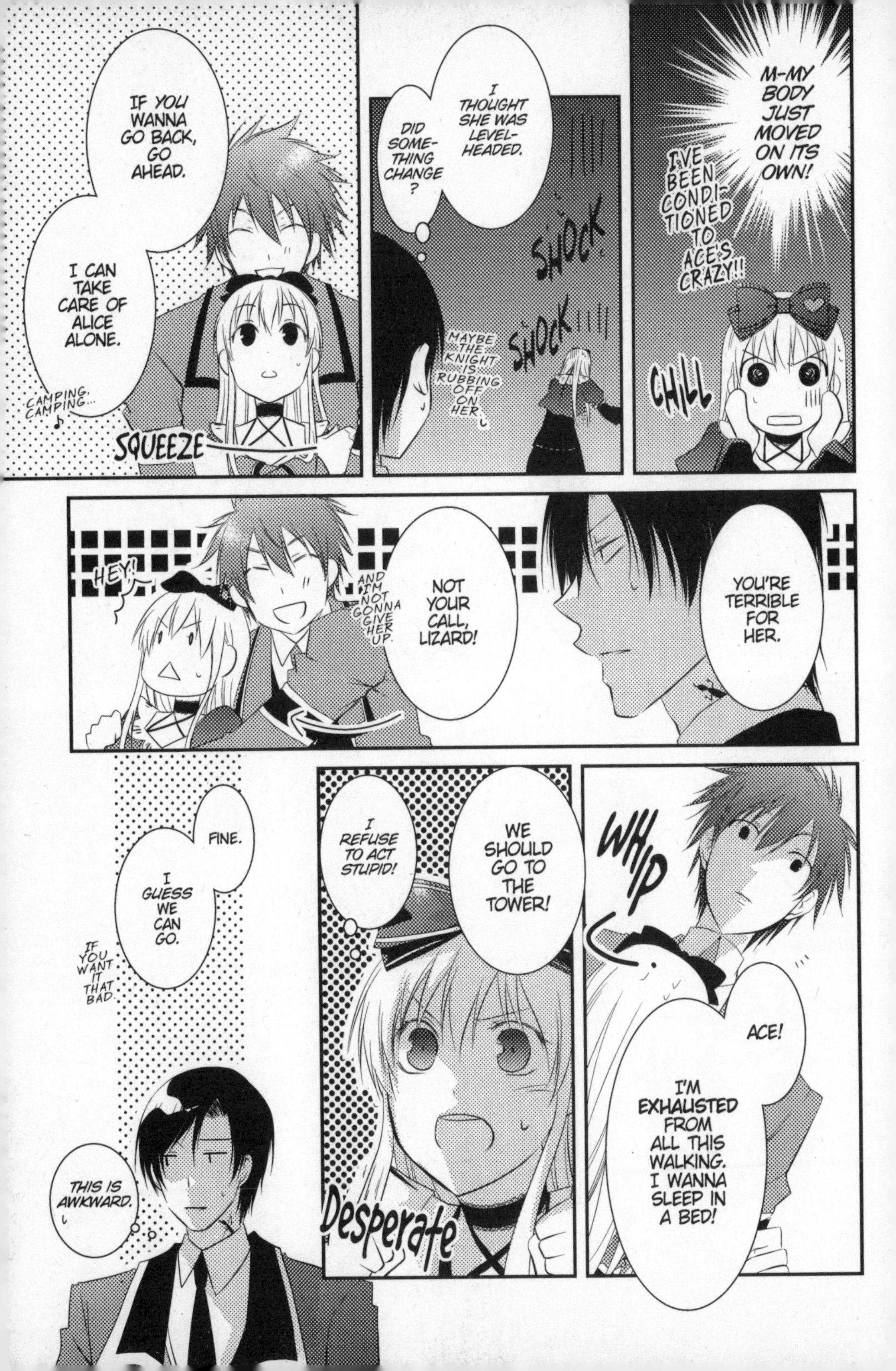
M-MY BODY JUST MOVED ON ITS OWN!
I'VE BEEN CONDITIONED TO ACE'S CRAZY!!
CHILL
I THOUGHT SHE WAS LEVEL-HEADED.
DID SOMETHING CHANGE?
SHOCK
SHOCK
MAYBE THE KNIGHT IS RUBBING OFF ON HER.
IF YOU WANNA GO BACK, GO AHEAD.
I CAN TAKE CARE OF ALICE ALONE.
CAMPING, CAMPING...
SQUEEZE
YOU'RE TERRIBLE FOR HER.
NOT YOUR CALL, LIZARD!
AND I'M NOT GONNA GIVE HER UP.
HEY!
WHIP
ACE!
I'M EXHAUSTED FROM ALL THIS WALKING. I WANNA SLEEP IN A BED!
WE SHOULD GO TO THE TOWER!
I REFUSE TO ACT STUPID!
Desperate
FINE.
I GUESS WE CAN GO.
IF YOU WANT IT THAT BAD.
THIS IS AWKWARD.

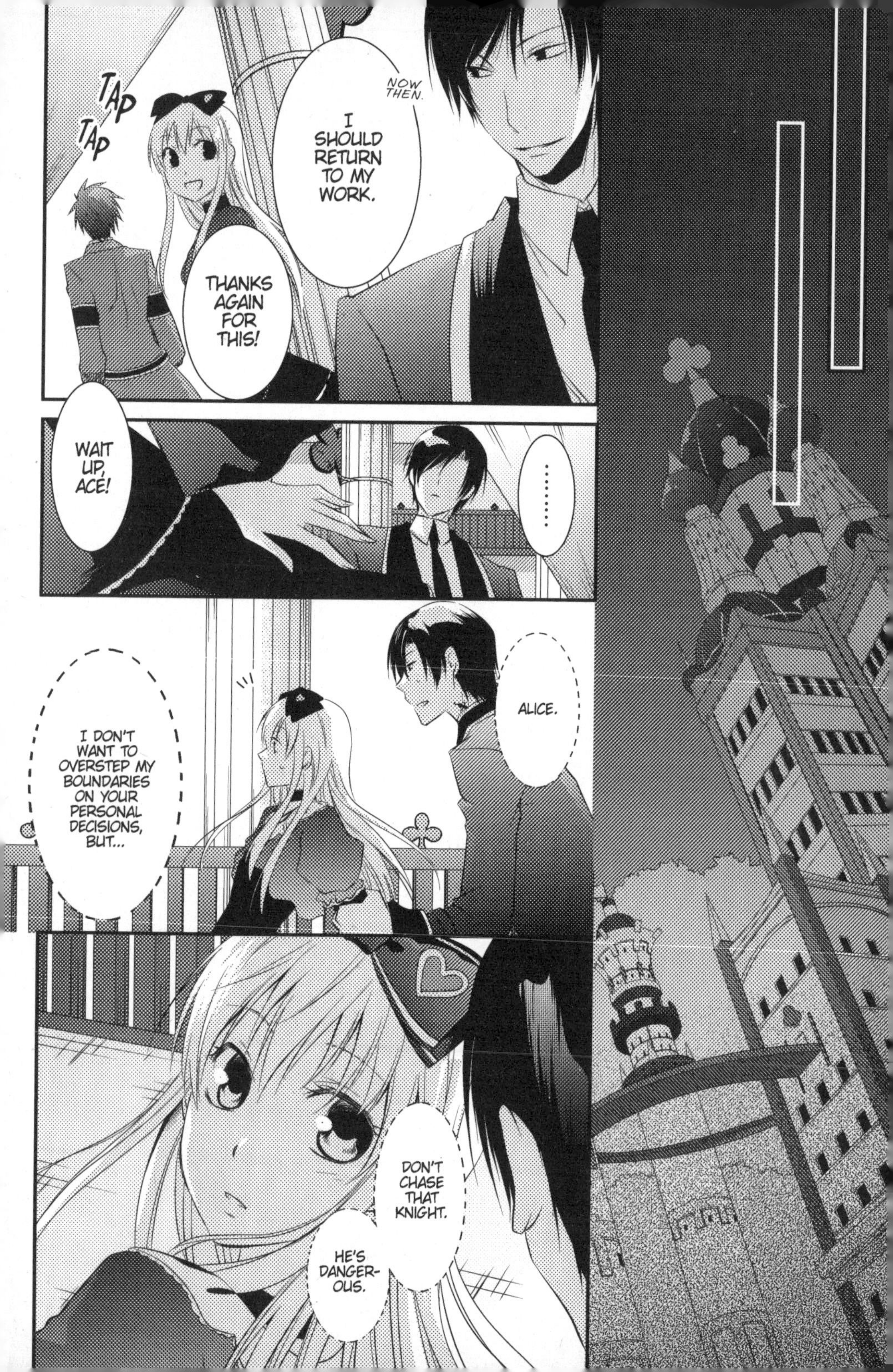
NOW THEN.
I SHOULD RETURN TO MY WORK.
THANKS AGAIN FOR THIS!
TAP TAP
......
WAIT UP, ACE!
ALICE.
I DON'T WANT TO OVERSTEP MY BOUNDARIES ON YOUR PERSONAL DECISIONS, BUT...
DON'T CHASE THAT KNIGHT.
HE'S DANGER-OUS.

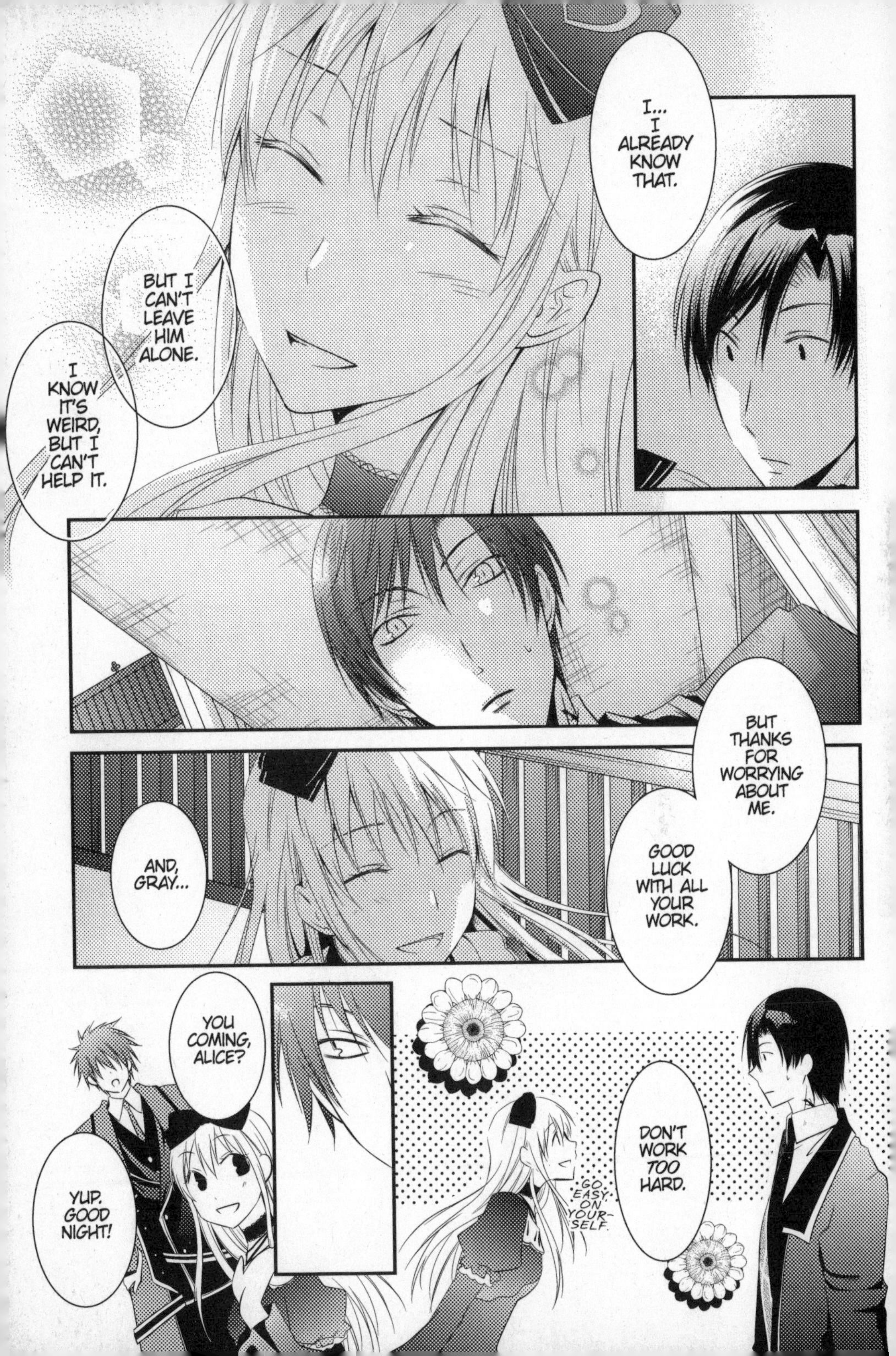
I... I ALREADY KNOW THAT.
BUT I CAN'T LEAVE HIM ALONE.
I KNOW IT'S WEIRD, BUT I CAN'T HELP IT.
BUT THANKS FOR WORRYING ABOUT ME.
GOOD LUCK WITH ALL YOUR WORK.
AND, GRAY...
DON'T WORK *TOO* HARD.
GO EASY ON YOURSELF.
YOU COMING, ALICE?
YUP. GOOD NIGHT!

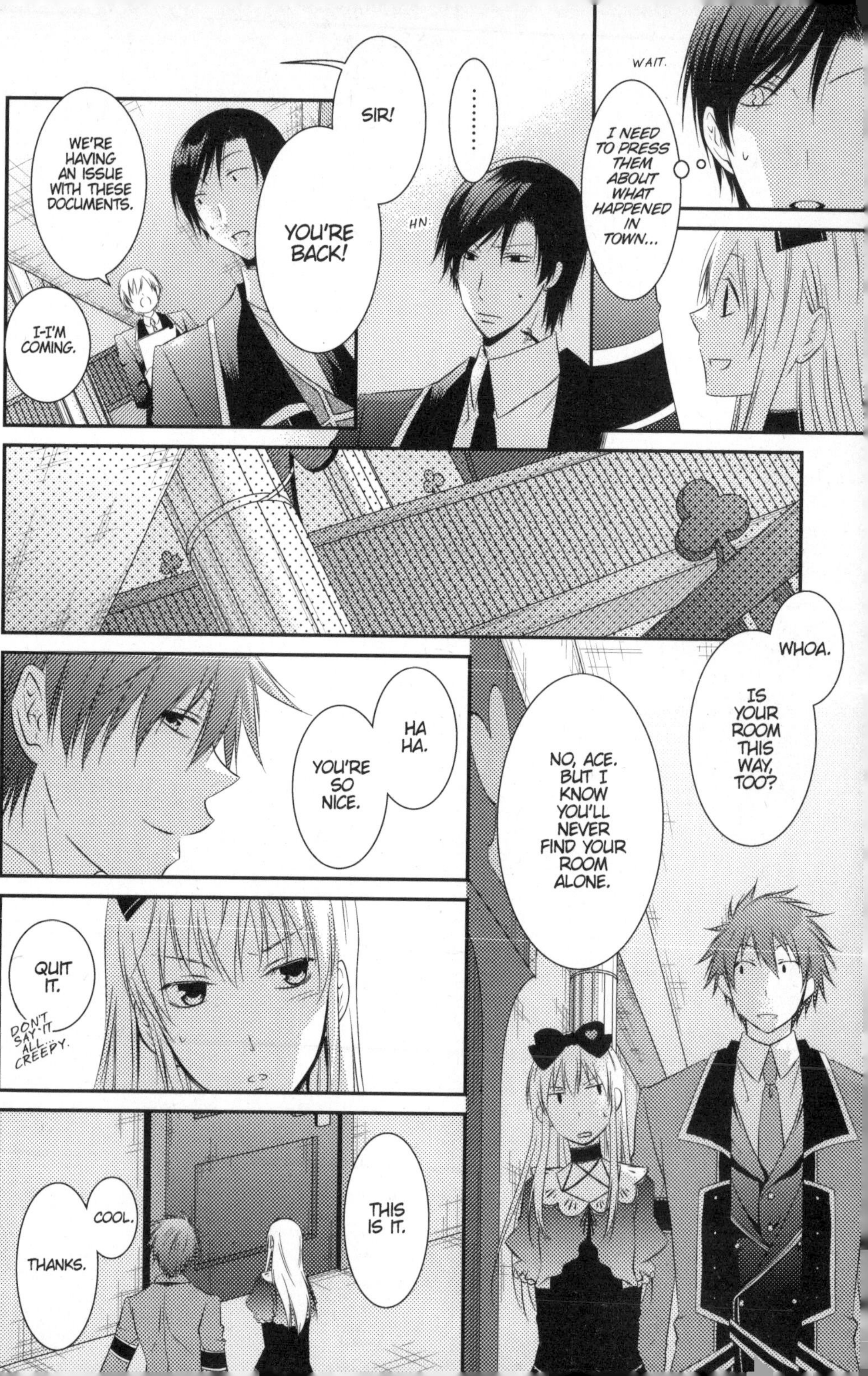
WAIT.
I NEED TO PRESS THEM ABOUT WHAT HAPPENED IN TOWN...
......
SIR!
YOU'RE BACK!
HN.
WE'RE HAVING AN ISSUE WITH THESE DOCUMENTS.
I-I'M COMING.
WHOA.
IS YOUR ROOM THIS WAY, TOO?
NO, ACE. BUT I KNOW YOU'LL NEVER FIND YOUR ROOM ALONE.
HA HA.
YOU'RE SO NICE.
QUIT IT.
DON'T SAY IT ALL... CREEPY.
THIS IS IT.
COOL.
THANKS.

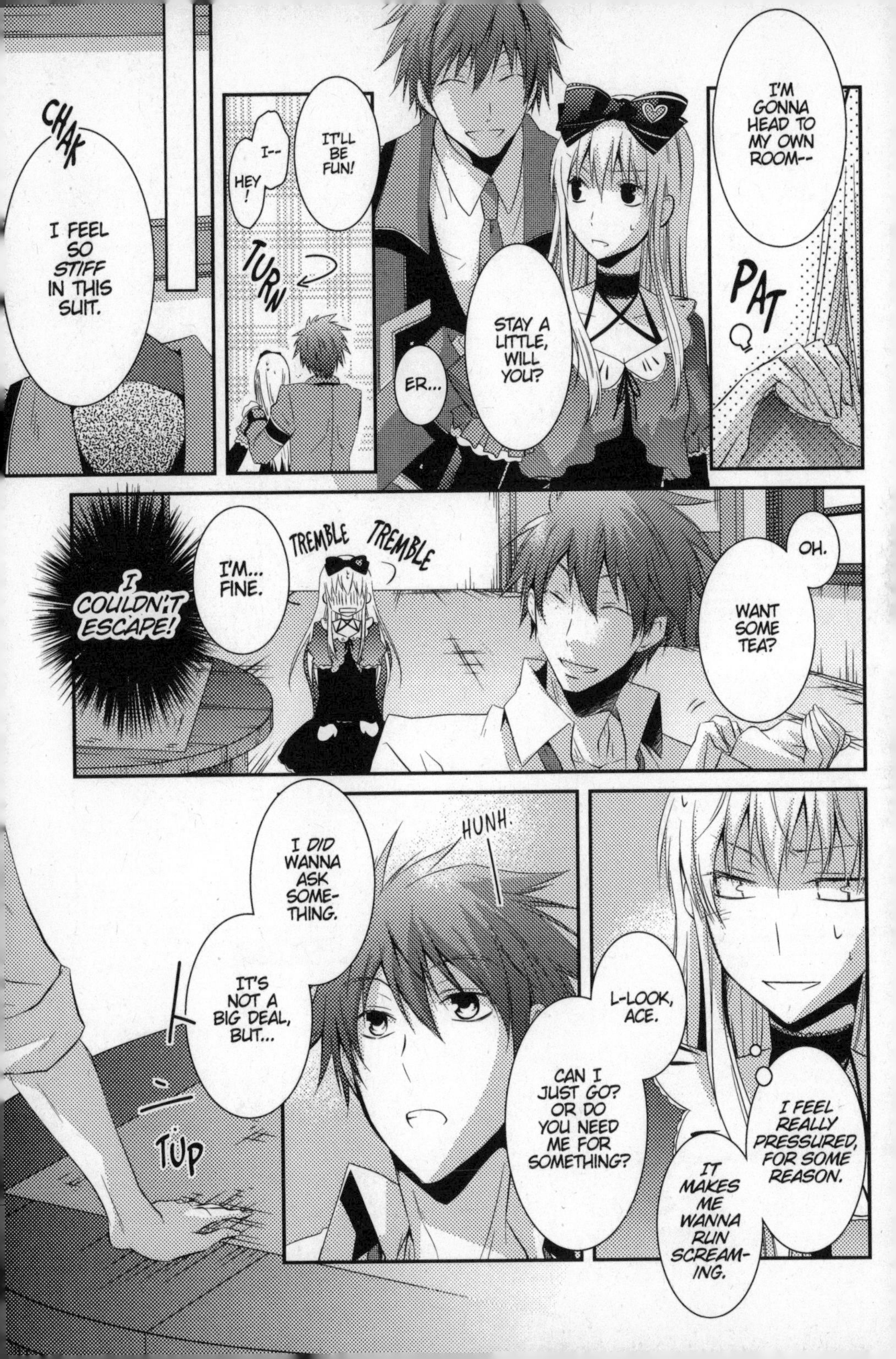
I'M GONNA HEAD TO MY OWN ROOM--
PAT
STAY A LITTLE, WILL YOU?
ER...
IT'LL BE FUN!
I-- HEY!
TURN
CHAK
I FEEL SO STIFF IN THIS SUIT.
OH.
WANT SOME TEA?
TREMBLE TREMBLE
I'M... FINE.
I COULDN'T ESCAPE!
L-LOOK, ACE.
CAN I JUST GO? OR DO YOU NEED ME FOR SOMETHING?
I FEEL REALLY PRESSURED, FOR SOME REASON.
IT MAKES ME WANNA RUN SCREAMING.
HUNH.
I DID WANNA ASK SOMETHING.
IT'S NOT A BIG DEAL, BUT...
TUP

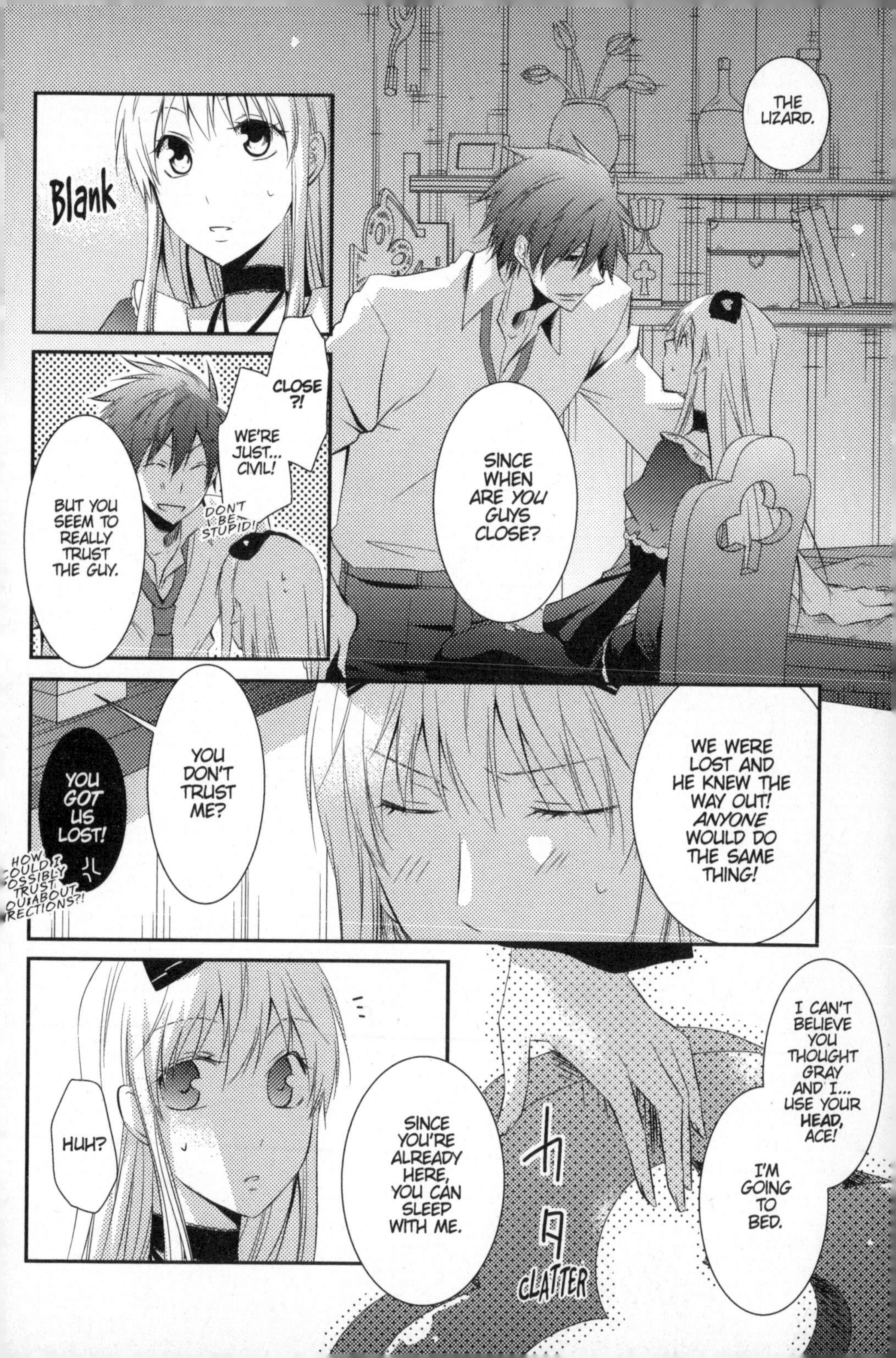
THE LIZARD.
SINCE WHEN ARE YOU GUYS CLOSE?
Blank
CLOSE?!
WE'RE JUST... CIVIL!
DON'T BE STUPID!
BUT YOU SEEM TO REALLY TRUST THE GUY.
WE WERE LOST AND HE KNEW THE WAY OUT! ANYONE WOULD DO THE SAME THING!
YOU DON'T TRUST ME?
YOU GOT US LOST!
HOW COULD I OSSIBLY TRUST OU ABOUT RECTIONS?!
I CAN'T BELIEVE YOU THOUGHT GRAY AND I... USE YOUR HEAD, ACE!
I'M GOING TO BED.
カタ
CLATTER
SINCE YOU'RE ALREADY HERE, YOU CAN SLEEP WITH ME.
HUH?

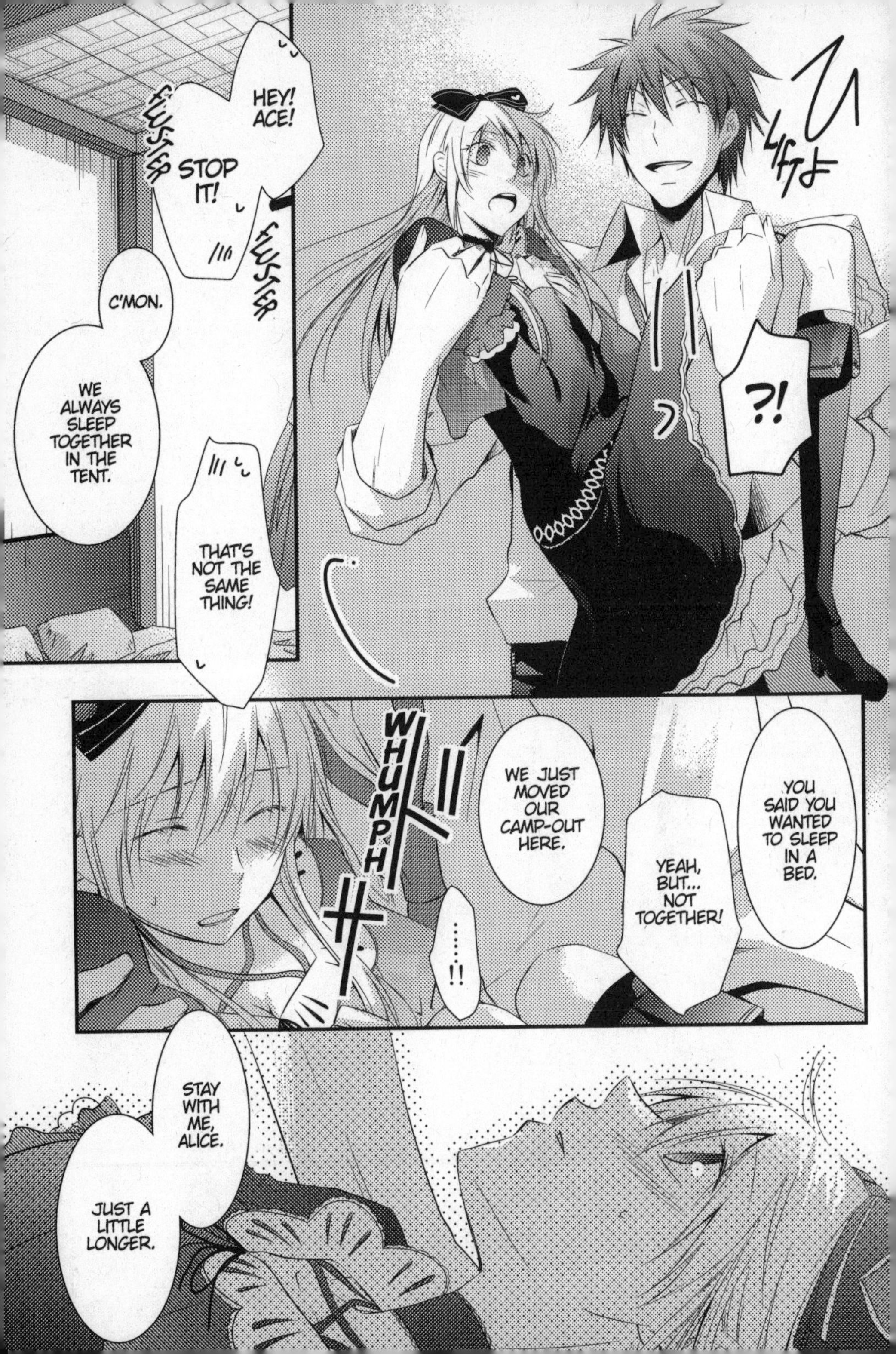
LIFT
?!
HEY! ACE!
STOP IT!
FLUSTER
FLUSTER
C'MON.
WE ALWAYS SLEEP TOGETHER IN THE TENT.
THAT'S NOT THE SAME THING!
YOU SAID YOU WANTED TO SLEEP IN A BED.
YEAH, BUT... NOT TOGETHER!
WE JUST MOVED OUR CAMP-OUT HERE.
WHUMPH
......!!
STAY WITH ME, ALICE.
JUST A LITTLE LONGER.

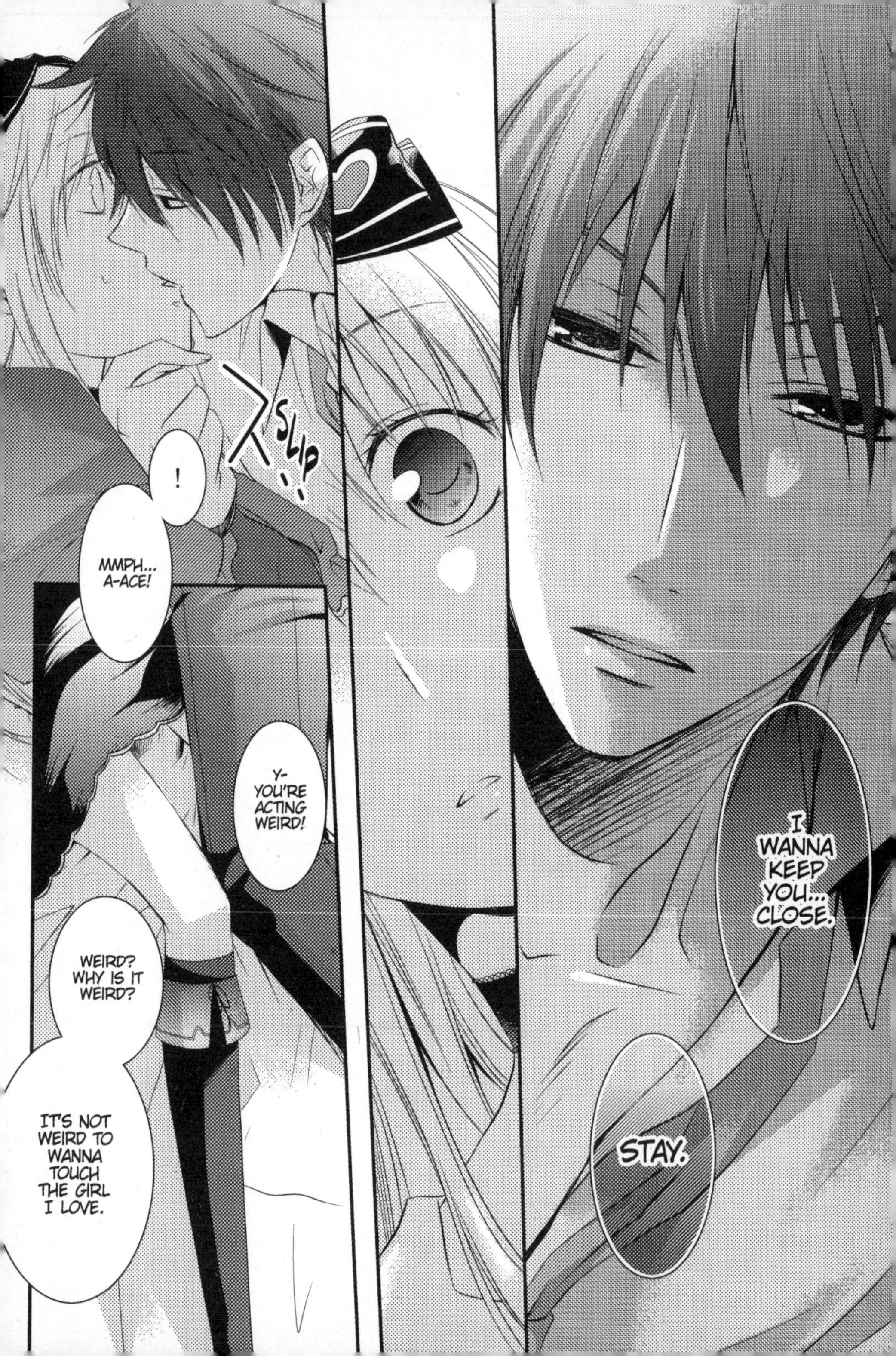
I WANNA KEEP YOU... CLOSE.
STAY.
SLIP
!
MMPH... A-ACE!
Y- YOU'RE ACTING WEIRD!
WEIRD? WHY IS IT WEIRD?
IT'S NOT WEIRD TO WANNA TOUCH THE GIRL I LOVE.

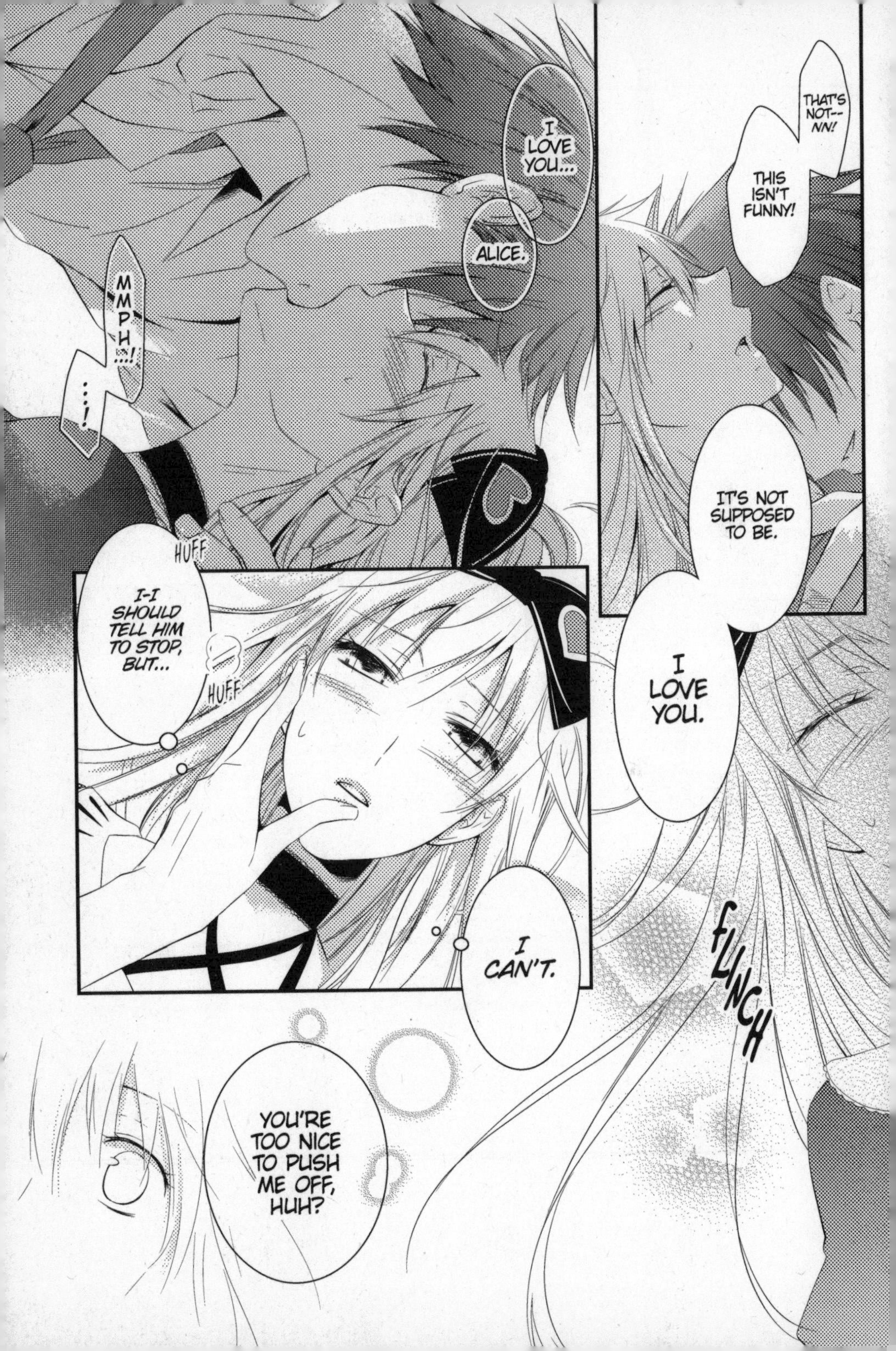
THAT'S NOT-- NN!
THIS ISN'T FUNNY!
IT'S NOT SUPPOSED TO BE.
I LOVE YOU.
I LOVE YOU...
ALICE.
MMPH...!
...!
HUFF
I-I SHOULD TELL HIM TO STOP, BUT...
HUFF
I CAN'T.
FLINCH
YOU'RE TOO NICE TO PUSH ME OFF, HUH?

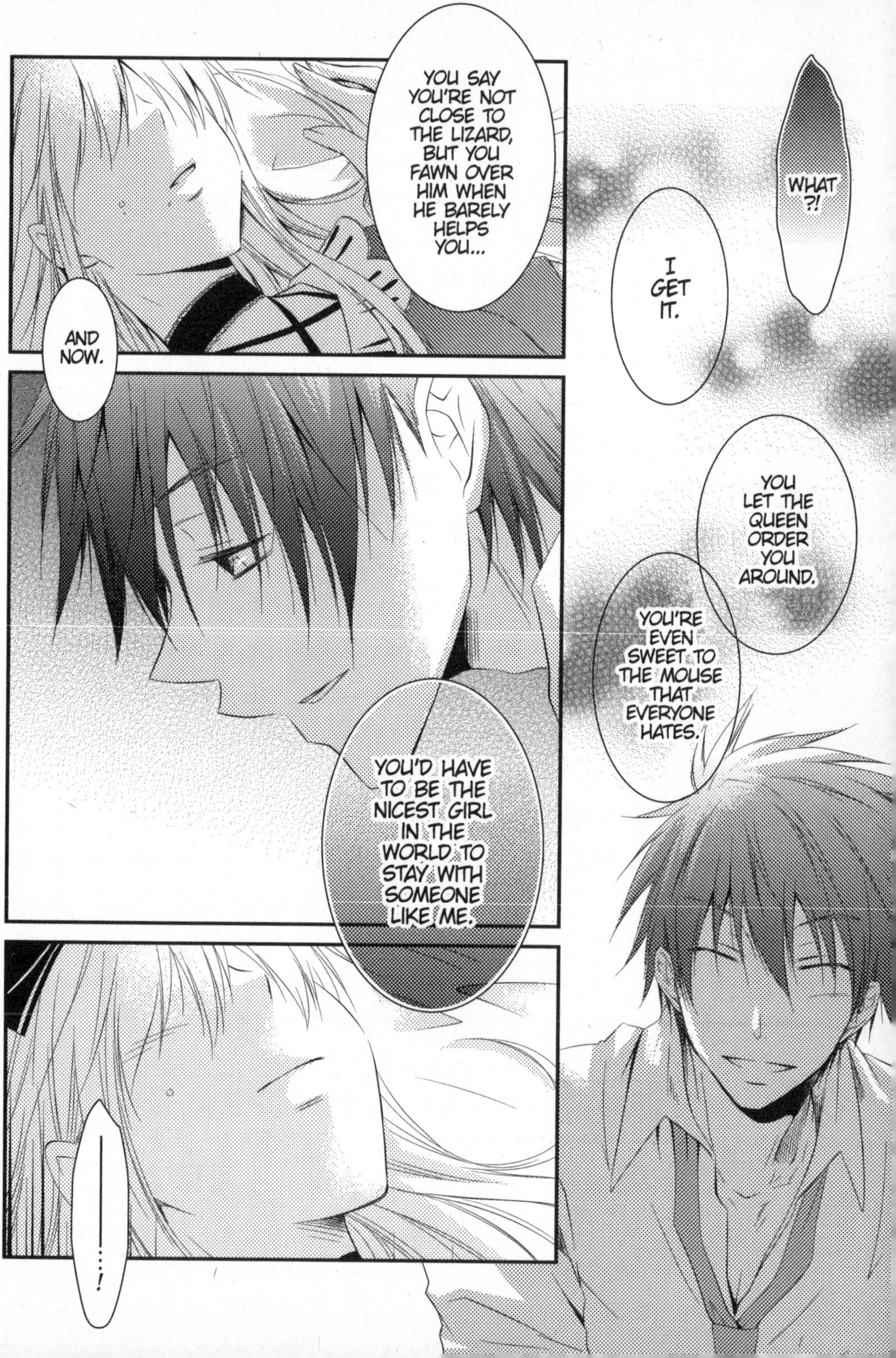
WHAT?!
I GET IT.
YOU SAY YOU'RE NOT CLOSE TO THE LIZARD, BUT YOU FAWN OVER HIM WHEN HE BARELY HELPS YOU...
AND NOW.
YOU LET THE QUEEN ORDER YOU AROUND.
YOU'RE EVEN SWEET TO THE MOUSE THAT EVERYONE HATES.
YOU'D HAVE TO BE THE NICEST GIRL IN THE WORLD TO STAY WITH SOMEONE LIKE ME.
......!

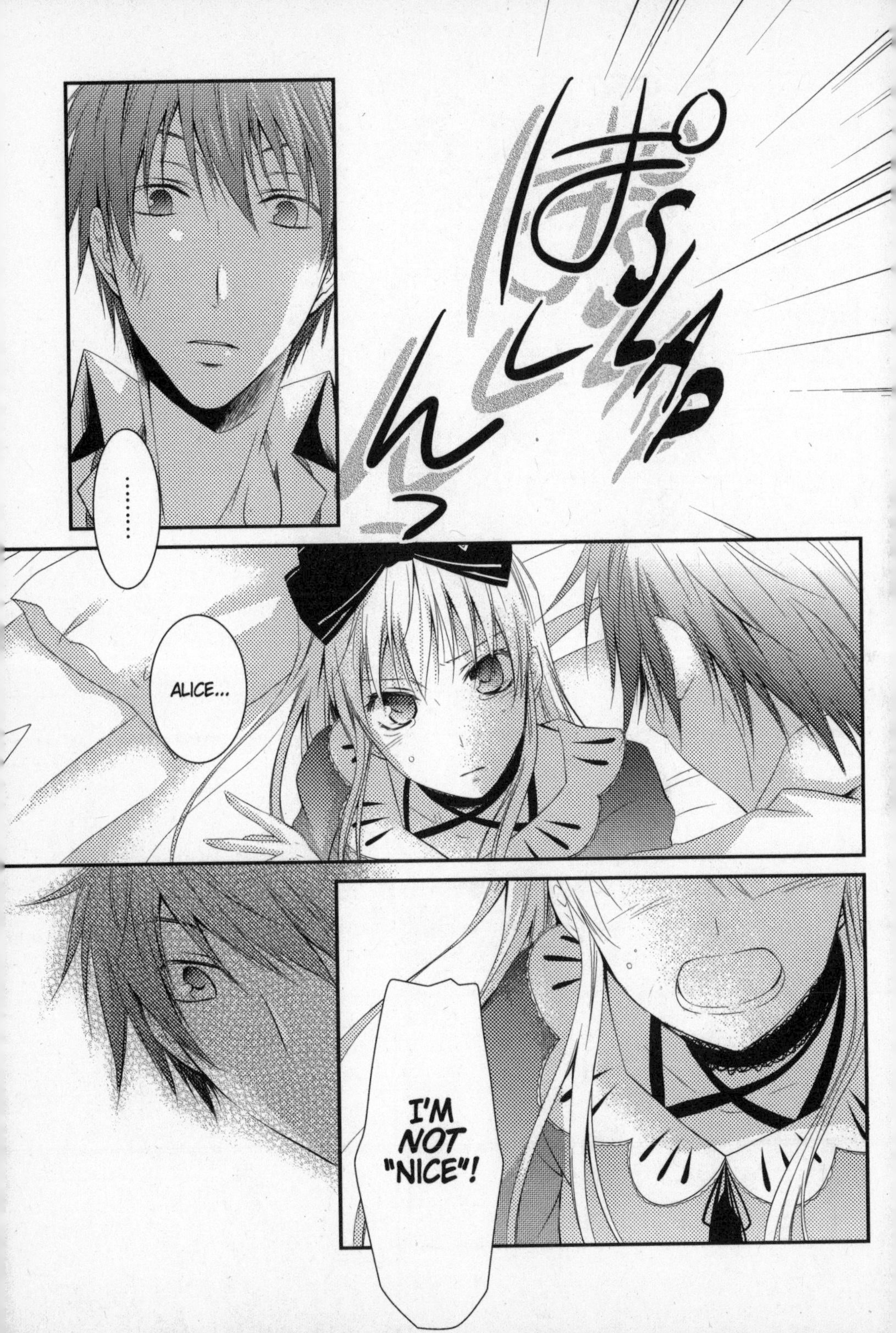
ぱしんっ
SLAP
......
ALICE...
I'M NOT "NICE"!

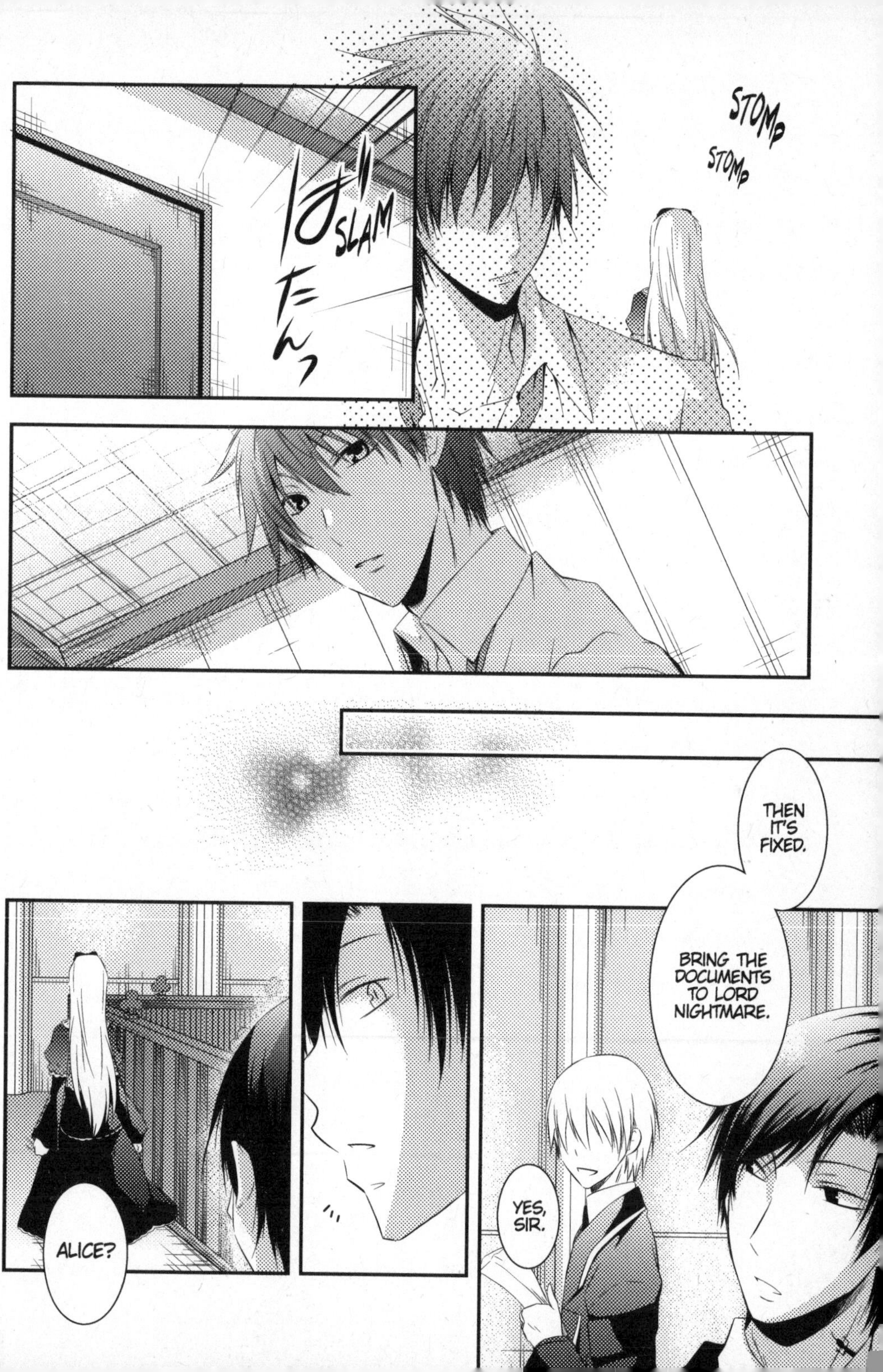
STOMP
STOMP
SLAM
THEN IT'S FIXED.
BRING THE DOCUMENTS TO LORD NIGHTMARE.
YES, SIR.
...
ALICE?

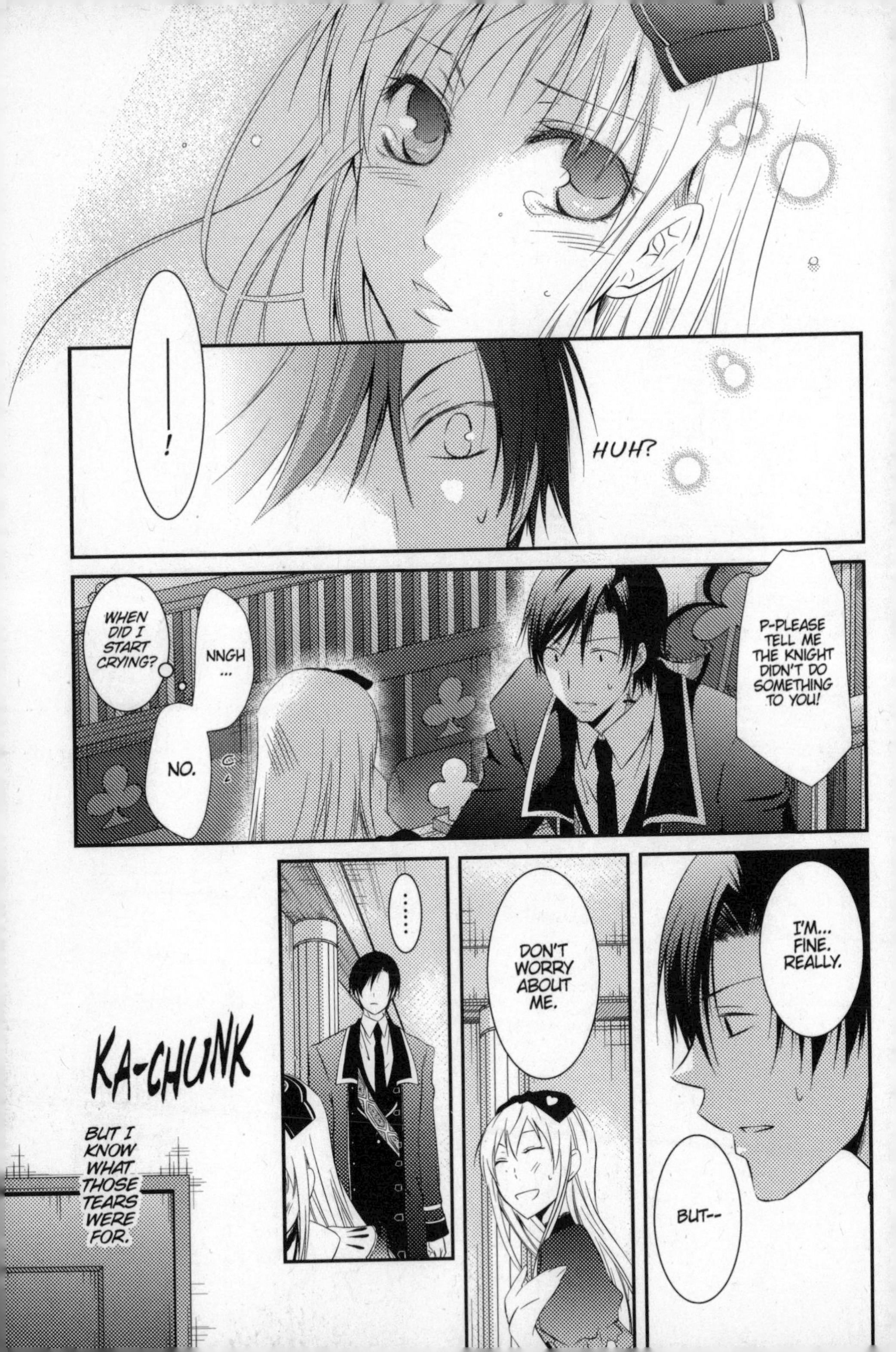
HUH?
!
P-PLEASE TELL ME THE KNIGHT DIDN'T DO SOMETHING TO YOU!
NNGH...
WHEN DID I START CRYING?
NO.
I'M... FINE. REALLY.
BUT--
DON'T WORRY ABOUT ME.
......
KA-CHUNK
BUT I KNOW WHAT THOSE TEARS WERE FOR.

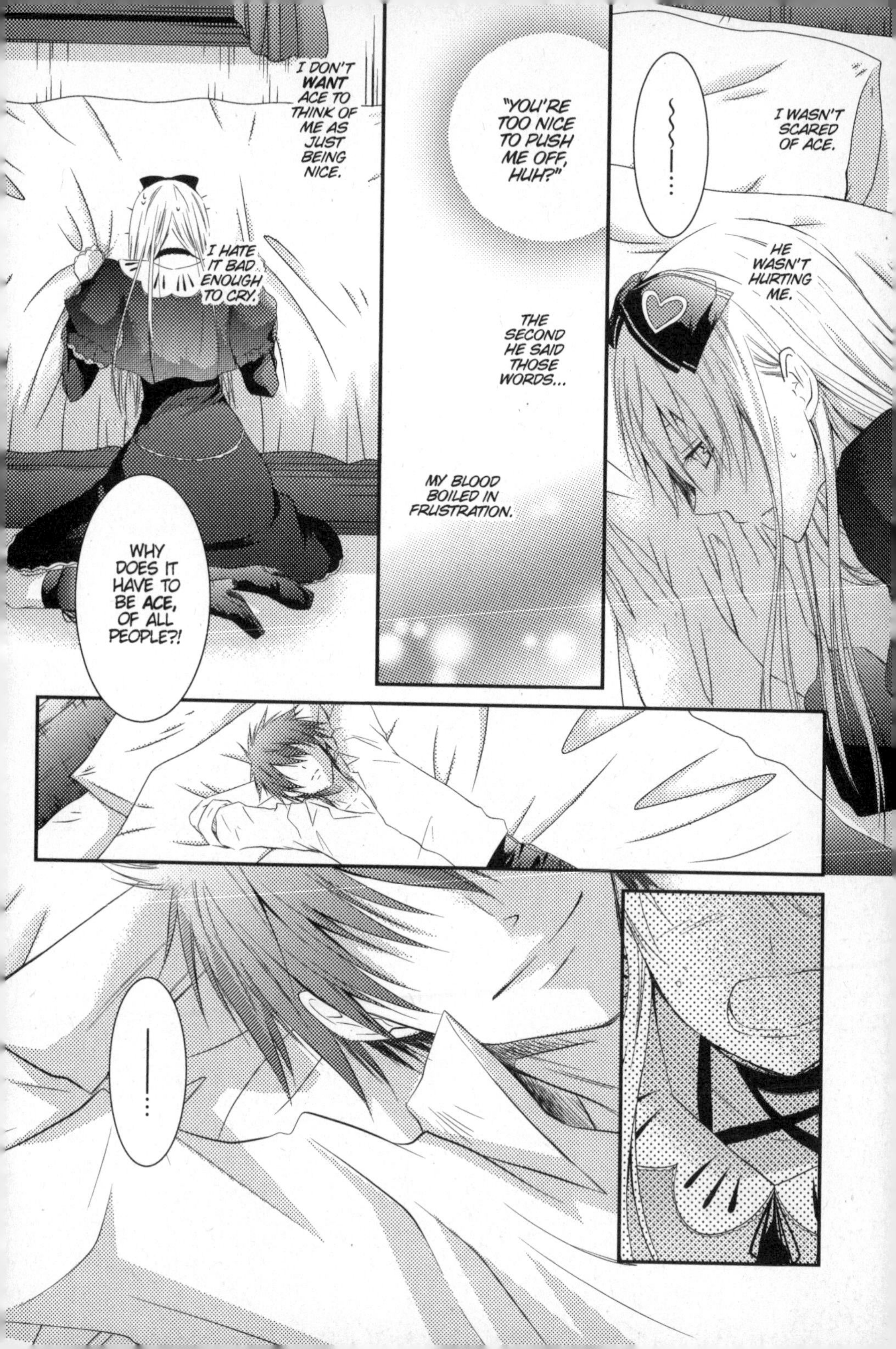
~~!...
I WASN'T SCARED OF ACE.
HE WASN'T HURTING ME.
"YOU'RE TOO NICE TO PUSH ME OFF, HUH?"
THE SECOND HE SAID THOSE WORDS...
MY BLOOD BOILED IN FRUSTRATION.
I DON'T WANT ACE TO THINK OF ME AS JUST BEING NICE.
I HATE IT BAD ENOUGH TO CRY.
WHY DOES IT HAVE TO BE ACE, OF ALL PEOPLE?!
—!...

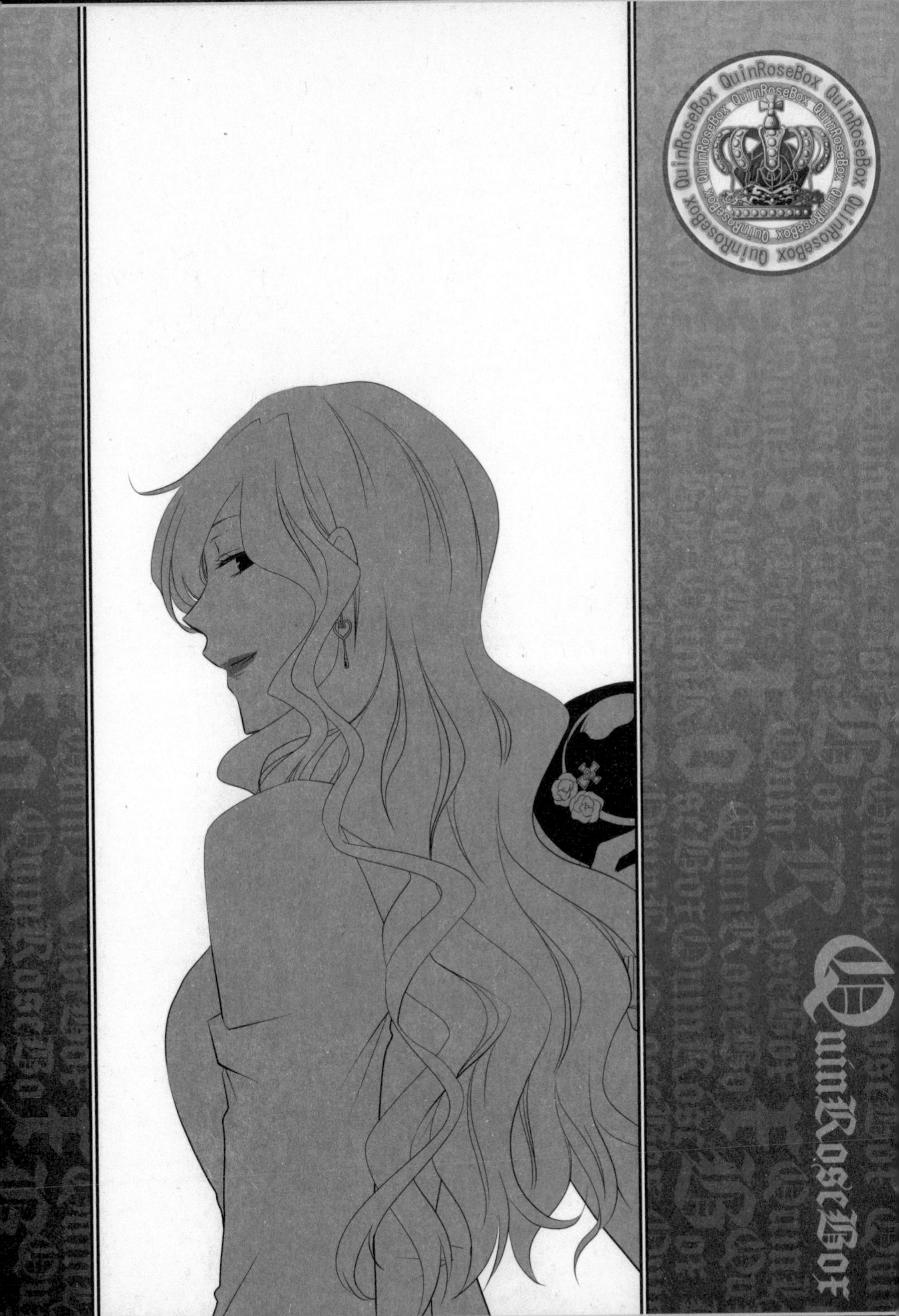
QuinRoseBox

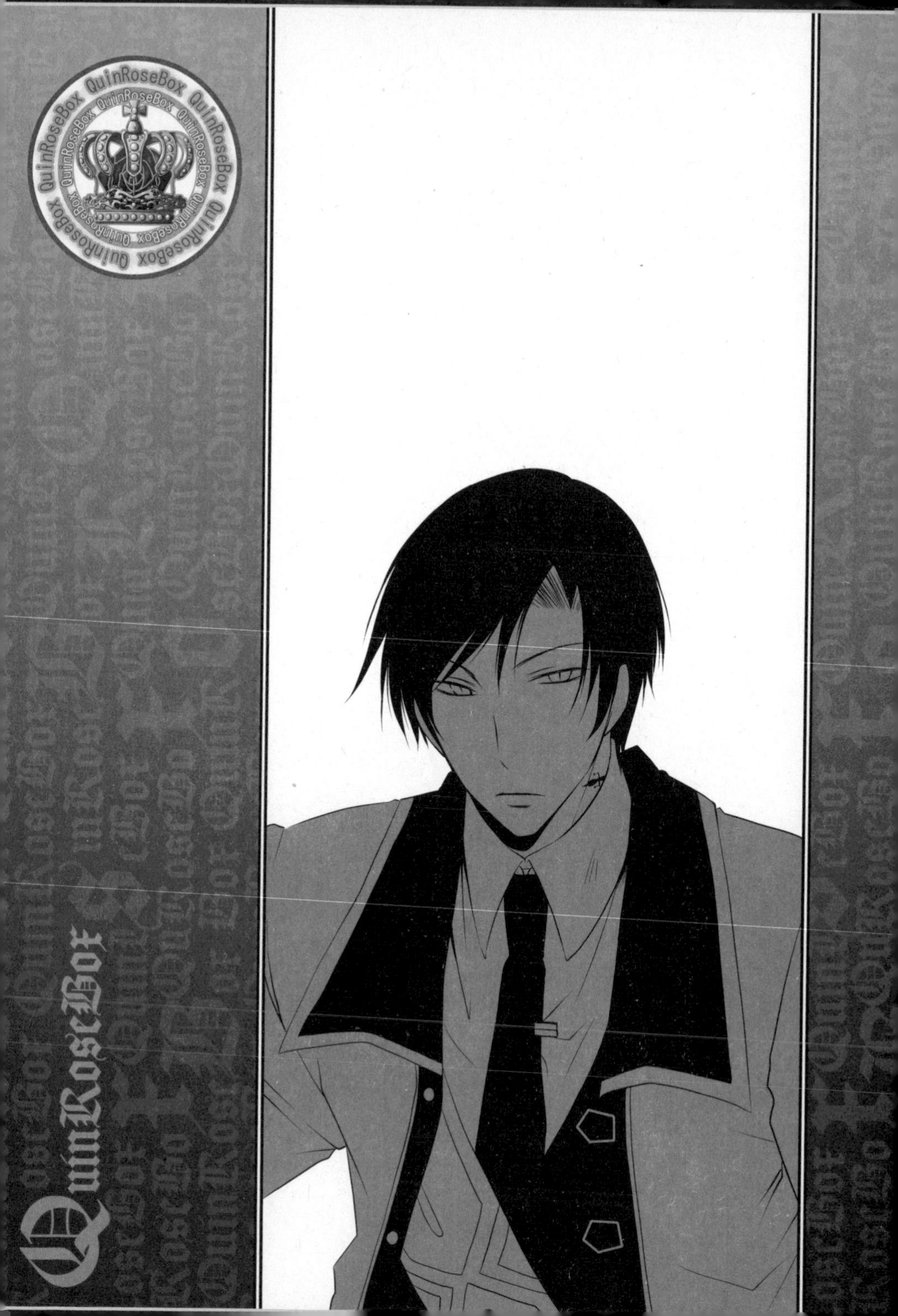
QuinRoseBox

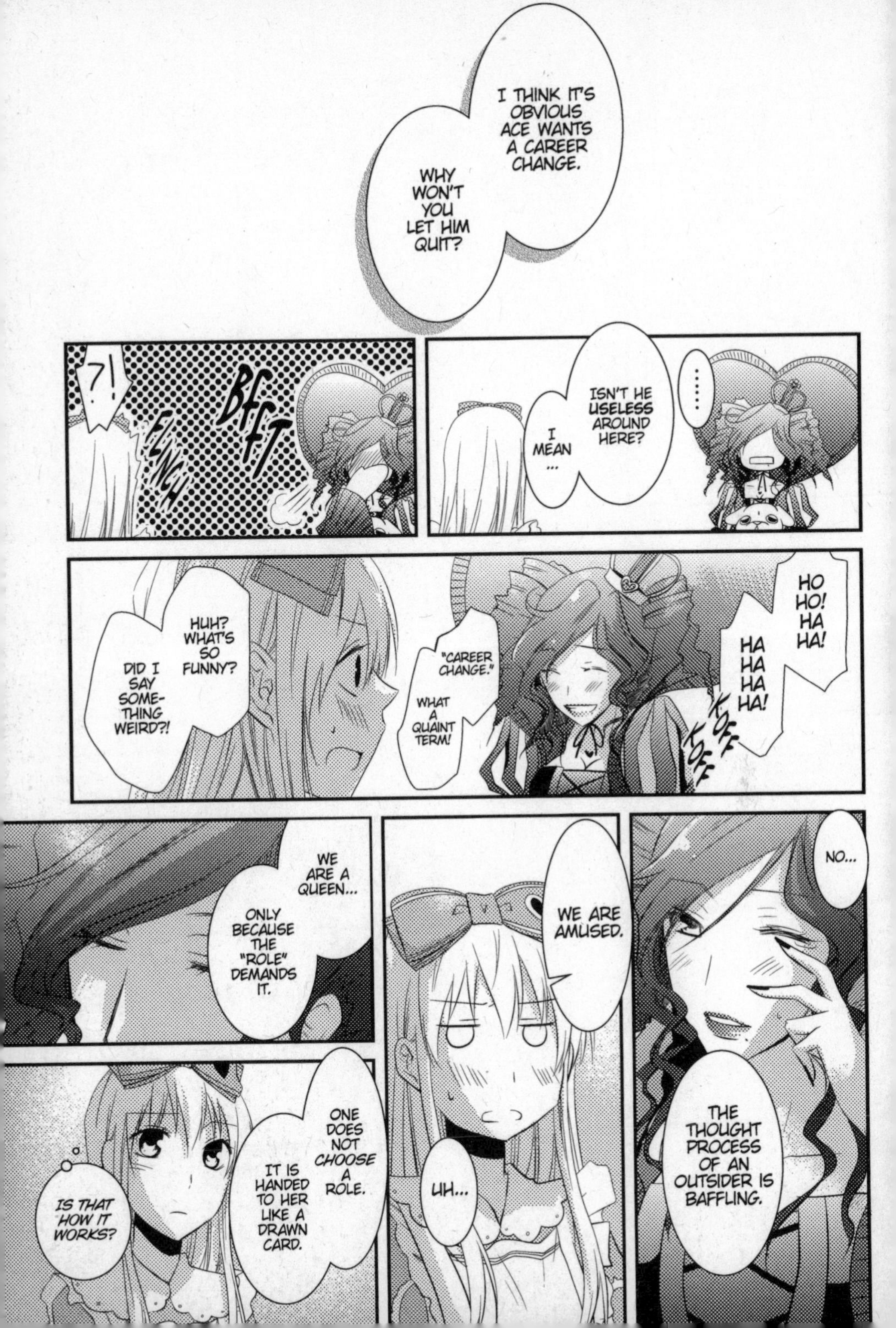
I THINK IT'S OBVIOUS ACE WANTS A CAREER CHANGE.
WHY WON'T YOU LET HIM QUIT?
......
ISN'T HE USELESS AROUND HERE?
I MEAN ...
BFFT
FLINCH
?!
HO HO! HA HA!
HA HA HA HA!
KOFF KOFF
"CAREER CHANGE."
WHAT A QUAINT TERM!
HUH? WHAT'S SO FUNNY?
DID I SAY SOME-THING WEIRD?!
NO...
THE THOUGHT PROCESS OF AN OUTSIDER IS BAFFLING.
WE ARE AMUSED.
UH...
WE ARE A QUEEN...
ONLY BECAUSE THE "ROLE" DEMANDS IT.
ONE DOES NOT CHOOSE A ROLE.
IT IS HANDED TO HER LIKE A DRAWN CARD.
IS THAT HOW IT WORKS?

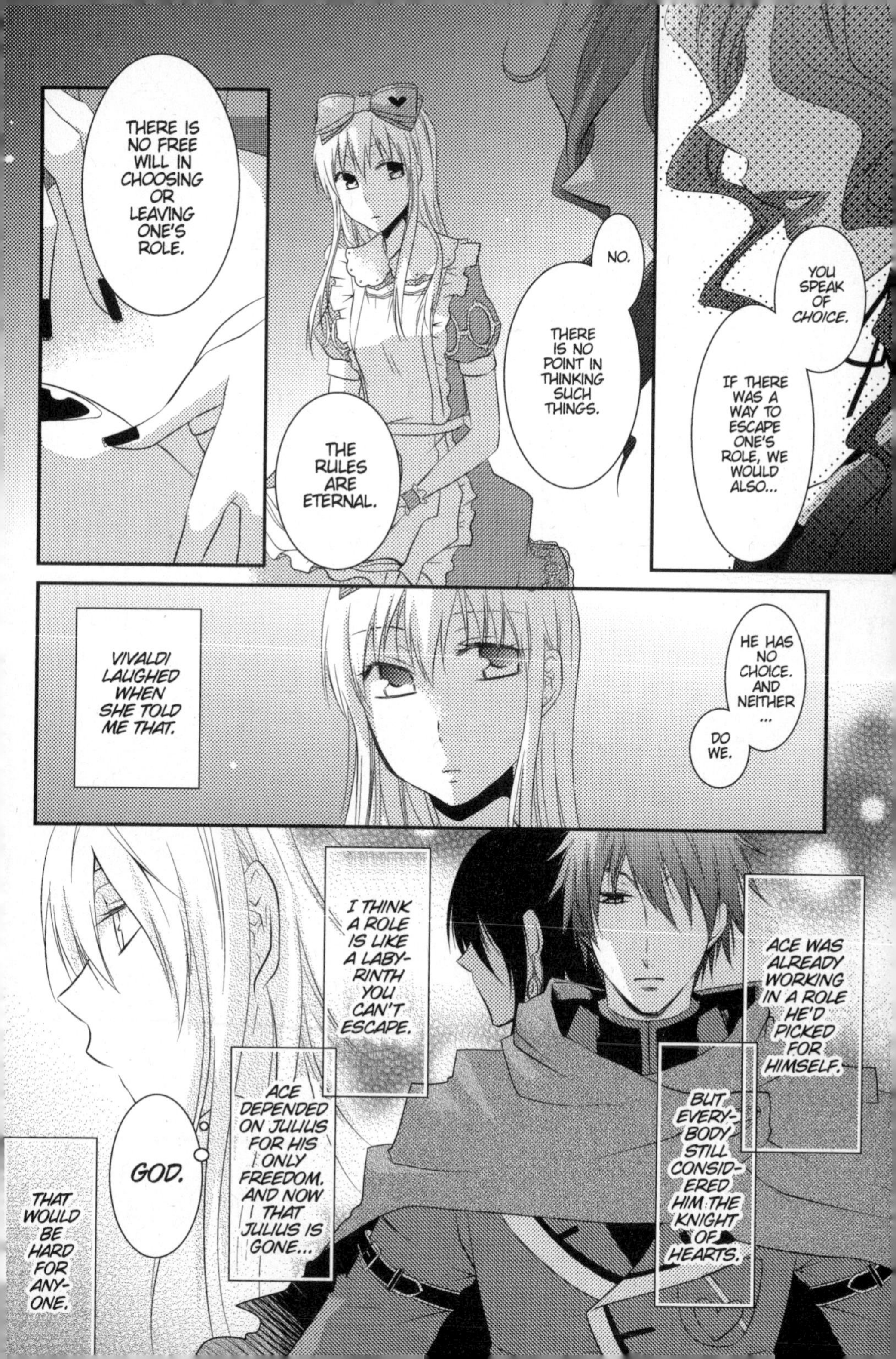
YOU SPEAK OF CHOICE.
IF THERE WAS A WAY TO ESCAPE ONE'S ROLE, WE WOULD ALSO...
NO.
THERE IS NO POINT IN THINKING SUCH THINGS.
THE RULES ARE ETERNAL.
THERE IS NO FREE WILL IN CHOOSING OR LEAVING ONE'S ROLE.
HE HAS NO CHOICE. AND NEITHER ...
DO WE.
VIVALDI LAUGHED WHEN SHE TOLD ME THAT.
ACE WAS ALREADY WORKING IN A ROLE HE'D PICKED FOR HIMSELF.
BUT EVERYBODY STILL CONSIDERED HIM THE KNIGHT OF HEARTS.
I THINK A ROLE IS LIKE A LABYRINTH YOU CAN'T ESCAPE.
ACE DEPENDED ON JULIUS FOR HIS ONLY FREEDOM. AND NOW THAT JULIUS IS GONE...
GOD.
THAT WOULD BE HARD FOR ANYONE.

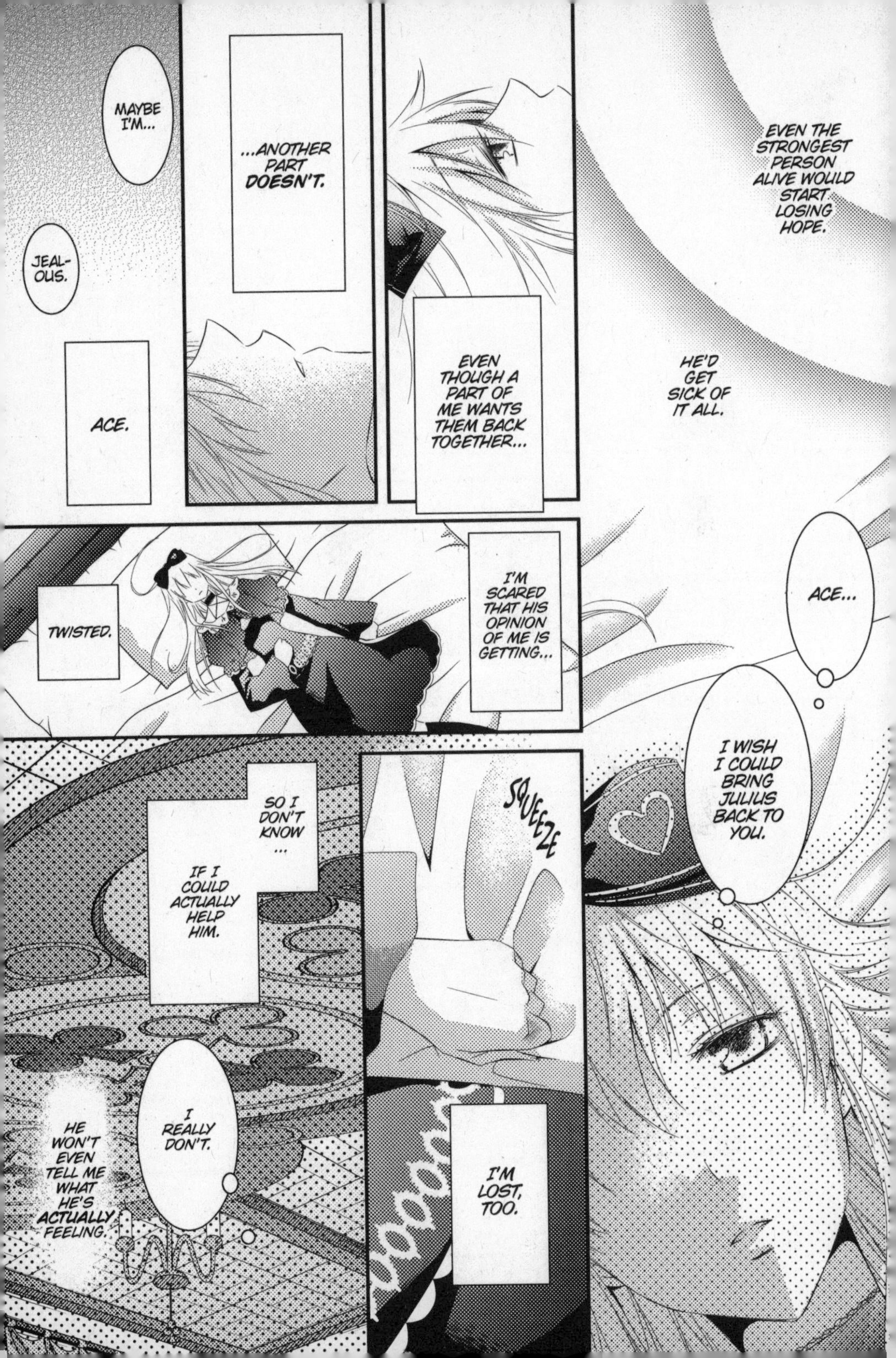
EVEN THE STRONGEST PERSON ALIVE WOULD START LOSING HOPE.
HE'D GET SICK OF IT ALL.
ACE...
I WISH I COULD BRING JULIUS BACK TO YOU.
EVEN THOUGH A PART OF ME WANTS THEM BACK TOGETHER...
...ANOTHER PART DOESN'T.
MAYBE I'M...
JEAL-OUS.
ACE.
I'M SCARED THAT HIS OPINION OF ME IS GETTING...
TWISTED.
SQUEEZE
I'M LOST, TOO.
SO I DON'T KNOW...
IF I COULD ACTUALLY HELP HIM.
I REALLY DON'T.
HE WON'T EVEN TELL ME WHAT HE'S ACTUALLY FEELING.

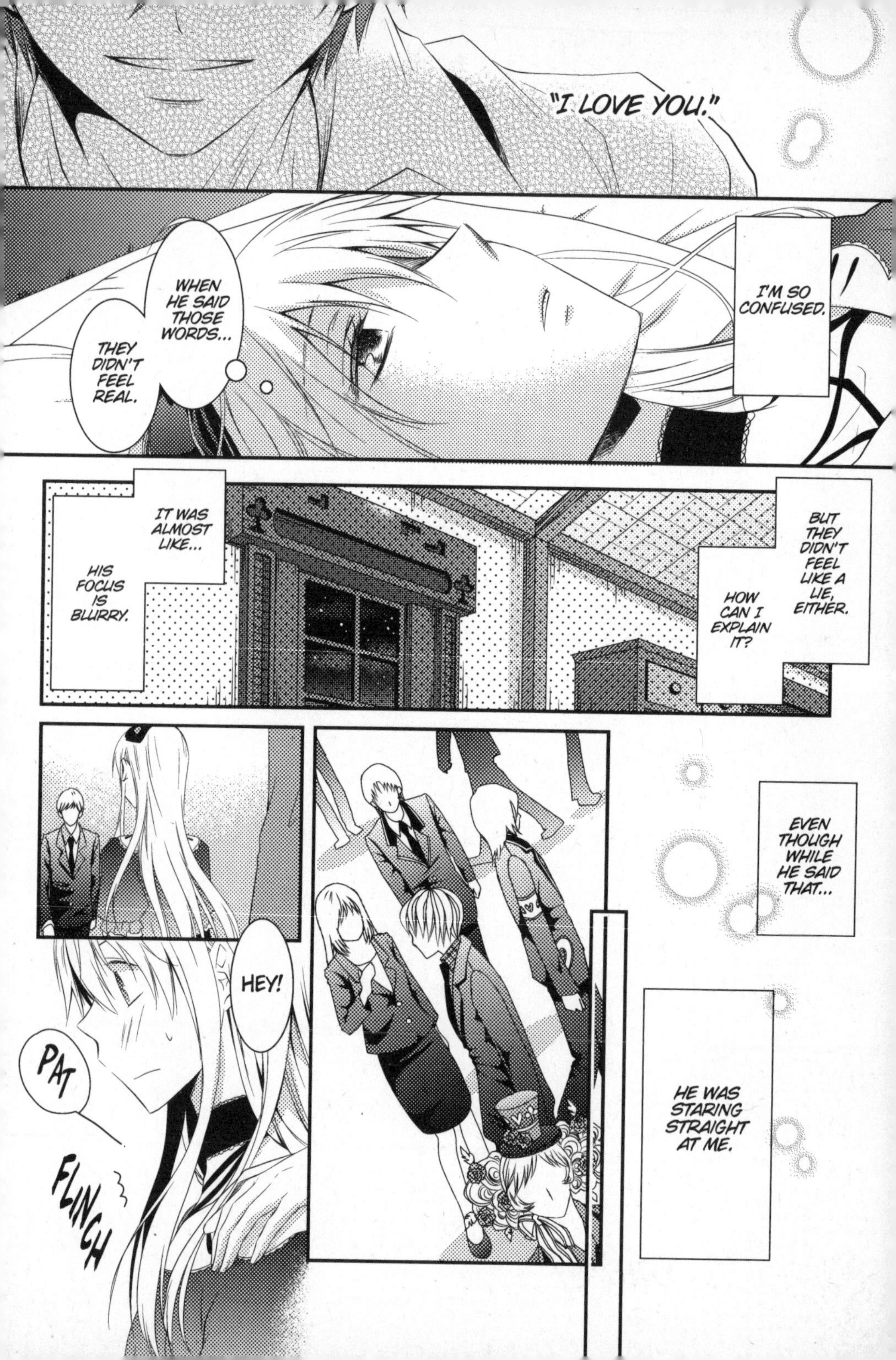
"I LOVE YOU."
I'M SO CONFUSED.
WHEN HE SAID THOSE WORDS...
THEY DIDN'T FEEL REAL.
BUT THEY DIDN'T FEEL LIKE A LIE, EITHER.
HOW CAN I EXPLAIN IT?
IT WAS ALMOST LIKE...
HIS FOCUS IS BLURRY.
EVEN THOUGH WHILE HE SAID THAT...
HE WAS STARING STRAIGHT AT ME.
HEY!
PAT
FLINCH

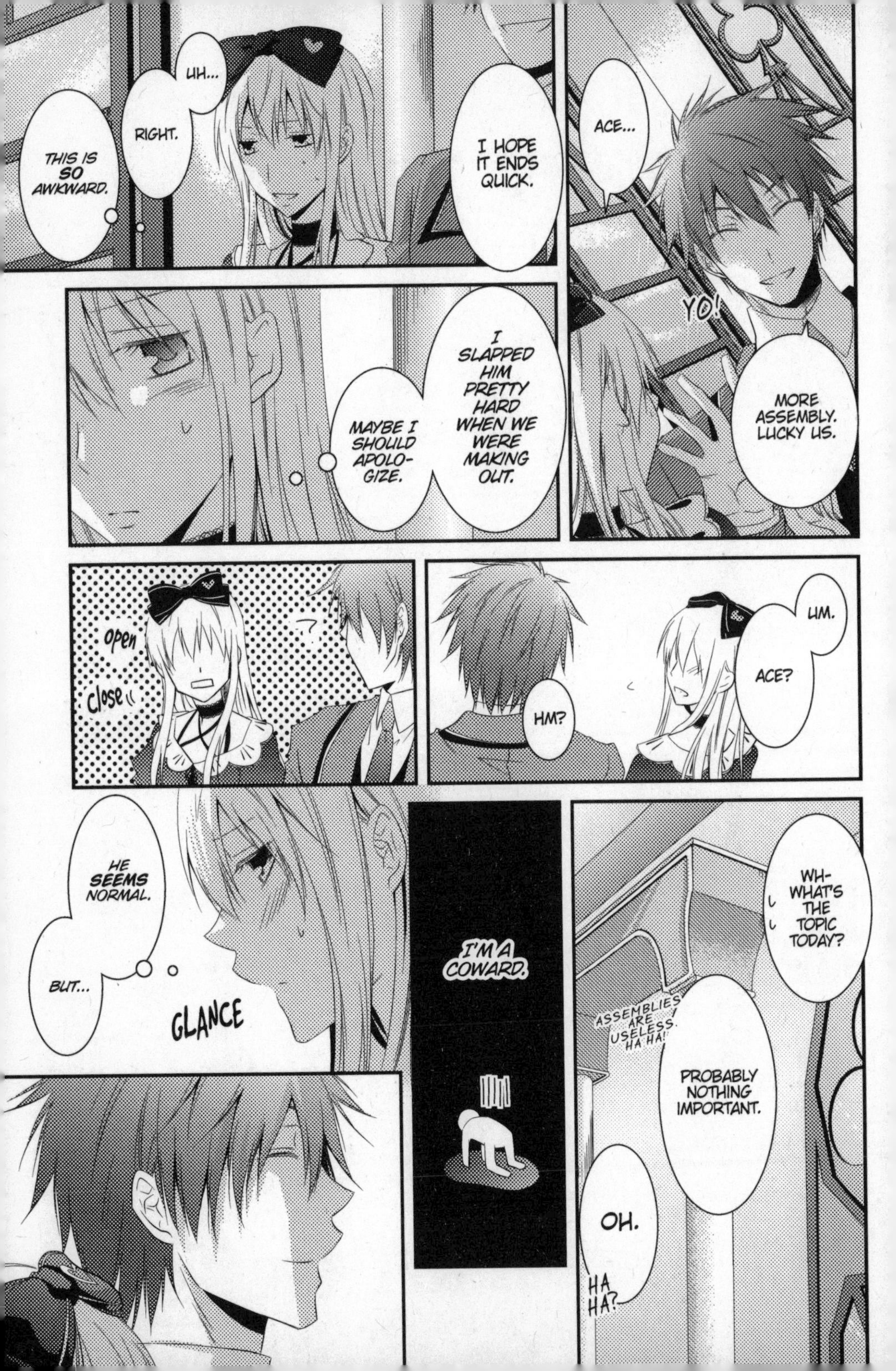

ACE...
YO!
MORE ASSEMBLY. LUCKY US.
I HOPE IT ENDS QUICK.
UH... RIGHT.
THIS IS SO AWKWARD.
I SLAPPED HIM PRETTY HARD WHEN WE WERE MAKING OUT.
MAYBE I SHOULD APOLOGIZE.
UM. ACE?
HM?
open
close
WH-WHAT'S THE TOPIC TODAY?
ASSEMBLIES ARE USELESS. HA HA!
PROBABLY NOTHING IMPORTANT.
OH.
HA HA?
I'M A COWARD.
HE SEEMS NORMAL.
BUT...
GLANCE

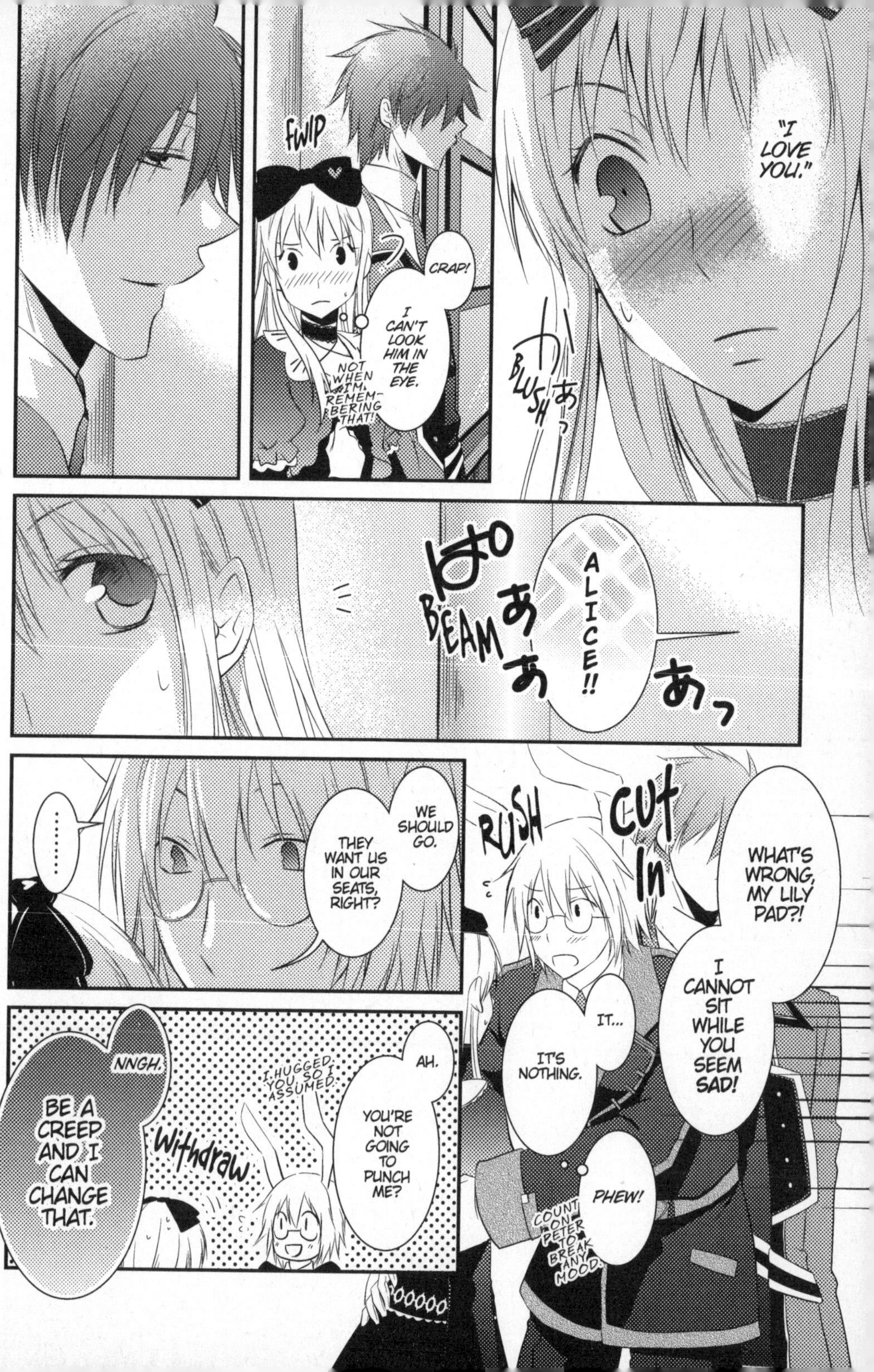

"I LOVE YOU."
BLUSH
あっ
FWIP
CRAP!
I CAN'T LOOK HIM IN THE EYE.
NOT WHEN I'M REMEMBERING THAT!
ALICE!!
BEAM
あああっ
CUT IN
RUSH
WHAT'S WRONG, MY LILY PAD?!
I CANNOT SIT WHILE YOU SEEM SAD!
IT...
IT'S NOTHING.
PHEW!
COUNT ON PETER TO BREAK ANY MOOD.
WE SHOULD GO.
THEY WANT US IN OUR SEATS, RIGHT?
......
AH.
YOU'RE NOT GOING TO PUNCH ME?
I HUGGED YOU SO I ASSUMED.
Withdraw
NNGH.
BE A CREEP AND I CAN CHANGE THAT.

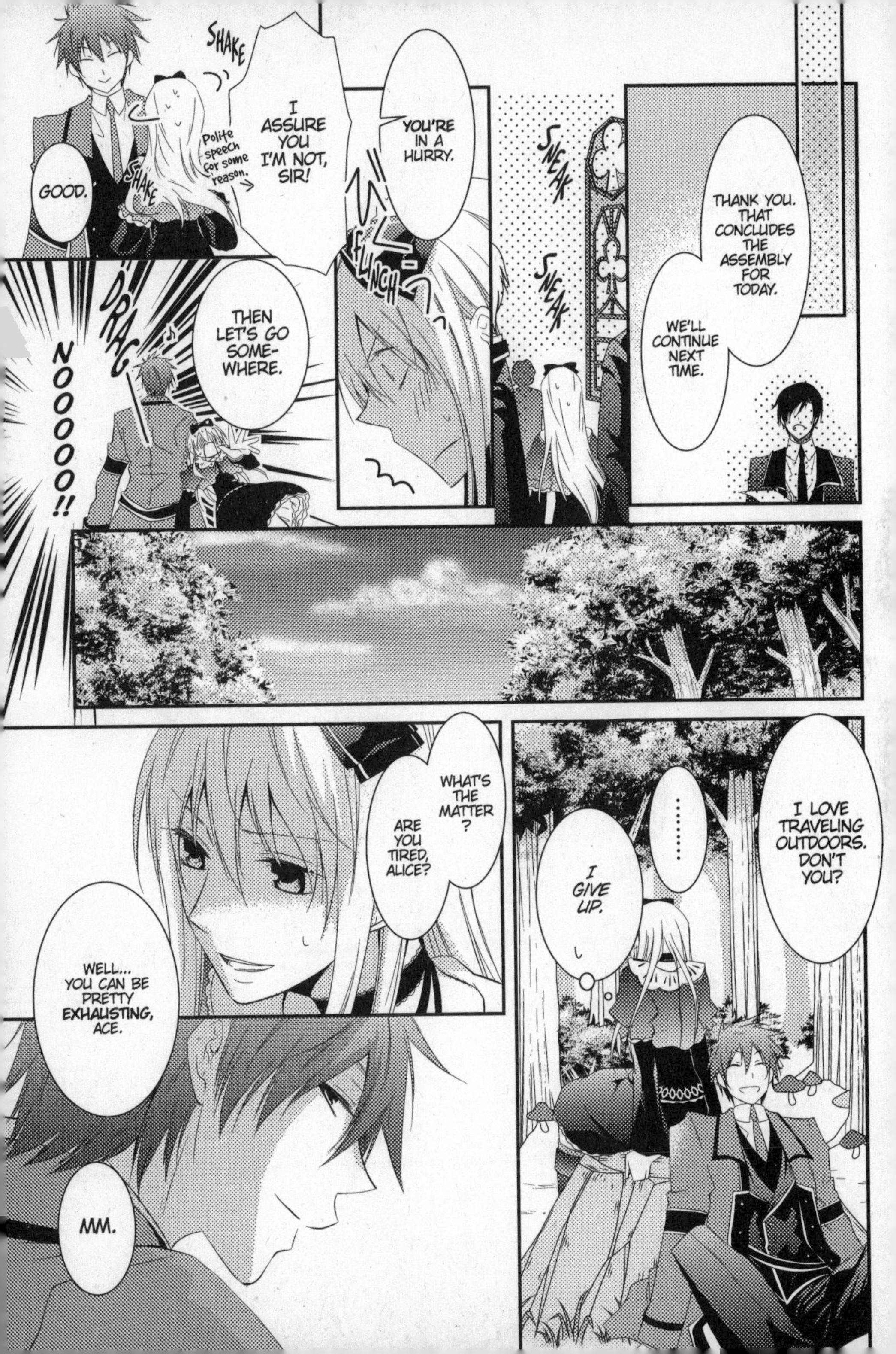
THANK YOU. THAT CONCLUDES THE ASSEMBLY FOR TODAY.
WE'LL CONTINUE NEXT TIME.
SNEAK
SNEAK
YOU'RE IN A HURRY.
FLINCH
I ASSURE YOU I'M NOT, SIR!
Polite speech for some reason.
SHAKE
SHAKE
GOOD.
THEN LET'S GO SOME-WHERE.
DRAG
NOOOOOO!!
I LOVE TRAVELING OUTDOORS. DON'T YOU?
......
I GIVE UP.
WHAT'S THE MATTER?
ARE YOU TIRED, ALICE?
WELL... YOU CAN BE PRETTY EXHAUSTING, ACE.
MM.

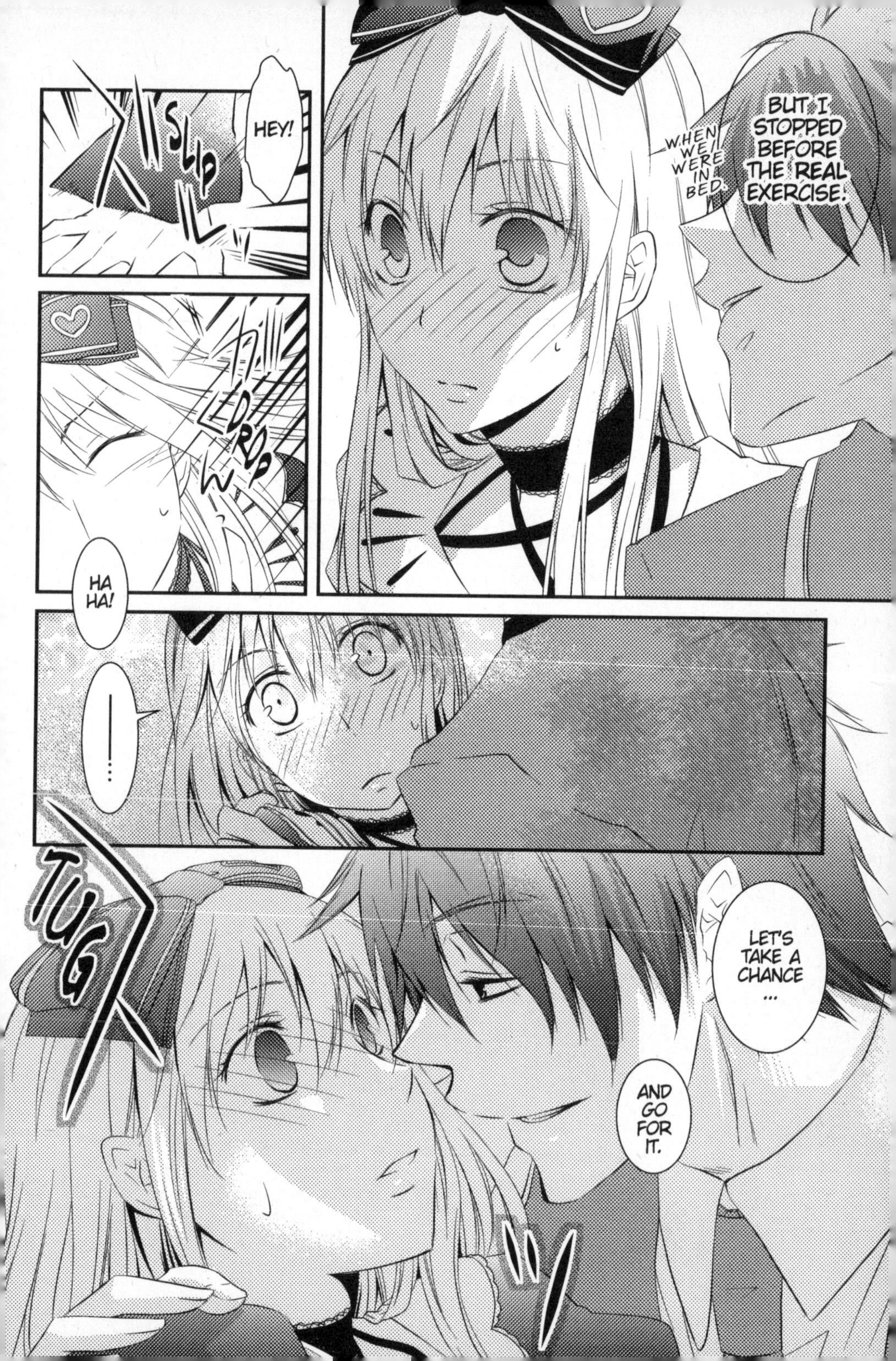
BUT I STOPPED BEFORE THE REAL EXERCISE.
WHEN WE WERE IN BED.
HEY!
SLIP
DROP
HA HA!
!...
LET'S TAKE A CHANCE ...
AND GO FOR IT.
TUG

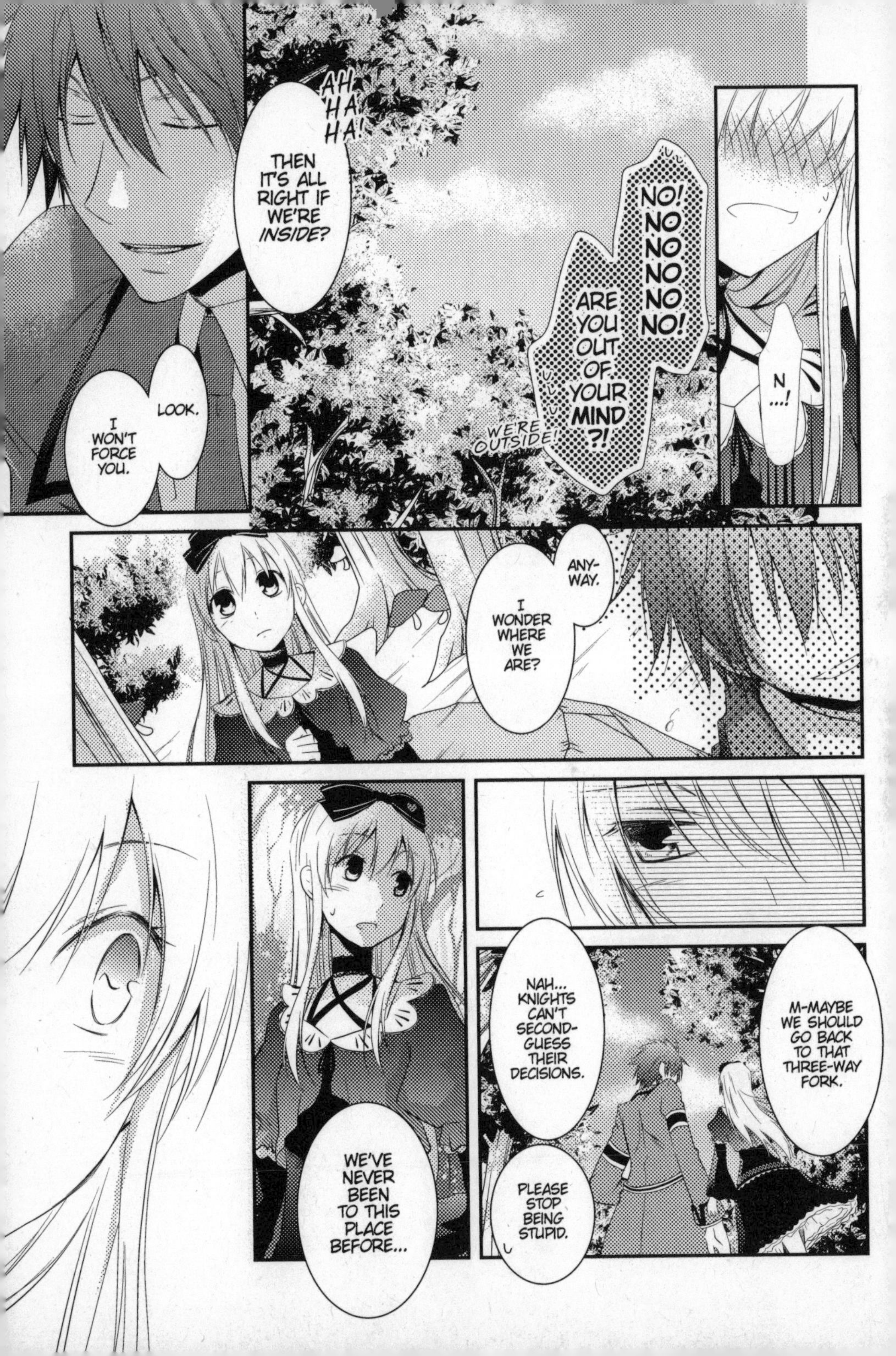
N...!
NO! NO NO NO NO NO!
ARE YOU OUT OF YOUR MIND?!
WE'RE OUTSIDE!
AH HA HA!
THEN IT'S ALL RIGHT IF WE'RE *INSIDE*?
LOOK.
I WON'T FORCE YOU.
ANY-WAY.
I WONDER WHERE WE ARE?
M-MAYBE WE SHOULD GO BACK TO THAT THREE-WAY FORK.
NAH... KNIGHTS CAN'T SECOND-GUESS THEIR DECISIONS.
PLEASE STOP BEING STUPID.
WE'VE NEVER BEEN TO THIS PLACE BEFORE...

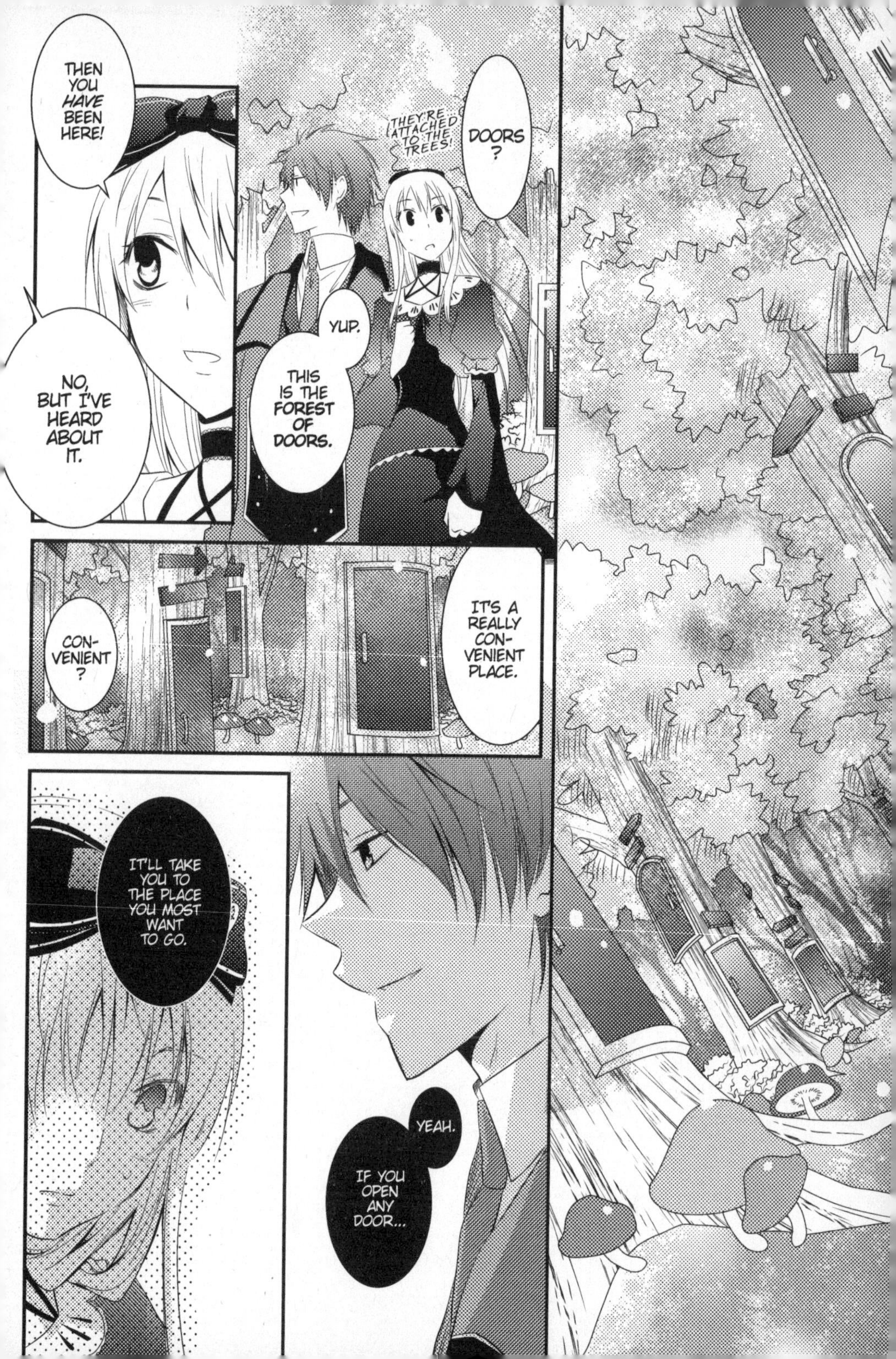
DOORS?
THEY'RE ATTACHED TO THE TREES!
YUP.
THIS IS THE FOREST OF DOORS.
THEN YOU *HAVE* BEEN HERE!
NO, BUT I'VE HEARD ABOUT IT.
IT'S A REALLY CON-VENIENT PLACE.
CON-VENIENT?
YEAH.
IF YOU OPEN ANY DOOR...
IT'LL TAKE YOU TO THE PLACE YOU MOST WANT TO GO.

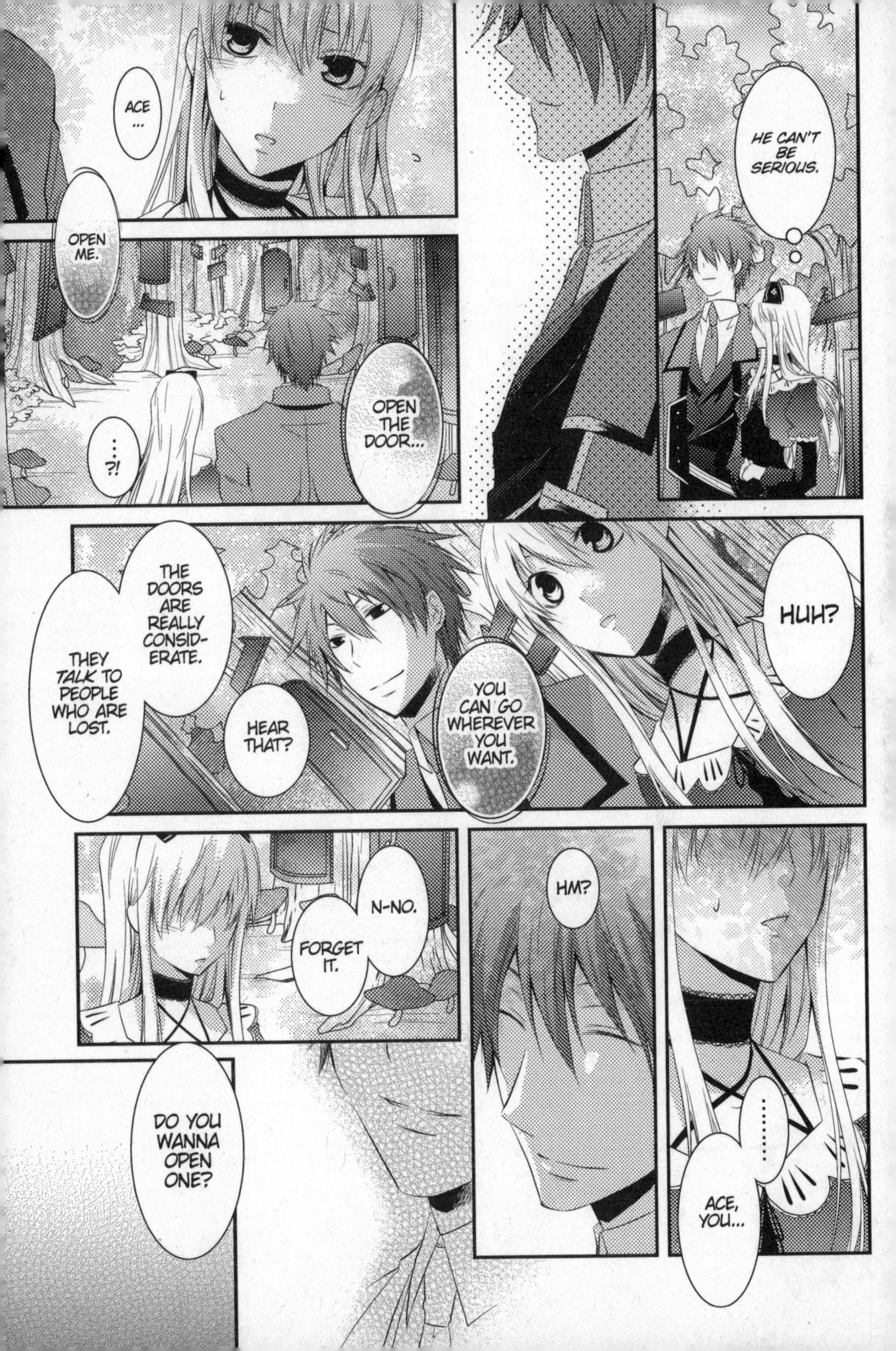
HE CAN'T BE SERIOUS.
ACE ...
OPEN ME.
OPEN THE DOOR...
...?!
HUH?
YOU CAN GO WHEREVER YOU WANT.
HEAR THAT?
THE DOORS ARE REALLY CONSID-ERATE.
THEY *TALK* TO PEOPLE WHO ARE LOST.
......
ACE, YOU...
HM?
N-NO.
FORGET IT.
DO YOU WANNA OPEN ONE?

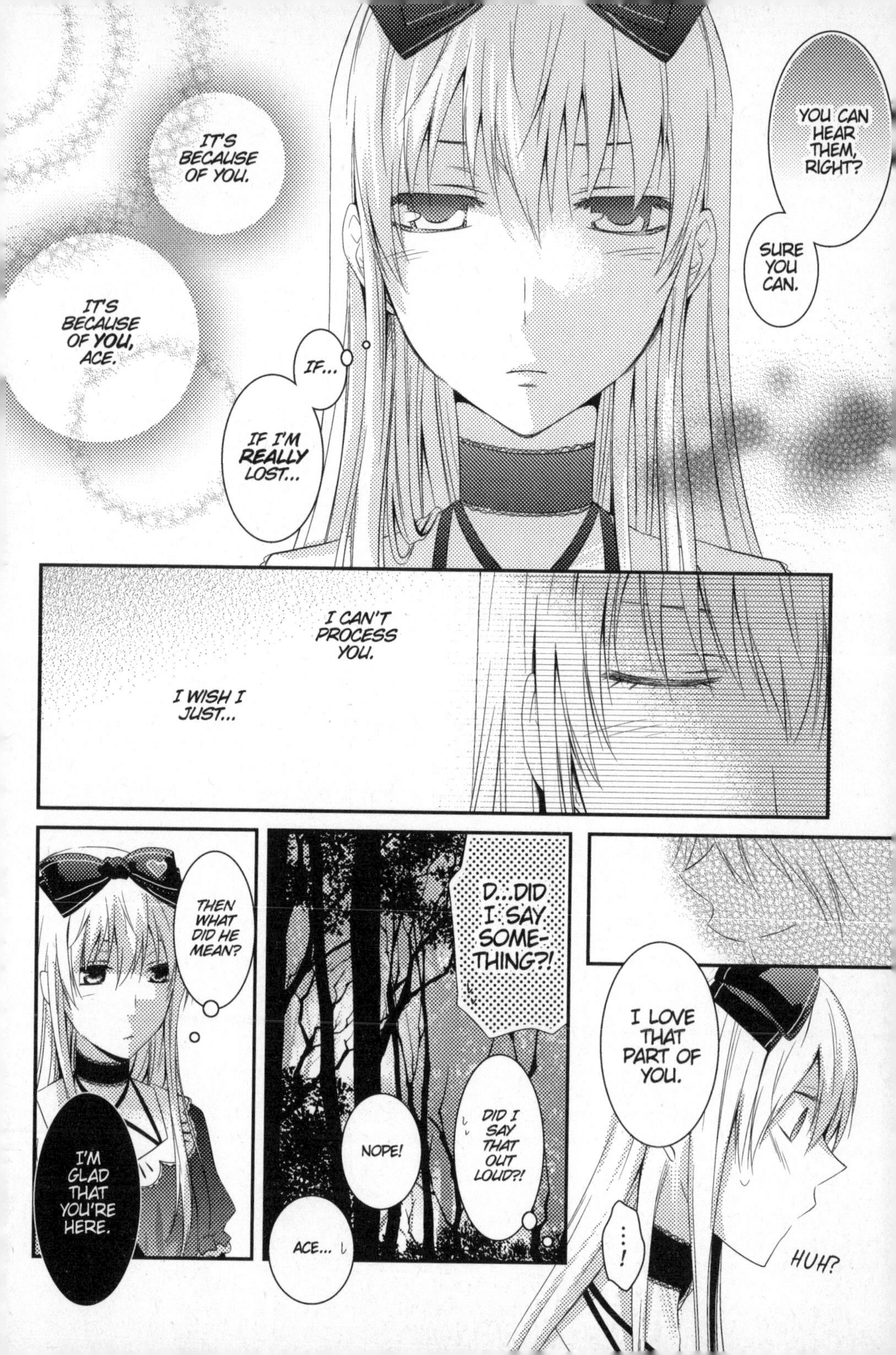
YOU CAN HEAR THEM, RIGHT?
SURE YOU CAN.
IF...
IF I'M REALLY LOST...
IT'S BECAUSE OF YOU.
IT'S BECAUSE OF YOU, ACE.
I CAN'T PROCESS YOU.
I WISH I JUST...
I LOVE THAT PART OF YOU.
...!
HUH?
D...DID I SAY SOMETHING?!
DID I SAY THAT OUT LOUD?!
NOPE!
ACE...
THEN WHAT DID HE MEAN?
I'M GLAD THAT YOU'RE HERE.

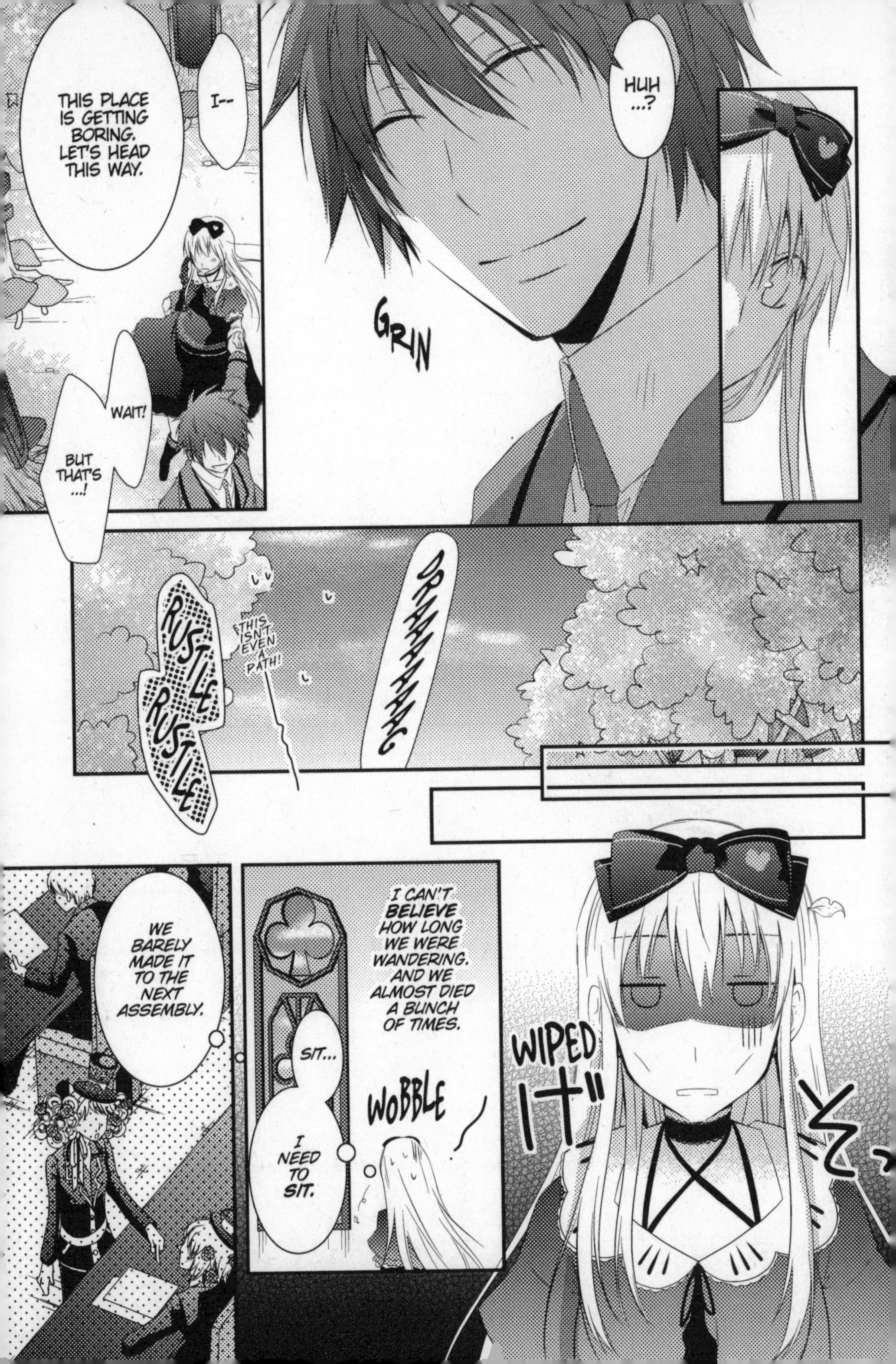
HUH ...?
GRIN
I--
THIS PLACE IS GETTING BORING. LET'S HEAD THIS WAY.
WAIT!
BUT THAT'S ...!
DRAAAAAAAG
THIS ISN'T EVEN A PATH!
RUSTLE RUSTLE
WIPED
I CAN'T BELIEVE HOW LONG WE WERE WANDERING. AND WE ALMOST DIED A BUNCH OF TIMES.
WOBBLE
SIT...
I NEED TO SIT.
WE BARELY MADE IT TO THE NEXT ASSEMBLY.

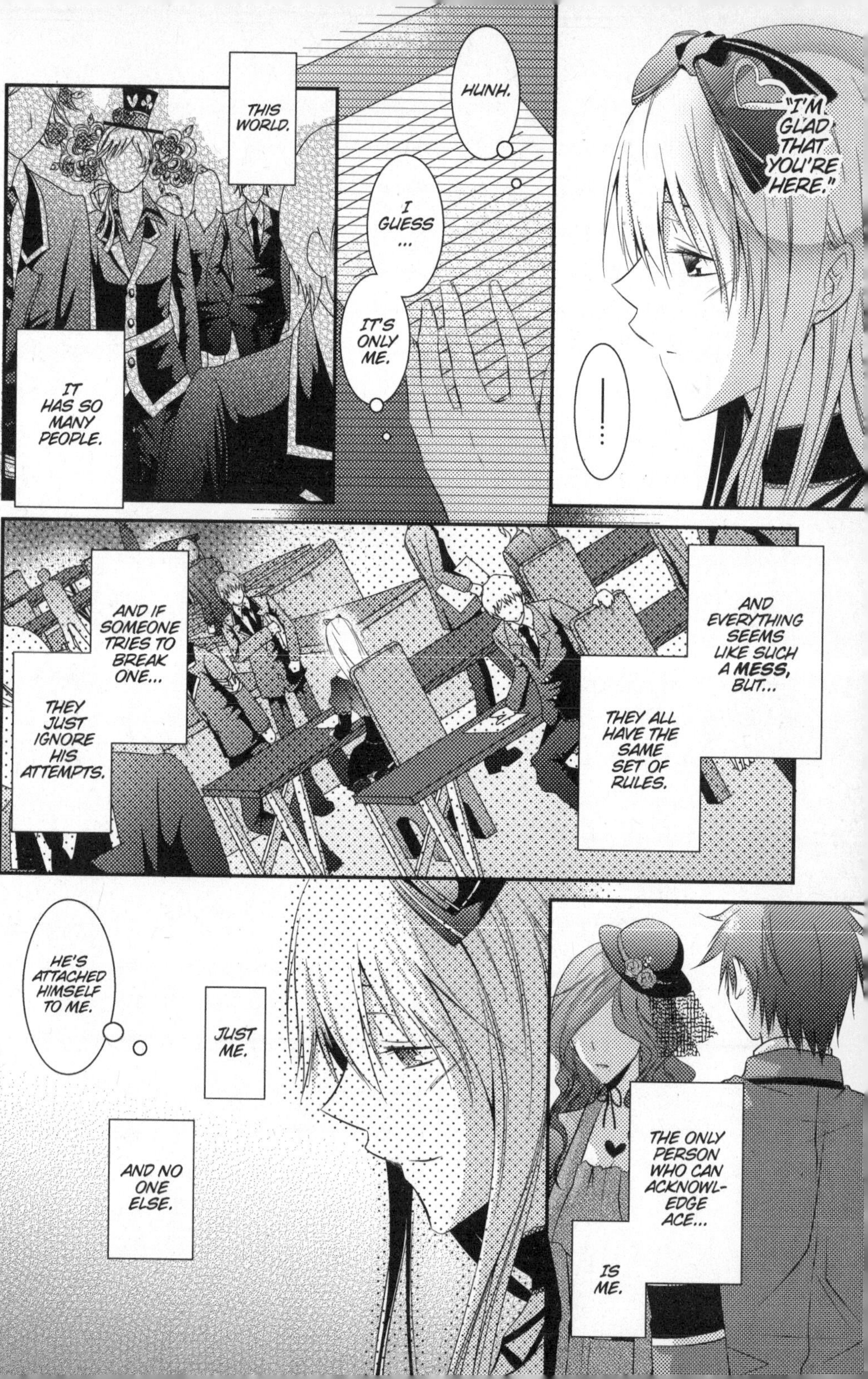
"I'M GLAD THAT YOU'RE HERE."
—…
HUNH.
I GUESS…
IT'S ONLY ME.
THIS WORLD.
IT HAS SO MANY PEOPLE.
AND EVERYTHING SEEMS LIKE SUCH A MESS, BUT…
THEY ALL HAVE THE SAME SET OF RULES.
AND IF SOMEONE TRIES TO BREAK ONE…
THEY JUST IGNORE HIS ATTEMPTS.
THE ONLY PERSON WHO CAN ACKNOWL-EDGE ACE…
IS ME.
HE'S ATTACHED HIMSELF TO ME.
JUST ME.
AND NO ONE ELSE.

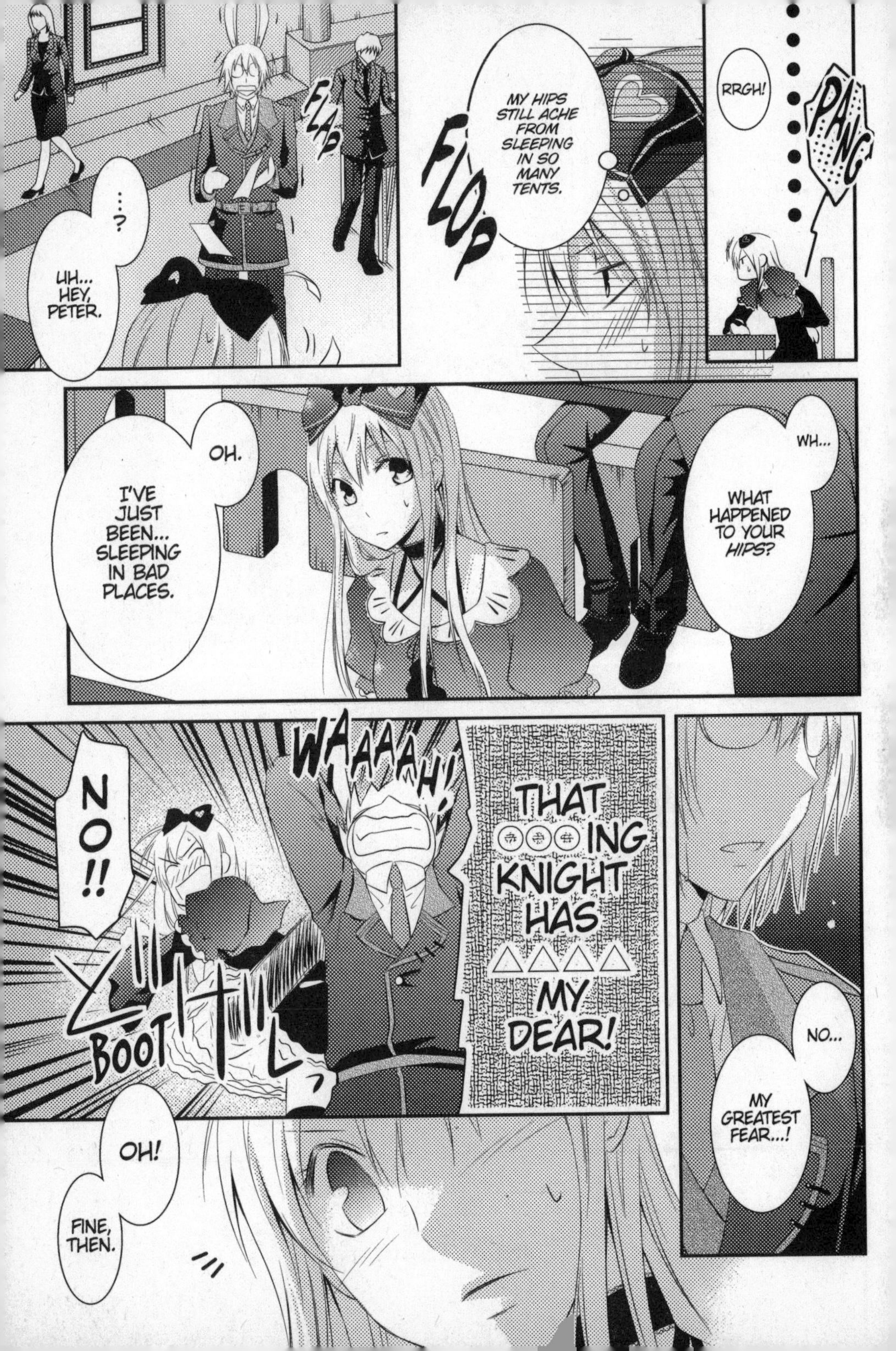
RRGH!
PANG
MY HIPS STILL ACHE FROM SLEEPING IN SO MANY TENTS.
FLOP
FLAP
...?
UH... HEY, PETER.
WH... WHAT HAPPENED TO YOUR HIPS?
OH.
I'VE JUST BEEN... SLEEPING IN BAD PLACES.
NO...
MY GREATEST FEAR...!
WAAAAH!
THAT ○○○ING KNIGHT HAS △△△△ MY DEAR!
NO!!
BOOT
OH!
FINE, THEN.

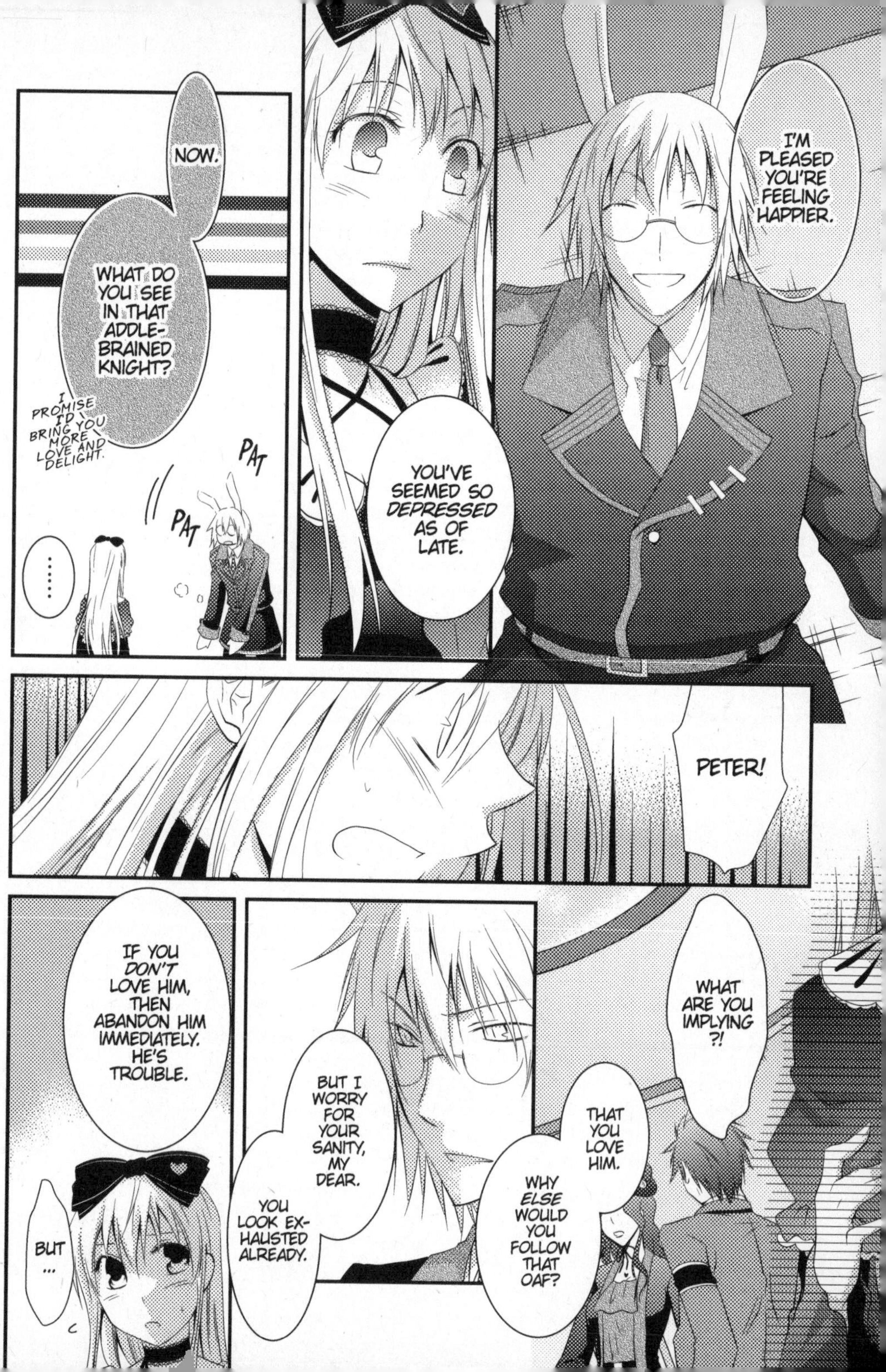
I'M PLEASED YOU'RE FEELING HAPPIER.
YOU'VE SEEMED SO DEPRESSED AS OF LATE.
NOW.
WHAT DO YOU SEE IN THAT ADDLE-BRAINED KNIGHT?
I PROMISE I'D BRING YOU MORE LOVE AND DELIGHT.
PAT
PAT
......
PETER!
WHAT ARE YOU IMPLYING?!
THAT YOU LOVE HIM.
WHY ELSE WOULD YOU FOLLOW THAT OAF?
BUT I WORRY FOR YOUR SANITY, MY DEAR.
YOU LOOK EX-HAUSTED ALREADY.
IF YOU DON'T LOVE HIM, THEN ABANDON HIM IMMEDIATELY. HE'S TROUBLE.
BUT ...

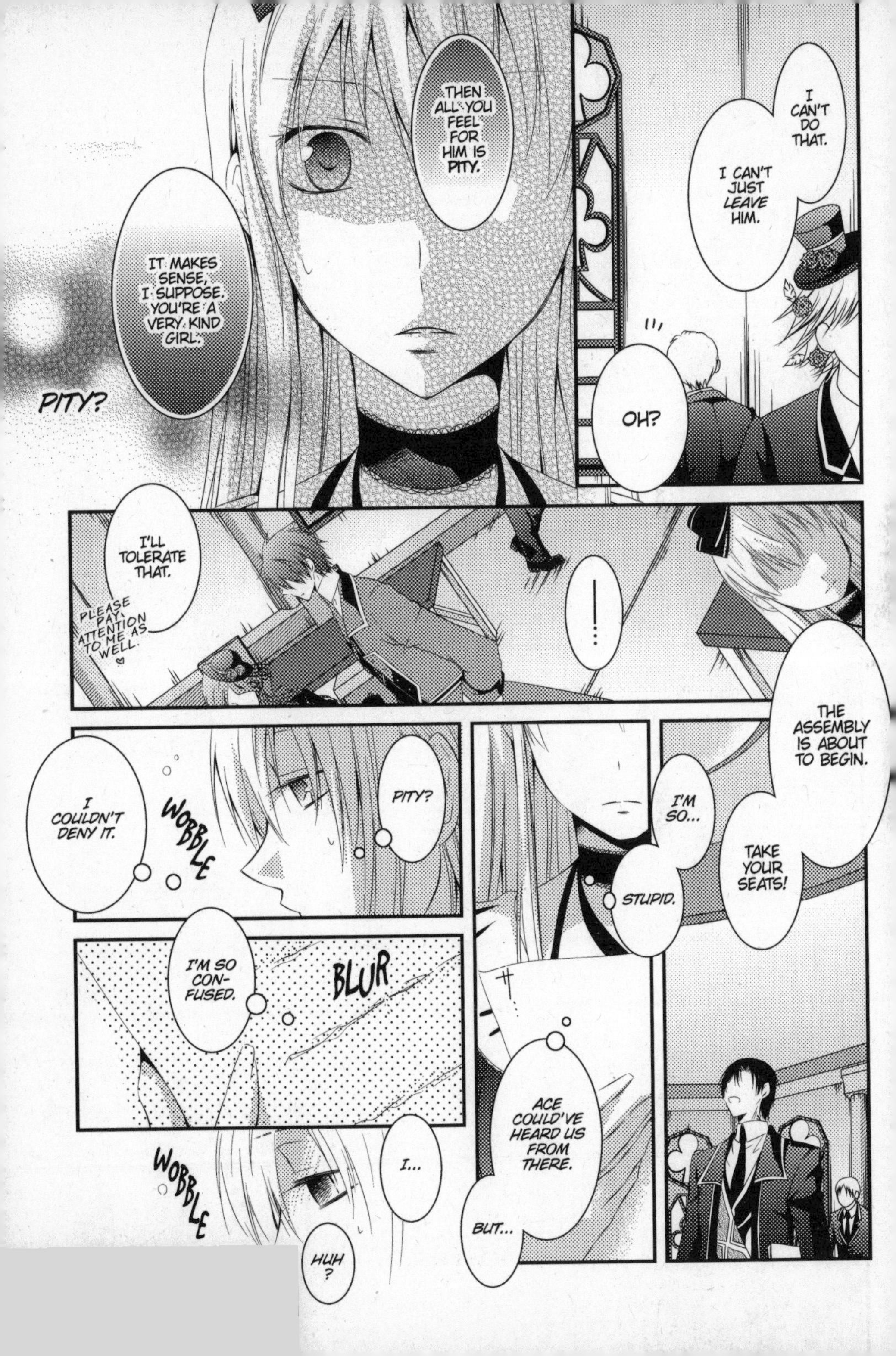

I CAN'T DO THAT.
I CAN'T JUST LEAVE HIM.
OH?
THEN ALL YOU FEEL FOR HIM IS PITY.
IT MAKES SENSE, I SUPPOSE. YOU'RE A VERY KIND GIRL.
PITY?
!...
I'LL TOLERATE THAT.
PLEASE PAY ATTENTION TO ME AS WELL. ♥
THE ASSEMBLY IS ABOUT TO BEGIN.
TAKE YOUR SEATS!
I'M SO...
STUPID.
PITY?
I COULDN'T DENY IT.
WOBBLE
ACE COULD'VE HEARD US FROM THERE.
BUT...
I'M SO CON-FUSED.
BLUR
I...
WOBBLE
HUH?

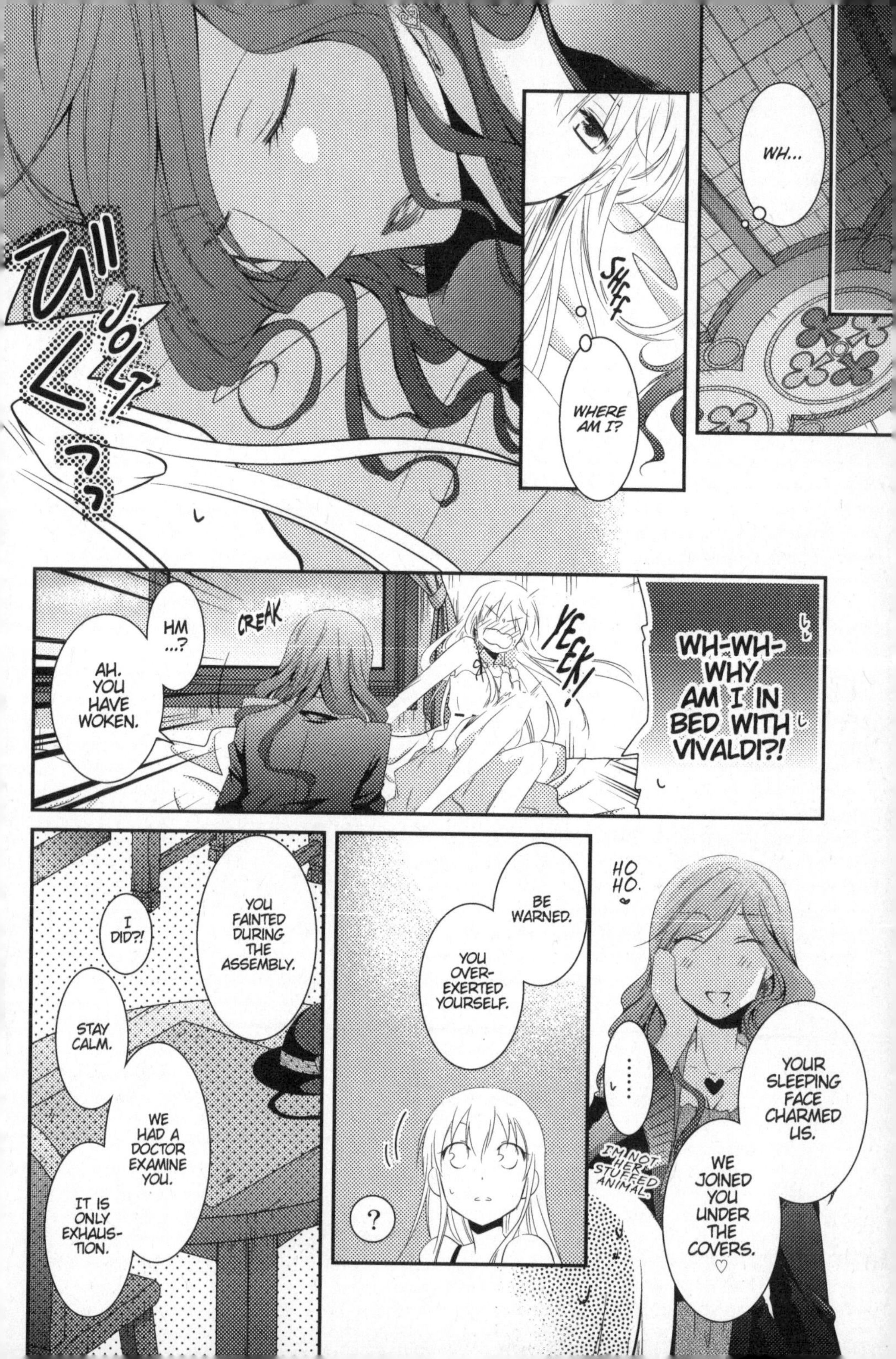
WH...
SHFF
WHERE AM I?
JOLT
WH-WH-WHY AM I IN BED WITH VIVALDI?!
YEEK!
CREAK
HM ...?
AH. YOU HAVE WOKEN.
HO HO.
YOUR SLEEPING FACE CHARMED US.
WE JOINED YOU UNDER THE COVERS. ♡
......
I'M NOT HER STUFFED ANIMAL.
BE WARNED.
YOU OVER-EXERTED YOURSELF.
?
YOU FAINTED DURING THE ASSEMBLY.
I DID?!
STAY CALM.
WE HAD A DOCTOR EXAMINE YOU.
IT IS ONLY EXHAUSTION.

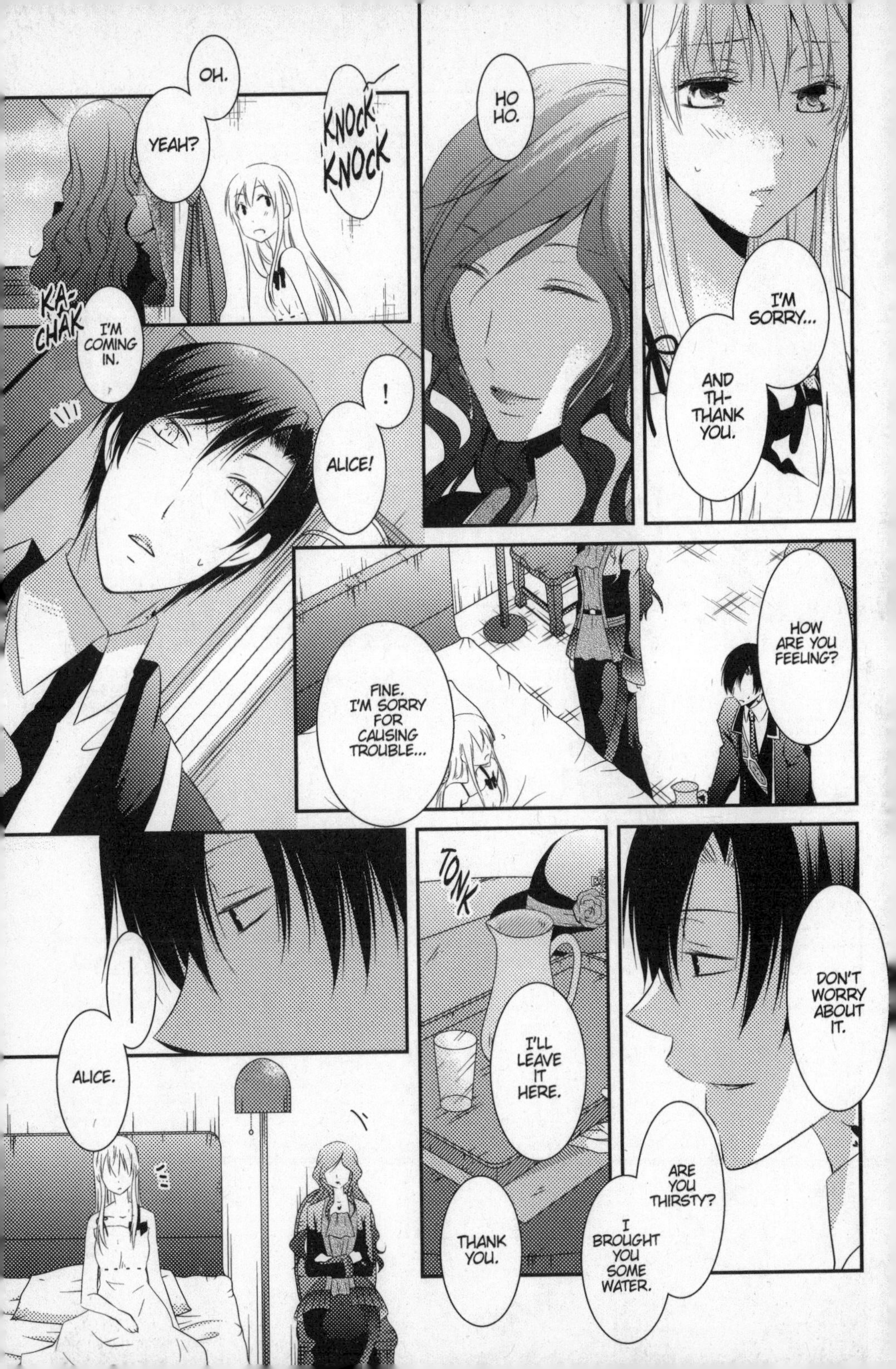
I'M SORRY...
AND TH-THANK YOU.
HO HO.
KNOCK KNOCK
OH.
YEAH?
KA-CHAK
I'M COMING IN.
!
ALICE!
HOW ARE YOU FEELING?
FINE. I'M SORRY FOR CAUSING TROUBLE...
DON'T WORRY ABOUT IT.
ARE YOU THIRSTY?
I BROUGHT YOU SOME WATER.
TONK
I'LL LEAVE IT HERE.
THANK YOU.
ALICE.

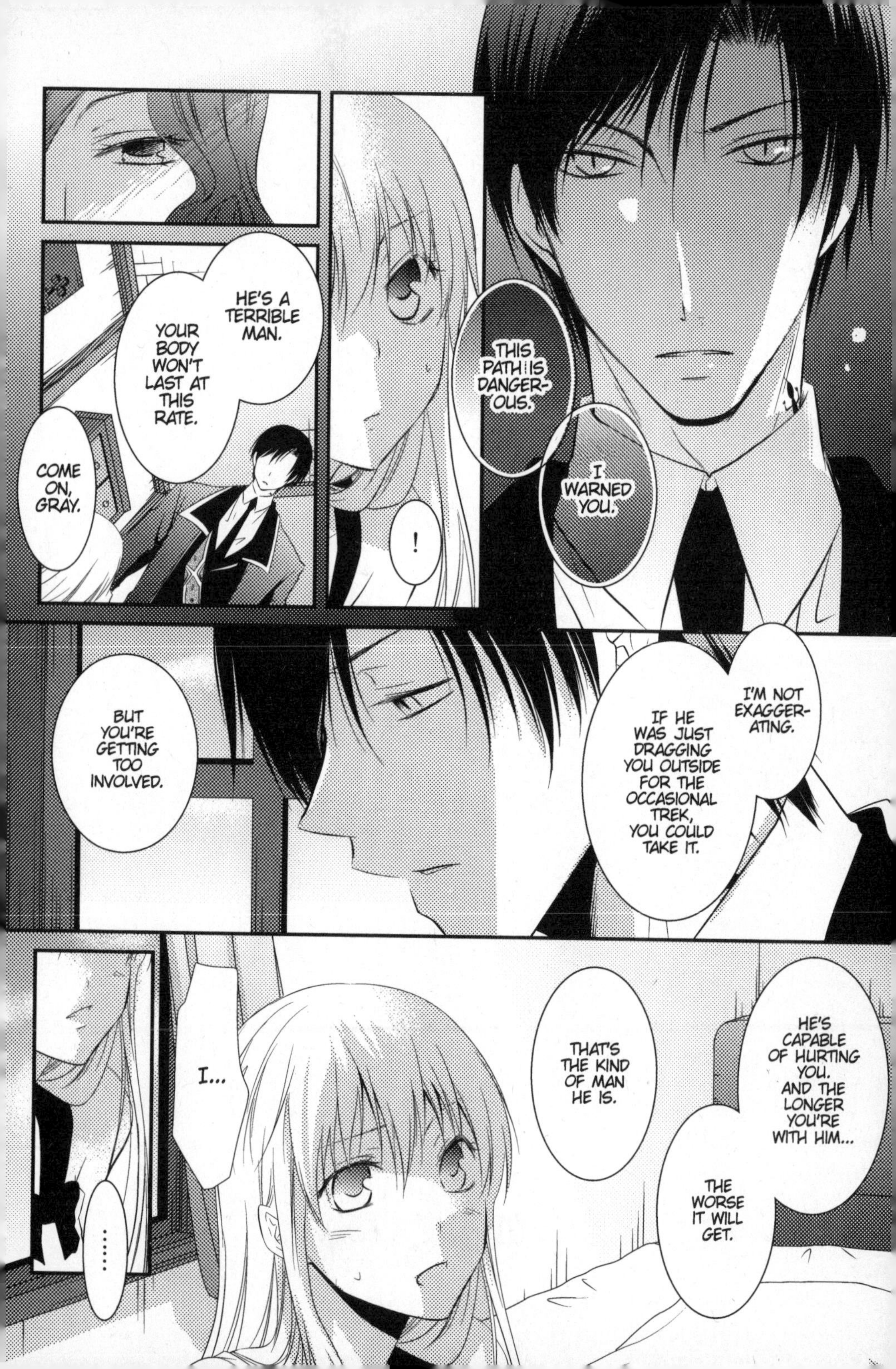
THIS PATH IS DANGEROUS.
I WARNED YOU.
!
HE'S A TERRIBLE MAN.
YOUR BODY WON'T LAST AT THIS RATE.
COME ON, GRAY.
I'M NOT EXAGGERATING.
IF HE WAS JUST DRAGGING YOU OUTSIDE FOR THE OCCASIONAL TREK, YOU COULD TAKE IT.
BUT YOU'RE GETTING TOO INVOLVED.
HE'S CAPABLE OF HURTING YOU. AND THE LONGER YOU'RE WITH HIM...
THE WORSE IT WILL GET.
THAT'S THE KIND OF MAN HE IS.
I...
......

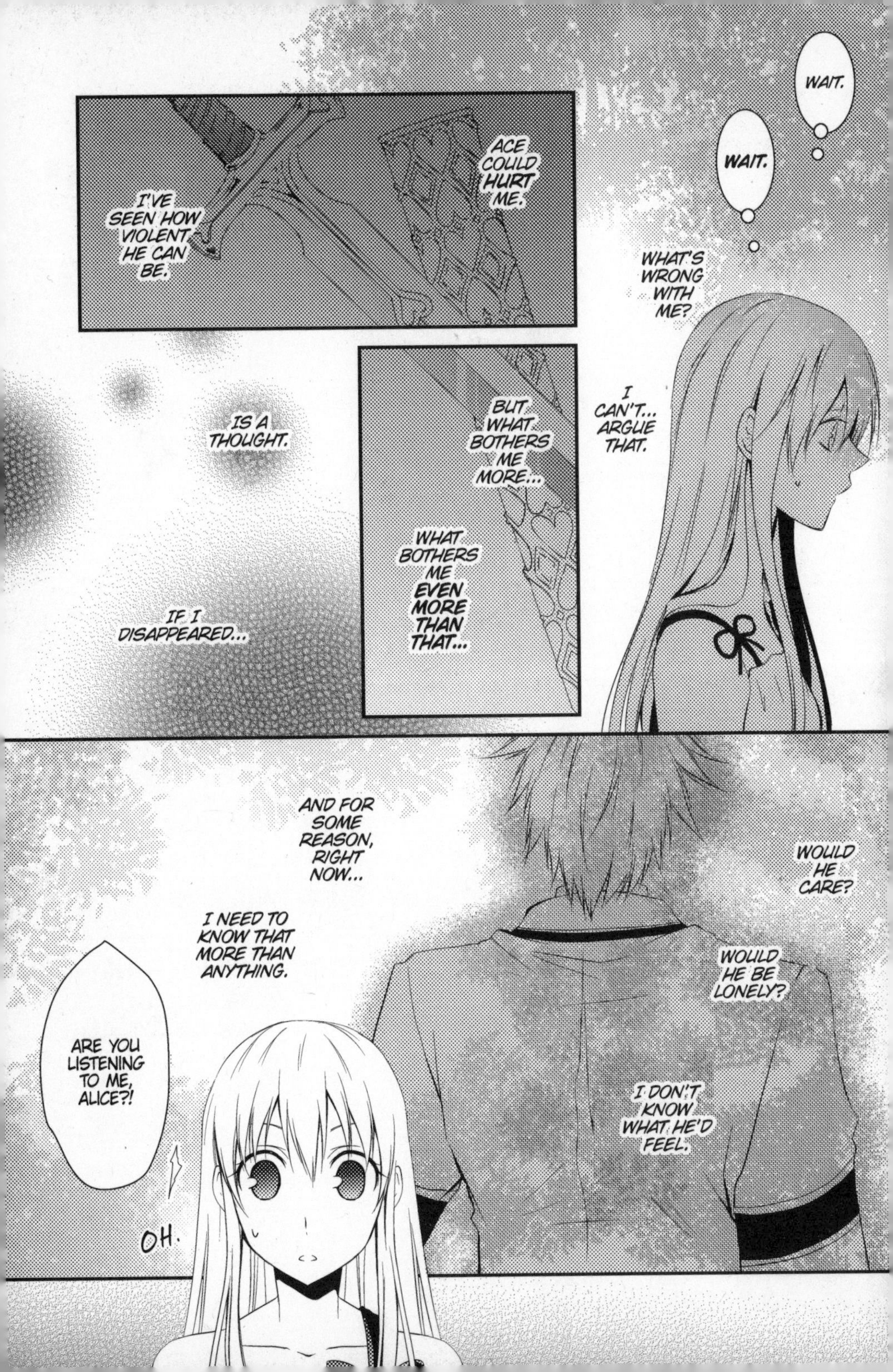
WAIT.
WAIT.
WHAT'S WRONG WITH ME?
I CAN'T... ARGUE THAT.
ACE COULD HURT ME.
I'VE SEEN HOW VIOLENT HE CAN BE.
BUT WHAT BOTHERS ME MORE...
WHAT BOTHERS ME EVEN MORE THAN THAT...
IS A THOUGHT.
IF I DISAPPEARED...
WOULD HE CARE?
WOULD HE BE LONELY?
I DON'T KNOW WHAT HE'D FEEL.
AND FOR SOME REASON, RIGHT NOW...
I NEED TO KNOW THAT MORE THAN ANYTHING.
ARE YOU LISTENING TO ME, ALICE?!
OH.

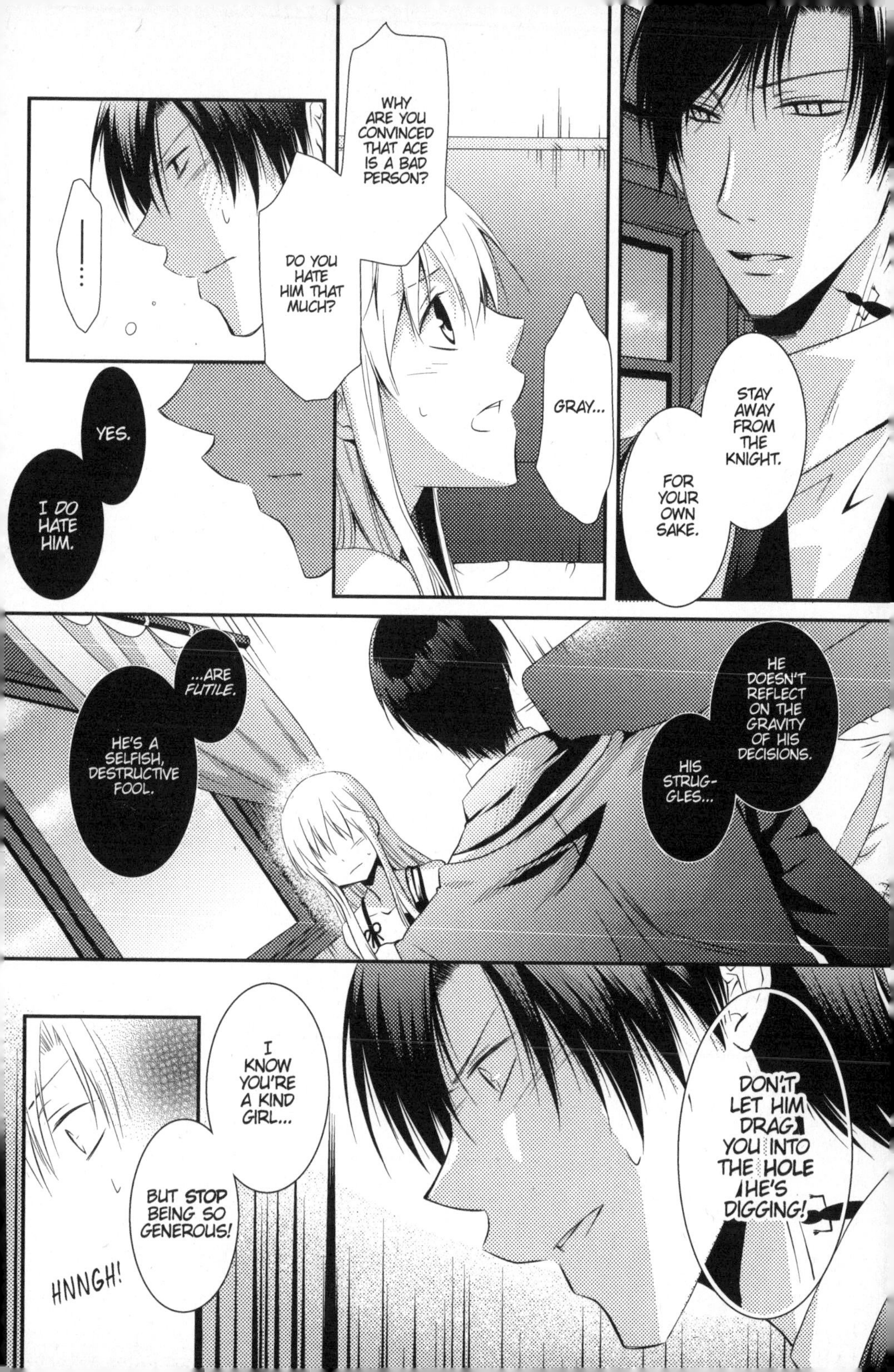

STAY AWAY FROM THE KNIGHT.
FOR YOUR OWN SAKE.
GRAY...
WHY ARE YOU CONVINCED THAT ACE IS A BAD PERSON?
DO YOU HATE HIM THAT MUCH?
—....
YES.
I *DO* HATE HIM.
HE DOESN'T REFLECT ON THE GRAVITY OF HIS DECISIONS.
HIS STRUGGLES...
...ARE *FUTILE*.
HE'S A SELFISH, DESTRUCTIVE FOOL.
DON'T LET HIM DRAG YOU INTO THE HOLE HE'S DIGGING!
I KNOW YOU'RE A KIND GIRL...
BUT **STOP** BEING SO GENEROUS!
HNNGH!

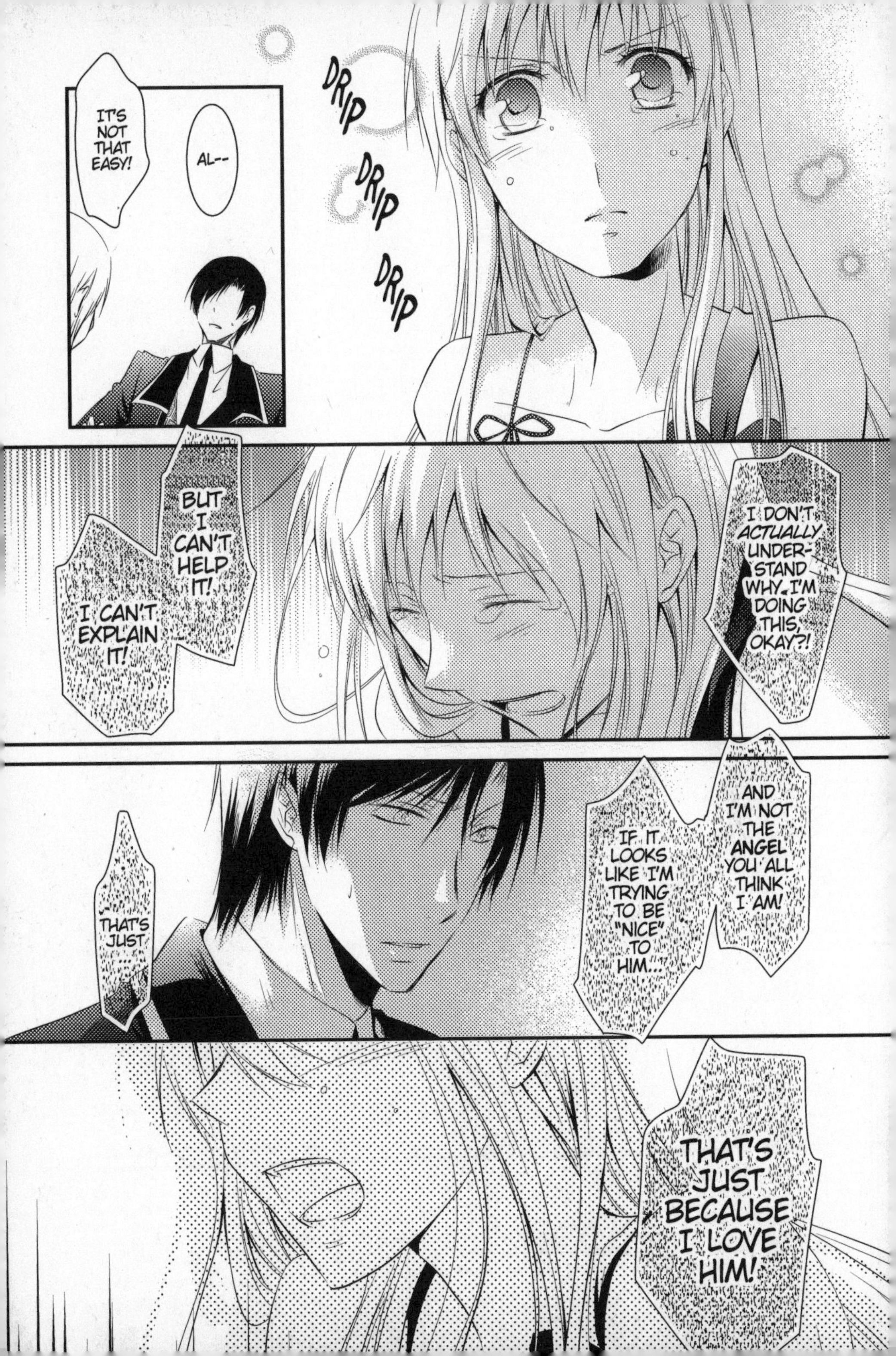
DRIP DRIP DRIP
AL--
IT'S NOT THAT EASY!
I DON'T ACTUALLY UNDERSTAND WHY I'M DOING THIS, OKAY?!
BUT I CAN'T HELP IT!
I CAN'T EXPLAIN IT!
AND I'M NOT THE ANGEL YOU ALL THINK I AM!
IF IT LOOKS LIKE I'M TRYING TO BE "NICE" TO HIM...
THAT'S JUST
THAT'S JUST BECAUSE I LOVE HIM!

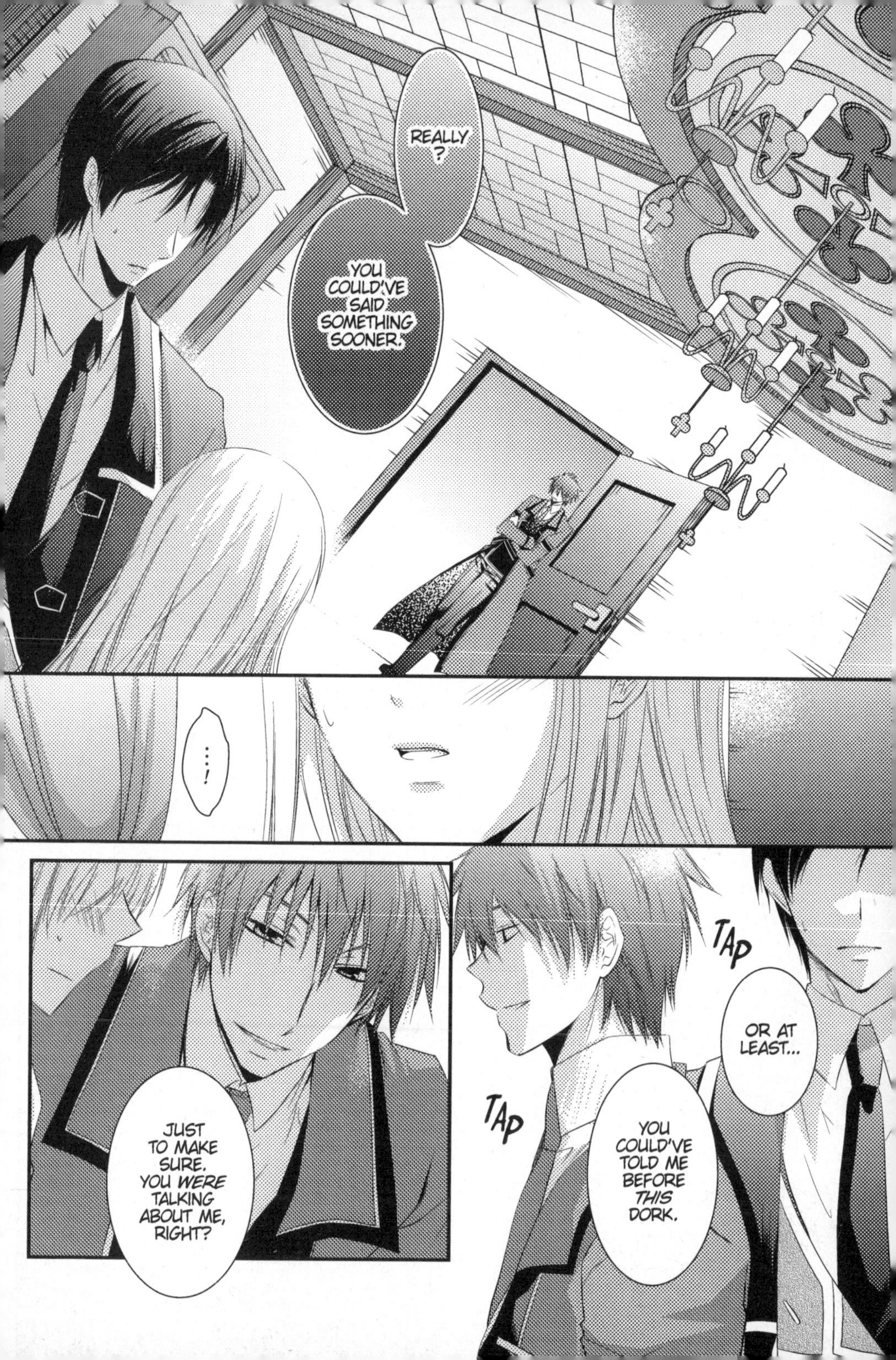

REALLY?
YOU COULD'VE SAID SOMETHING SOONER.
...!
TAP
OR AT LEAST...
TAP
YOU COULD'VE TOLD ME BEFORE THIS DORK.
JUST TO MAKE SURE. YOU WERE TALKING ABOUT ME, RIGHT?

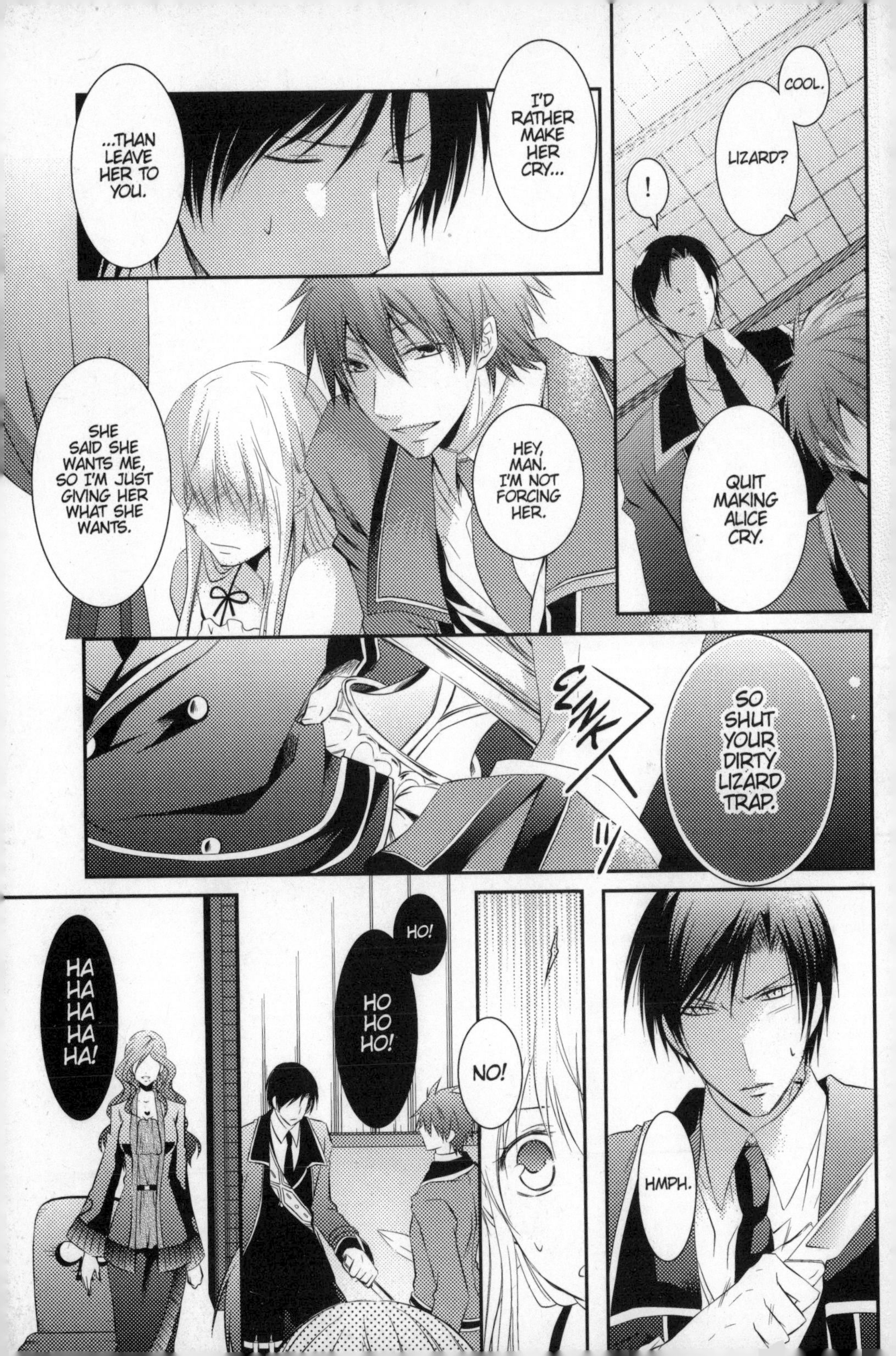
COOL.
LIZARD?
!
QUIT MAKING ALICE CRY.
I'D RATHER MAKE HER CRY...
...THAN LEAVE HER TO YOU.
HEY, MAN. I'M NOT FORCING HER.
SHE SAID SHE WANTS ME, SO I'M JUST GIVING HER WHAT SHE WANTS.
SO SHUT YOUR DIRTY LIZARD TRAP.
CLINK
HMPH.
NO!
HO!
HO HO HO!
HA HA HA HA HA!

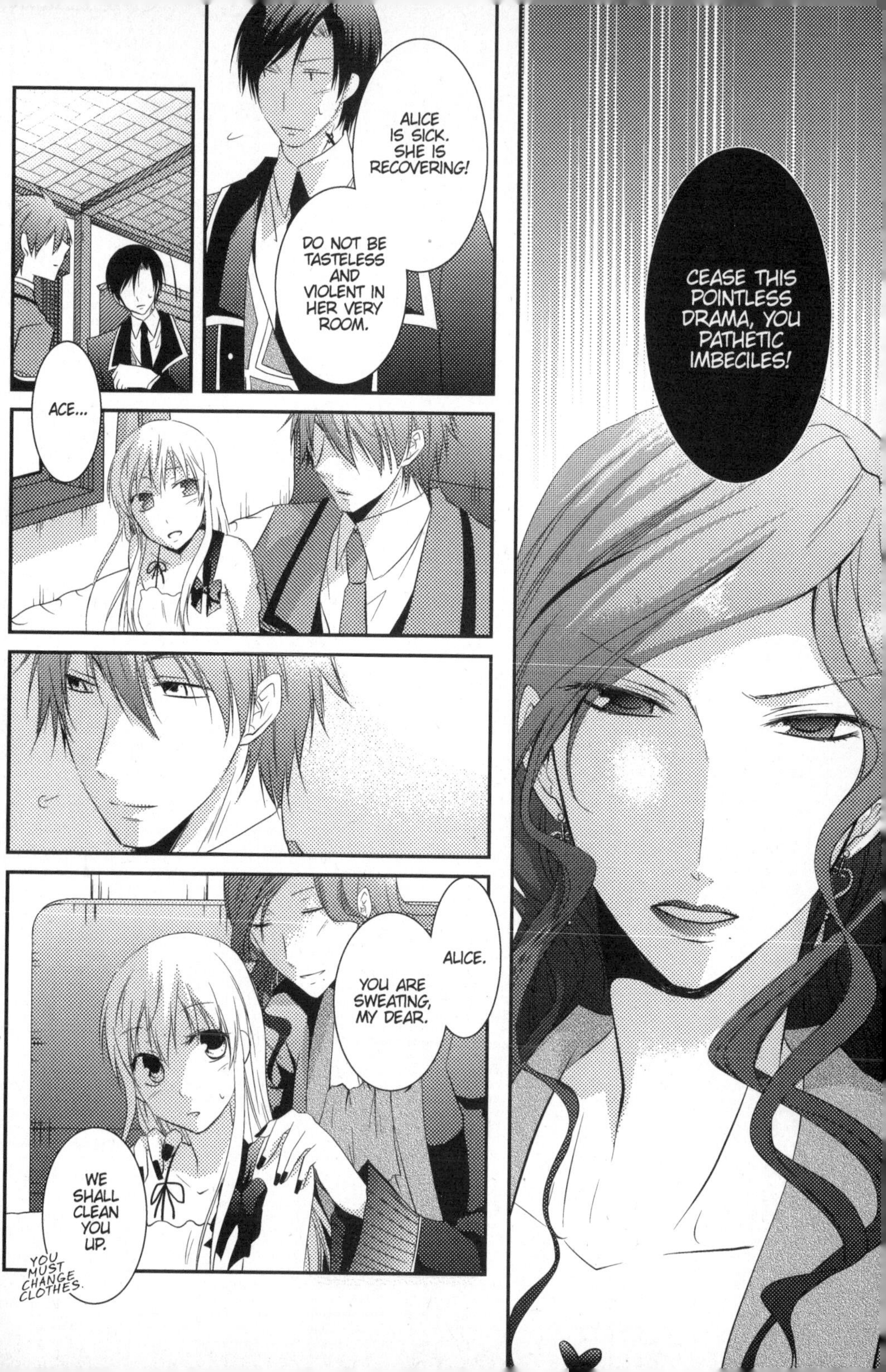
CEASE THIS POINTLESS DRAMA, YOU PATHETIC IMBECILES!
ALICE IS SICK. SHE IS RECOVERING!
DO NOT BE TASTELESS AND VIOLENT IN HER VERY ROOM.
ACE...
ALICE.
YOU ARE SWEATING, MY DEAR.
WE SHALL CLEAN YOU UP.
YOU MUST CHANGE CLOTHES.

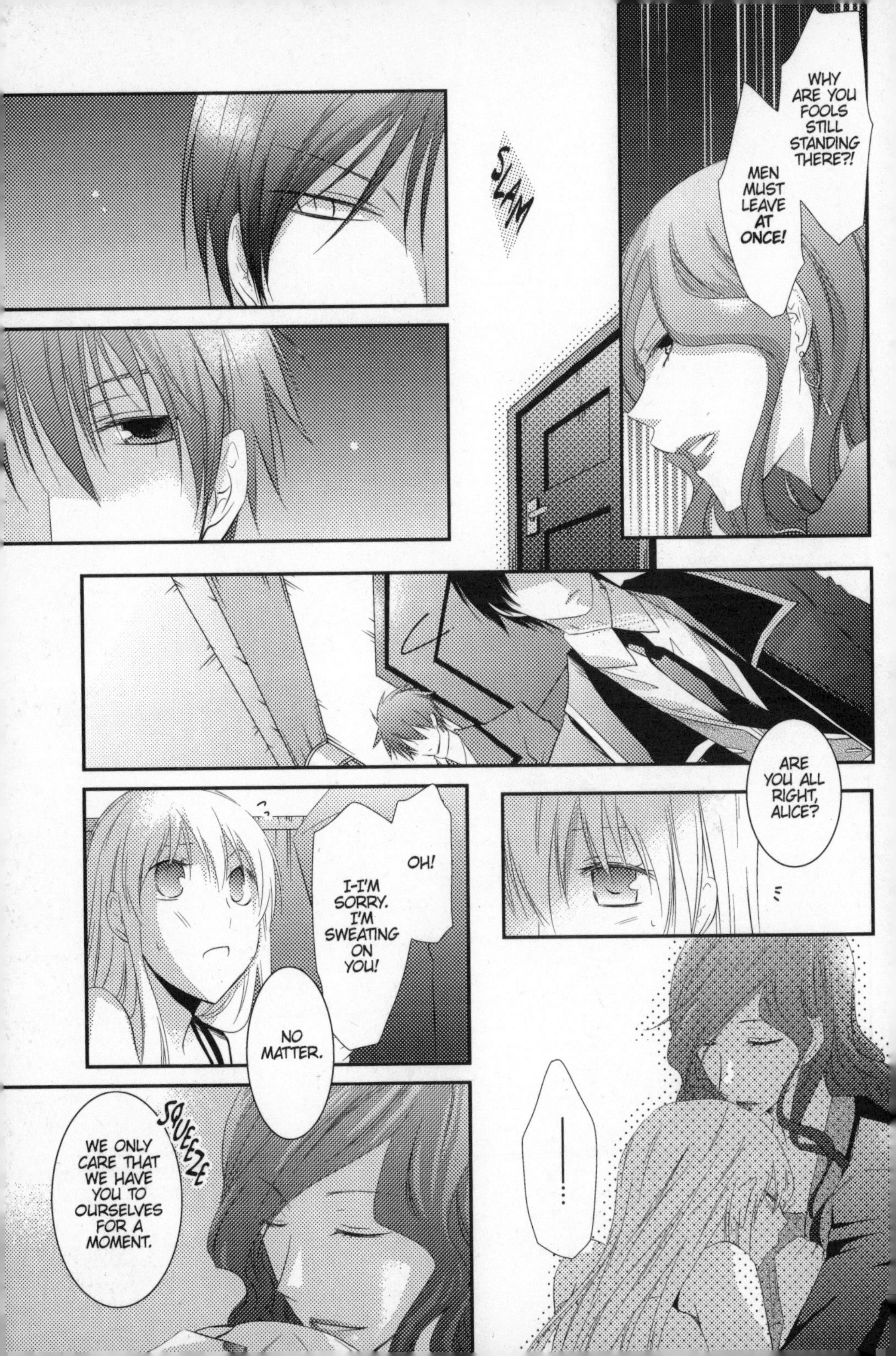
WHY ARE YOU FOOLS STILL STANDING THERE?!
MEN MUST LEAVE AT ONCE!
SLAM
ARE YOU ALL RIGHT, ALICE?
OH!
I-I'M SORRY. I'M SWEATING ON YOU!
NO MATTER.
——!...
SQUEEZE
WE ONLY CARE THAT WE HAVE YOU TO OURSELVES FOR A MOMENT.

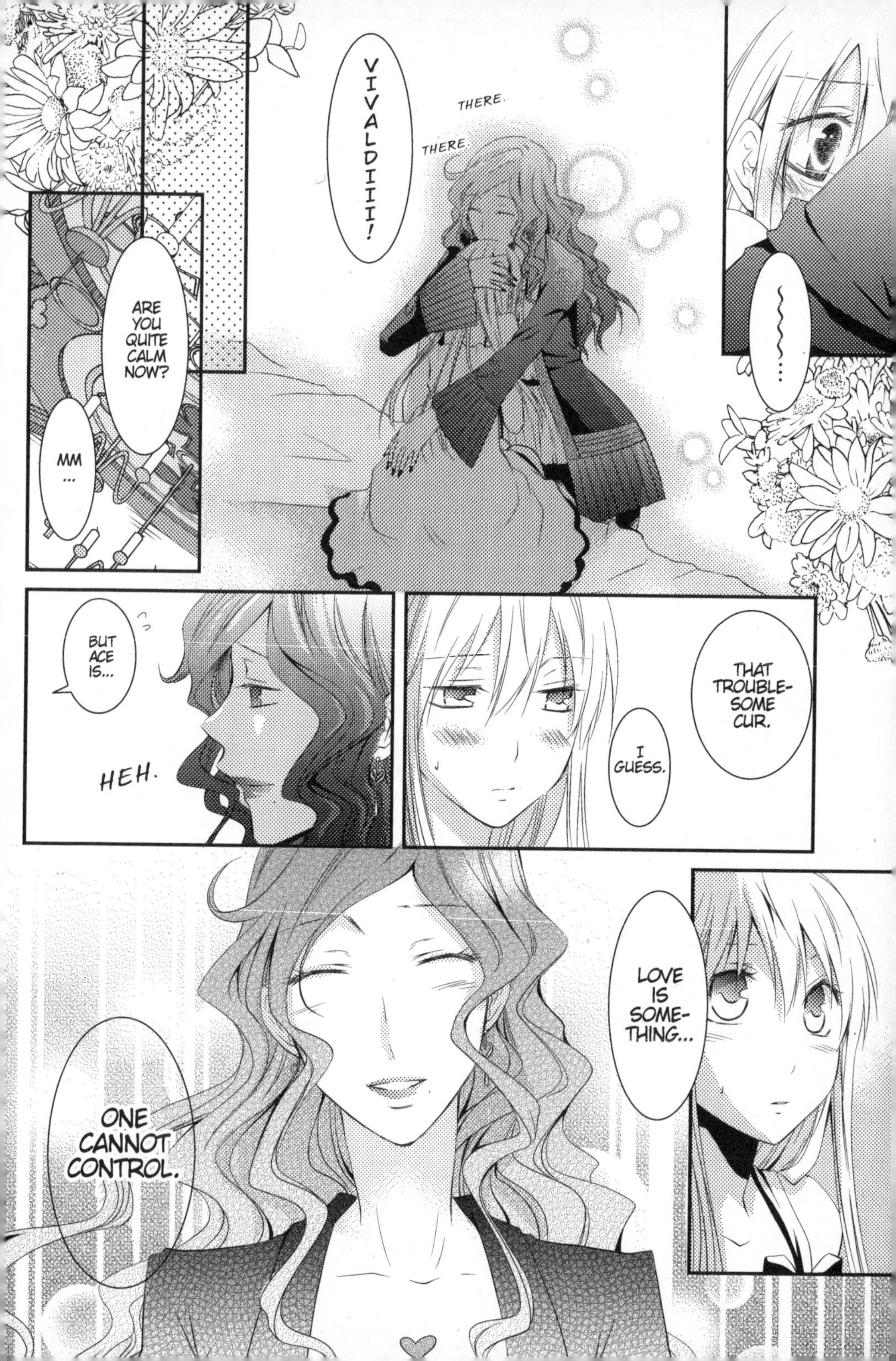

VIVALDIII!
THERE.
THERE.
ARE YOU QUITE CALM NOW?
MM...
THAT TROUBLE-SOME CUR.
I GUESS.
BUT ACE IS...
HEH.
LOVE IS SOME-THING...
ONE CANNOT CONTROL.

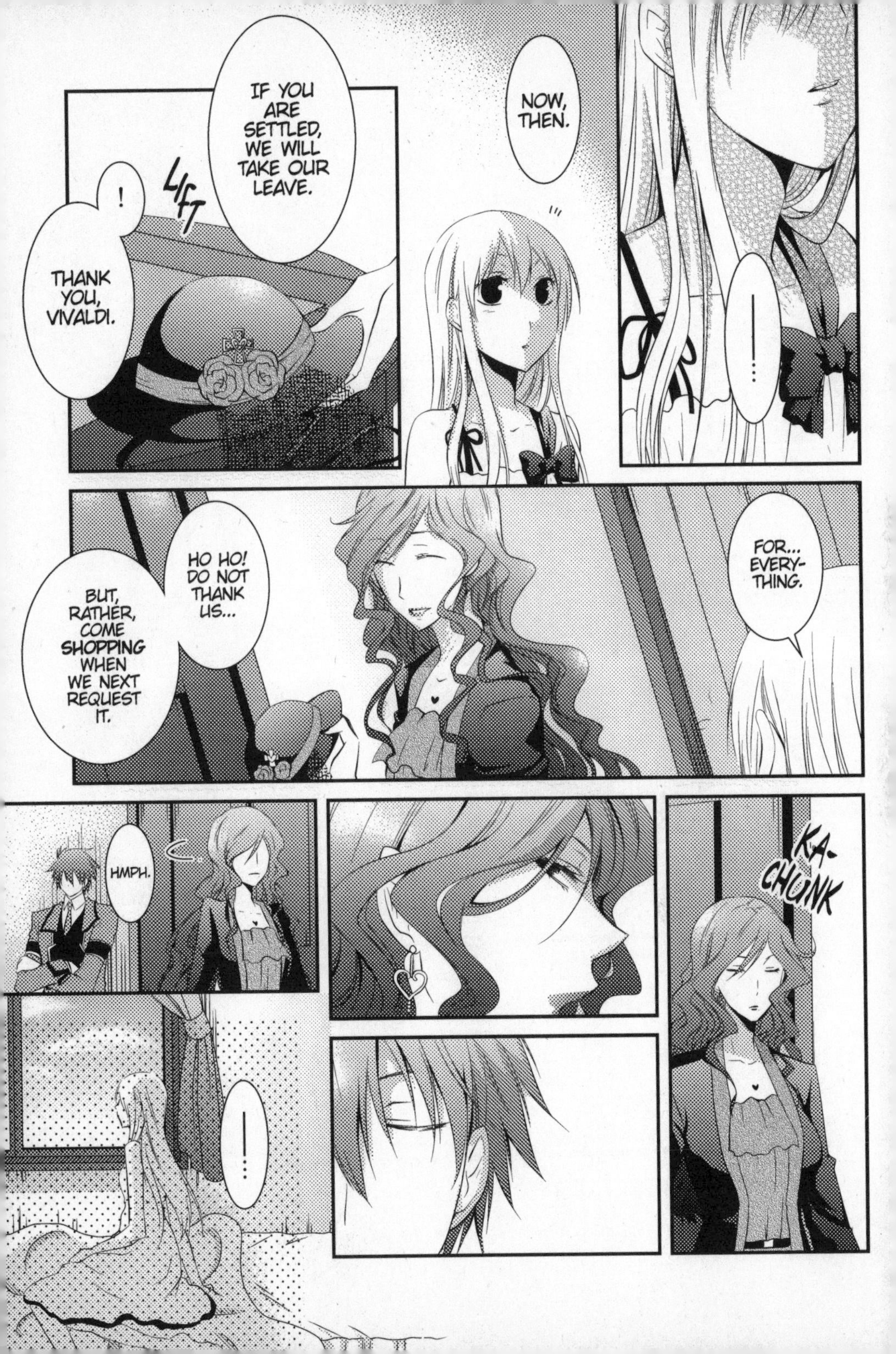

!...
NOW, THEN.
IF YOU ARE SETTLED, WE WILL TAKE OUR LEAVE.
LIFT
!
THANK YOU, VIVALDI.
FOR... EVERYTHING.
HO HO! DO NOT THANK US...
BUT, RATHER, COME SHOPPING WHEN WE NEXT REQUEST IT.
KA-CHUNK
HMPH.
!...

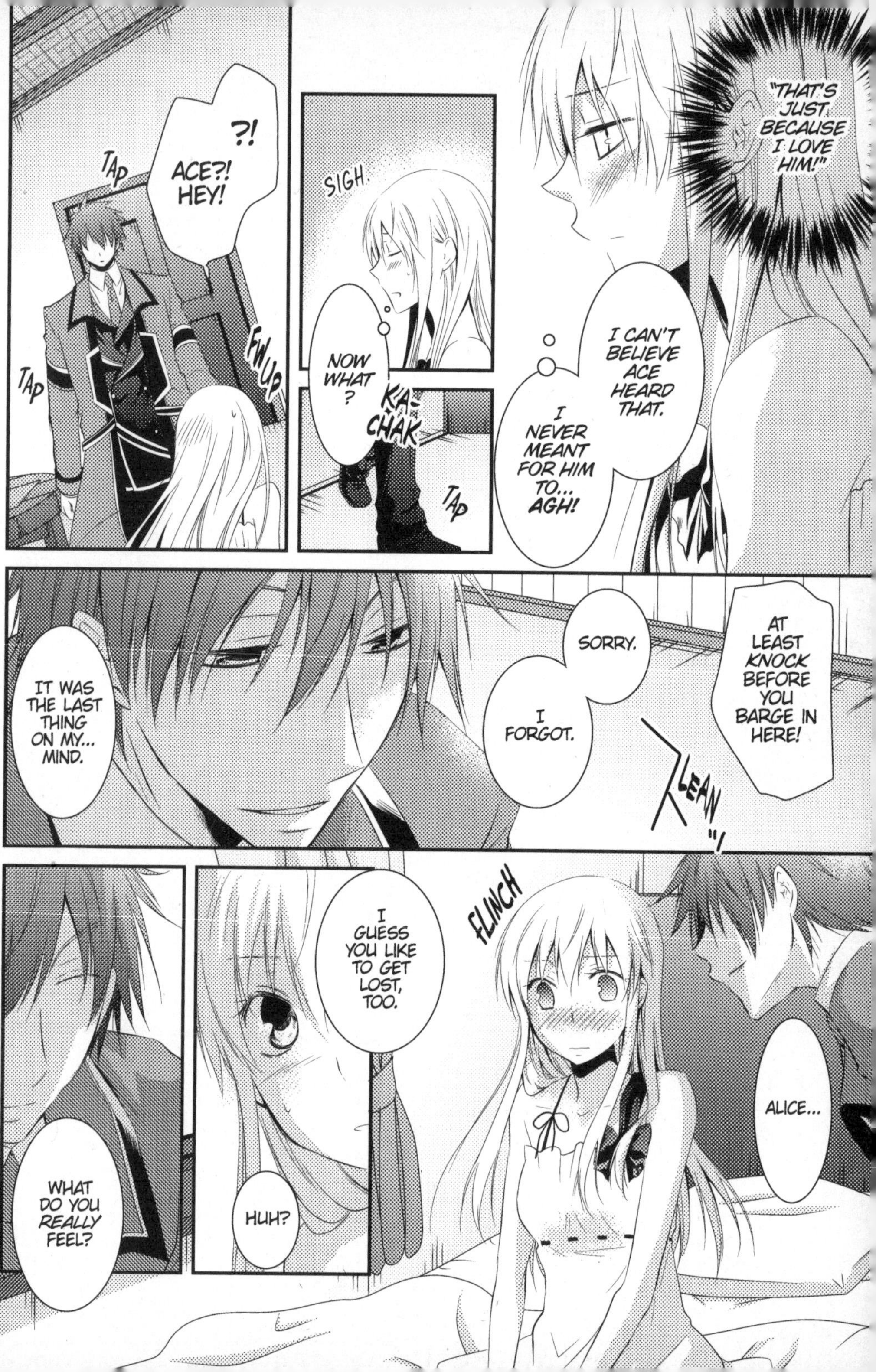
"THAT'S JUST BECAUSE I LOVE HIM!"
I CAN'T BELIEVE ACE HEARD THAT.
I NEVER MEANT FOR HIM TO... AGH!
SIGH.
NOW WHAT?
KA-CHAK
TAP
TAP
?!
ACE?! HEY!
FWUP
TAP
AT LEAST KNOCK BEFORE YOU BARGE IN HERE!
LEAN
SORRY.
I FORGOT.
IT WAS THE LAST THING ON MY... MIND.
ALICE...
FLINCH
I GUESS YOU LIKE TO GET LOST, TOO.
HUH?
WHAT DO YOU *REALLY* FEEL?

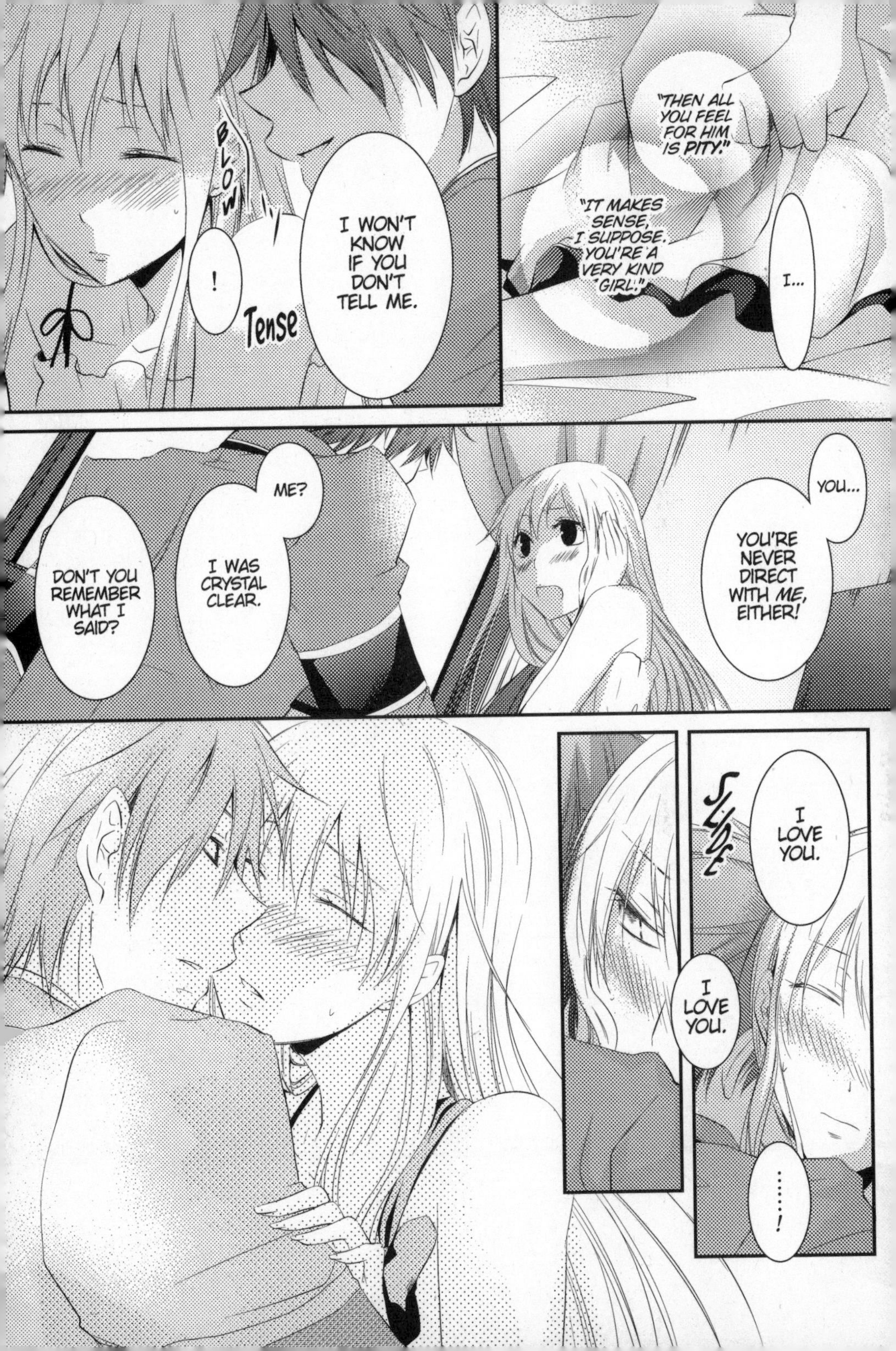
"THEN ALL YOU FEEL FOR HIM IS PITY."
"IT MAKES SENSE, I SUPPOSE. YOU'RE A VERY KIND GIRL."
I...
I WON'T KNOW IF YOU DON'T TELL ME.
BLOW
!
Tense
YOU...
YOU'RE NEVER DIRECT WITH ME, EITHER!
ME?
I WAS CRYSTAL CLEAR.
DON'T YOU REMEMBER WHAT I SAID?
SLIDE
I LOVE YOU.
I LOVE YOU.
......!

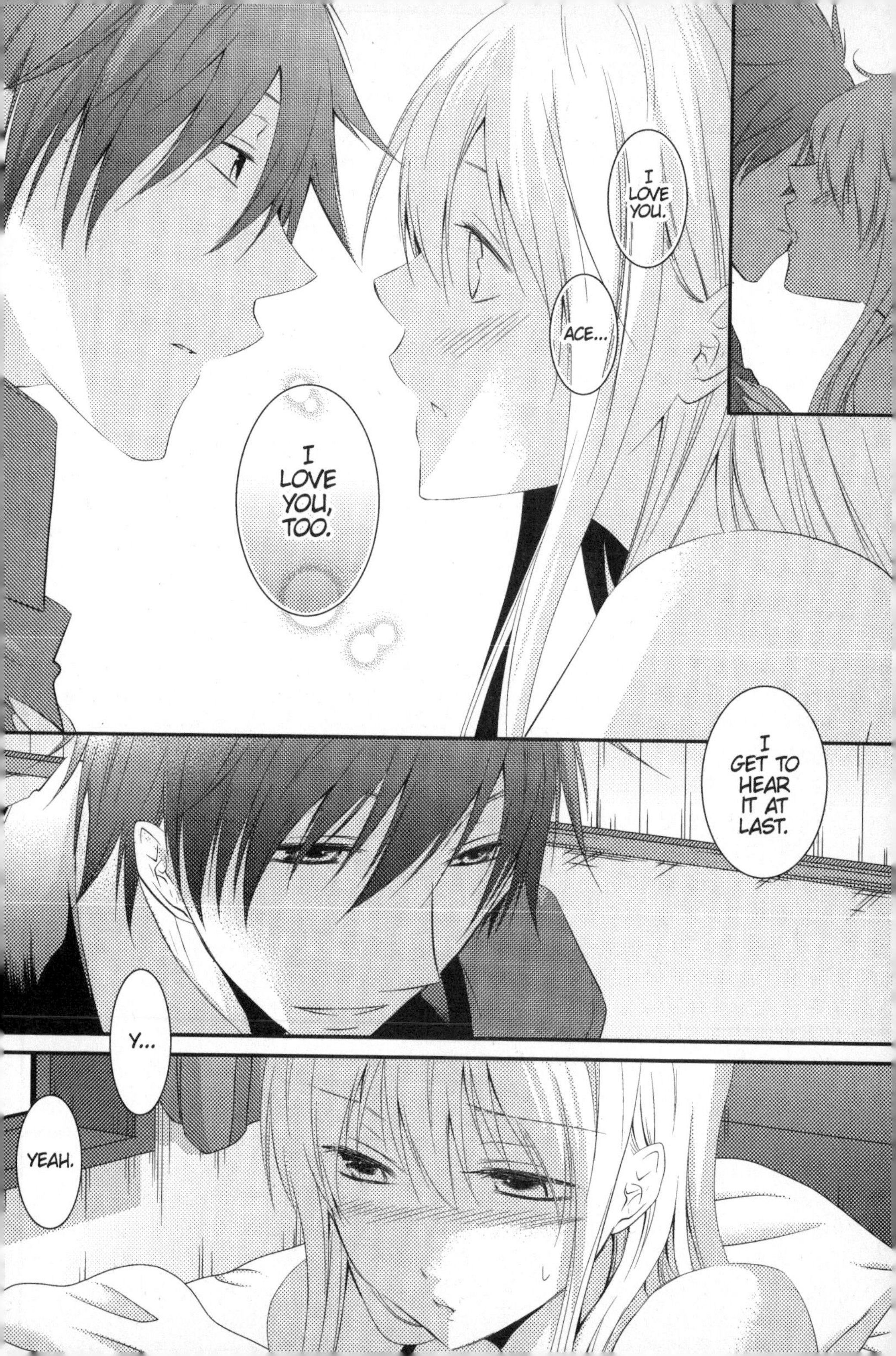
I LOVE YOU.
ACE...
I LOVE YOU, TOO.
I GET TO HEAR IT AT LAST.
Y...
YEAH.

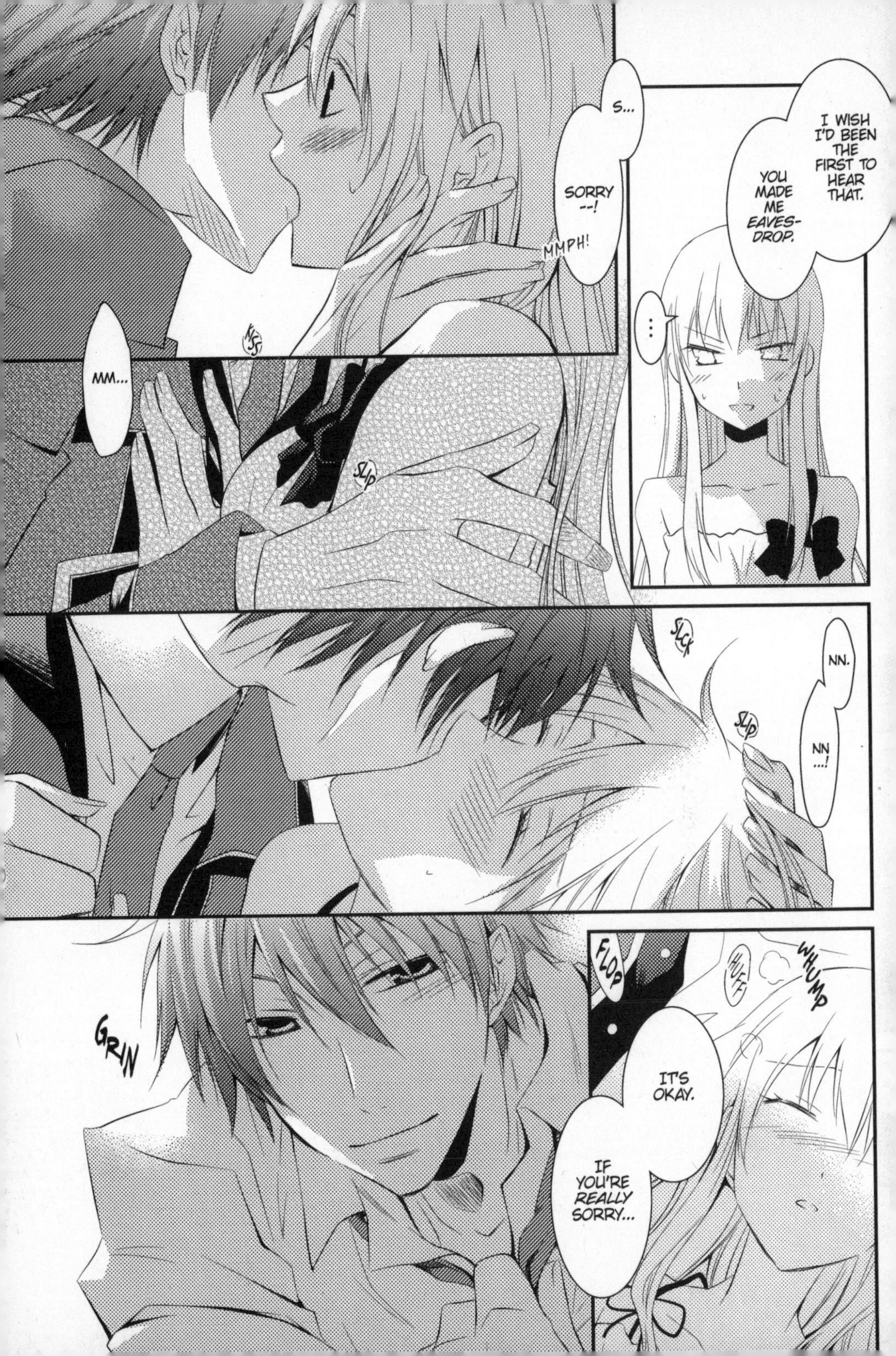

I WISH I'D BEEN THE FIRST TO HEAR THAT.
YOU MADE ME EAVES-DROP.
...
S...
SORRY --!
MMPH!
KISS
SLIP
MM...
SLCK
NN.
SLIP
NN ...!
WHUMP
HUFF
FLOP
IT'S OKAY.
IF YOU'RE *REALLY* SORRY...
GRIN

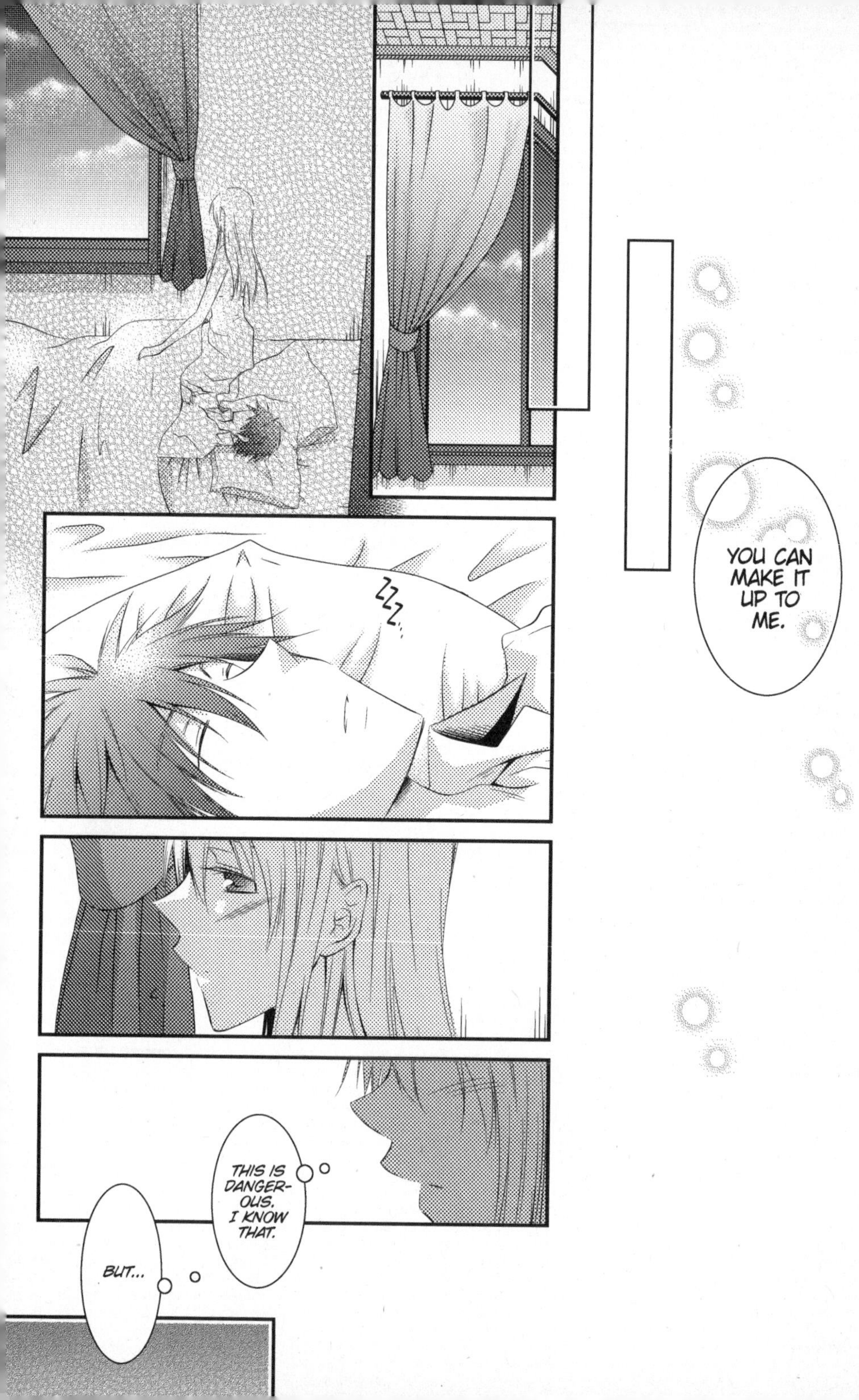
YOU CAN MAKE IT UP TO ME.
THIS IS DANGER-OUS. I KNOW THAT.
BUT...

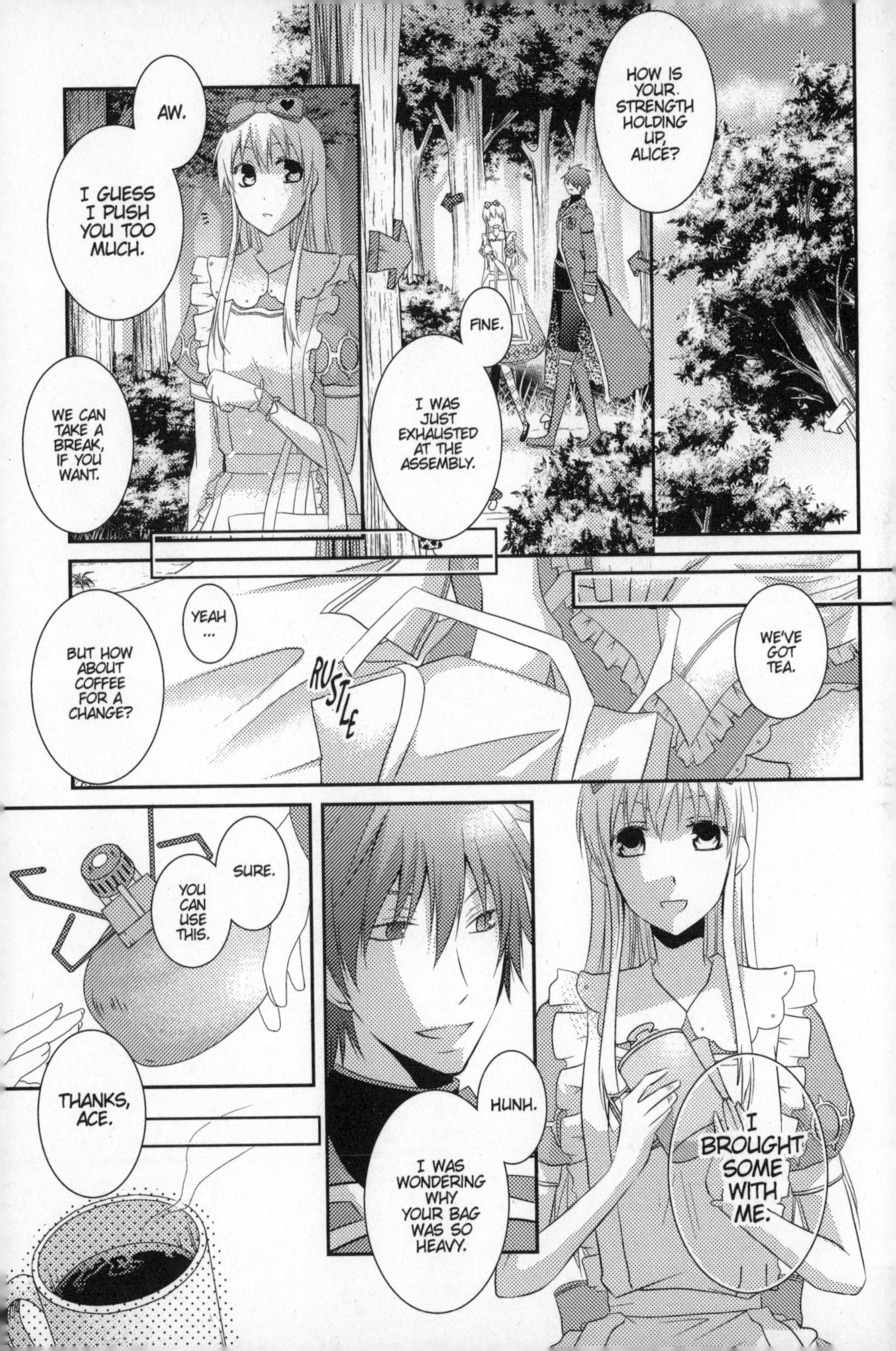
HOW IS YOUR STRENGTH HOLDING UP, ALICE?
FINE.
I WAS JUST EXHAUSTED AT THE ASSEMBLY.
AW.
I GUESS I PUSH YOU TOO MUCH.
WE CAN TAKE A BREAK, IF YOU WANT.
WE'VE GOT TEA.
YEAH...
BUT HOW ABOUT COFFEE FOR A CHANGE?
RUSTLE
I BROUGHT SOME WITH ME.
HUNH.
I WAS WONDERING WHY YOUR BAG WAS SO HEAVY.
SURE.
YOU CAN USE THIS.
THANKS, ACE.

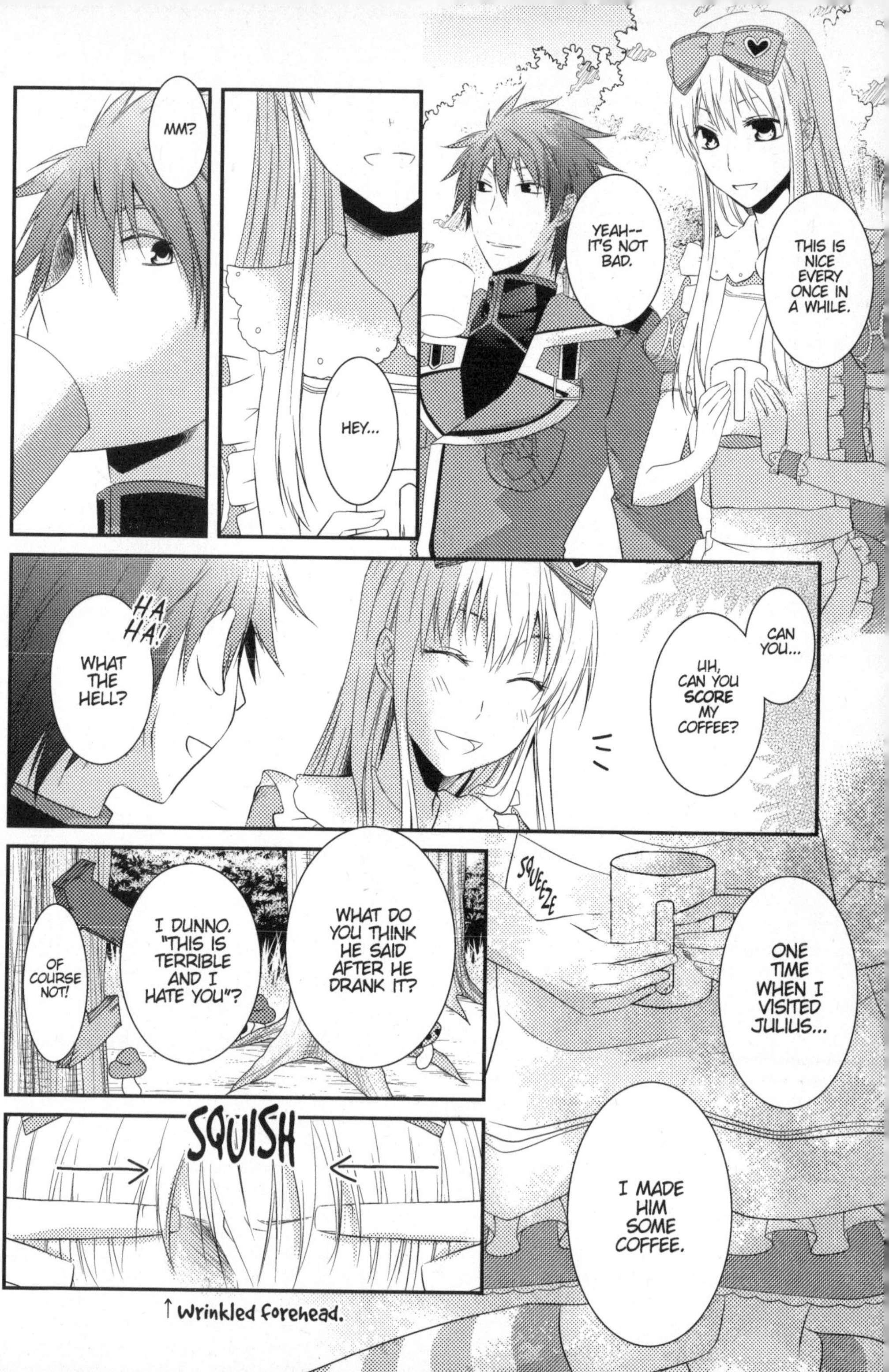
THIS IS NICE EVERY ONCE IN A WHILE.
YEAH-- IT'S NOT BAD.
HEY...
MM?
CAN YOU...
UH, CAN YOU SCORE MY COFFEE?
HA HA!
WHAT THE HELL?
SQUEEZE
ONE TIME WHEN I VISITED JULIUS...
I MADE HIM SOME COFFEE.
WHAT DO YOU THINK HE SAID AFTER HE DRANK IT?
I DUNNO. "THIS IS TERRIBLE AND I HATE YOU"?
OF COURSE NOT!
SQUISH
↑ Wrinkled forehead.

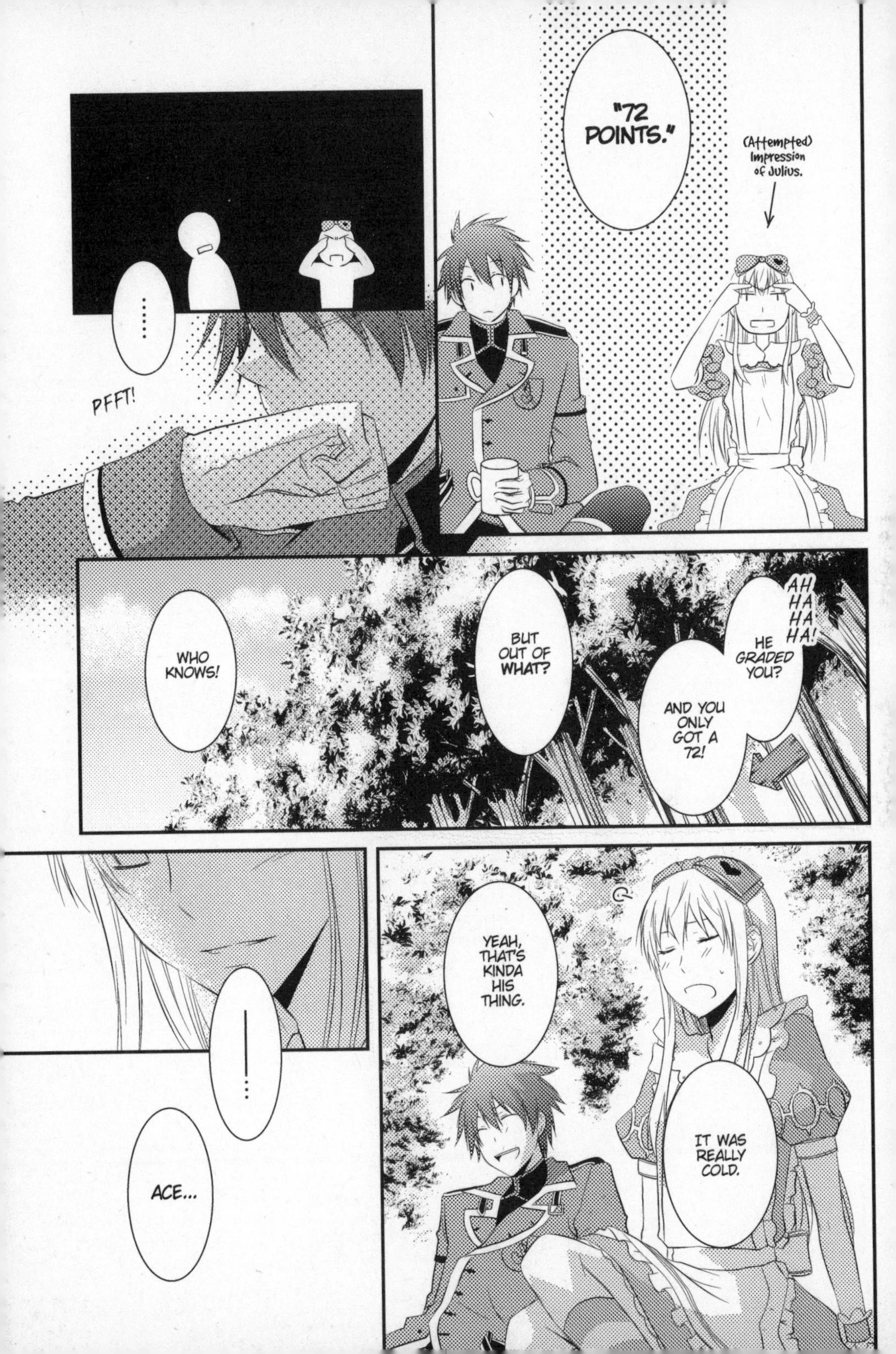
"72 POINTS."
(Attempted) Impression of Julius.
......
PFFT!
AH HA HA HA!
HE GRADED YOU?
AND YOU ONLY GOT A 72!
BUT OUT OF WHAT?
WHO KNOWS!
YEAH, THAT'S KINDA HIS THING.
IT WAS REALLY COLD.
—!...
ACE...

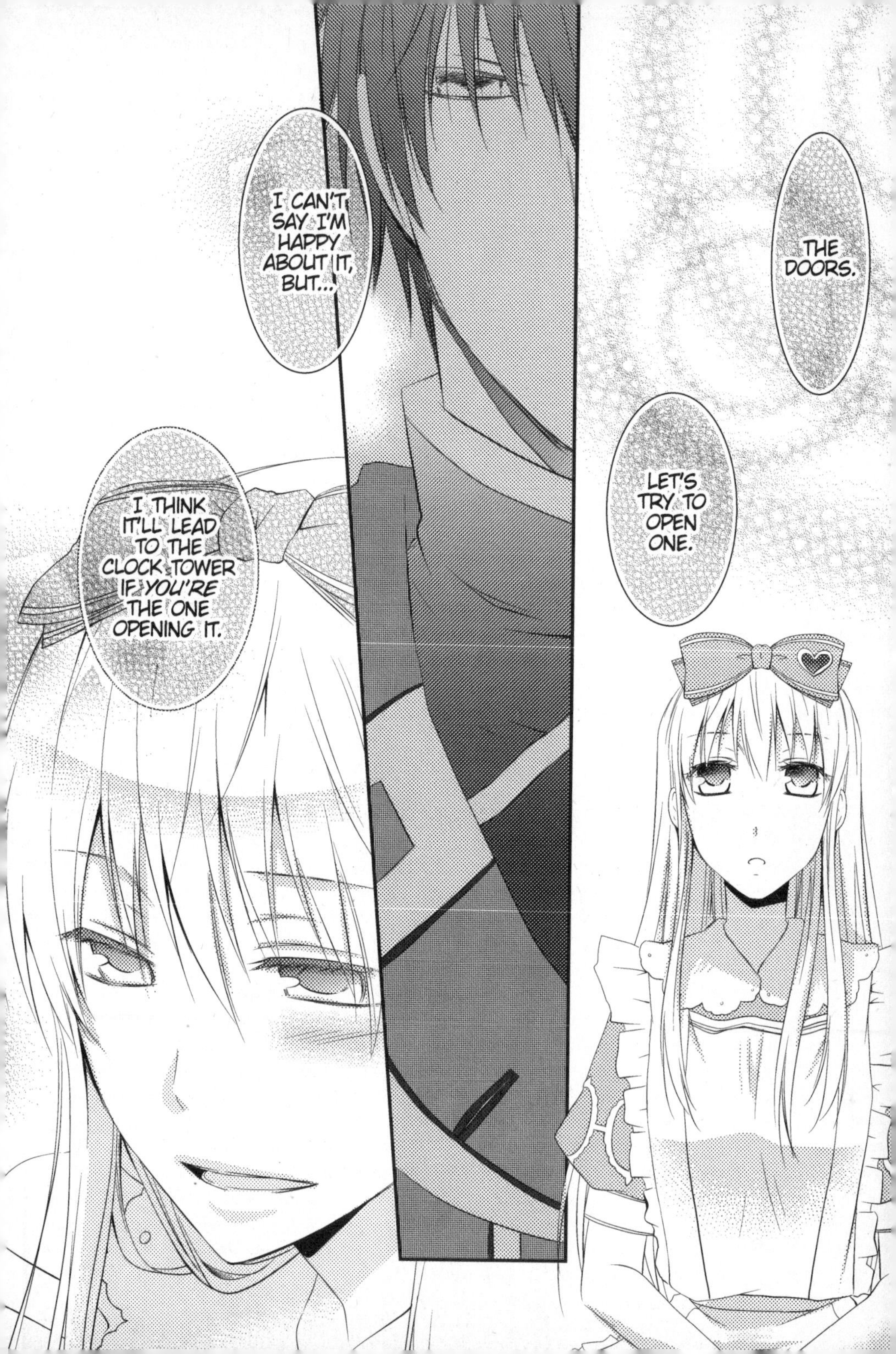
THE DOORS.
LET'S TRY TO OPEN ONE.
I CAN'T SAY I'M HAPPY ABOUT IT, BUT...
I THINK IT'LL LEAD TO THE CLOCK TOWER IF *YOU'RE* THE ONE OPENING IT.

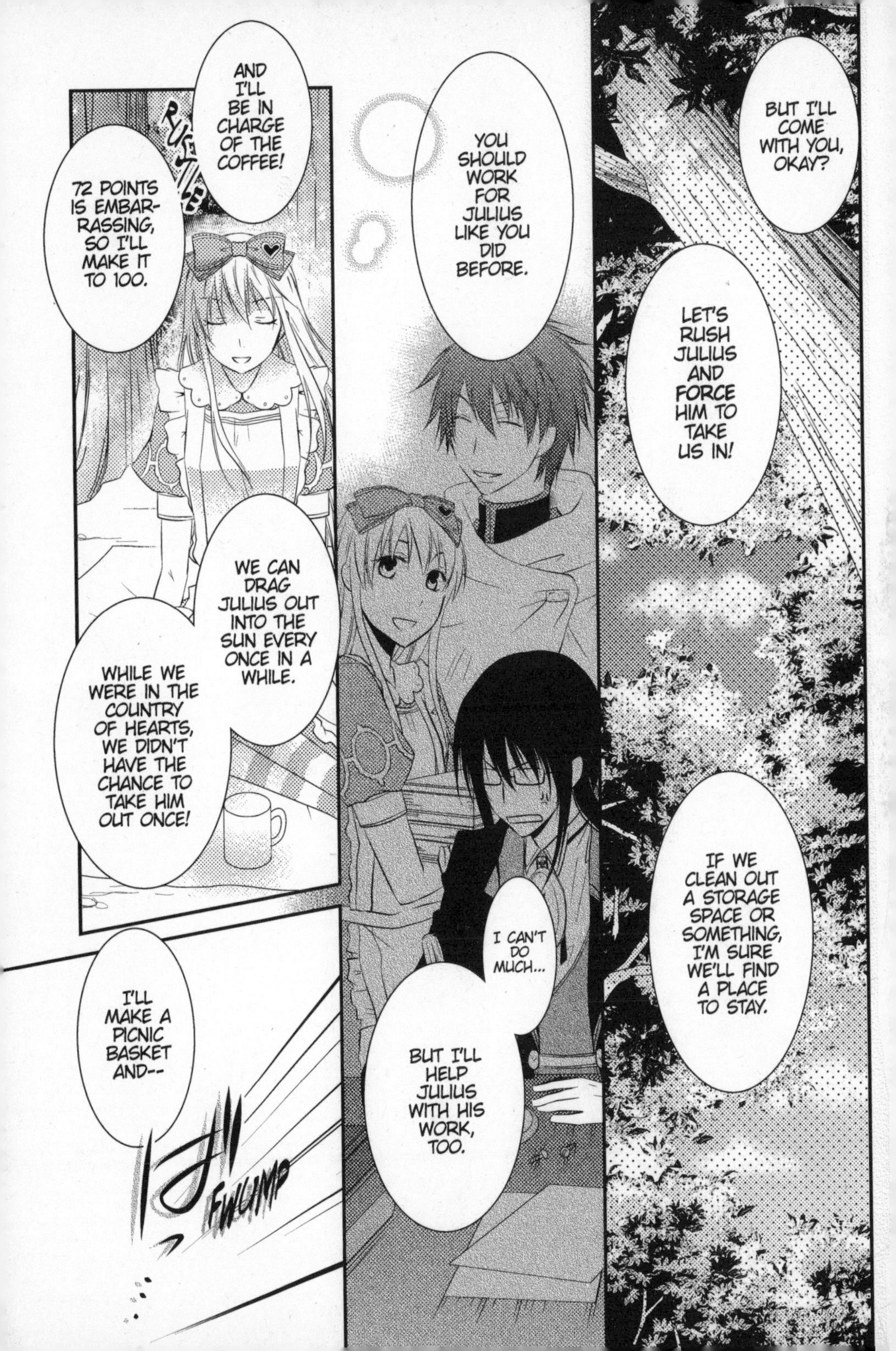

BUT I'LL COME WITH YOU, OKAY?
LET'S RUSH JULIUS AND FORCE HIM TO TAKE US IN!
IF WE CLEAN OUT A STORAGE SPACE OR SOMETHING, I'M SURE WE'LL FIND A PLACE TO STAY.
YOU SHOULD WORK FOR JULIUS LIKE YOU DID BEFORE.
I CAN'T DO MUCH...
BUT I'LL HELP JULIUS WITH HIS WORK, TOO.
AND I'LL BE IN CHARGE OF THE COFFEE!
RUSTLE
72 POINTS IS EMBARRASSING, SO I'LL MAKE IT TO 100.
WE CAN DRAG JULIUS OUT INTO THE SUN EVERY ONCE IN A WHILE.
WHILE WE WERE IN THE COUNTRY OF HEARTS, WE DIDN'T HAVE THE CHANCE TO TAKE HIM OUT ONCE!
I'LL MAKE A PICNIC BASKET AND--
!!
FWUMP

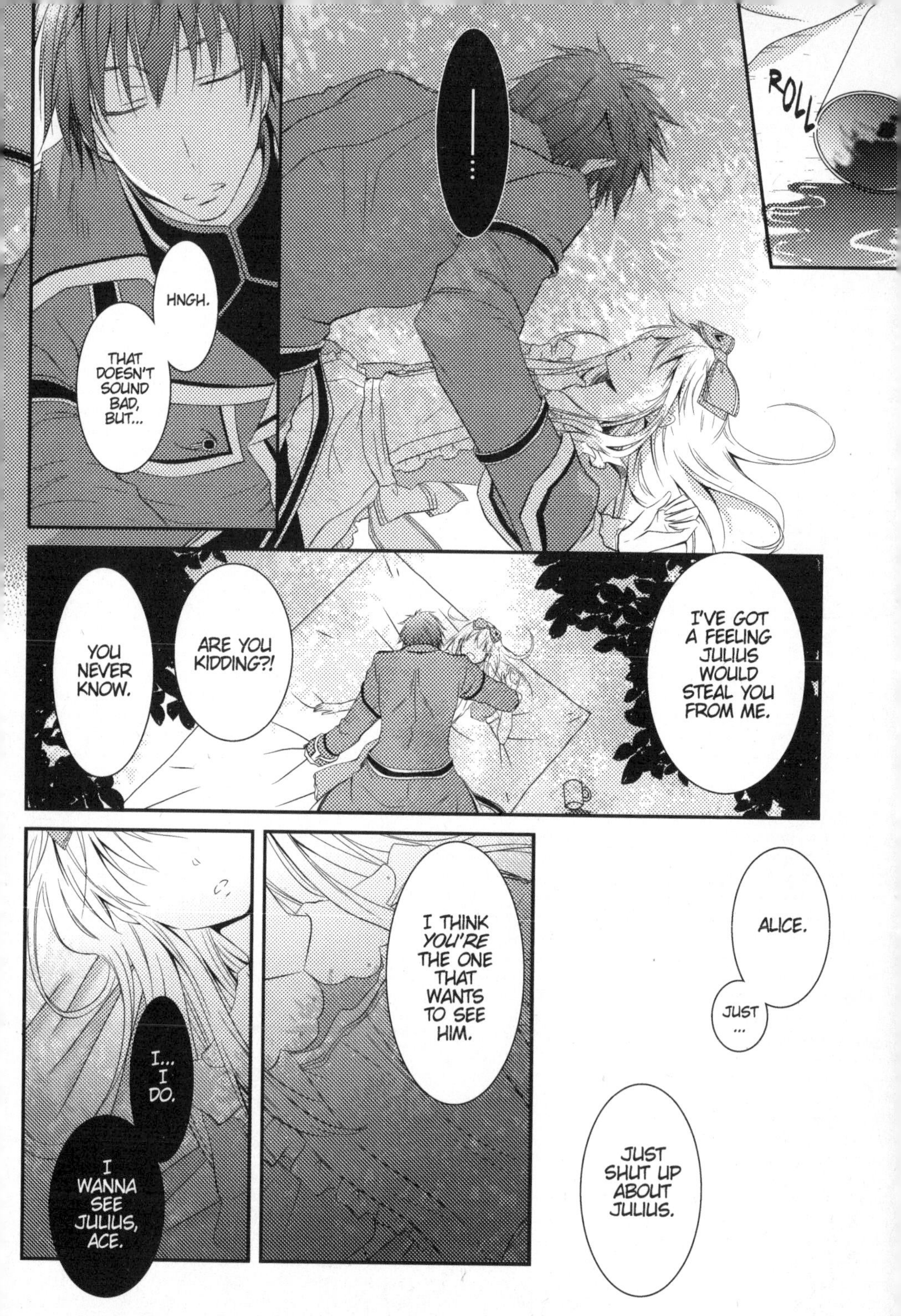

ROLL
—...
HNGH.
THAT DOESN'T SOUND BAD, BUT...
I'VE GOT A FEELING JULIUS WOULD STEAL YOU FROM ME.
ARE YOU KIDDING?!
YOU NEVER KNOW.
ALICE.
JUST ...
JUST SHUT UP ABOUT JULIUS.
I THINK *YOU'RE* THE ONE THAT WANTS TO SEE HIM.
I... I DO.
I WANNA SEE JULIUS, ACE.

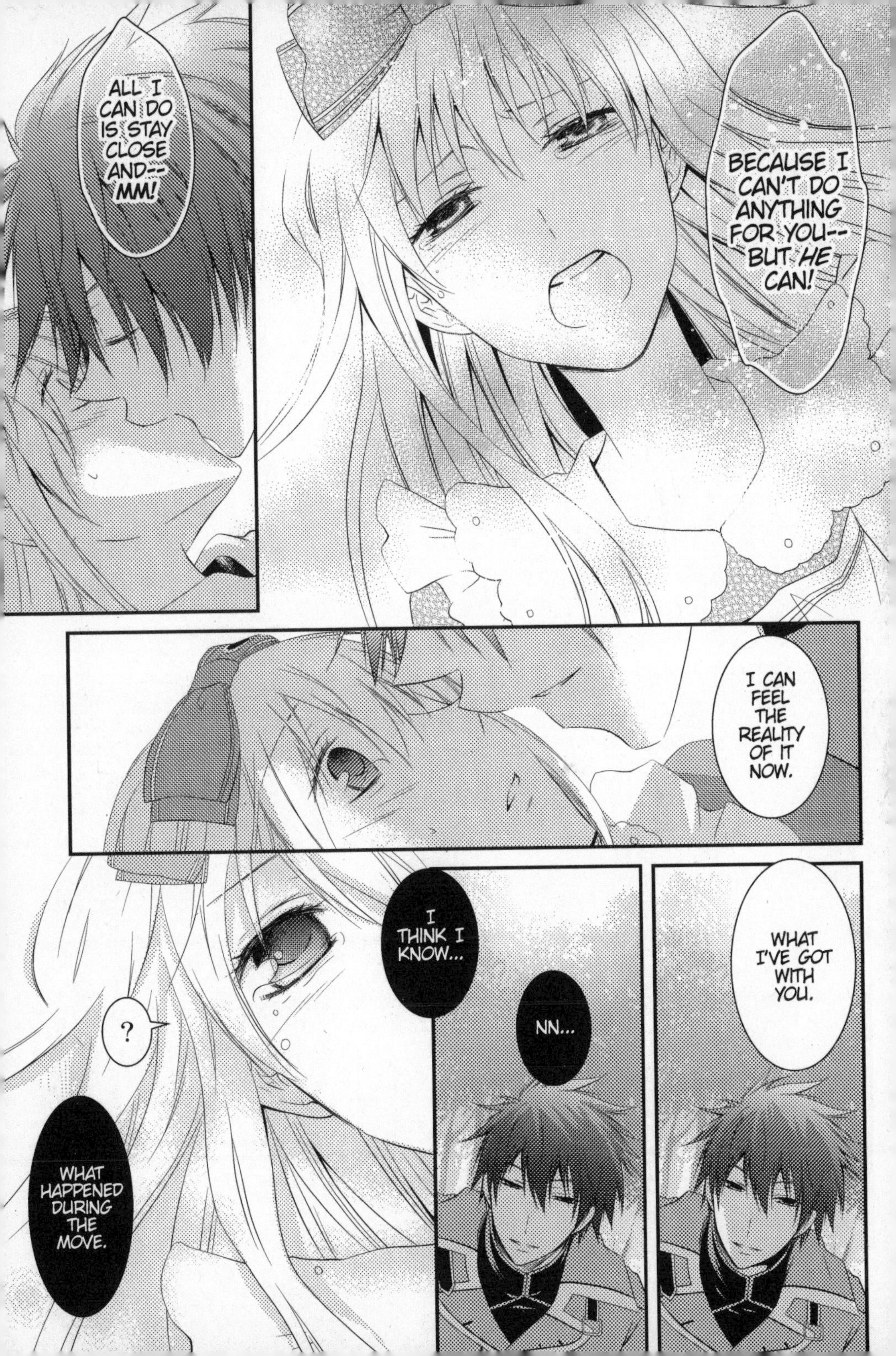
BECAUSE I CAN'T DO ANYTHING FOR YOU-- BUT *HE* CAN!
ALL I CAN DO IS STAY CLOSE AND-- MM!
I CAN FEEL THE REALITY OF IT NOW.
WHAT I'VE GOT WITH YOU.
I THINK I KNOW...
NN...
?
WHAT HAPPENED DURING THE MOVE.

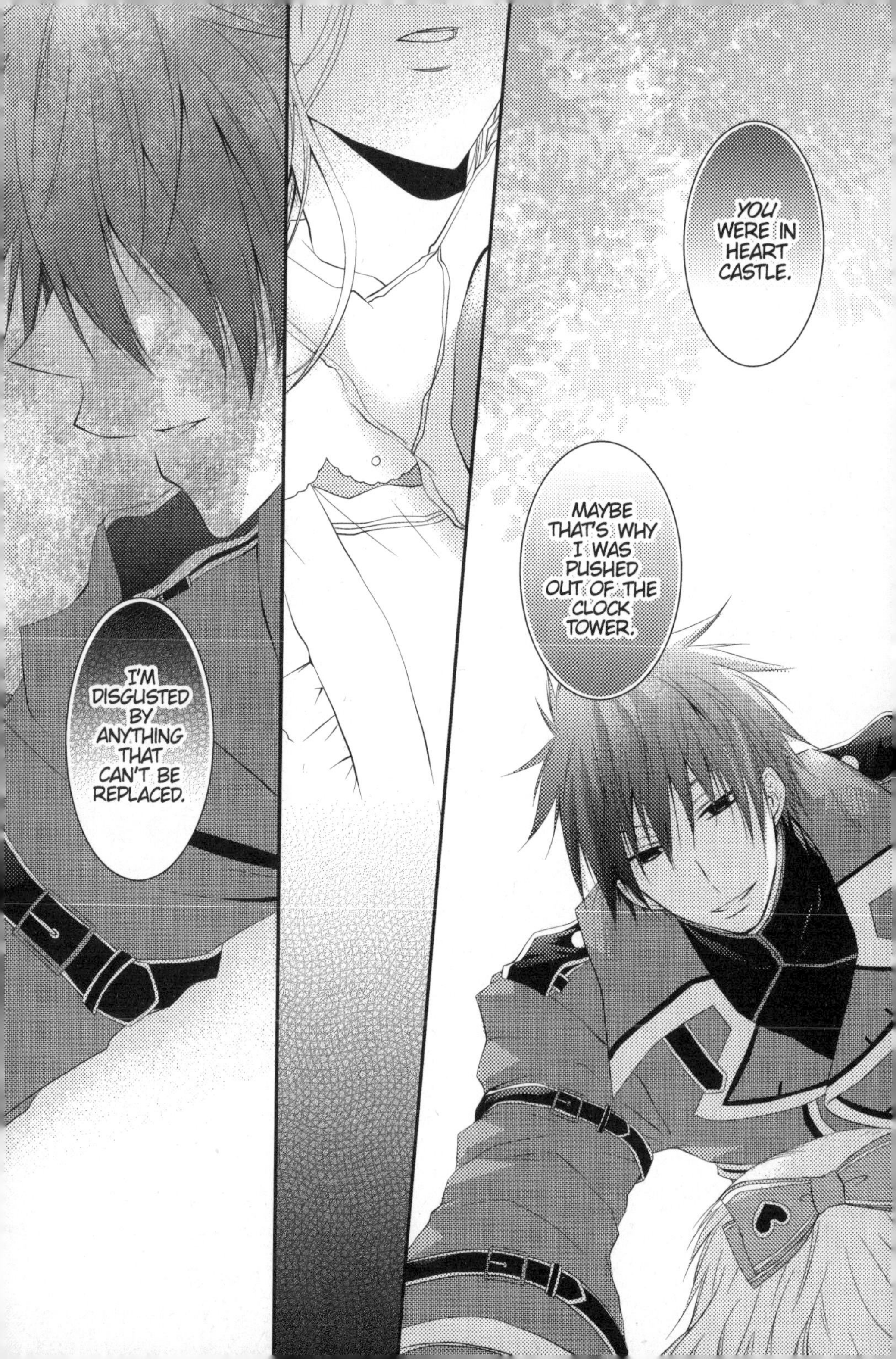
YOU WERE IN HEART CASTLE.
MAYBE THAT'S WHY I WAS PUSHED OUT OF THE CLOCK TOWER.
I'M DISGUSTED BY ANYTHING THAT CAN'T BE REPLACED.

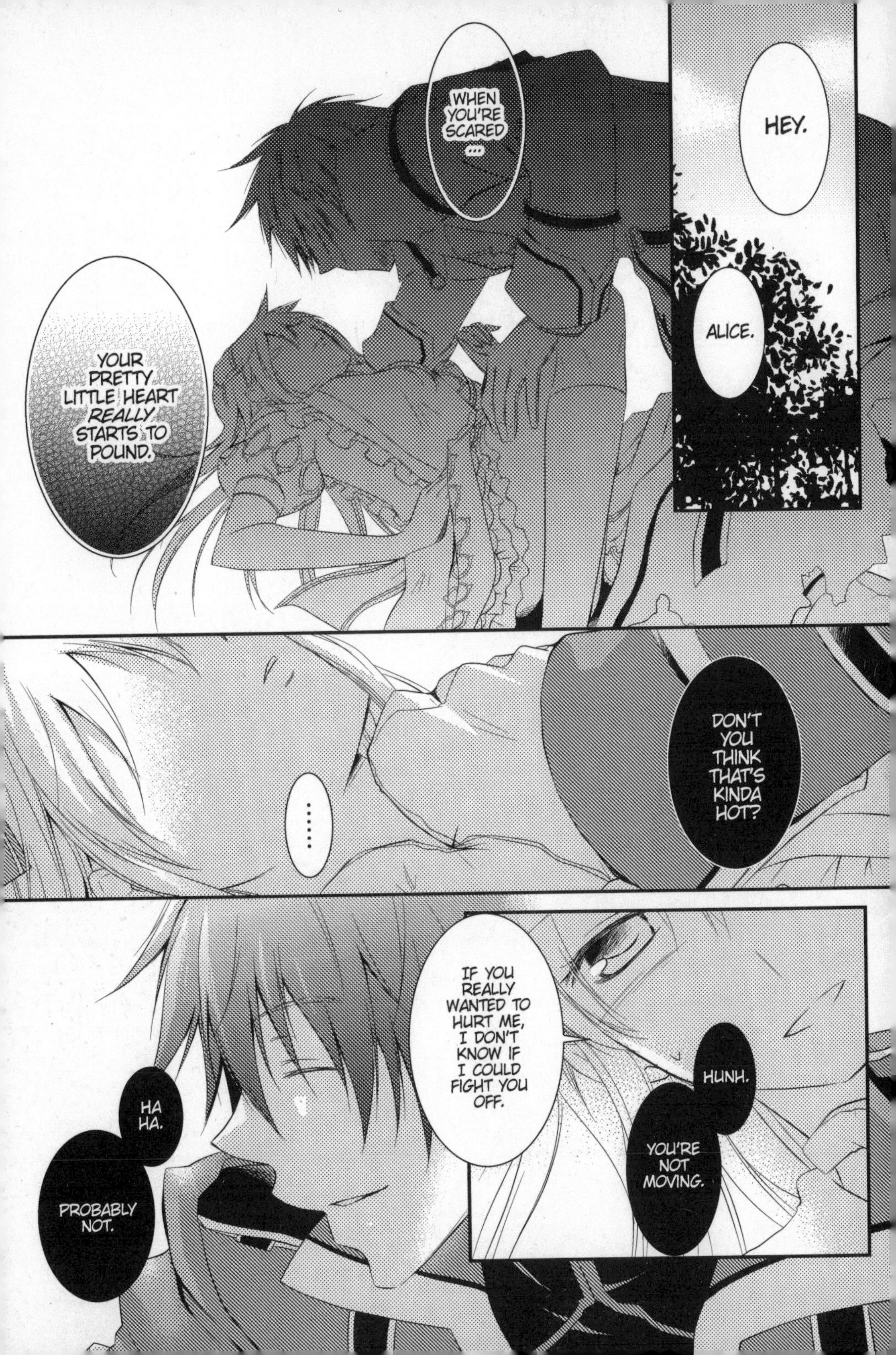
HEY.
ALICE.
WHEN YOU'RE SCARED ...
YOUR PRETTY LITTLE HEART *REALLY* STARTS TO POUND.
DON'T YOU THINK THAT'S KINDA HOT?
......
IF YOU REALLY WANTED TO HURT ME, I DON'T KNOW IF I COULD FIGHT YOU OFF.
HUNH.
YOU'RE NOT MOVING.
HA HA.
PROBABLY NOT.

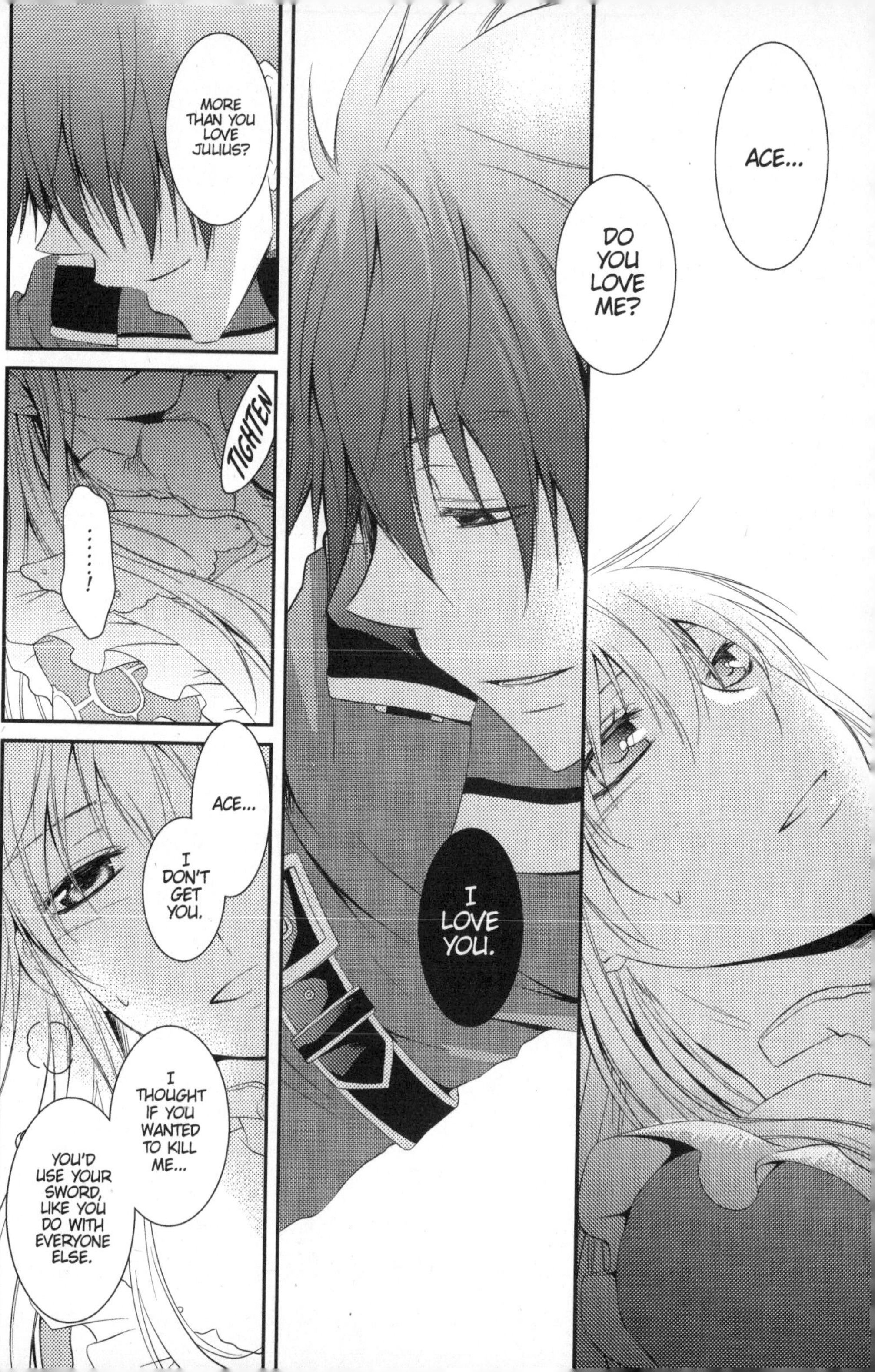
ACE...
DO YOU LOVE ME?
I LOVE YOU.
MORE THAN YOU LOVE JULIUS?
TIGHTEN
......!
ACE...
I DON'T GET YOU.
I THOUGHT IF YOU WANTED TO KILL ME...
YOU'D USE YOUR SWORD, LIKE YOU DO WITH EVERYONE ELSE.

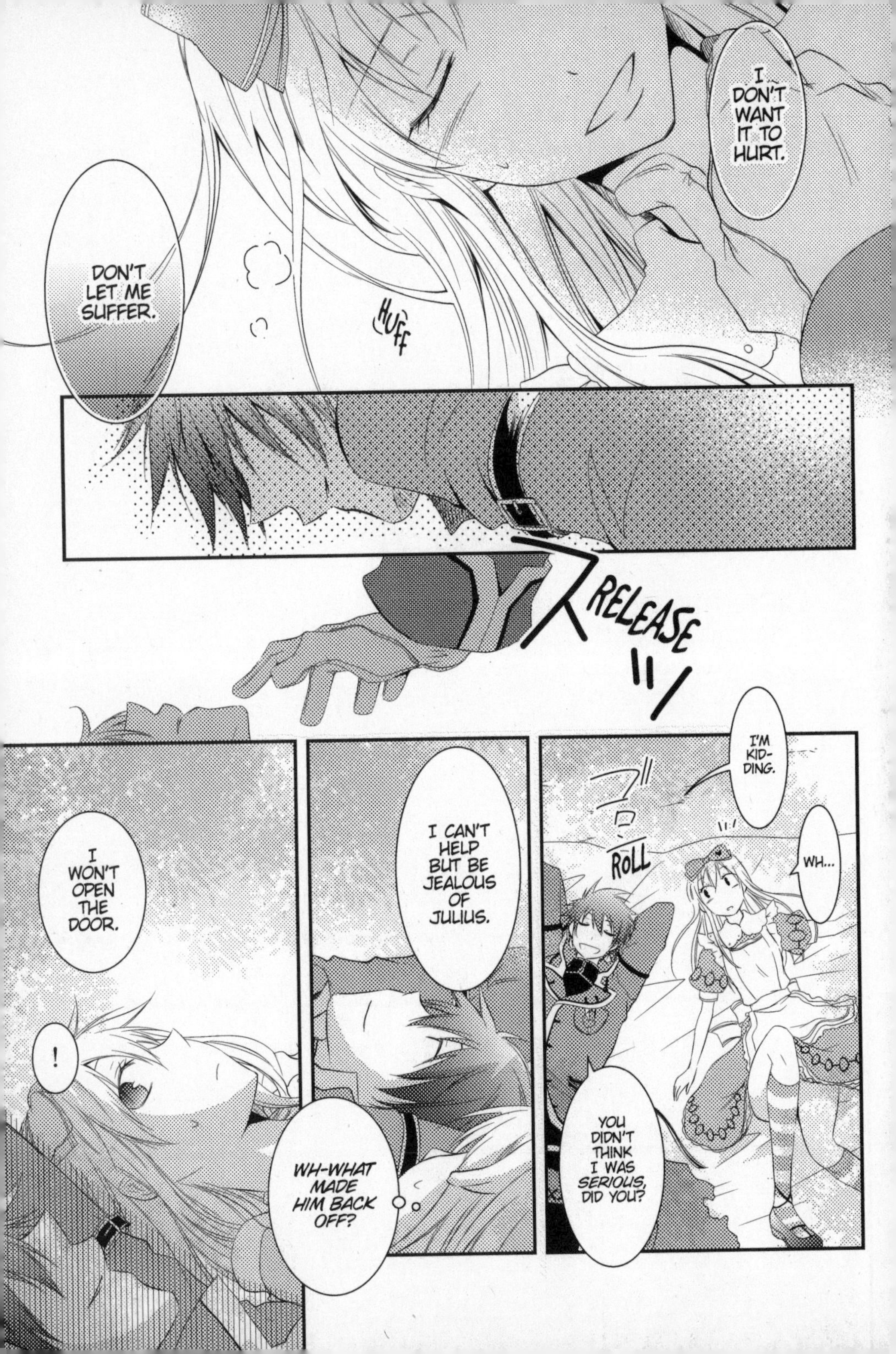
I DON'T WANT IT TO HURT.
DON'T LET ME SUFFER.
HUFF
RELEASE
I'M KIDDING.
ROLL
WH...
YOU DIDN'T THINK I WAS SERIOUS, DID YOU?
I CAN'T HELP BUT BE JEALOUS OF JULIUS.
WH-WHAT MADE HIM BACK OFF?
I WON'T OPEN THE DOOR.
!

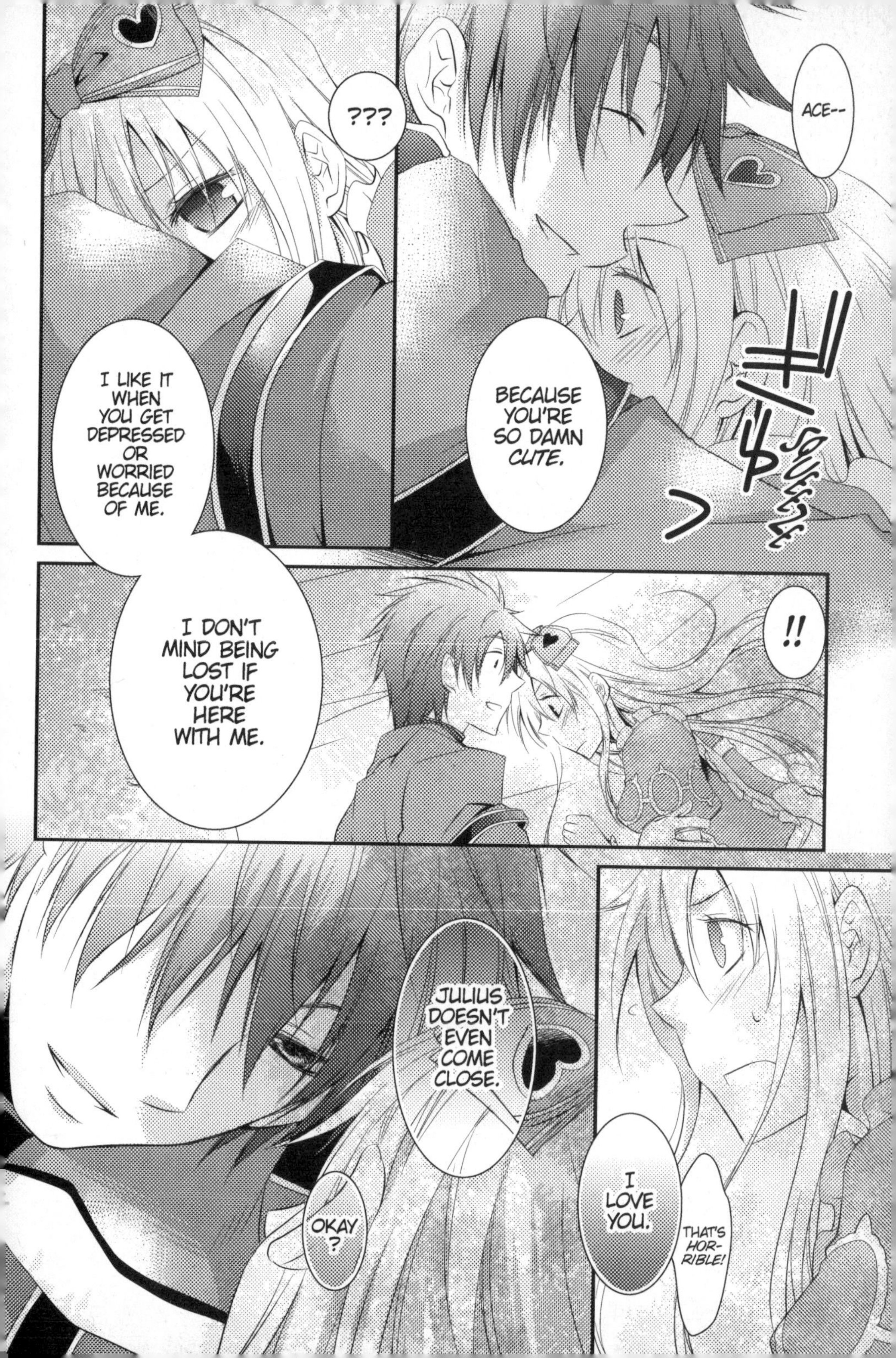
ACE--
SQUEEZE
BECAUSE YOU'RE SO DAMN CUTE.
???
I LIKE IT WHEN YOU GET DEPRESSED OR WORRIED BECAUSE OF ME.
!!
I DON'T MIND BEING LOST IF YOU'RE HERE WITH ME.
JULIUS DOESN'T EVEN COME CLOSE.
THAT'S HOR-RIBLE!
I LOVE YOU.
OKAY?

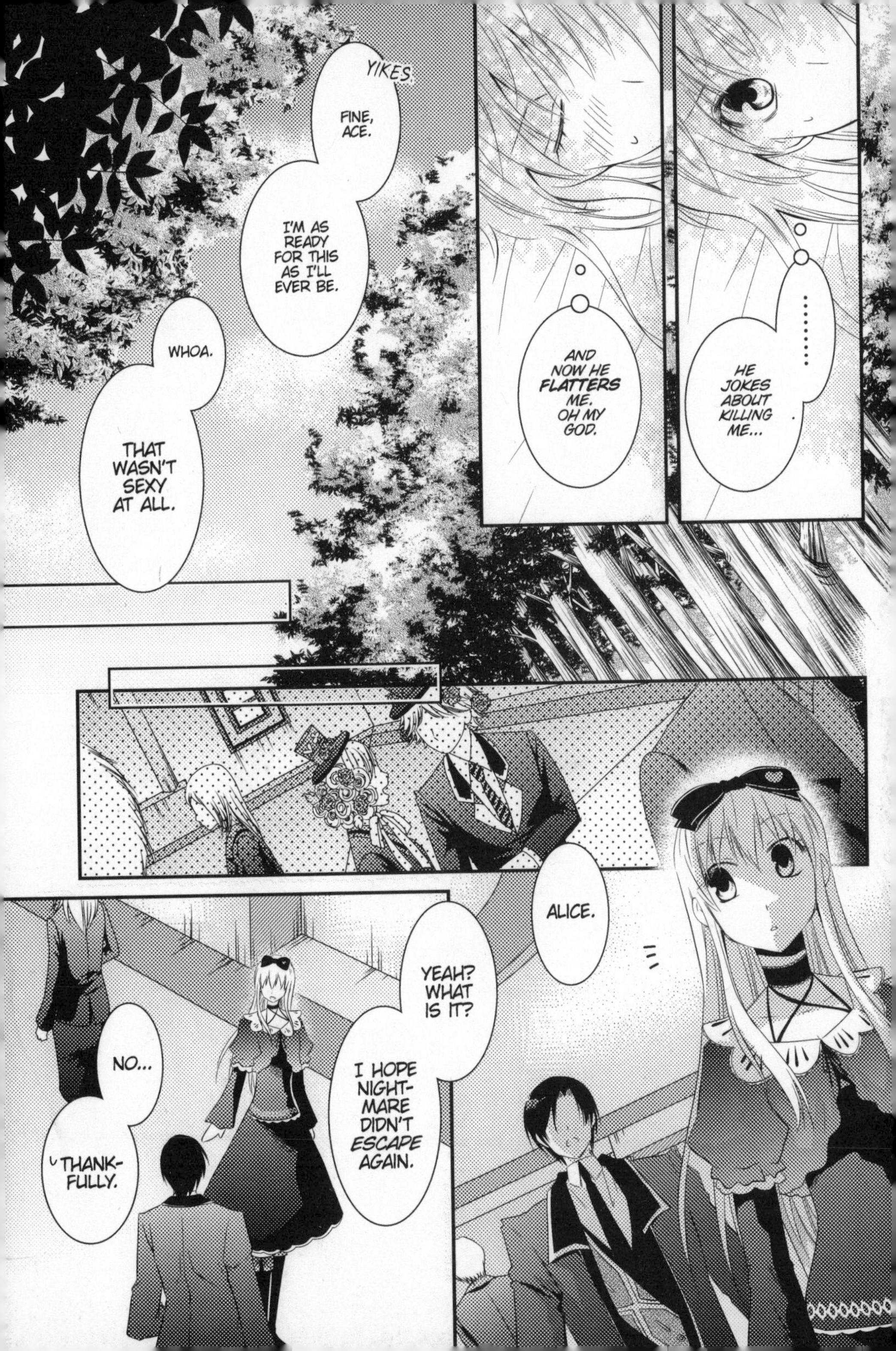
......
HE JOKES ABOUT KILLING ME...
AND NOW HE FLATTERS ME. OH MY GOD.
YIKES
FINE, ACE.
I'M AS READY FOR THIS AS I'LL EVER BE.
WHOA.
THAT WASN'T SEXY AT ALL.
ALICE.
YEAH? WHAT IS IT?
I HOPE NIGHTMARE DIDN'T ESCAPE AGAIN.
NO...
THANKFULLY.

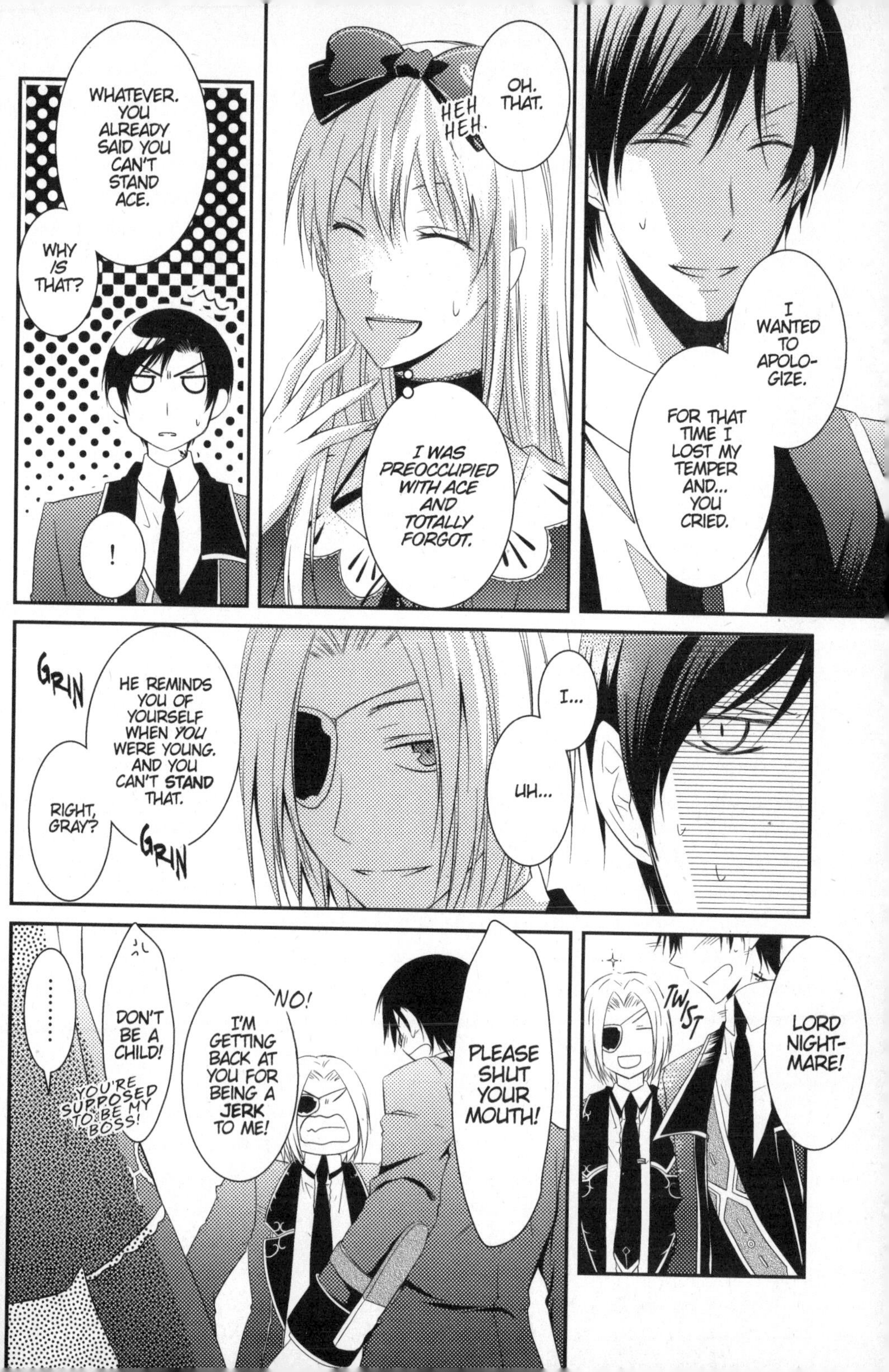
I WANTED TO APOLOGIZE.
FOR THAT TIME I LOST MY TEMPER AND... YOU CRIED.
OH. THAT.
HEH HEH.
I WAS PREOCCUPIED WITH ACE AND TOTALLY FORGOT.
WHATEVER. YOU ALREADY SAID YOU CAN'T STAND ACE.
WHY IS THAT?
!
I...
UH...
GRIN
HE REMINDS YOU OF YOURSELF WHEN YOU WERE YOUNG. AND YOU CAN'T STAND THAT.
RIGHT, GRAY?
GRIN
LORD NIGHTMARE!
TWIST
PLEASE SHUT YOUR MOUTH!
NO!
I'M GETTING BACK AT YOU FOR BEING A JERK TO ME!
DON'T BE A CHILD!
YOU'RE SUPPOSED TO BE MY BOSS!
....

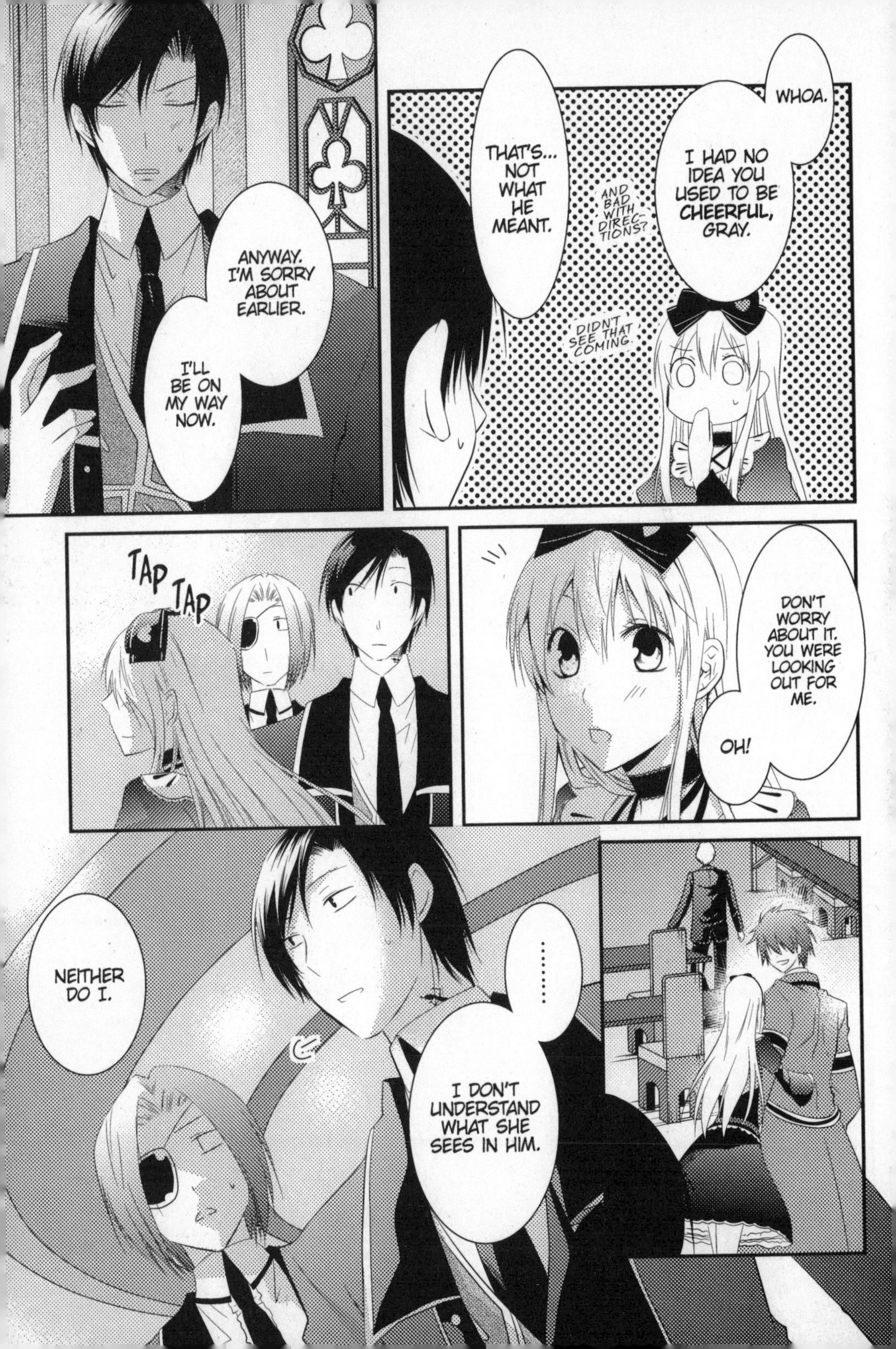
WHOA.
I HAD NO IDEA YOU USED TO BE CHEERFUL, GRAY.
AND BAD WITH DIRECTIONS?
DIDN'T SEE THAT COMING.
THAT'S... NOT WHAT HE MEANT.
ANYWAY. I'M SORRY ABOUT EARLIER.
I'LL BE ON MY WAY NOW.
DON'T WORRY ABOUT IT. YOU WERE LOOKING OUT FOR ME.
OH!
TAP TAP
......
I DON'T UNDERSTAND WHAT SHE SEES IN HIM.
NEITHER DO I.

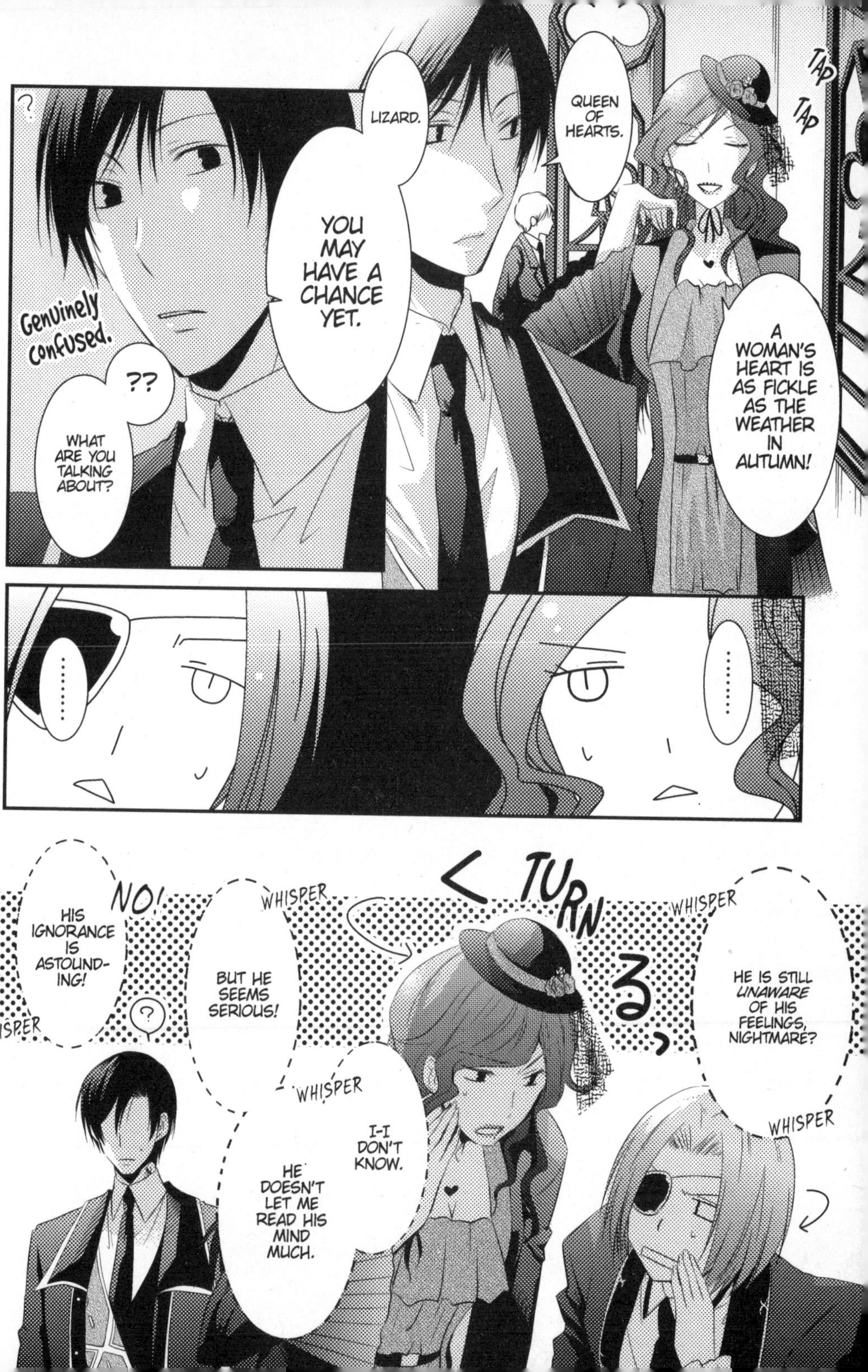
TAP TAP
QUEEN OF HEARTS.
A WOMAN'S HEART IS AS FICKLE AS THE WEATHER IN AUTUMN!
LIZARD.
YOU MAY HAVE A CHANCE YET.
?
Genuinely confused.
??
WHAT ARE YOU TALKING ABOUT?
......
......
TURN
WHISPER
HE IS STILL *UNAWARE* OF HIS FEELINGS, NIGHTMARE?
WHISPER
I-I DON'T KNOW.
HE DOESN'T LET ME READ HIS MIND MUCH.
WHISPER
BUT HE SEEMS SERIOUS!
NO!
HIS IGNORANCE IS ASTOUND-ING!
WHISPER
?

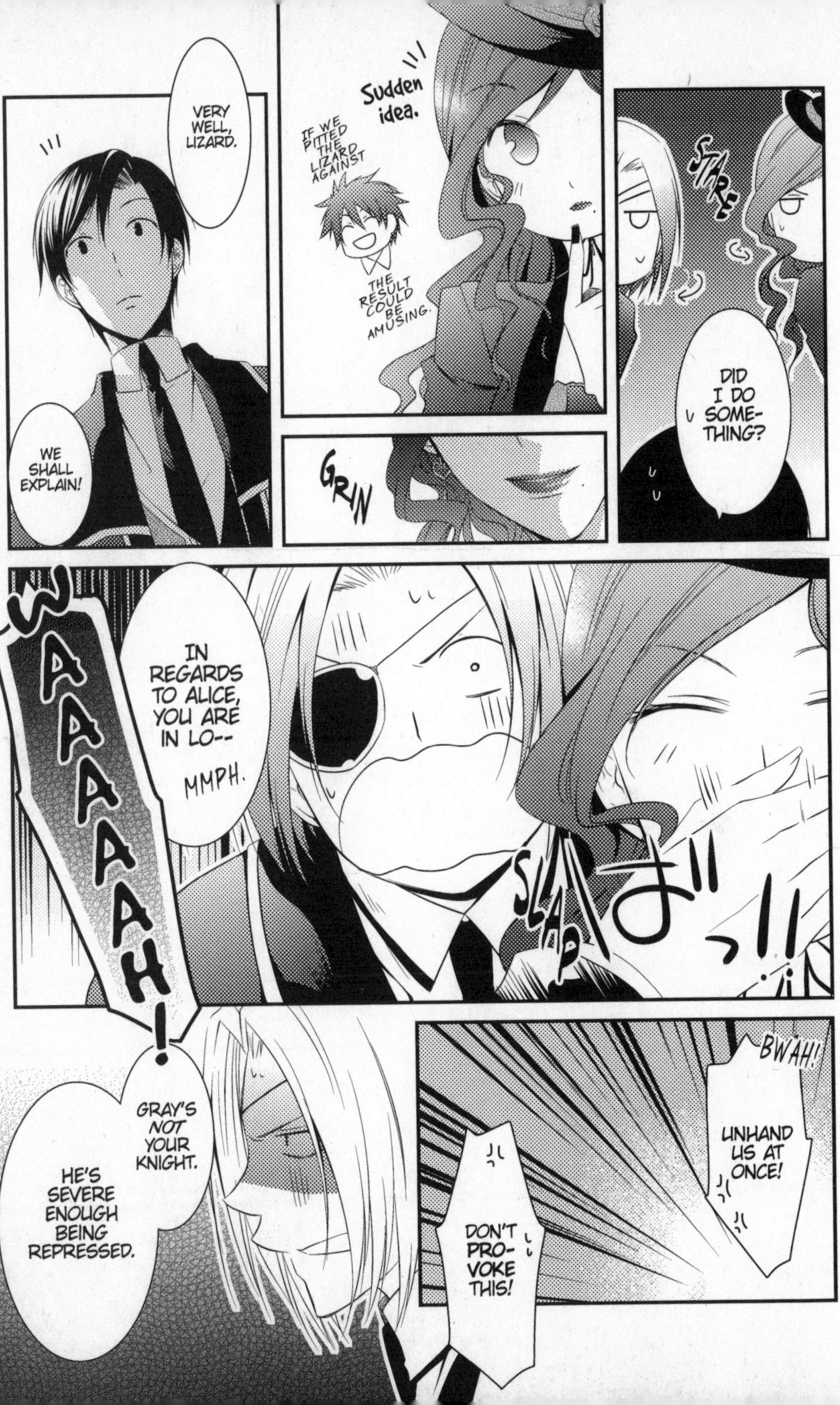
STARE
DID I DO SOMETHING?
Sudden idea.
IF WE PITTED THE LIZARD AGAINST
THE RESULT COULD BE AMUSING.
GRIN
VERY WELL, LIZARD.
WE SHALL EXPLAIN!
IN REGARDS TO ALICE, YOU ARE IN LO--
MMPH.
SLAP
WAAAAAAH!
BWAH!
UNHAND US AT ONCE!
DON'T PRO-VOKE THIS!
GRAY'S NOT YOUR KNIGHT.
HE'S SEVERE ENOUGH BEING REPRESSED.

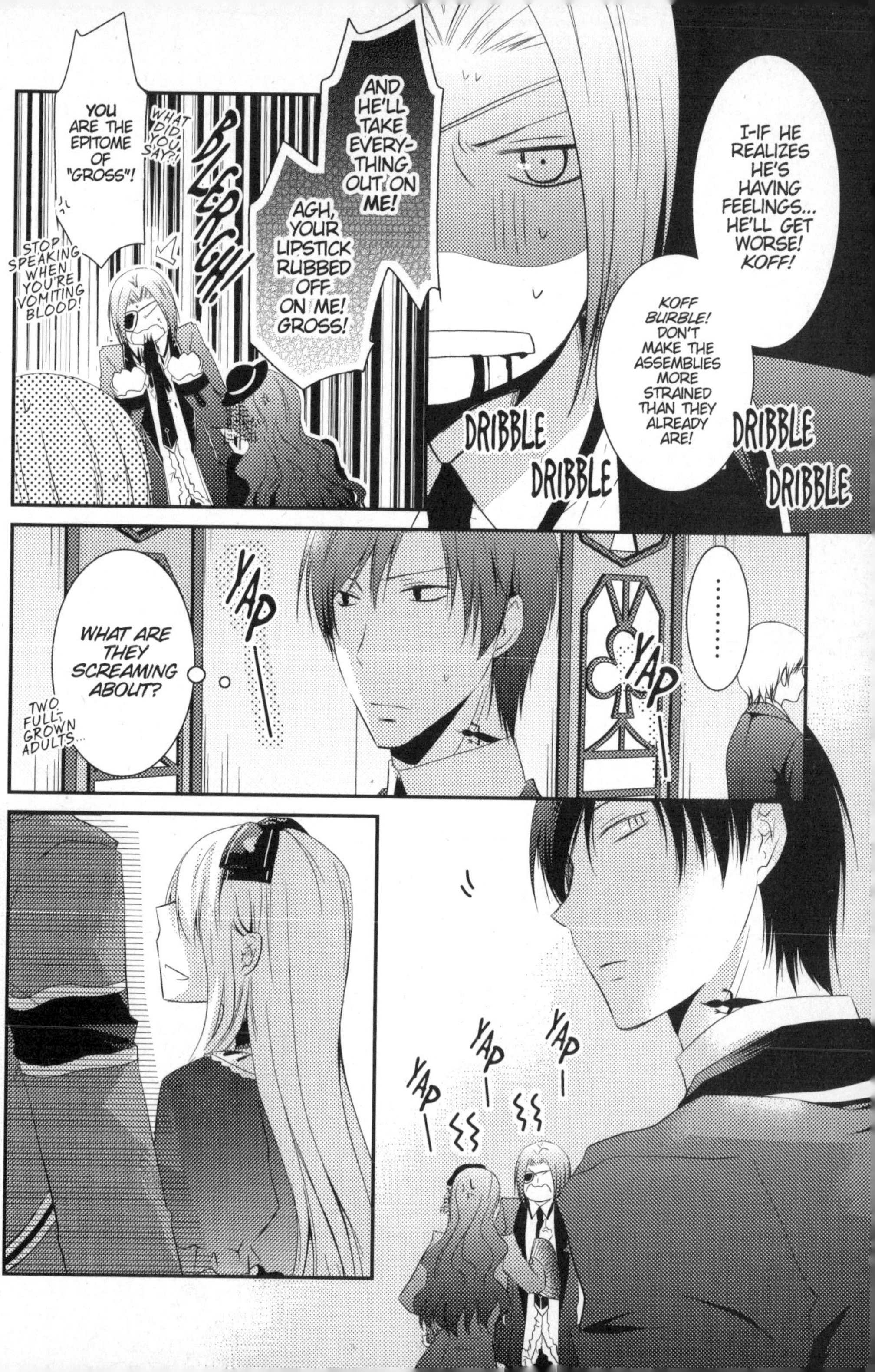
I-IF HE REALIZES HE'S HAVING FEELINGS... HE'LL GET WORSE! KOFF!
KOFF BURBLE! DON'T MAKE THE ASSEMBLIES MORE STRAINED THAN THEY ALREADY ARE!
DRIBBLE
DRIBBLE
DRIBBLE
DRIBBLE
AND HE'LL TAKE EVERYTHING OUT ON ME!
AGH, YOUR LIPSTICK RUBBED OFF ON ME! GROSS!
BLERGH!!
WHAT DID YOU SAY?!
YOU ARE THE EPITOME OF "GROSS"!
STOP SPEAKING WHEN YOU'RE VOMITING BLOOD!
......
YAP
YAP
WHAT ARE THEY SCREAMING ABOUT?
TWO FULL-GROWN ADULTS...
YAP
YAP
YAP

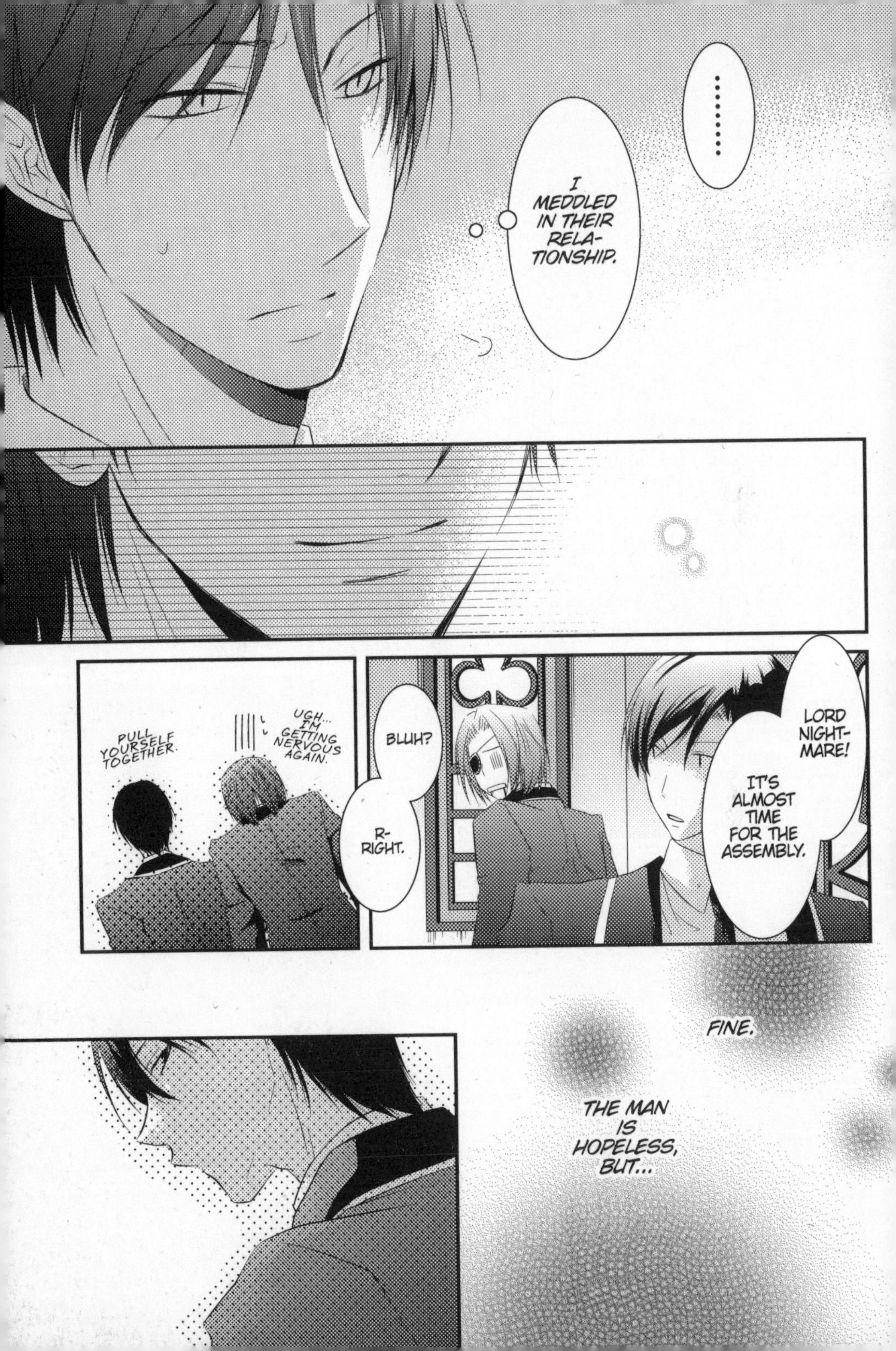
……
I MEDDLED IN THEIR RELATIONSHIP.
LORD NIGHTMARE!
IT'S ALMOST TIME FOR THE ASSEMBLY.
BLUH?
R-RIGHT.
UGH... I'M GETTING NERVOUS AGAIN.
PULL YOURSELF TOGETHER.
FINE.
THE MAN IS HOPELESS, BUT...

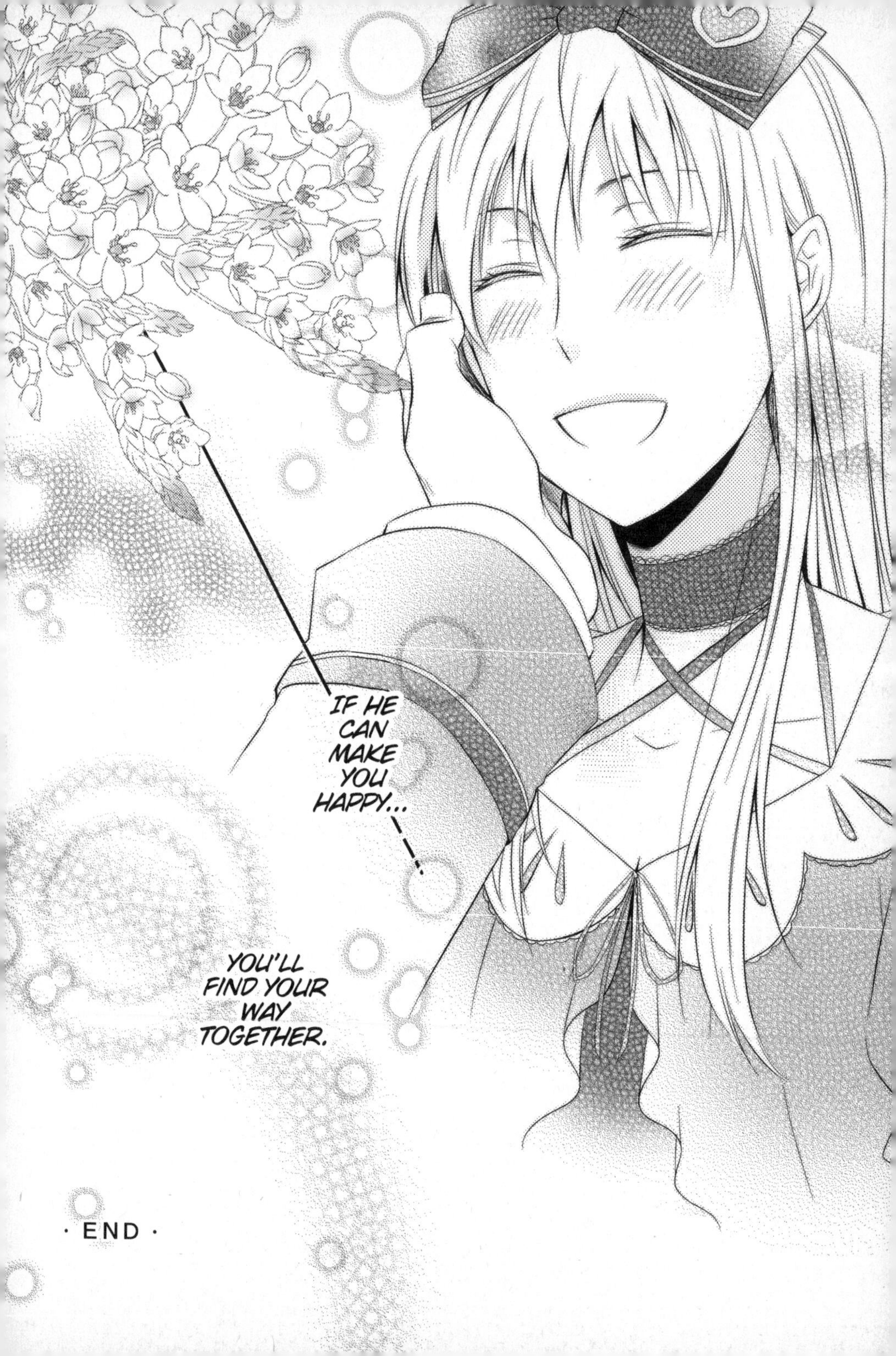
IF HE CAN MAKE YOU HAPPY...
YOU'LL FIND YOUR WAY TOGETHER.
· END ·

CRIMSON EMPIRE

クリムゾン・エンパイア

~Circumstances to serve a noble~

We devote our life proudly.
my life for you. For all you.

Quin Rose 2008

- STORY -

The setting is a country of aristocrats: a tributary nation for Luxonne. *Crimson Empire* is a love adventure game about a maid, Sheila, who works in the luxurious royal castle. But behind the lavish façade, the castle is home to a savage—and bloody—political war.

Strong and skilled, Sheila uses her position as a maid to hide her true profession: bodyguard to Prince Edvard. Sheila carries a dark past of enslavement and murder. Now she survives day to day, with only a small wish in her heart.

While navigating the power struggle between Prince Edvard and his brother, the deceptive Prince Justin, Sheila must understand and use the dangerous people who surround her. But although a brilliant fighter and tactician, Sheila is unskilled when it comes to love and friendships. Such a gap between her power and her heart could lead to a dire ending indeed!

Crimson Empire Character Information

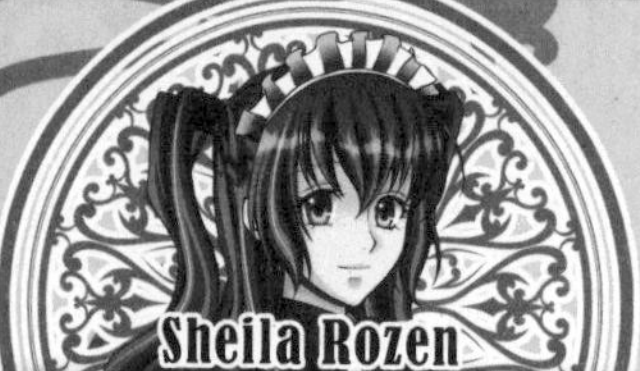

Sheila Rozen

The intensely loyal head maid to Prince Edvard—and his secret bodyguard. She's a skilled leader and shrewdly political, in addition to being fierce in combat. She doesn't hide her roots as a slave.

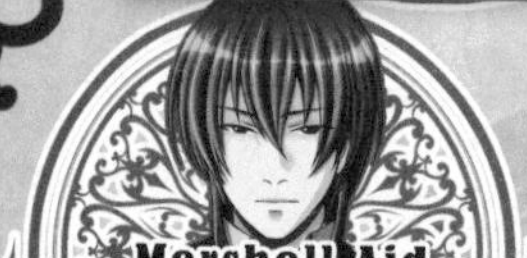

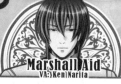

Marshall Aid

VA: Ken Narita

Prince Justin's head servant. He argues with Sheila in public but doesn't dislike her. In private, they're intimate enough to spar peacefully.

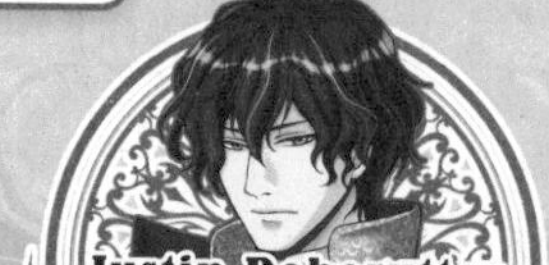

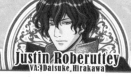

Justin Roberuttey

VA: Daisuke Hirakawa

The eldest prince, and Edvard's older half-brother. Since his mother is of lower status, Justin falls below his younger brother in line for the throne.

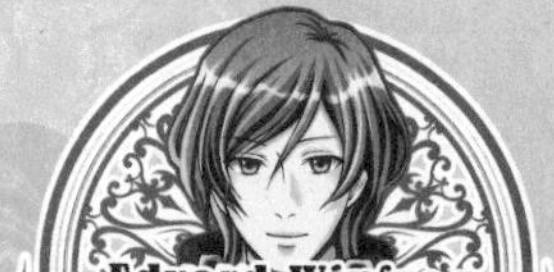

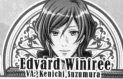

Edvard Winfree

VA: Kenichi Suzumura

Sheila's master. While friendly and regal on the surface, he's very condescending. He thinks of Sheila as more than a subordinate and loves her more than his own family... or so he *claims*.

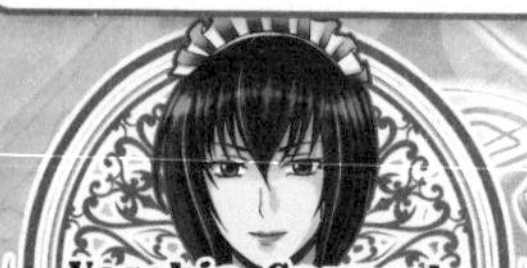

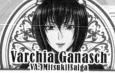

Varchia Ganasch

VA: Mitsuki Saiga

Varchia, the vice-maid, is a close friend of Sheila's, and is a former slave. Her actions and words are always painfully neutral. She's trustworthy and helps Sheila in both public and private.

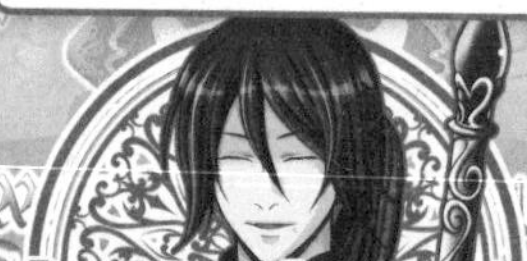

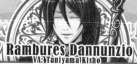

Rambures Dannunzio

VA: Taniyama Kisho

A commoner who was knighted after saving the king. He loves to lurk in his room and brew concoctions—which often stink and explode—instead of interacting with the nobility.

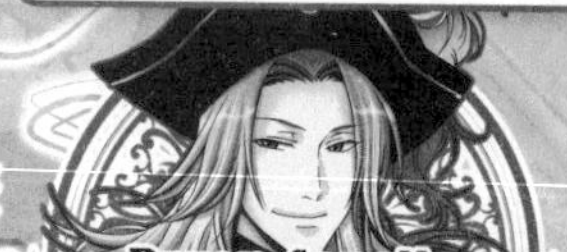

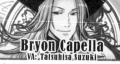

Bryon Capella

VA: Tatsuhisa Suzuki

Son of the marquis who one day will inherit the position and become an important pillar of the country. He seems cheerful and carefree, but rather guarded. Like his sister, he adores Sheila.

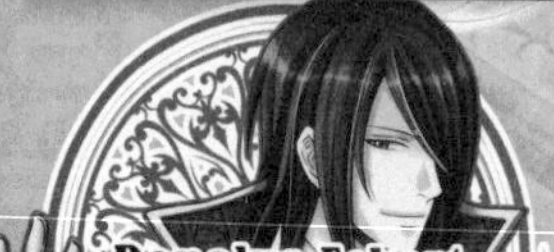

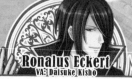

Ronalus Eckert

VA: Daisuke Kisho

Another guest in the royal castle, Ronalus is the servant to the Queen of Luxonne. Although he enjoys a higher status by serving the queen, he has a good relationship with other servants. His role is to monitor Meissen.

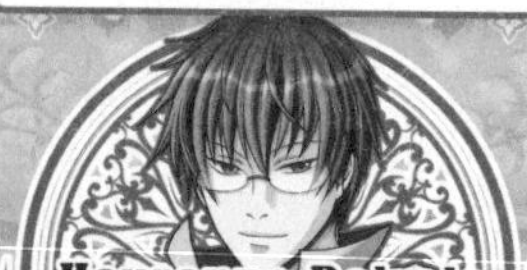

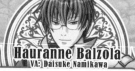

Hauranne Balzola

VA: Daisuke Namikawa

A wizard staying in the royal castle who is treated as a guest, but he's been in the castle longer than anyone. He's lived a *long* life...and his real age doesn't match his looks.

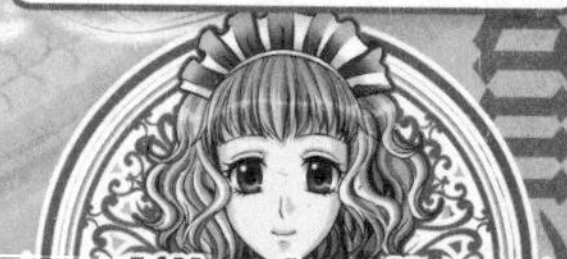

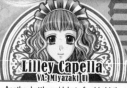

Lilley Capella

VA: Miyazaki Ui

Another battle maid, but of noble birth, Lilley is fiercely loyal to Sheila. She has innate skill, and her strength is second only to Sheila's. She and her brother Bryon are very close.

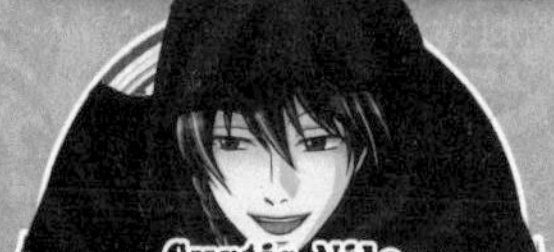

Curtis Nile

VA: Akira Ishida

A deadly assassin who specializes in poisons. He raised Sheila, and nearly killed her with his vicious training. Ever since, their relationship has been strained, to say the least.

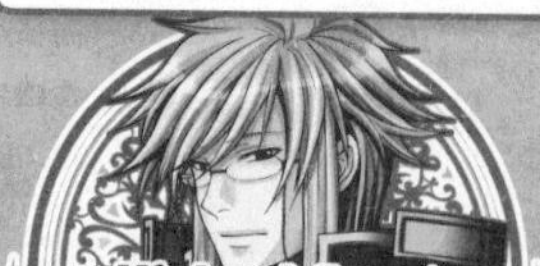

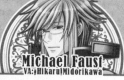

Michael Faust

VA: Hikaru Midorikawa

A demon who made a contract with Meissen. He's dangerously strong, monologues frequently, and is oddly nervous. His mental instability feeds his pessimism.

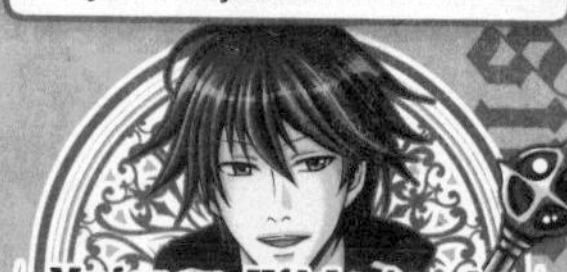

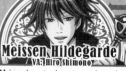

Meissen Hildegarde

VA: Hiro Shimono

Meissen has a tendency to wander, and he's traveled all over the world. His ladykiller persona hides a powerful wizard. He's searching for the truth and is trying to become a sage...supposedly.

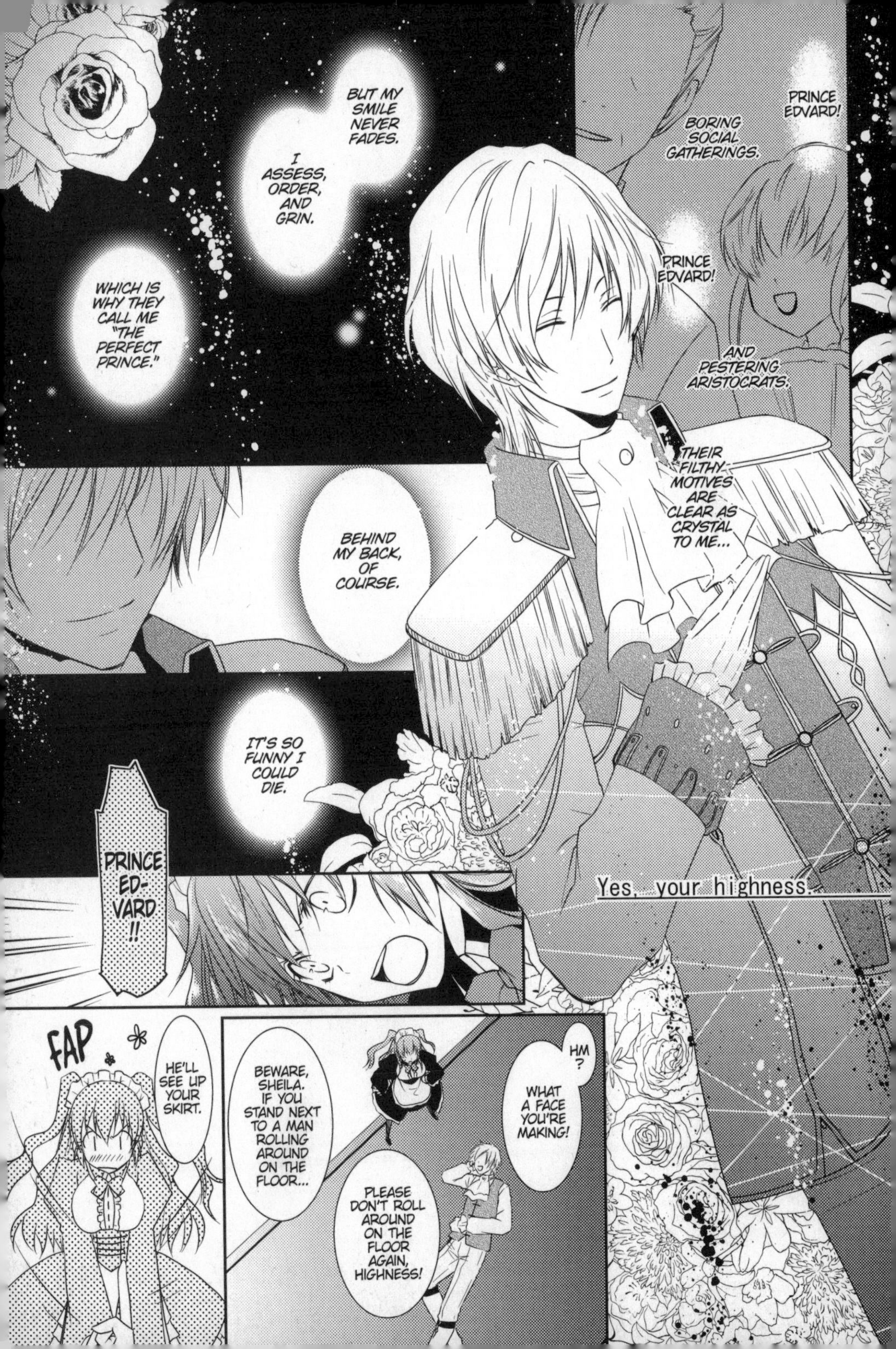
PRINCE EDVARD!
BORING SOCIAL GATHERINGS.
PRINCE EDVARD!
AND PESTERING ARISTOCRATS.
THEIR FILTHY MOTIVES ARE CLEAR AS CRYSTAL TO ME...
BUT MY SMILE NEVER FADES.
I ASSESS, ORDER, AND GRIN.
WHICH IS WHY THEY CALL ME "THE PERFECT PRINCE."
BEHIND MY BACK, OF COURSE.
IT'S SO FUNNY I COULD DIE.
PRINCE ED-VARD!!
Yes, your highness.
HM?
WHAT A FACE YOU'RE MAKING!
BEWARE, SHEILA. IF YOU STAND NEXT TO A MAN ROLLING AROUND ON THE FLOOR...
PLEASE DON'T ROLL AROUND ON THE FLOOR AGAIN, HIGHNESS!
HE'LL SEE UP YOUR SKIRT.
FAP

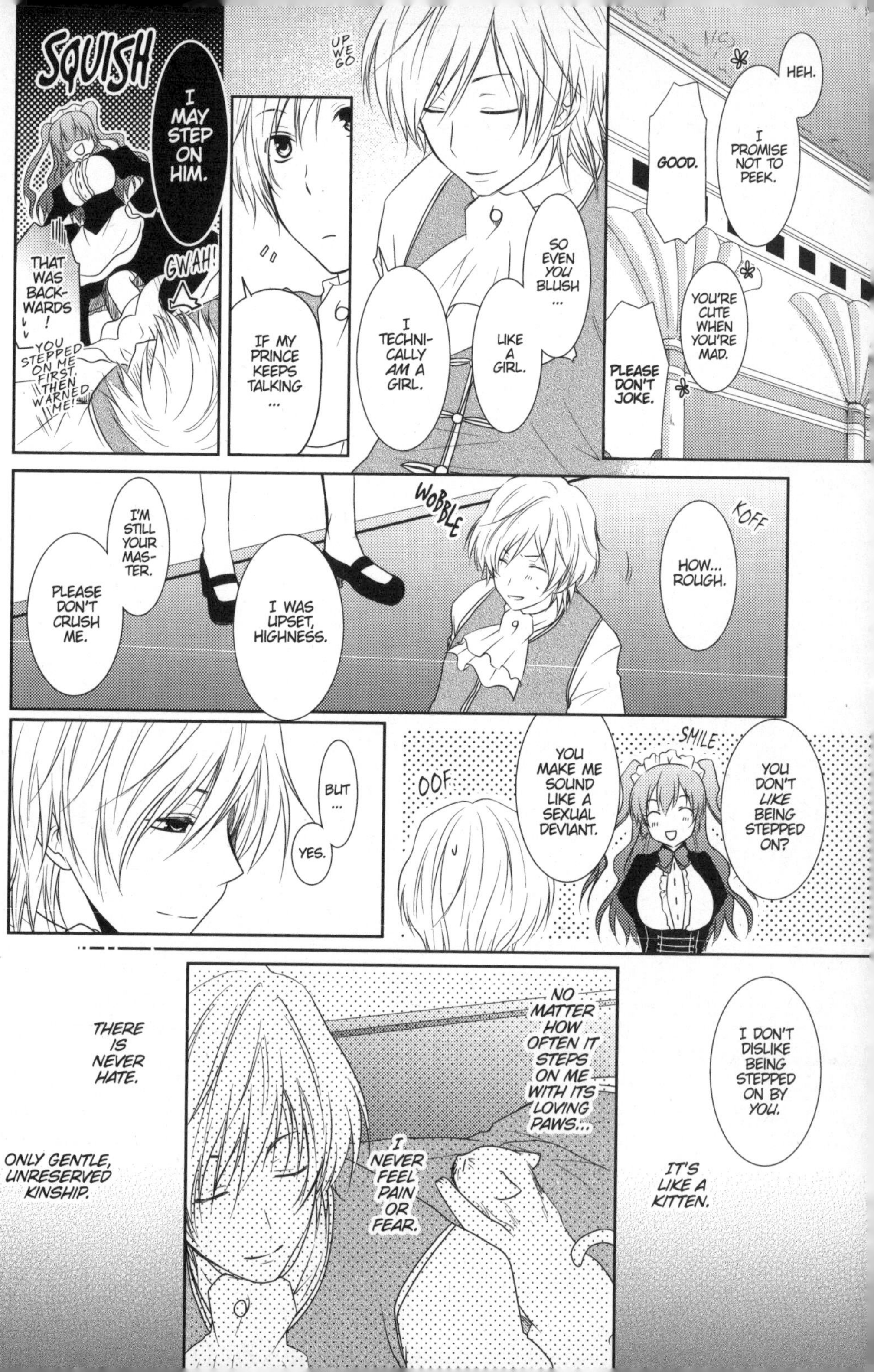
HEH.
I PROMISE NOT TO PEEK.
GOOD.
YOU'RE CUTE WHEN YOU'RE MAD.
PLEASE DON'T JOKE.
UP WE GO
SO EVEN YOU BLUSH ...
LIKE A GIRL.
I TECHNICALLY AM A GIRL.
IF MY PRINCE KEEPS TALKING ...
SQUISH
I MAY STEP ON HIM.
GWAH!
THAT WAS BACKWARDS!
YOU STEPPED ON ME FIRST, THEN WARNED ME!
KOFF
HOW... ROUGH.
WOBBLE
I WAS UPSET, HIGHNESS.
I'M STILL YOUR MASTER.
PLEASE DON'T CRUSH ME.
SMILE
YOU DON'T LIKE BEING STEPPED ON?
YOU MAKE ME SOUND LIKE A SEXUAL DEVIANT.
OOF
BUT ...
YES.
I DON'T DISLIKE BEING STEPPED ON BY YOU.
IT'S LIKE A KITTEN.
NO MATTER HOW OFTEN IT STEPS ON ME WITH ITS LOVING PAWS...
I NEVER FEEL PAIN OR FEAR.
THERE IS NEVER HATE.
ONLY GENTLE, UNRESERVED KINSHIP.

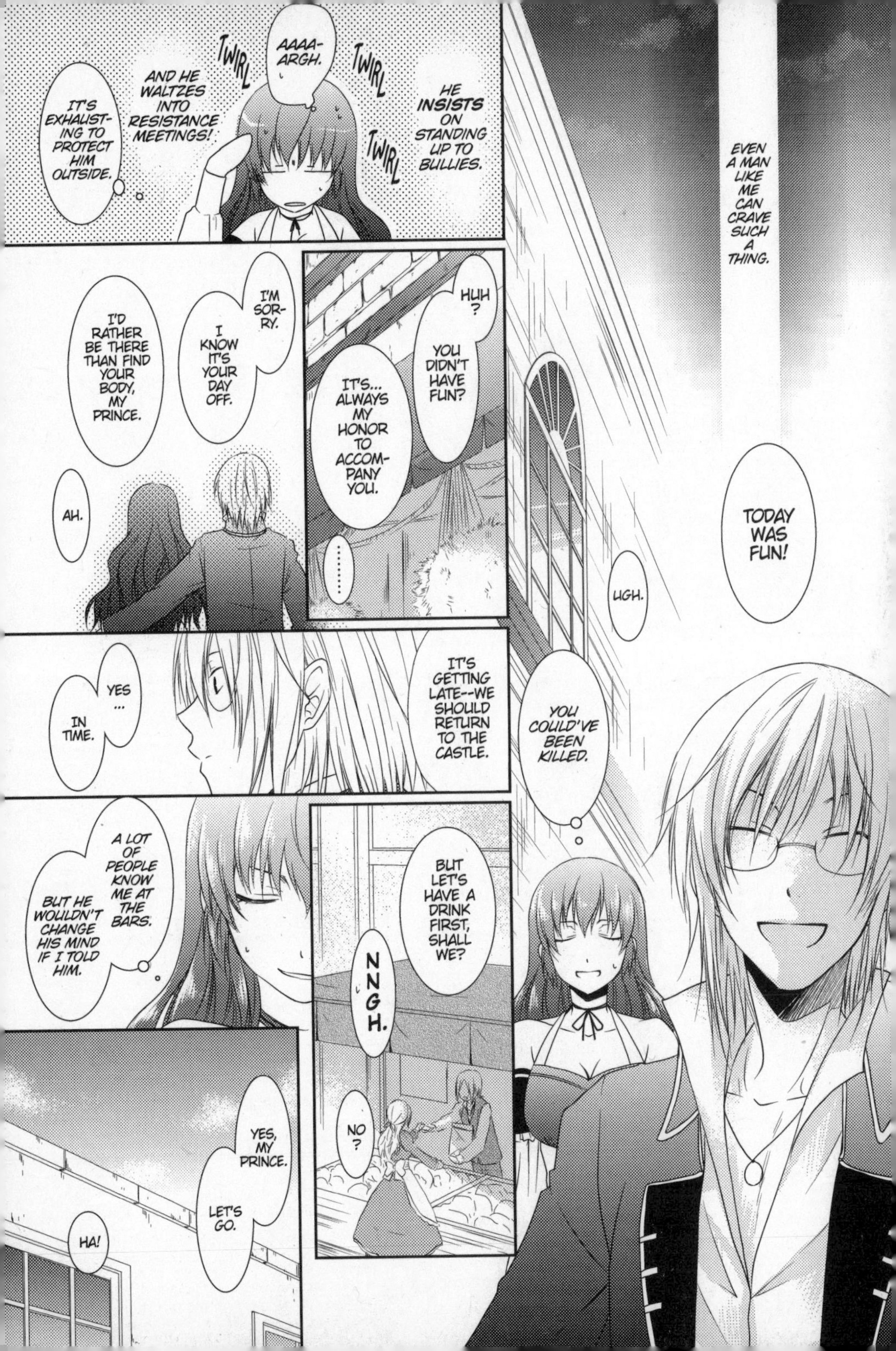
EVEN A MAN LIKE ME CAN CRAVE SUCH A THING.
TODAY WAS FUN!
UGH.
YOU COULD'VE BEEN KILLED.
HE INSISTS ON STANDING UP TO BULLIES.
AAAA-ARGH.
TWIRL
TWIRL
TWIRL
AND HE WALTZES INTO RESISTANCE MEETINGS!
IT'S EXHAUSTING TO PROTECT HIM OUTSIDE.
HUH? YOU DIDN'T HAVE FUN?
IT'S... ALWAYS MY HONOR TO ACCOMPANY YOU.
......
I'M SORRY.
I KNOW IT'S YOUR DAY OFF.
I'D RATHER BE THERE THAN FIND YOUR BODY, MY PRINCE.
AH.
IT'S GETTING LATE--WE SHOULD RETURN TO THE CASTLE.
YES ... IN TIME.
BUT LET'S HAVE A DRINK FIRST, SHALL WE?
NNGH.
NO?
A LOT OF PEOPLE KNOW ME AT THE BARS.
BUT HE WOULDN'T CHANGE HIS MIND IF I TOLD HIM.
YES, MY PRINCE.
LET'S GO.
HA!

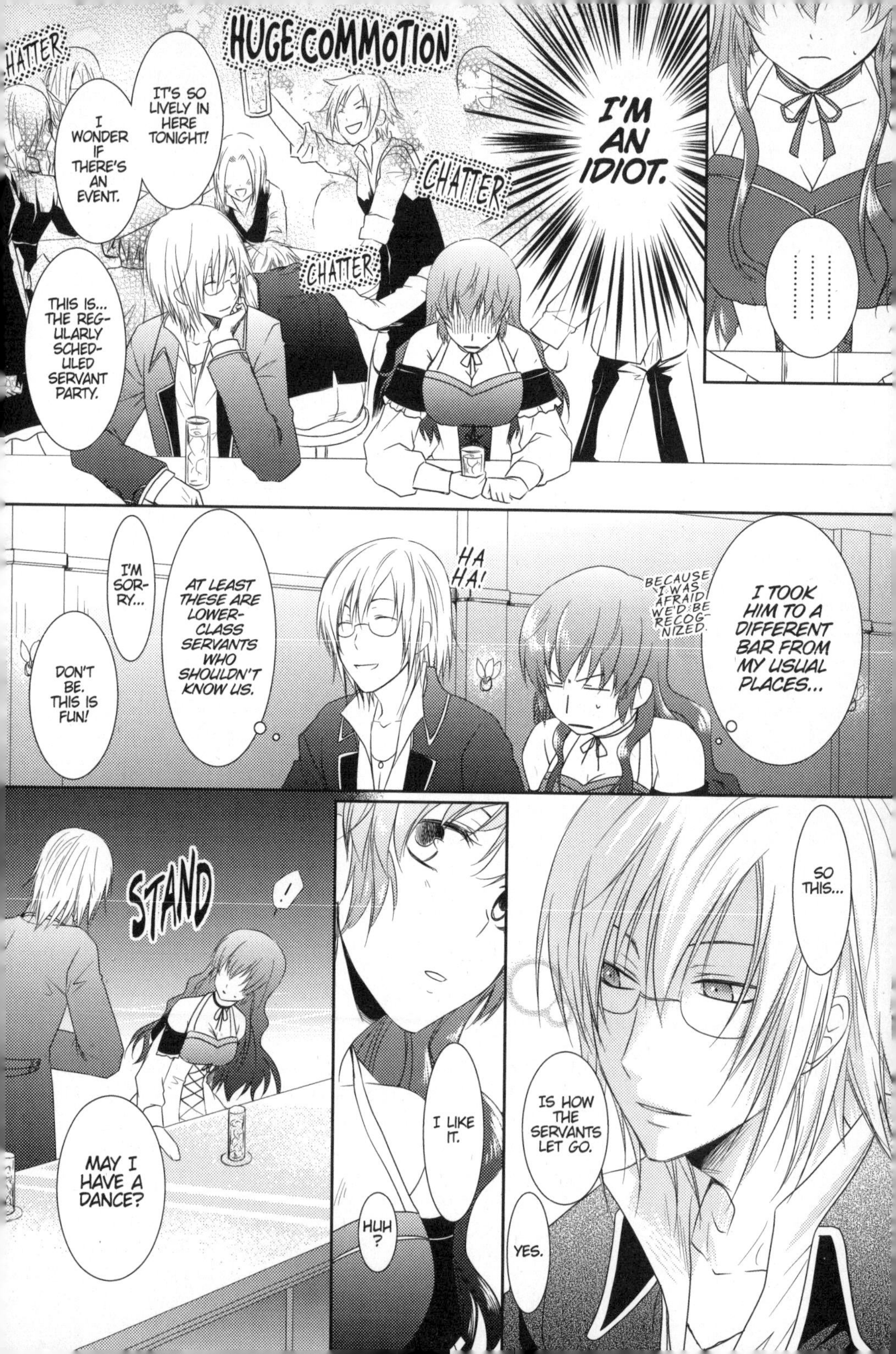

......
I'M AN IDIOT.
HUGE COMMOTION
CHATTER
IT'S SO LIVELY IN HERE TONIGHT!
I WONDER IF THERE'S AN EVENT.
CHATTER
CHATTER
THIS IS... THE REGULARLY SCHEDULED SERVANT PARTY.
I TOOK HIM TO A DIFFERENT BAR FROM MY USUAL PLACES...
BECAUSE I WAS AFRAID WE'D BE RECOGNIZED.
HA HA!
AT LEAST THESE ARE LOWER-CLASS SERVANTS WHO SHOULDN'T KNOW US.
I'M SORRY...
DON'T BE. THIS IS FUN!
SO THIS...
IS HOW THE SERVANTS LET GO.
YES.
I LIKE IT.
HUH?
STAND
!
MAY I HAVE A DANCE?

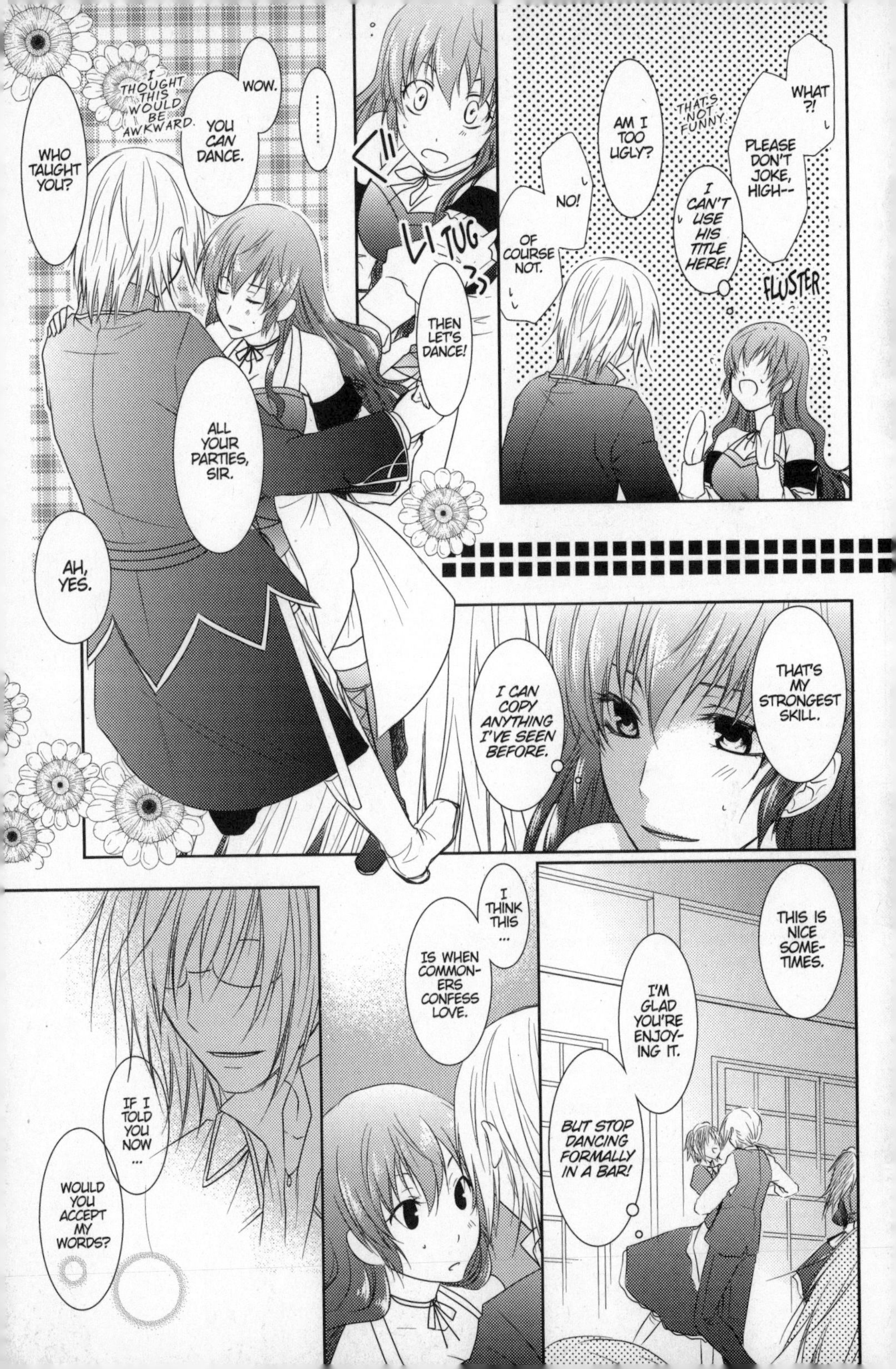
WHAT?!
PLEASE DON'T JOKE, HIGH--
I CAN'T USE HIS TITLE HERE!
FLUSTER
THAT'S NOT FUNNY.
AM I TOO UGLY?
NO!
OF COURSE NOT.
TUG
THEN LET'S DANCE!
......
WOW.
YOU CAN DANCE.
I THOUGHT THIS WOULD BE AWKWARD.
WHO TAUGHT YOU?
ALL YOUR PARTIES, SIR.
AH, YES.
THAT'S MY STRONGEST SKILL.
I CAN COPY ANYTHING I'VE SEEN BEFORE.
THIS IS NICE SOMETIMES.
I'M GLAD YOU'RE ENJOYING IT.
BUT STOP DANCING FORMALLY IN A BAR!
I THINK THIS ...
IS WHEN COMMONERS CONFESS LOVE.
IF I TOLD YOU NOW ...
WOULD YOU ACCEPT MY WORDS?

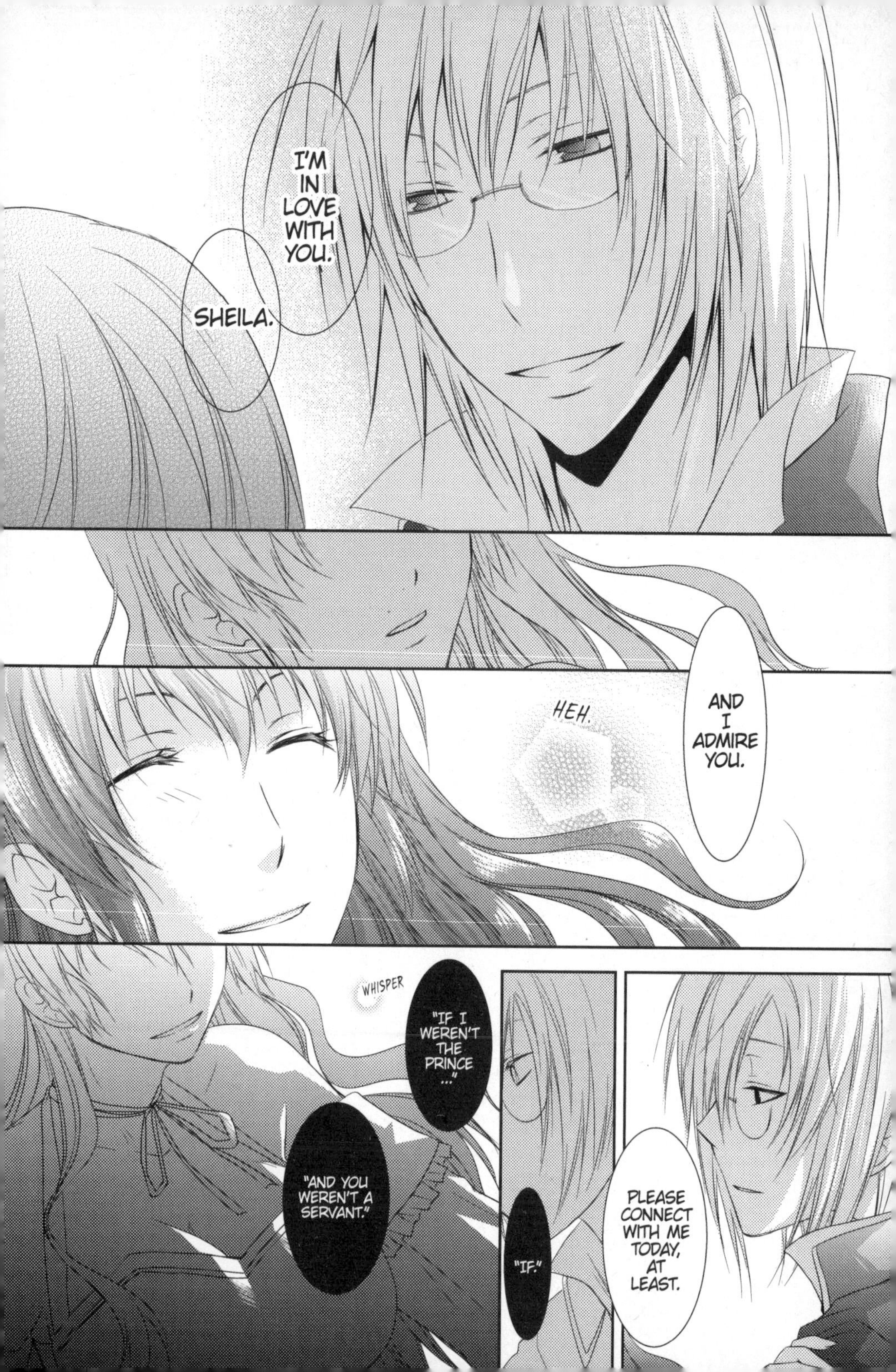
I'M IN LOVE WITH YOU.
SHEILA.
AND I ADMIRE YOU.
HEH.
PLEASE CONNECT WITH ME TODAY, AT LEAST.
"IF."
WHISPER
"IF I WEREN'T THE PRINCE ..."
"AND YOU WEREN'T A SERVANT."

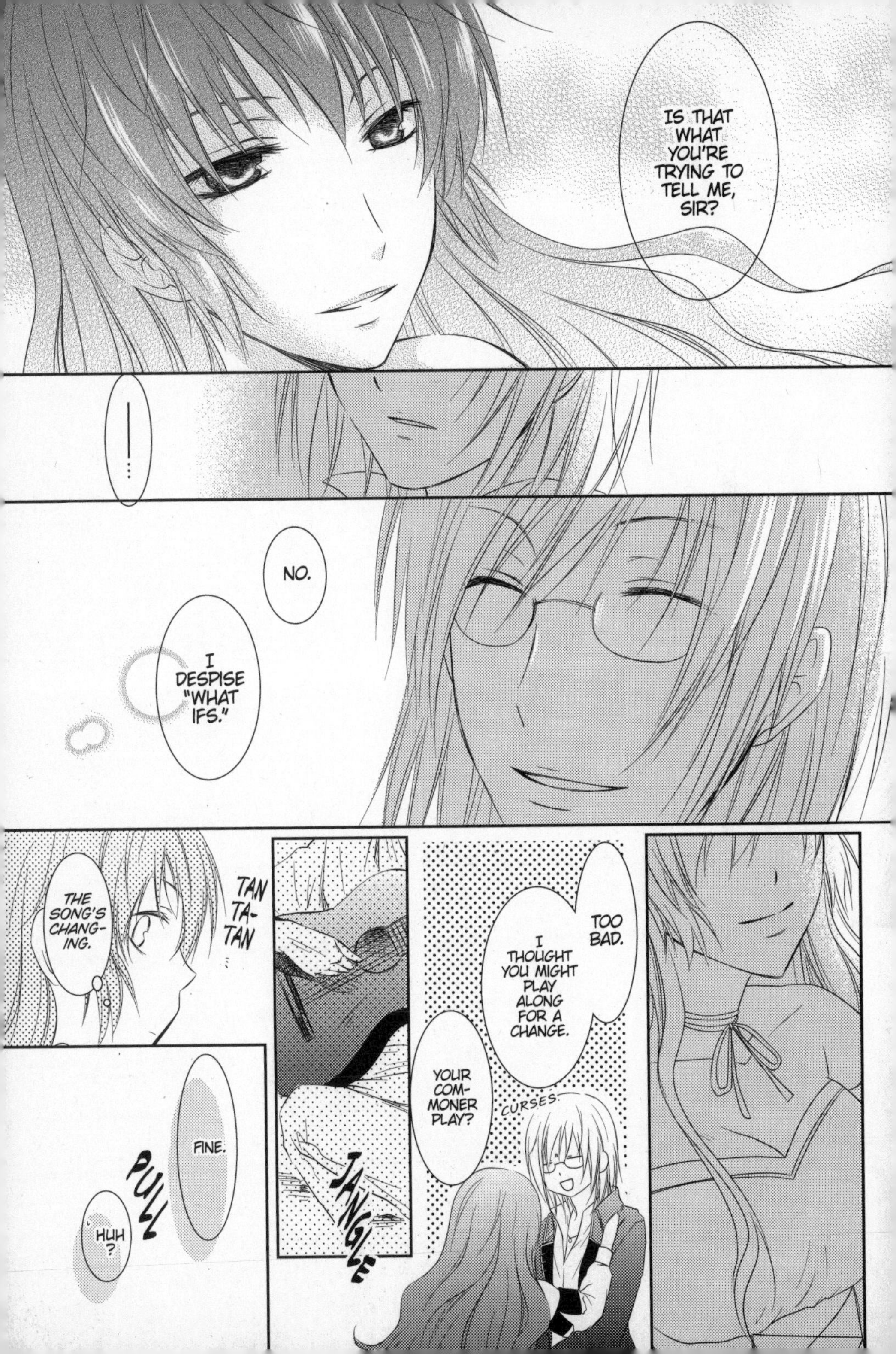
IS THAT WHAT YOU'RE TRYING TO TELL ME, SIR?
—……
NO.
I DESPISE "WHAT IFS."
TOO BAD.
I THOUGHT YOU MIGHT PLAY ALONG FOR A CHANGE.
YOUR COMMONER PLAY?
CURSES.
JANGLE
THE SONG'S CHANGING.
TAN TA-TAN…
FINE.
PULL
HUH?

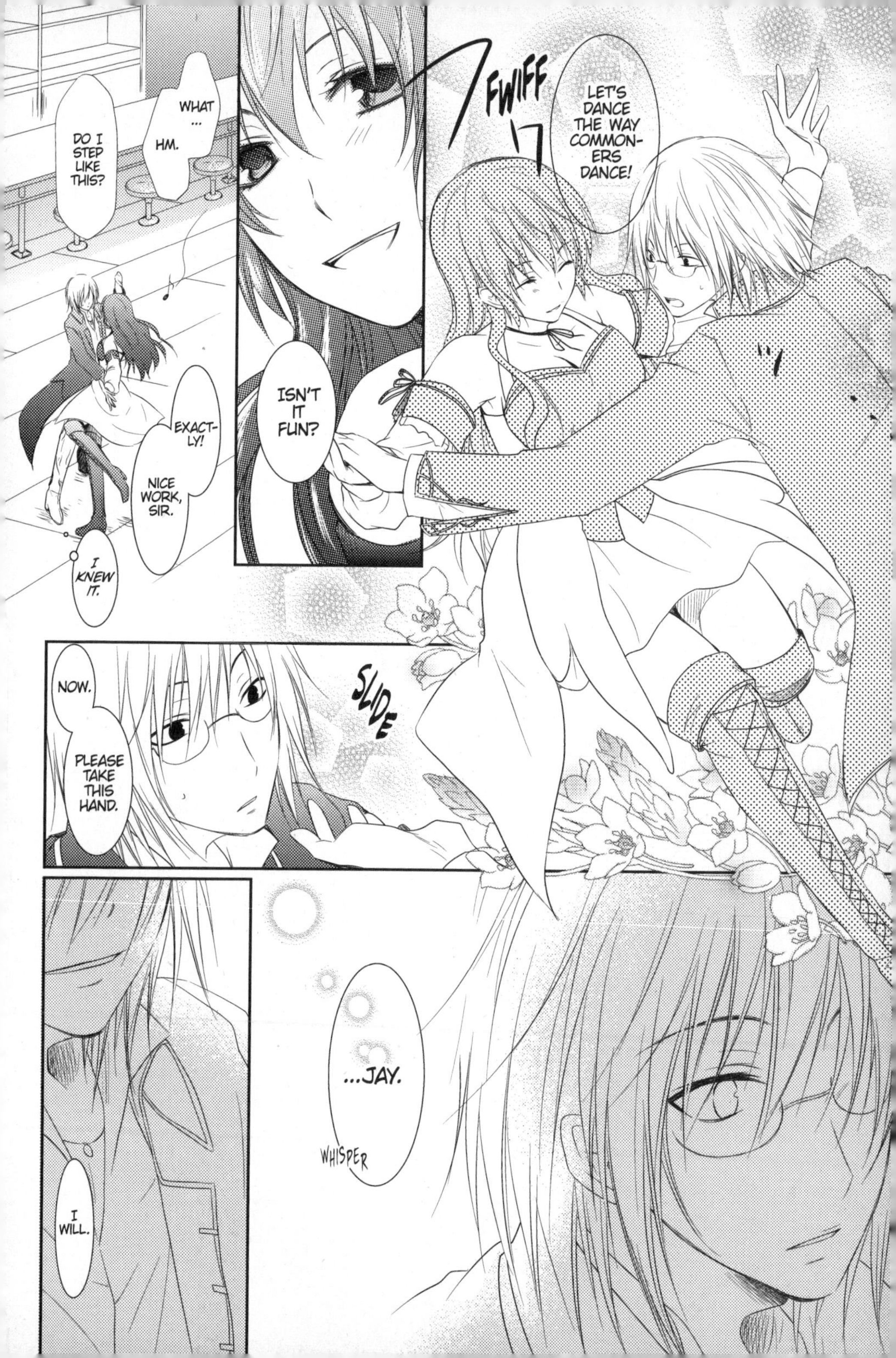
FWIFF
LET'S DANCE THE WAY COMMONERS DANCE!
ISN'T IT FUN?
WHAT ... HM.
DO I STEP LIKE THIS?
EXACTLY!
NICE WORK, SIR.
I KNEW IT.
SLIDE
NOW.
PLEASE TAKE THIS HAND.
...JAY.
WHISPER
I WILL.

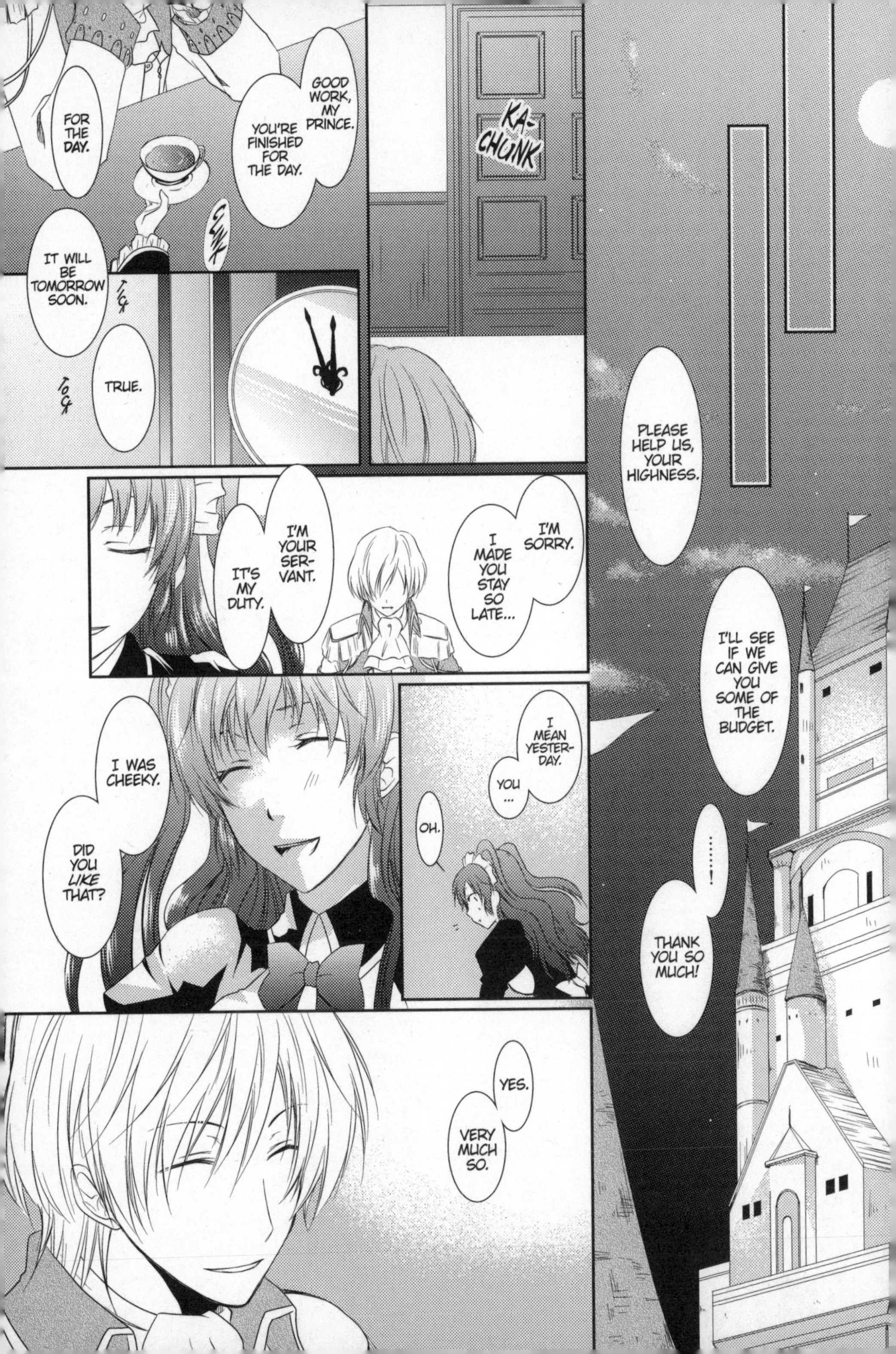
PLEASE HELP US, YOUR HIGHNESS.
I'LL SEE IF WE CAN GIVE YOU SOME OF THE BUDGET.
......!
THANK YOU SO MUCH!
KA-CHUNK
GOOD WORK, MY PRINCE.
YOU'RE FINISHED FOR THE DAY.
FOR THE DAY.
CLINK
IT WILL BE TOMORROW SOON.
TOCK
TRUE.
TOCK
I'M SORRY.
I MADE YOU STAY SO LATE...
I'M YOUR SER-VANT.
IT'S MY DUTY.
I MEAN YESTER-DAY.
YOU ...
OH.
I WAS CHEEKY.
DID YOU LIKE THAT?
YES.
VERY MUCH SO.

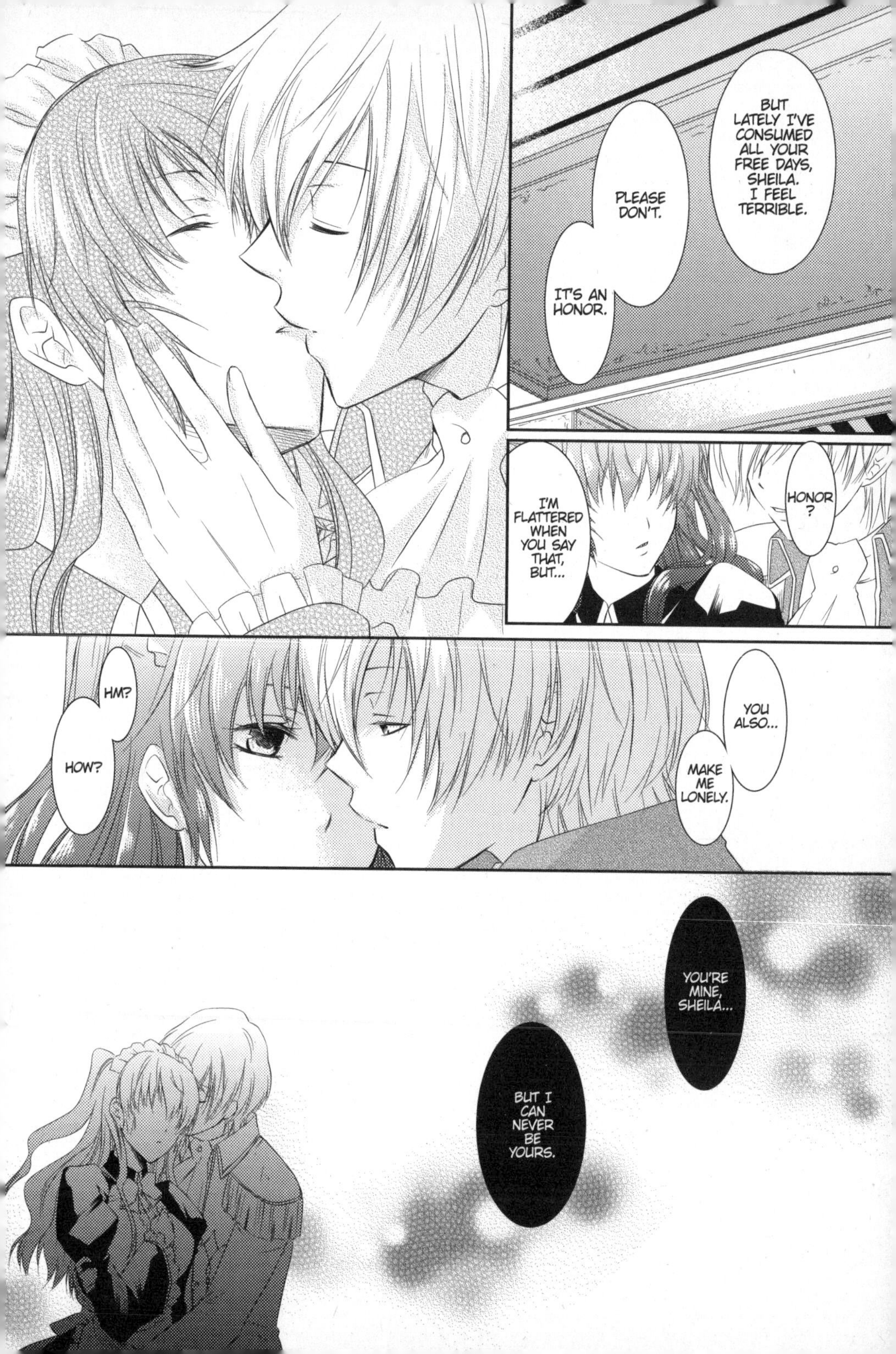
BUT LATELY I'VE CONSUMED ALL YOUR FREE DAYS, SHEILA. I FEEL TERRIBLE.
PLEASE DON'T.
IT'S AN HONOR.
HONOR?
I'M FLATTERED WHEN YOU SAY THAT, BUT...
YOU ALSO...
MAKE ME LONELY.
HM?
HOW?
YOU'RE MINE, SHEILA...
BUT I CAN NEVER BE YOURS.

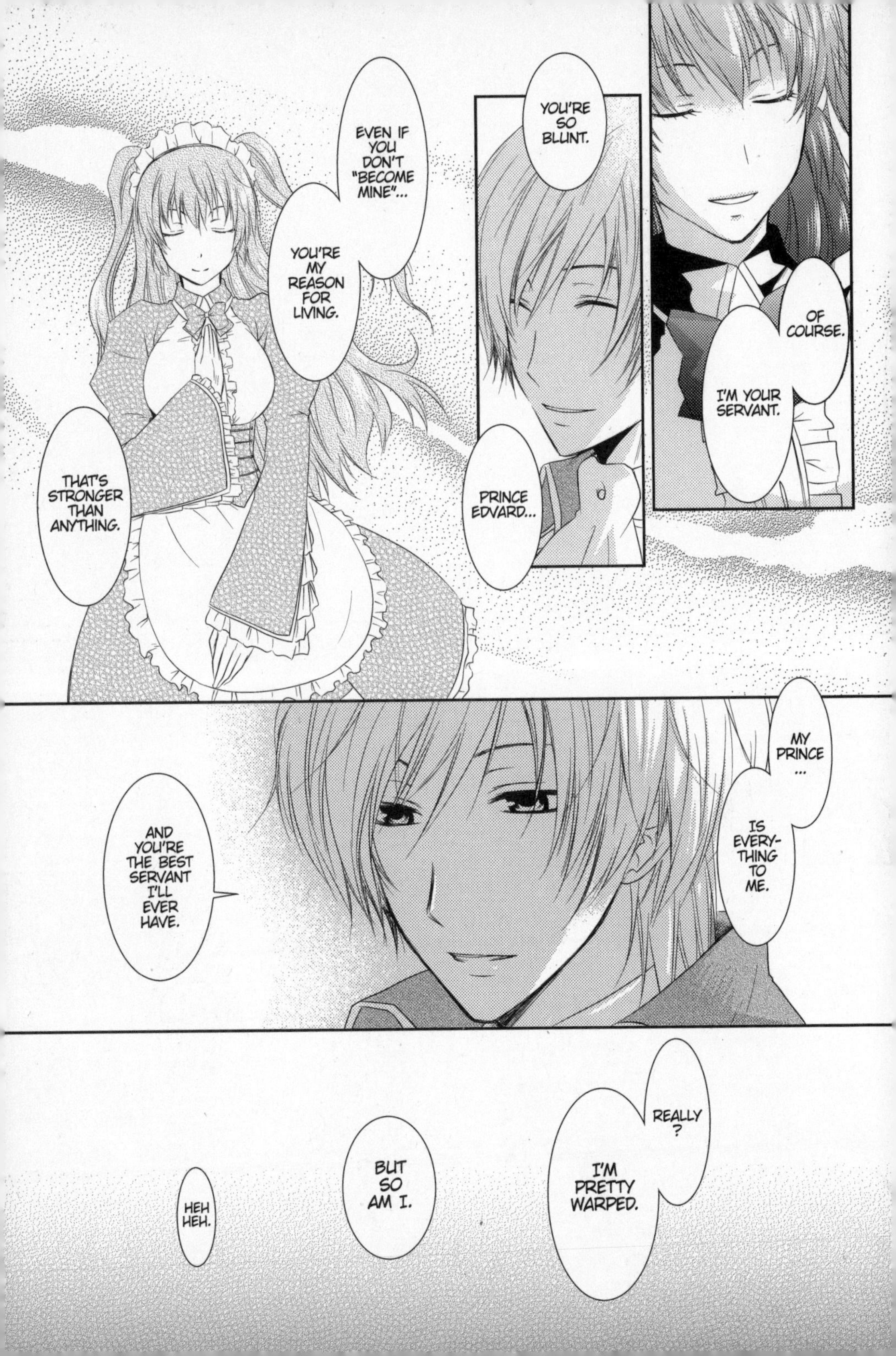
OF COURSE.
I'M YOUR SERVANT.
YOU'RE SO BLUNT.
PRINCE EDVARD...
EVEN IF YOU DON'T "BECOME MINE"...
YOU'RE MY REASON FOR LIVING.
THAT'S STRONGER THAN ANYTHING.
MY PRINCE ...
IS EVERY-THING TO ME.
AND YOU'RE THE BEST SERVANT I'LL EVER HAVE.
REALLY ?
I'M PRETTY WARPED.
BUT SO AM I.
HEH HEH.

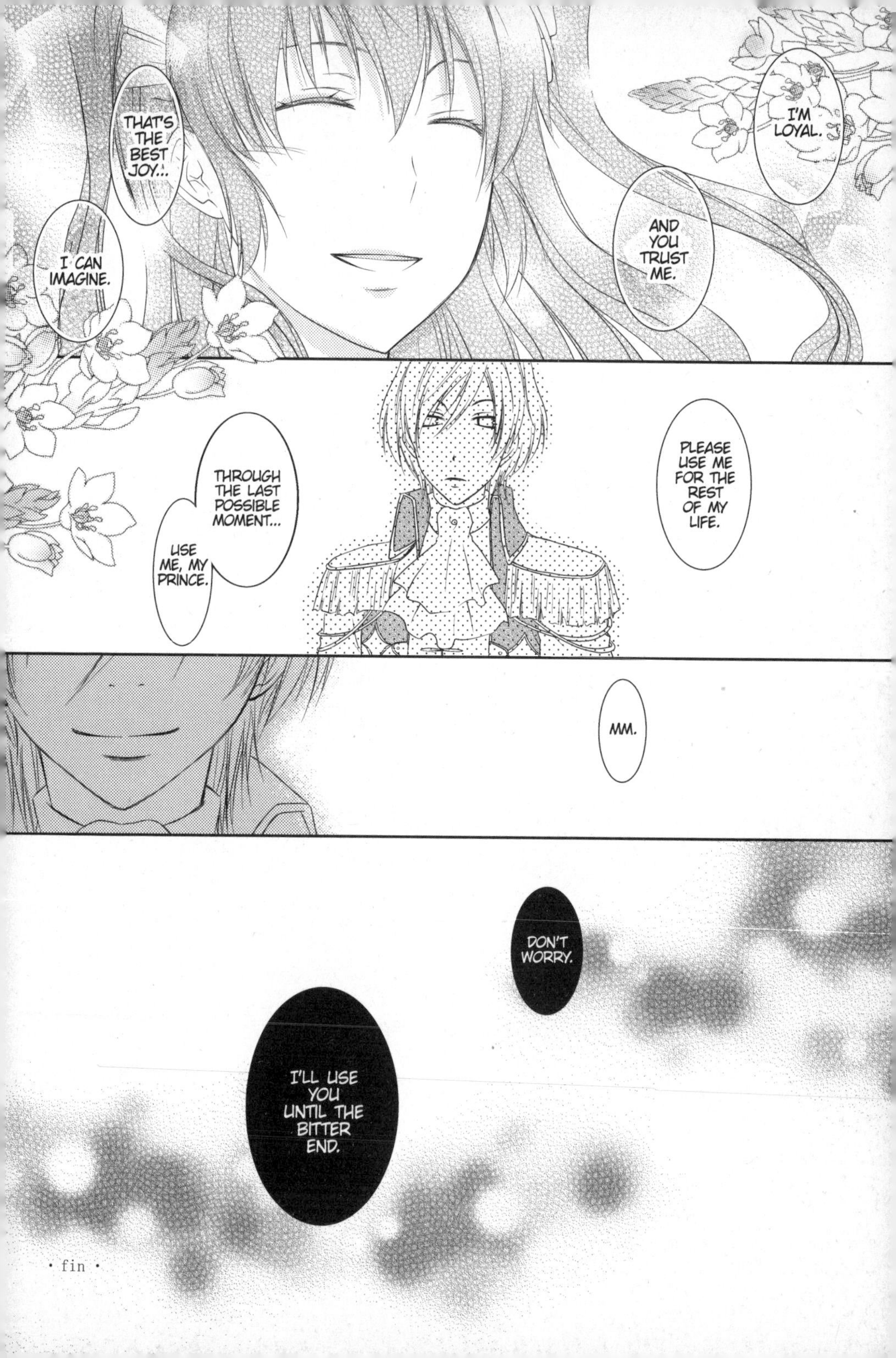
I'M LOYAL.
AND YOU TRUST ME.
THAT'S THE BEST JOY...
I CAN IMAGINE.
PLEASE USE ME FOR THE REST OF MY LIFE.
THROUGH THE LAST POSSIBLE MOMENT...
USE ME, MY PRINCE.
MM.
DON'T WORRY.
I'LL USE YOU UNTIL THE BITTER END.
• fin •

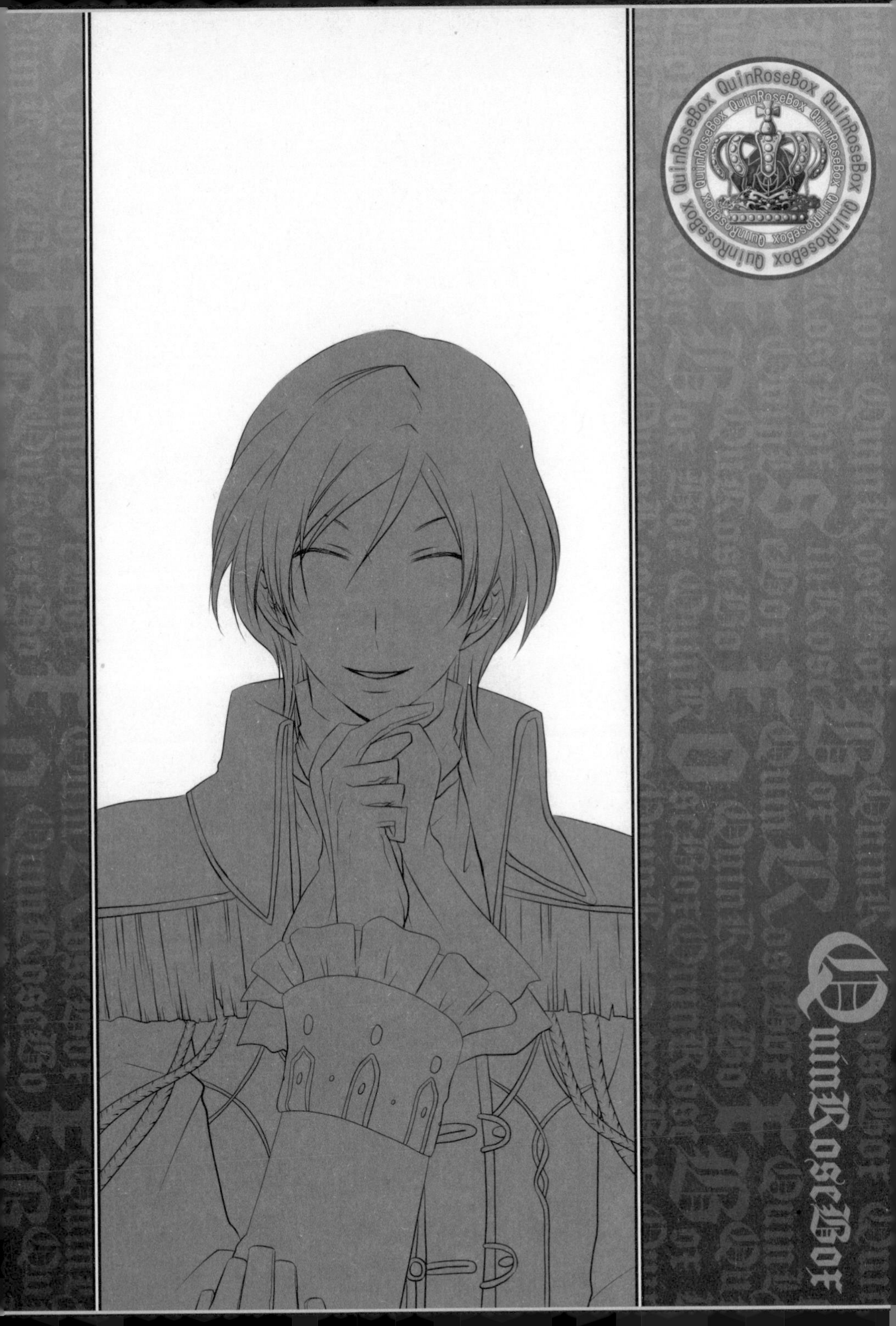
QuinRoseBox

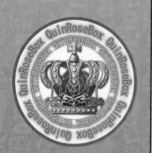

NOTE: The preceding *Crimson Empire* short story and the one that follows feature love routes for Sheila & Prince Edvard and Sheila & Count Bryon, respectively.

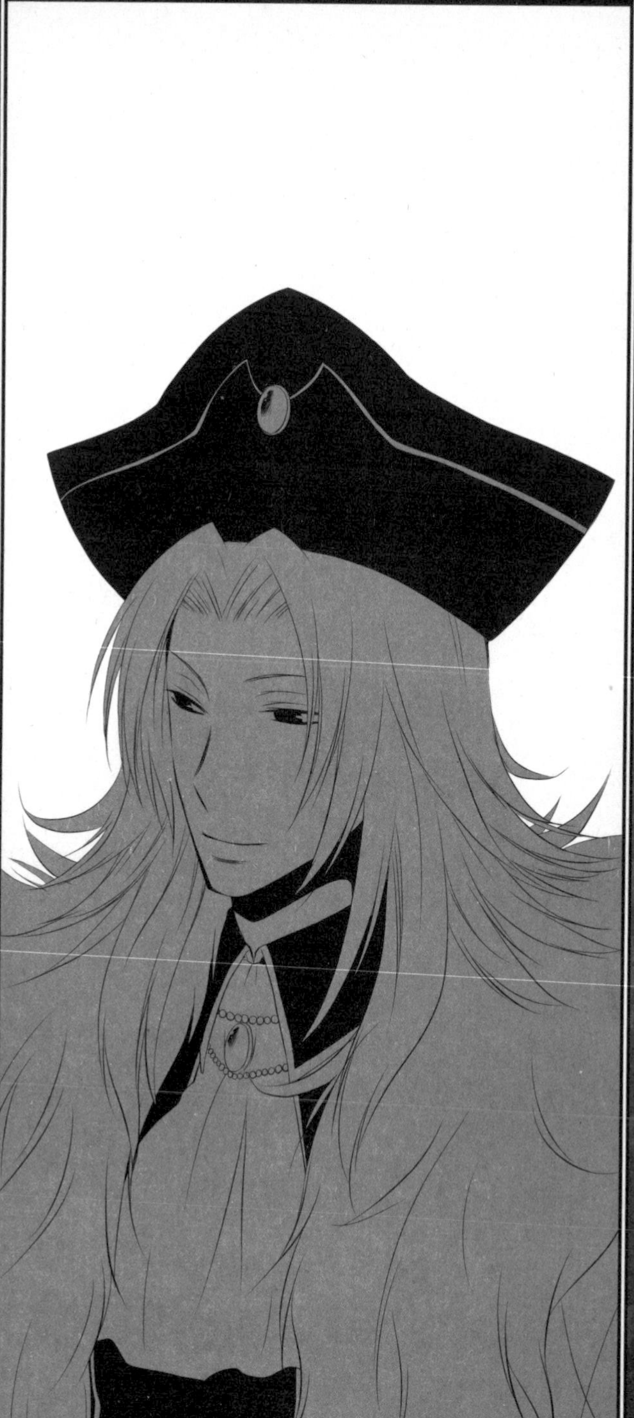

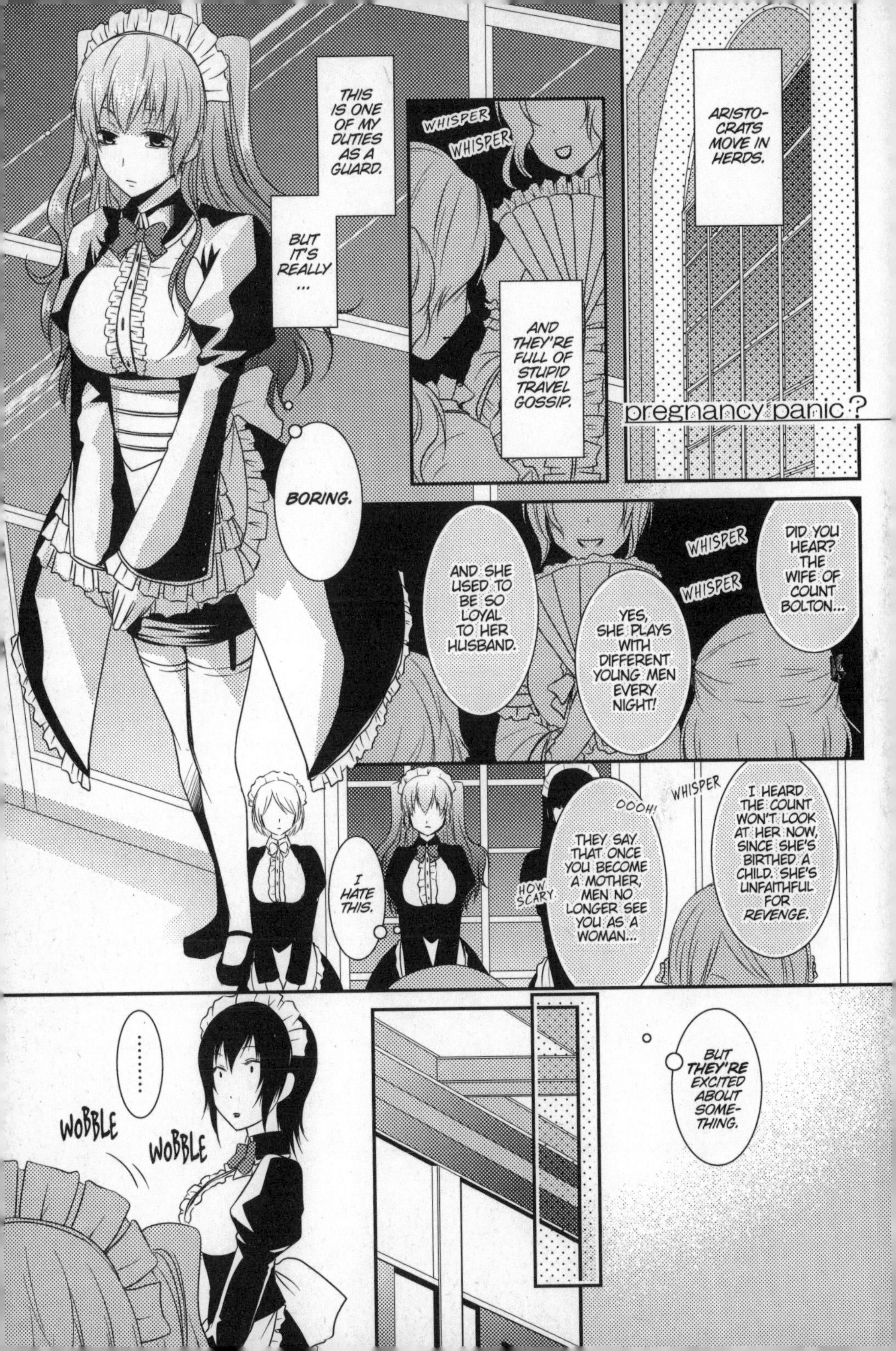
ARISTO-CRATS MOVE IN HERDS.
pregnancy panic?
WHISPER
WHISPER
AND THEY'RE FULL OF STUPID TRAVEL GOSSIP.
DID YOU HEAR? THE WIFE OF COUNT BOLTON...
WHISPER
WHISPER
YES, SHE PLAYS WITH DIFFERENT YOUNG MEN EVERY NIGHT!
AND SHE USED TO BE SO LOYAL TO HER HUSBAND.
I HEARD THE COUNT WON'T LOOK AT HER NOW, SINCE SHE'S BIRTHED A CHILD. SHE'S UNFAITHFUL FOR REVENGE.
WHISPER
OOOH!
THEY SAY THAT ONCE YOU BECOME A MOTHER, MEN NO LONGER SEE YOU AS A WOMAN...
HOW SCARY.
I HATE THIS.
THIS IS ONE OF MY DUTIES AS A GUARD.
BUT IT'S REALLY ...
BORING.
BUT THEY'RE EXCITED ABOUT SOME-THING.
......
WOBBLE
WOBBLE

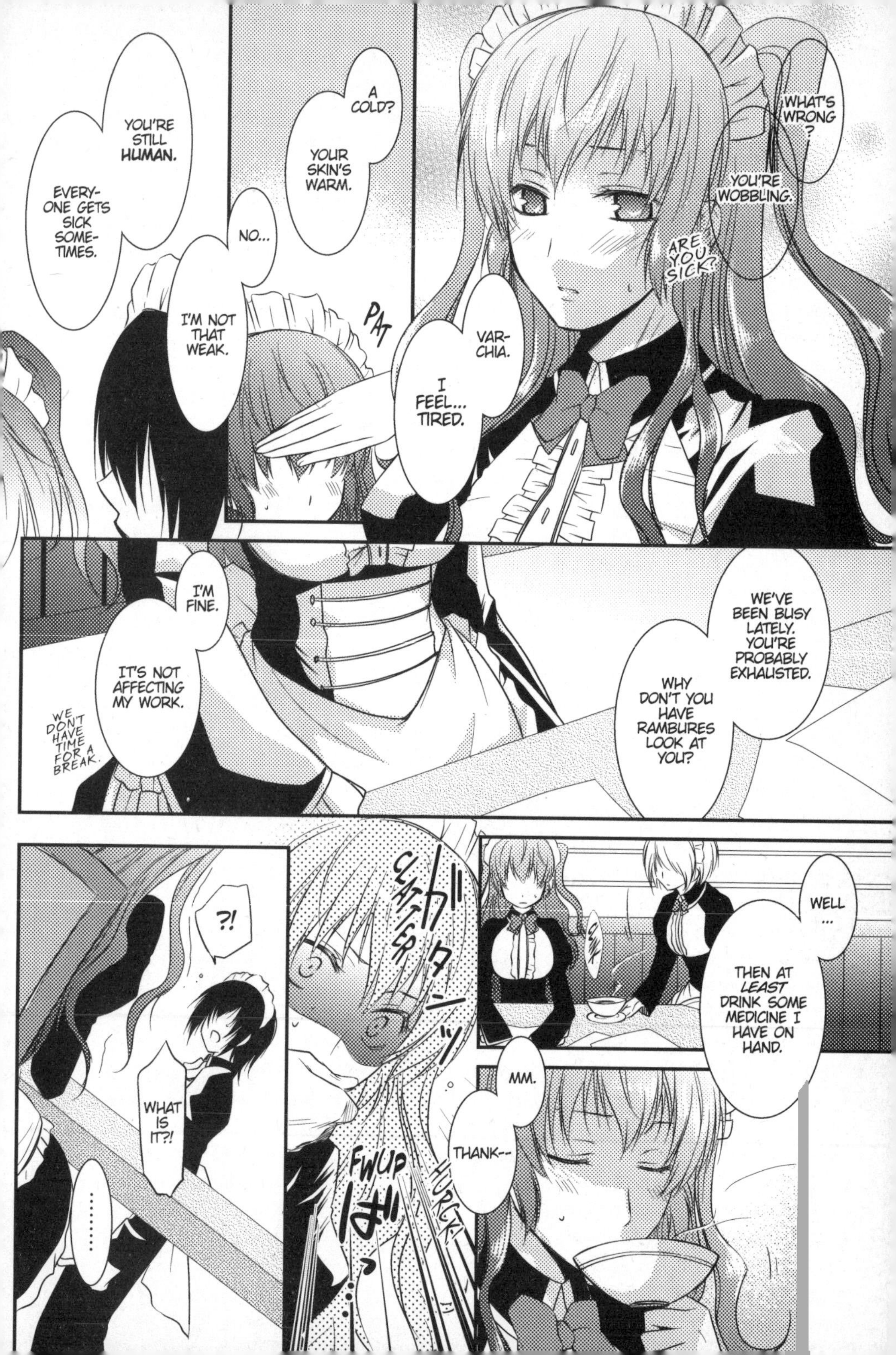
WHAT'S WRONG?
YOU'RE WOBBLING.
ARE YOU SICK?
VAR-CHIA.
I FEEL... TIRED.
PAT
A COLD?
YOUR SKIN'S WARM.
NO...
I'M NOT THAT WEAK.
YOU'RE STILL HUMAN.
EVERY-ONE GETS SICK SOME-TIMES.
WE'VE BEEN BUSY LATELY. YOU'RE PROBABLY EXHAUSTED.
WHY DON'T YOU HAVE RAMBURES LOOK AT YOU?
I'M FINE.
IT'S NOT AFFECTING MY WORK.
WE DON'T HAVE TIME FOR A BREAK.
WELL...
THEN AT LEAST DRINK SOME MEDICINE I HAVE ON HAND.
MM.
THANK--
CLATTER
HURGK!
FWUP
?!
WHAT IS IT?!
......

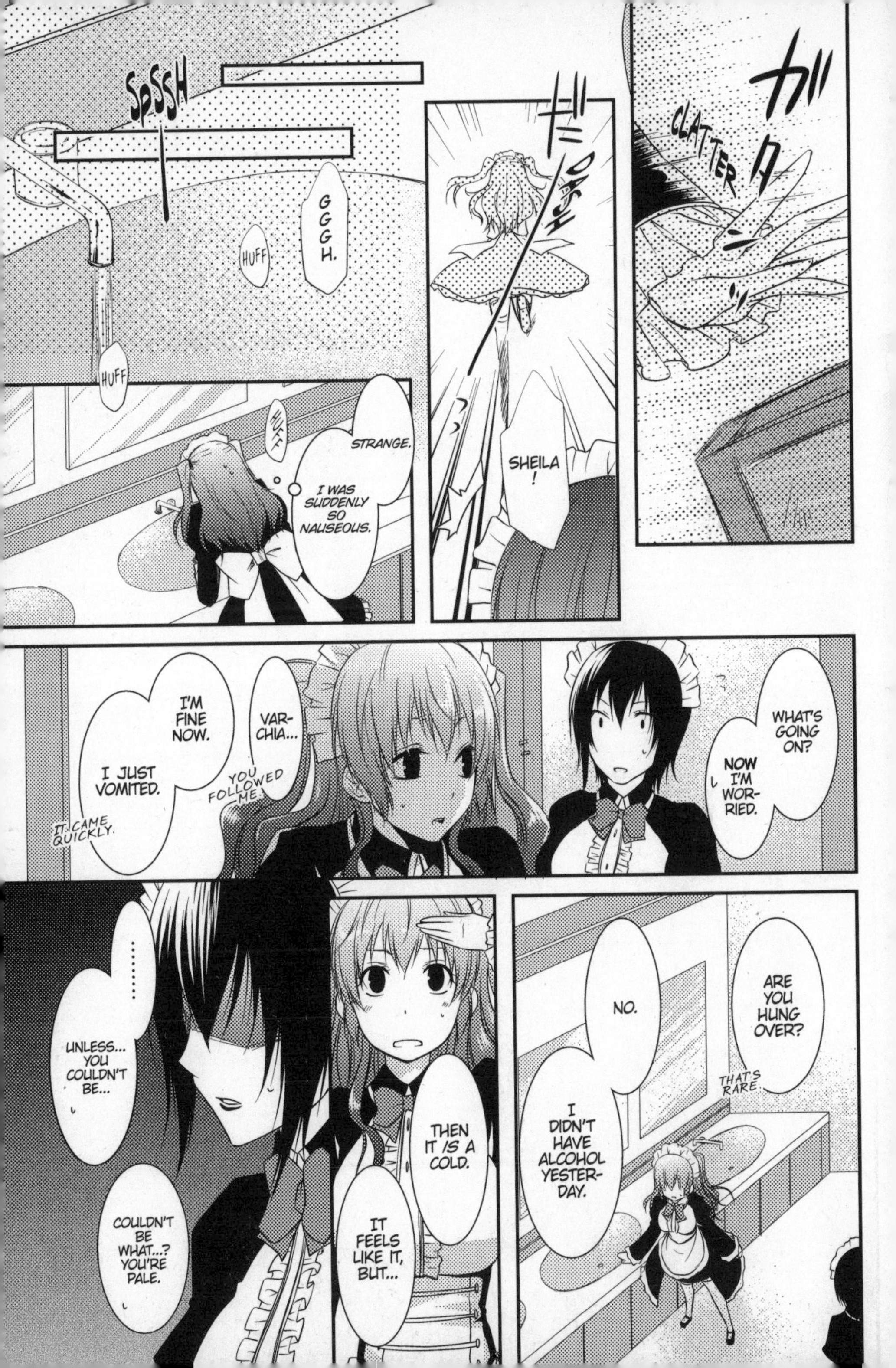
CLATTER
DASH
SHEILA!
SPSSH
GGGH.
HUFF
HUFF
HUFF HUFF
STRANGE.
I WAS SUDDENLY SO NAUSEOUS.
WHAT'S GOING ON?
NOW I'M WORRIED.
VARCHIA...
YOU FOLLOWED ME.
I'M FINE NOW.
I JUST VOMITED.
IT CAME QUICKLY.
ARE YOU HUNG OVER?
THAT'S RARE.
NO.
I DIDN'T HAVE ALCOHOL YESTERDAY.
THEN IT IS A COLD.
IT FEELS LIKE IT, BUT...
......
UNLESS... YOU COULDN'T BE...
COULDN'T BE WHAT...? YOU'RE PALE.

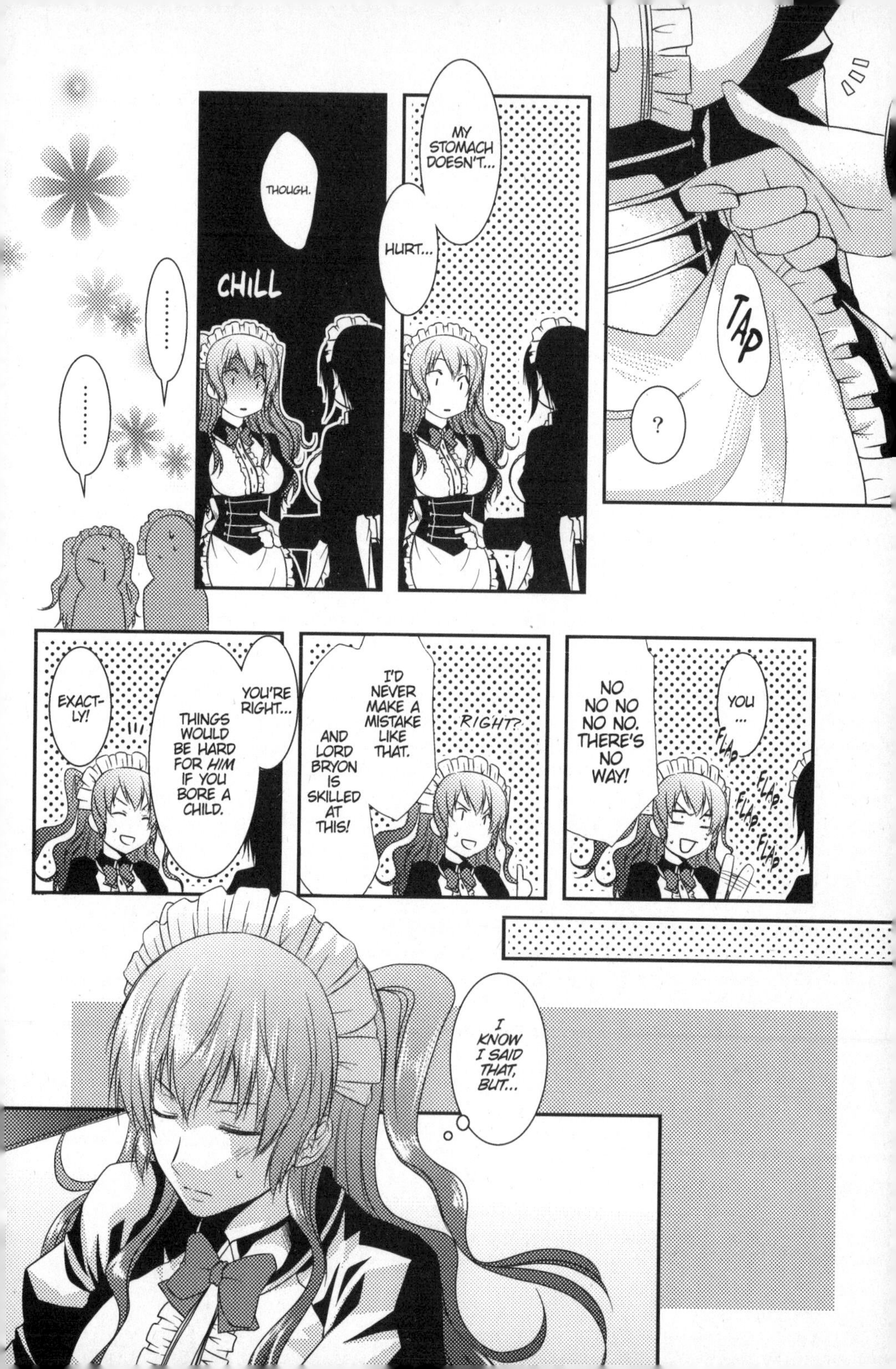
TAP
?
MY STOMACH DOESN'T...
HURT...
THOUGH.
CHILL
......
......
YOU ...
FLAP FLAP FLAP FLAP
NO NO NO NO NO. THERE'S NO WAY!
RIGHT?
I'D NEVER MAKE A MISTAKE LIKE THAT.
AND LORD BRYON IS SKILLED AT THIS!
YOU'RE RIGHT...
THINGS WOULD BE HARD FOR *HIM* IF YOU BORE A CHILD.
EXACT-LY!
I KNOW I SAID THAT, BUT...

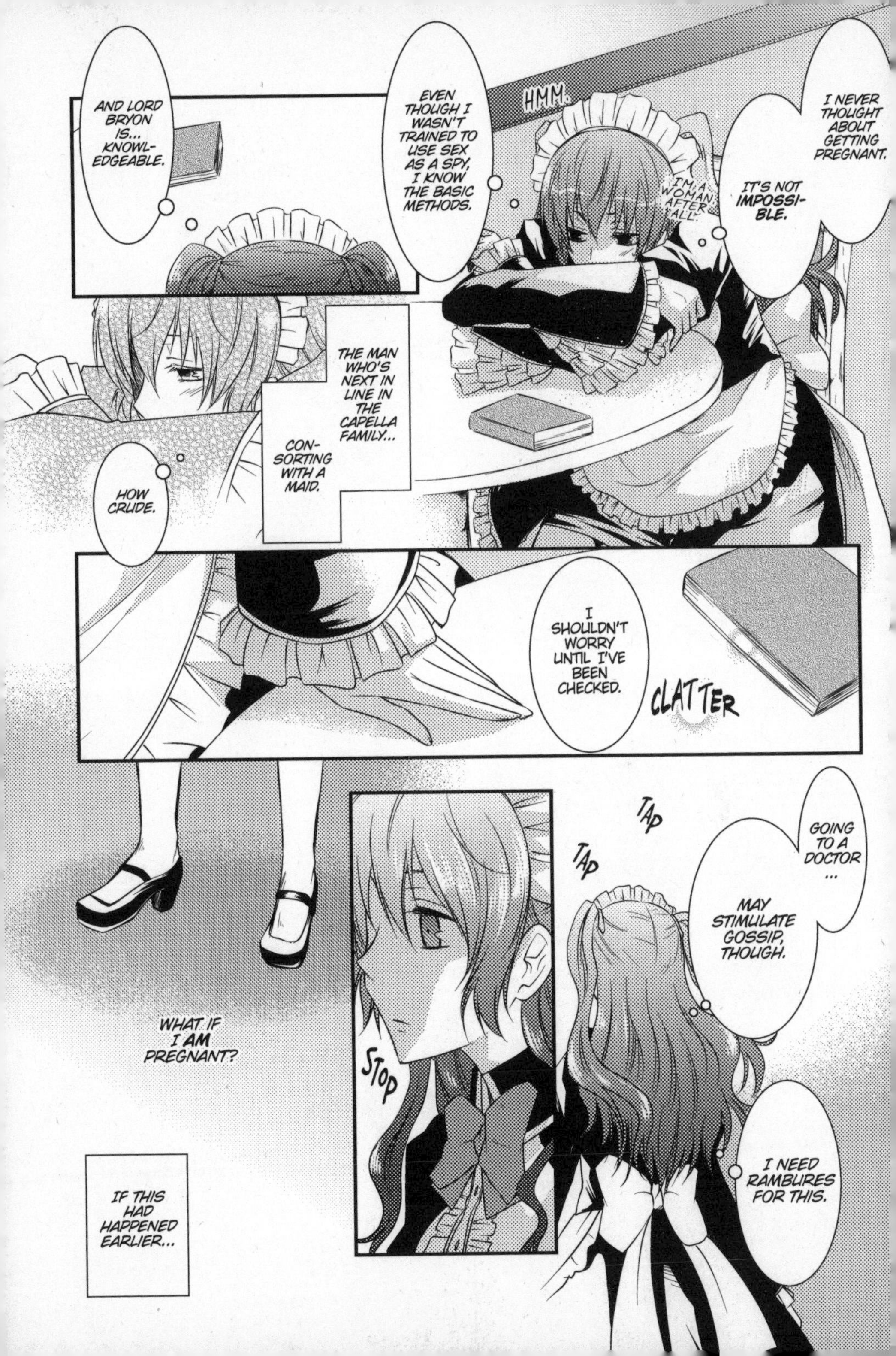
HMM.
I NEVER THOUGHT ABOUT GETTING PREGNANT.
IT'S NOT IMPOSSIBLE.
I'M A WOMAN AFTER ALL.
EVEN THOUGH I WASN'T TRAINED TO USE SEX AS A SPY, I KNOW THE BASIC METHODS.
AND LORD BRYON IS... KNOWLEDGEABLE.
THE MAN WHO'S NEXT IN LINE IN THE CAPELLA FAMILY...
CONSORTING WITH A MAID.
HOW CRUDE.
I SHOULDN'T WORRY UNTIL I'VE BEEN CHECKED.
CLATTER
TAP
TAP
GOING TO A DOCTOR...
MAY STIMULATE GOSSIP, THOUGH.
STOP
I NEED RAMBURES FOR THIS.
WHAT IF I AM PREGNANT?
IF THIS HAD HAPPENED EARLIER...

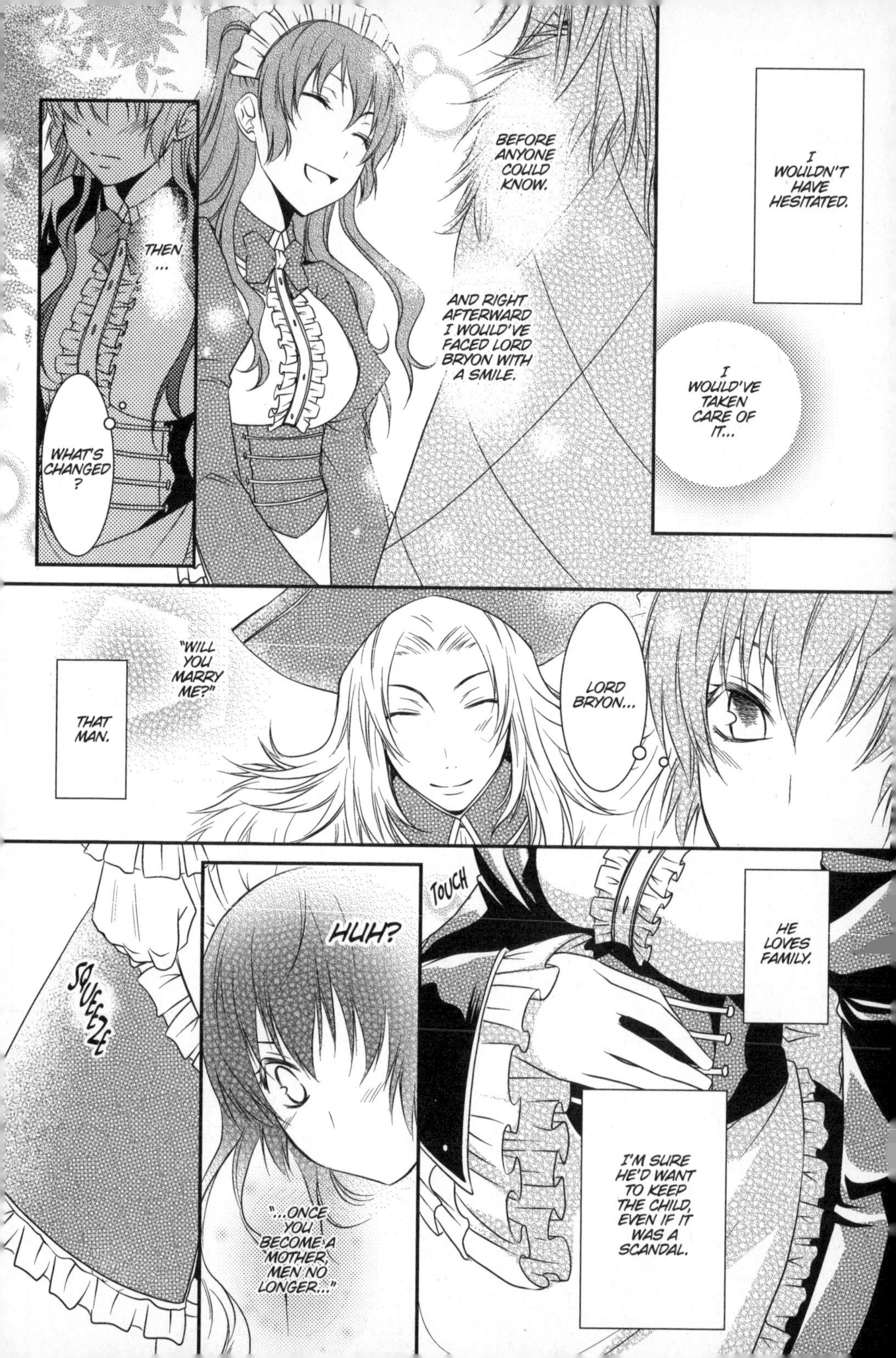
I WOULDN'T HAVE HESITATED.
I WOULD'VE TAKEN CARE OF IT...
BEFORE ANYONE COULD KNOW.
AND RIGHT AFTERWARD I WOULD'VE FACED LORD BRYON WITH A SMILE.
THEN...
WHAT'S CHANGED?
LORD BRYON...
"WILL YOU MARRY ME?"
THAT MAN.
HE LOVES FAMILY.
I'M SURE HE'D WANT TO KEEP THE CHILD, EVEN IF IT WAS A SCANDAL.
TOUCH
HUH?
"...ONCE YOU BECOME A MOTHER, MEN NO LONGER..."
SQUEEZE

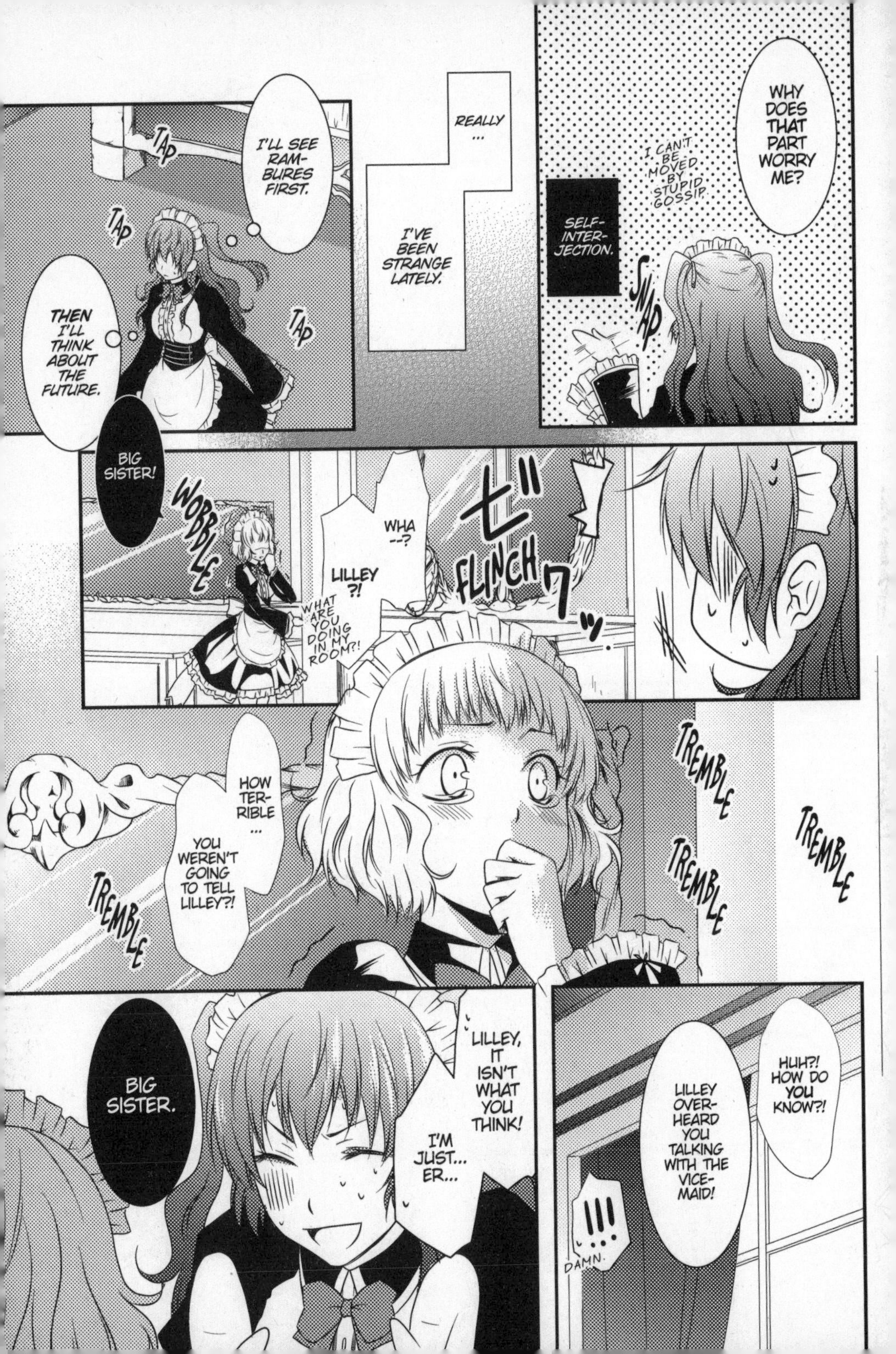
WHY DOES THAT PART WORRY ME?
I CAN'T BE MOVED BY STUPID GOSSIP.
SELF-INTERJECTION.
SNAP
REALLY ...
I'VE BEEN STRANGE LATELY.
I'LL SEE RAM-BURES FIRST.
TAP
TAP
TAP
THEN I'LL THINK ABOUT THE FUTURE.
BIG SISTER!
WOBBLE
FLINCH
WHA --?
LILLEY ?!
WHAT ARE YOU DOING IN MY ROOM?!
TREMBLE
TREMBLE
TREMBLE
HOW TER-RIBLE ...
YOU WEREN'T GOING TO TELL LILLEY?!
TREMBLE
HUH?! HOW DO YOU KNOW?!
LILLEY OVER-HEARD YOU TALKING WITH THE VICE-MAID!
!!!
...
DAMN.
LILLEY, IT ISN'T WHAT YOU THINK!
I'M JUST... ER...
BIG SISTER.

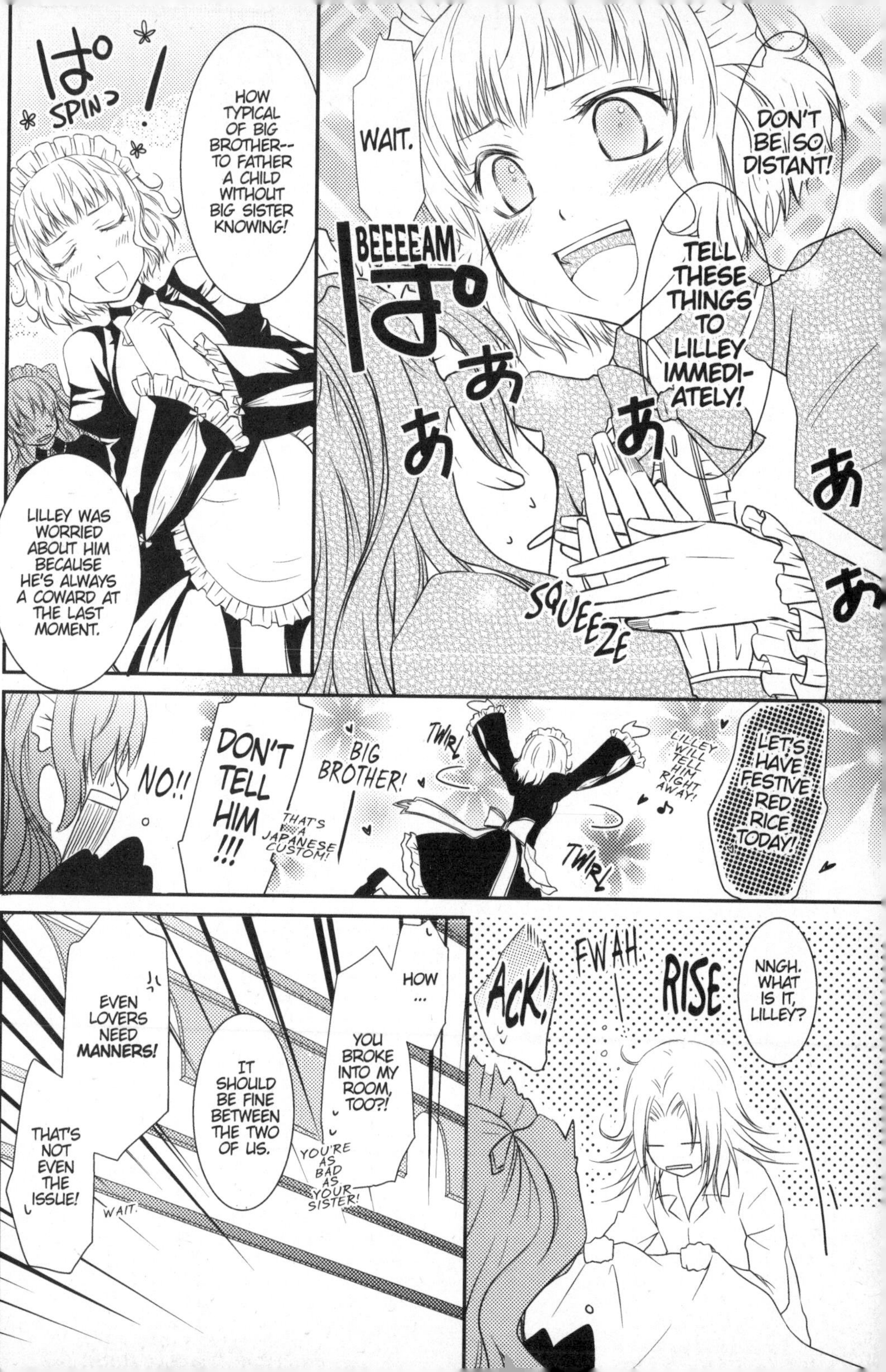
DON'T BE SO DISTANT!
WAIT.
TELL THESE THINGS TO LILLEY IMMEDIATELY!
BEEEEAM
ぱぁぁぁぁぁ
SQUEEZE
ぱっ SPIN !
HOW TYPICAL OF BIG BROTHER-- TO FATHER A CHILD WITHOUT BIG SISTER KNOWING!
LILLEY WAS WORRIED ABOUT HIM BECAUSE HE'S ALWAYS A COWARD AT THE LAST MOMENT.
LET'S HAVE FESTIVE RED RICE TODAY!
LILLEY WILL TELL HIM RIGHT AWAY!
TWIRL
TWIRL
BIG BROTHER!
THAT'S A JAPANESE CUSTOM!
DON'T TELL HIM !!!
NO!!
NNGH. WHAT IS IT, LILLEY?
RISE
FWAH
ACK!
HOW ...
YOU BROKE INTO MY ROOM, TOO?!
YOU'RE AS BAD AS YOUR SISTER!
IT SHOULD BE FINE BETWEEN THE TWO OF US.
EVEN LOVERS NEED MANNERS!
THAT'S NOT EVEN THE ISSUE!
WAIT.

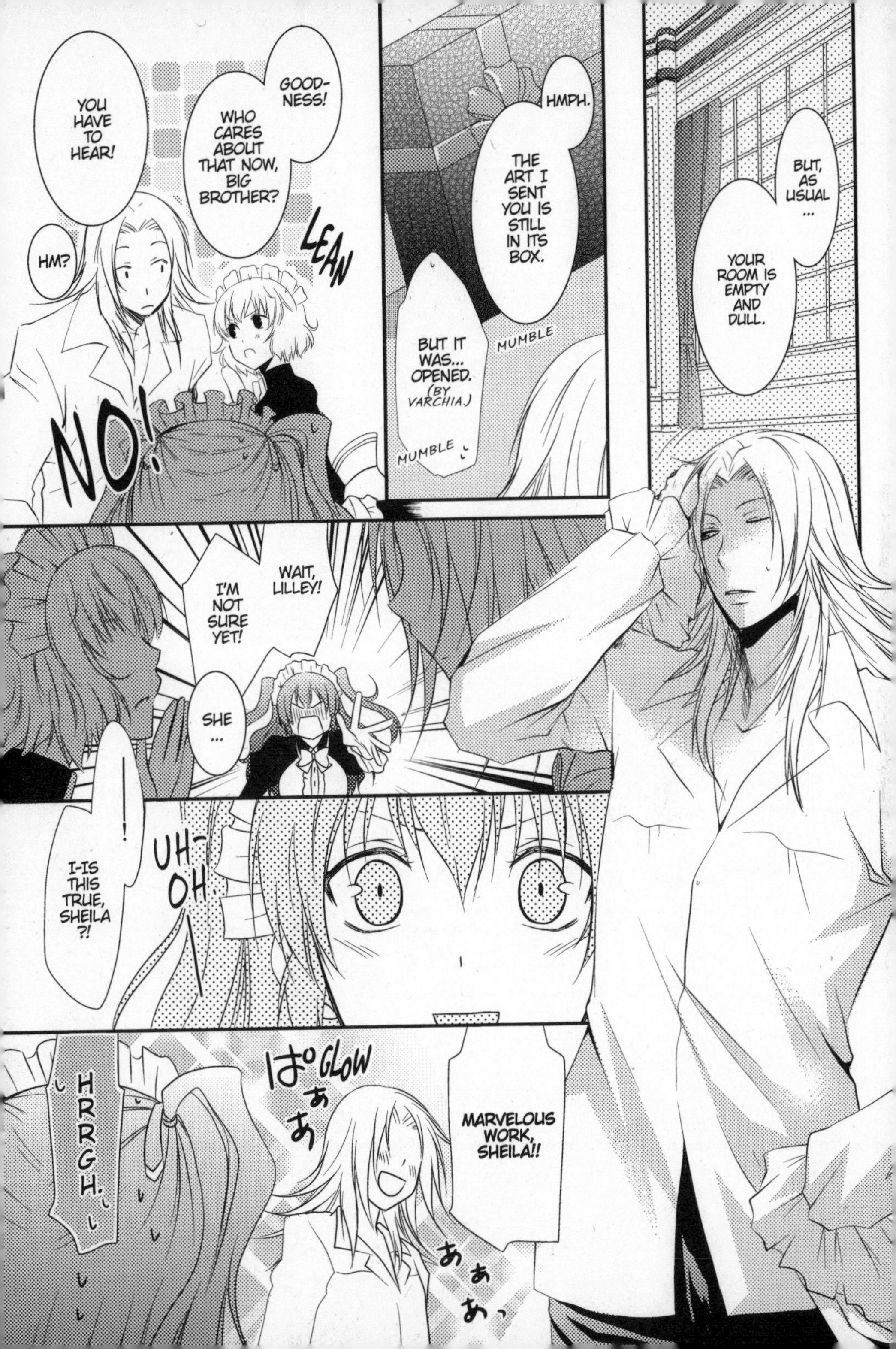

BUT, AS USUAL...
YOUR ROOM IS EMPTY AND DULL.
HMPH.
THE ART I SENT YOU IS STILL IN ITS BOX.
MUMBLE
BUT IT WAS... OPENED. (BY VARCHIA)
MUMBLE
GOODNESS!
WHO CARES ABOUT THAT NOW, BIG BROTHER?
LEAN
YOU HAVE TO HEAR!
HM?
NO!
WAIT, LILLEY!
I'M NOT SURE YET!
SHE...
UH-OH!
!
I-IS THIS TRUE, SHEILA?!
MARVELOUS WORK, SHEILA!!
ぱぁぁ GLOW
あぁぁっ
HRRGH.

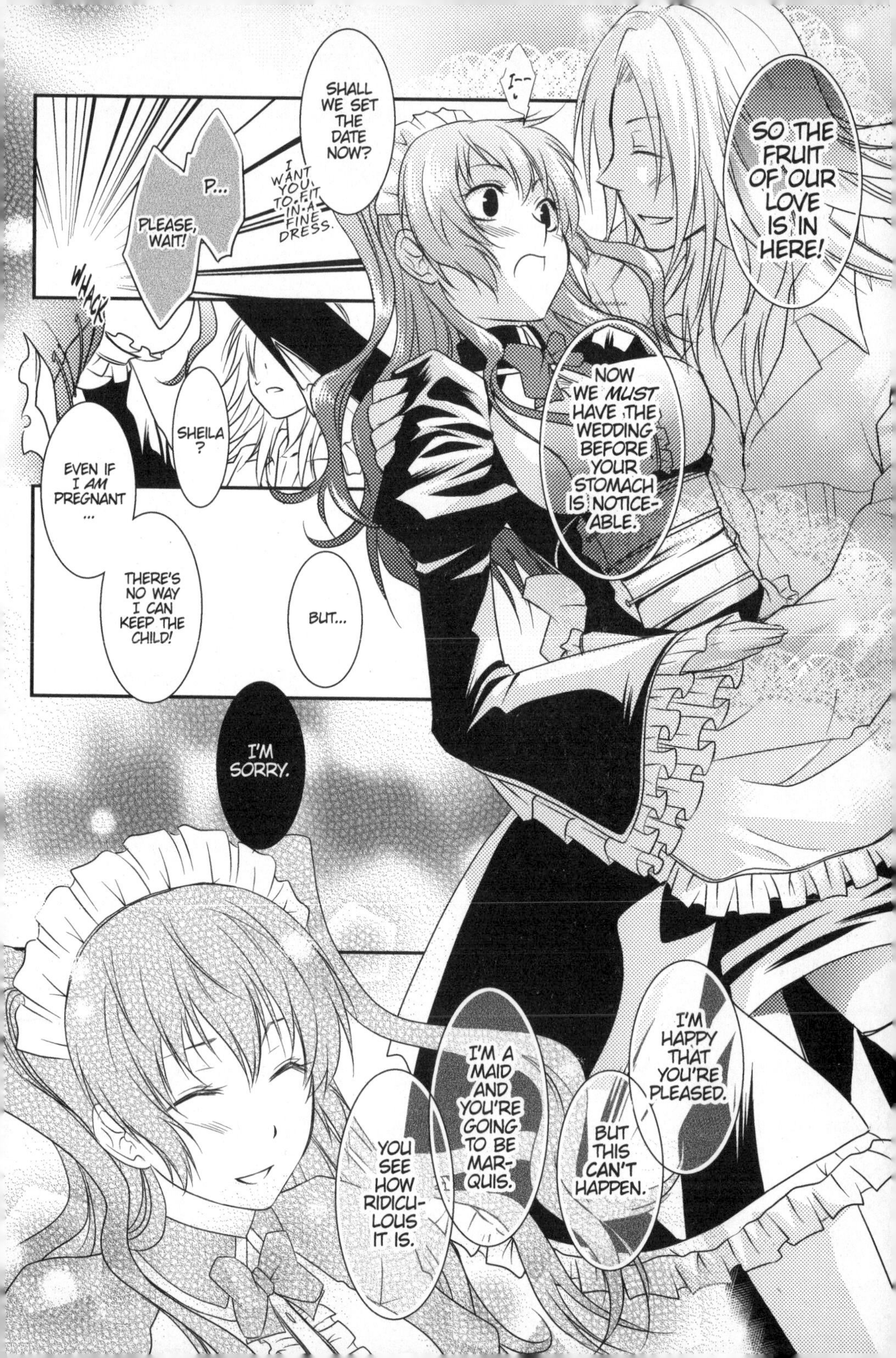

SO THE FRUIT OF OUR LOVE IS IN HERE!
I--!
NOW WE *MUST* HAVE THE WEDDING BEFORE YOUR STOMACH IS NOTICE-ABLE.
SHALL WE SET THE DATE NOW?
I WANT YOU TO FIT IN A FINE DRESS.
P...
PLEASE, WAIT!
WHACK
SHEILA?
EVEN IF I *AM* PREGNANT...
THERE'S NO WAY I CAN KEEP THE CHILD!
BUT...
I'M SORRY.
I'M HAPPY THAT YOU'RE PLEASED.
BUT THIS CAN'T HAPPEN.
I'M A MAID AND YOU'RE GOING TO BE MAR-QUIS.
YOU SEE HOW RIDICULOUS IT IS.

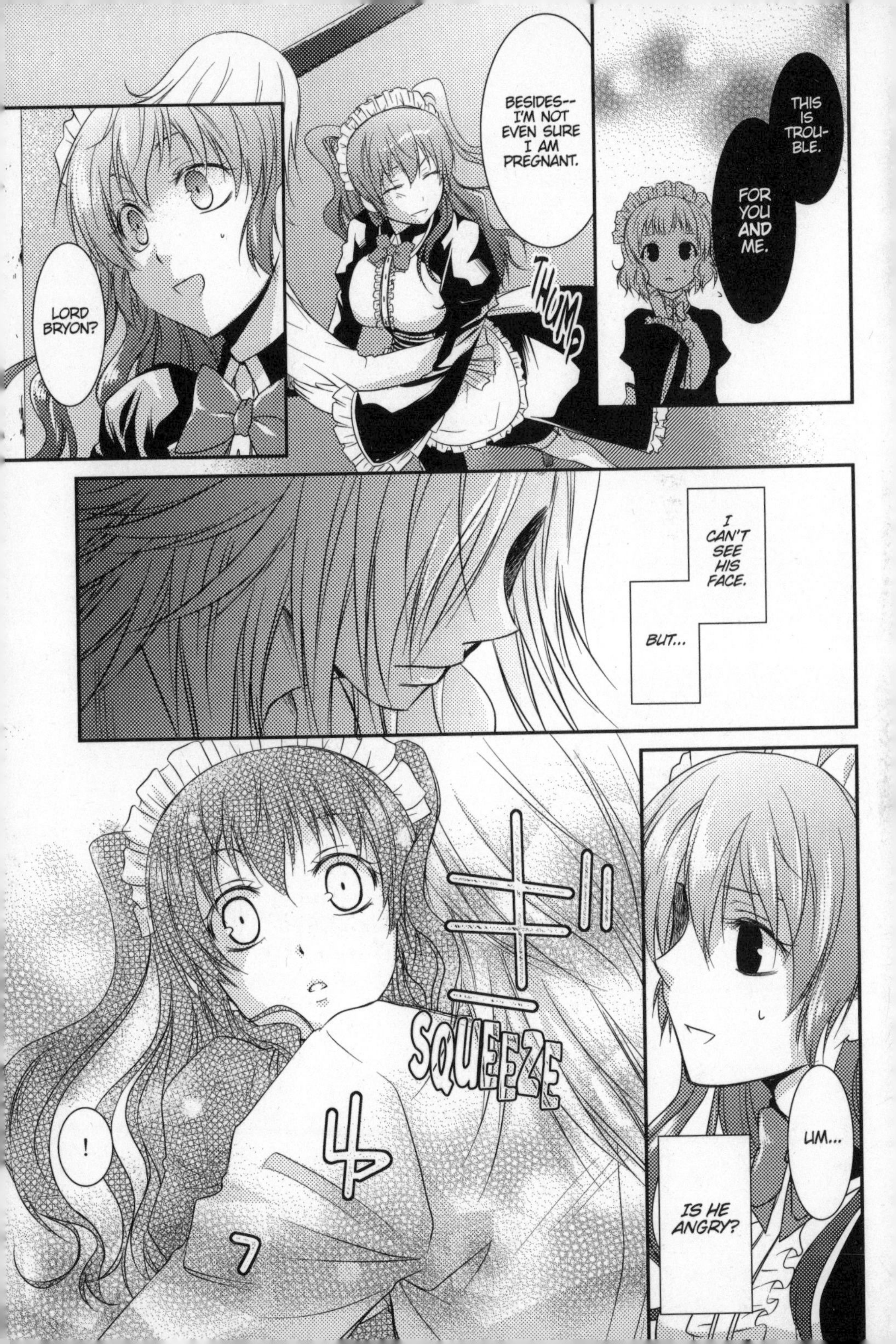
THIS IS TROUBLE.
FOR YOU AND ME.
BESIDES-- I'M NOT EVEN SURE I AM PREGNANT.
THUMP
LORD BRYON?
I CAN'T SEE HIS FACE.
BUT...
UM...
IS HE ANGRY?
SQUEEZE
!

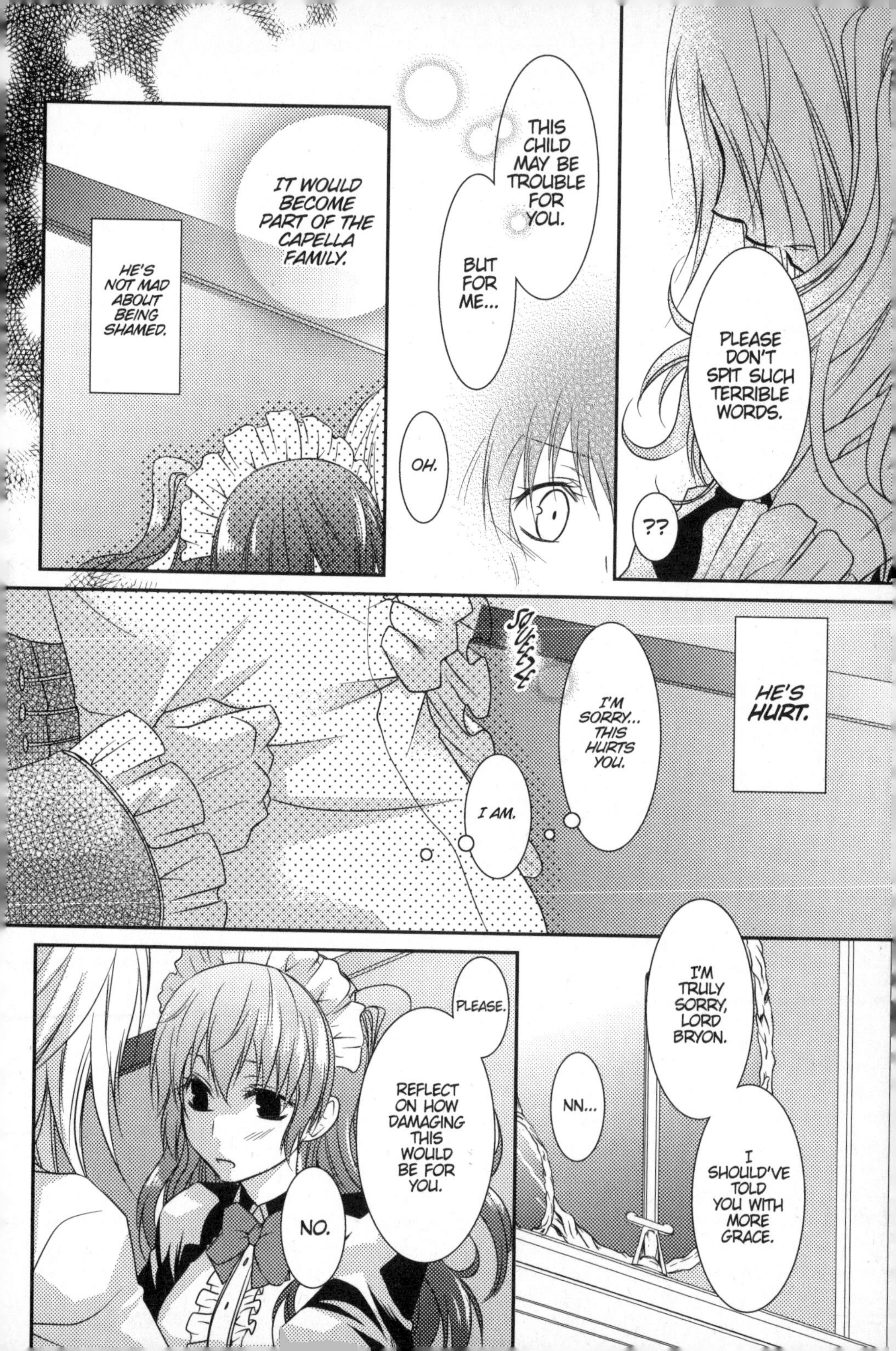
PLEASE DON'T SPIT SUCH TERRIBLE WORDS.
??
THIS CHILD MAY BE TROUBLE FOR YOU.
BUT FOR ME...
OH.
IT WOULD BECOME PART OF THE CAPELLA FAMILY.
HE'S NOT MAD ABOUT BEING SHAMED.
HE'S HURT.
SQUEEZE
I'M SORRY... THIS HURTS YOU.
I AM.
I'M TRULY SORRY, LORD BRYON.
I SHOULD'VE TOLD YOU WITH MORE GRACE.
NN...
PLEASE.
REFLECT ON HOW DAMAGING THIS WOULD BE FOR YOU.
NO.

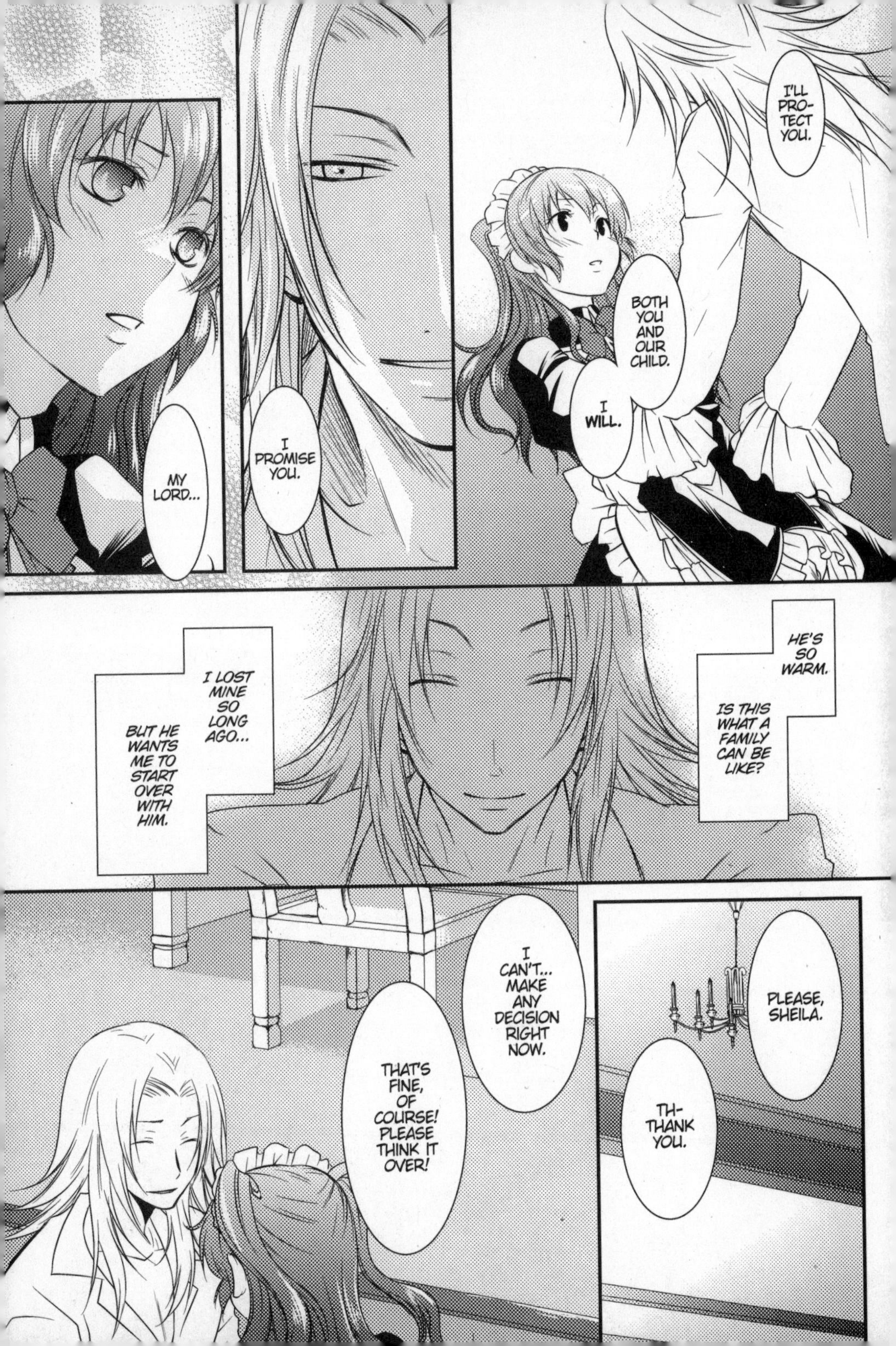
I'LL PROTECT YOU.
BOTH YOU AND OUR CHILD.
I WILL.
I PROMISE YOU.
MY LORD...
HE'S SO WARM.
IS THIS WHAT A FAMILY CAN BE LIKE?
I LOST MINE SO LONG AGO...
BUT HE WANTS ME TO START OVER WITH HIM.
PLEASE, SHEILA.
TH-THANK YOU.
I CAN'T... MAKE ANY DECISION RIGHT NOW.
THAT'S FINE, OF COURSE! PLEASE THINK IT OVER!

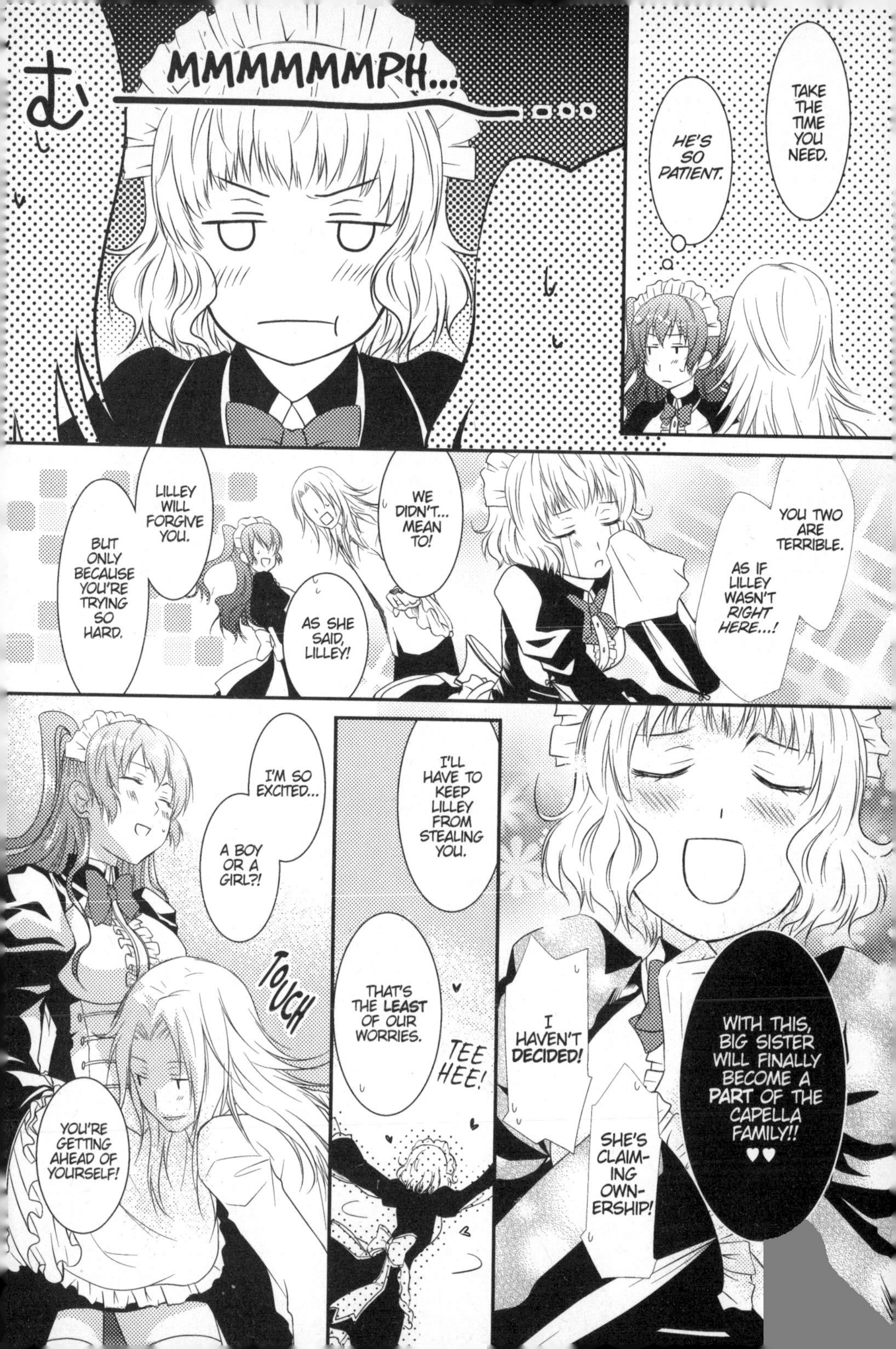
TAKE THE TIME YOU NEED.
HE'S SO PATIENT.
MMMMMMPH...
YOU TWO ARE TERRIBLE.
AS IF LILLEY WASN'T RIGHT HERE...!
WE DIDN'T... MEAN TO!
AS SHE SAID, LILLEY!
LILLEY WILL FORGIVE YOU.
BUT ONLY BECAUSE YOU'RE TRYING SO HARD.
WITH THIS, BIG SISTER WILL FINALLY BECOME A PART OF THE CAPELLA FAMILY!! ♥♥
I HAVEN'T DECIDED!
SHE'S CLAIMING OWNERSHIP!
I'LL HAVE TO KEEP LILLEY FROM STEALING YOU.
THAT'S THE LEAST OF OUR WORRIES.
TEE HEE!
I'M SO EXCITED...
A BOY OR A GIRL?!
TOUCH
YOU'RE GETTING AHEAD OF YOURSELF!

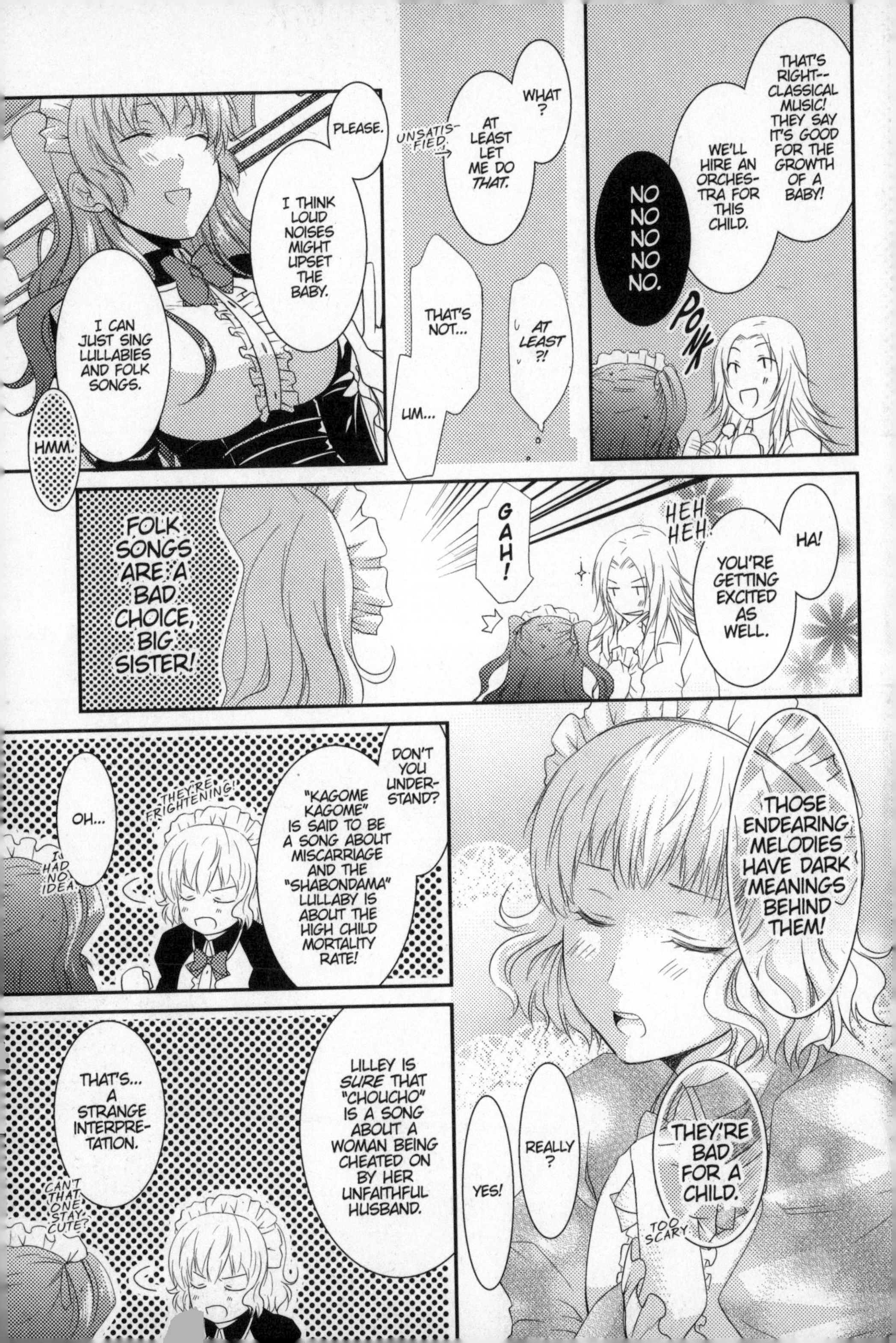
THAT'S RIGHT-- CLASSICAL MUSIC! THEY SAY IT'S GOOD FOR THE GROWTH OF A BABY!
WE'LL HIRE AN ORCHESTRA FOR THIS CHILD.
NO NO NO NO NO.
PONK
WHAT?
UNSATIS-FIED
AT LEAST LET ME DO *THAT*.
AT LEAST?!
THAT'S NOT...
UM...
PLEASE.
I THINK LOUD NOISES MIGHT UPSET THE BABY.
I CAN JUST SING LULLABIES AND FOLK SONGS.
HMM.
HEH HEH
HA!
YOU'RE GETTING EXCITED AS WELL.
GAH!
FOLK SONGS ARE A BAD CHOICE, BIG SISTER!
THOSE ENDEARING MELODIES HAVE DARK MEANINGS BEHIND THEM!
THEY'RE BAD FOR A CHILD.
TOO SCARY
REALLY?
YES!
DON'T YOU UNDERSTAND?
"KAGOME KAGOME" IS SAID TO BE A SONG ABOUT MISCARRIAGE AND THE "SHABONDAMA" LULLABY IS ABOUT THE HIGH CHILD MORTALITY RATE!
THEY'RE FRIGHTENING!
OH...
I HAD NO IDEA.
LILLEY IS *SURE* THAT "CHOUCHO" IS A SONG ABOUT A WOMAN BEING CHEATED ON BY HER UNFAITHFUL HUSBAND.
THAT'S... A STRANGE INTERPRETATION.
CAN'T THAT ONE STAY CUTE?

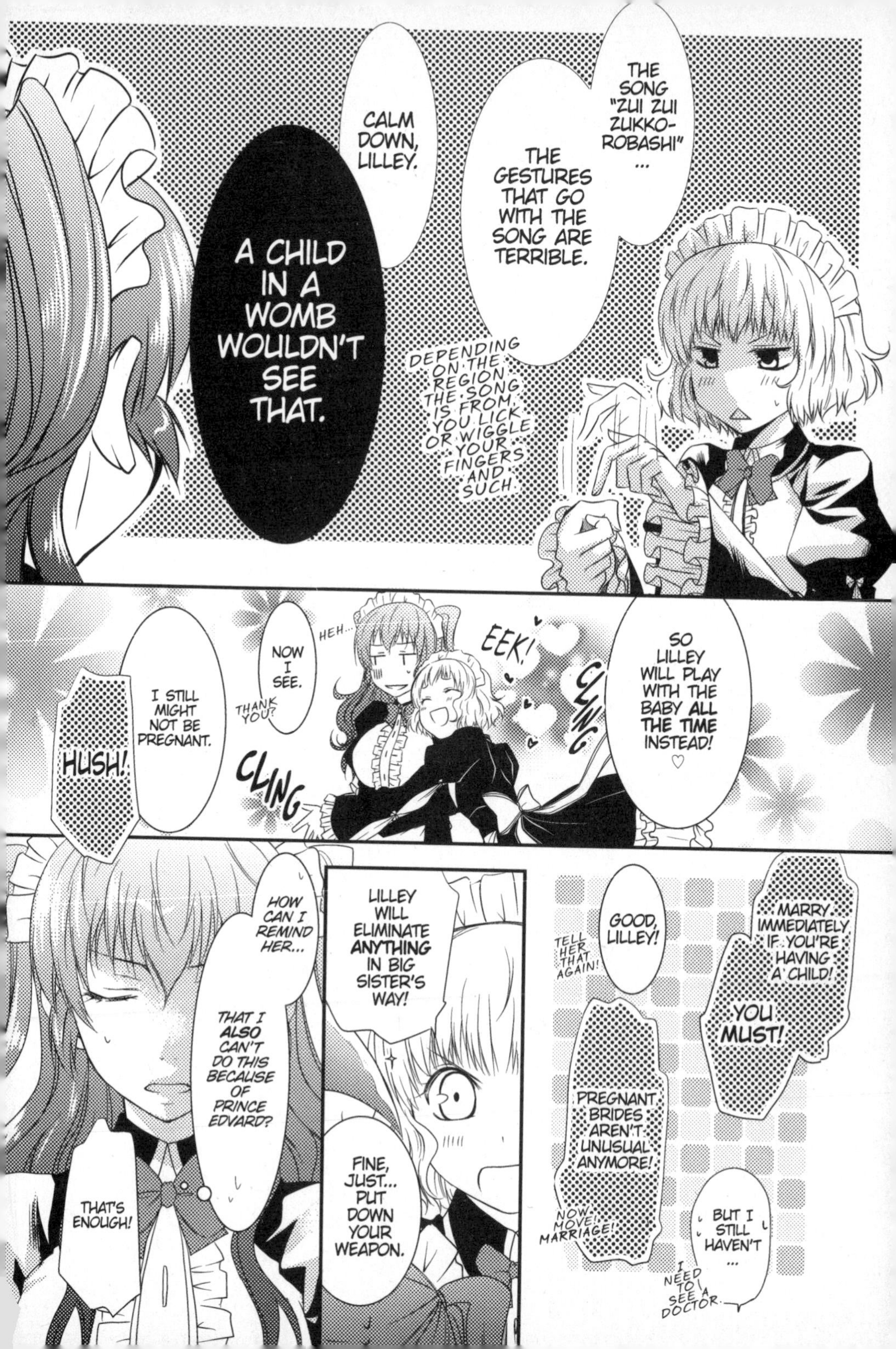
THE SONG "ZUI ZUI ZUKKO-ROBASHI" ...
THE GESTURES THAT GO WITH THE SONG ARE TERRIBLE.
DEPENDING ON THE REGION THE SONG IS FROM, YOU LICK OR WIGGLE YOUR FINGERS AND SUCH.
CALM DOWN, LILLEY.
A CHILD IN A WOMB WOULDN'T SEE THAT.
SO LILLEY WILL PLAY WITH THE BABY ALL THE TIME INSTEAD! ♡
CLING
EEK!
HEH...
NOW I SEE.
THANK YOU?
CLING
I STILL MIGHT NOT BE PREGNANT.
HUSH!
MARRY IMMEDIATELY IF YOU'RE HAVING A CHILD!
YOU MUST!
GOOD, LILLEY!
TELL HER THAT AGAIN!
PREGNANT BRIDES AREN'T UNUSUAL ANYMORE!
NOW! MOVE! MARRIAGE!
BUT I STILL HAVEN'T ...
I NEED TO SEE A DOCTOR.
LILLEY WILL ELIMINATE ANYTHING IN BIG SISTER'S WAY!
FINE, JUST... PUT DOWN YOUR WEAPON.
HOW CAN I REMIND HER...
THAT I ALSO CAN'T DO THIS BECAUSE OF PRINCE EDVARD?
THAT'S ENOUGH!

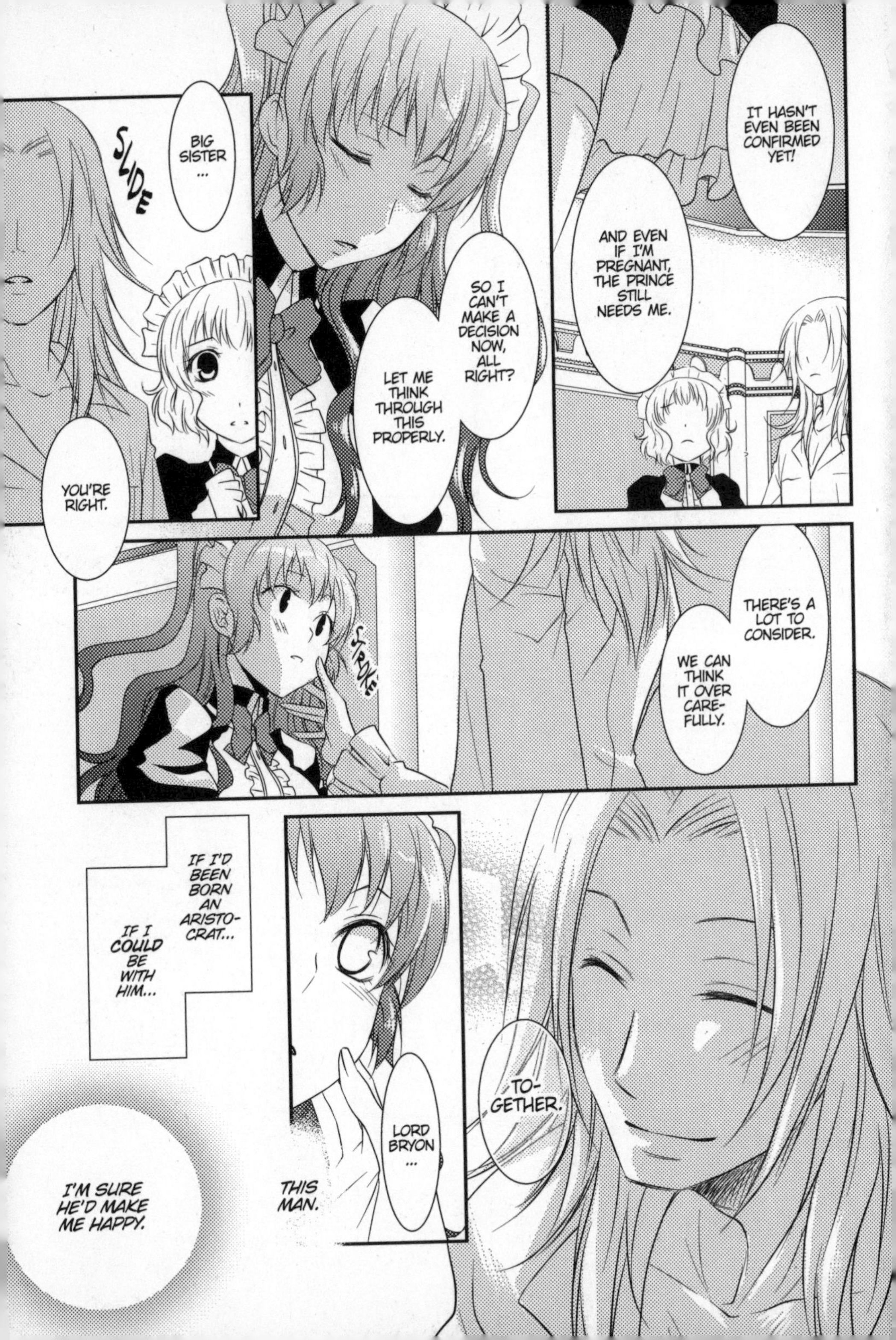
IT HASN'T EVEN BEEN CONFIRMED YET!
AND EVEN IF I'M PREGNANT, THE PRINCE STILL NEEDS ME.
SO I CAN'T MAKE A DECISION NOW, ALL RIGHT?
LET ME THINK THROUGH THIS PROPERLY.
BIG SISTER ...
SLIDE
YOU'RE RIGHT.
THERE'S A LOT TO CONSIDER.
WE CAN THINK IT OVER CARE-FULLY.
STROKE
TO-GETHER.
LORD BRYON ...
IF I'D BEEN BORN AN ARISTO-CRAT...
IF I COULD BE WITH HIM...
THIS MAN.
I'M SURE HE'D MAKE ME HAPPY.

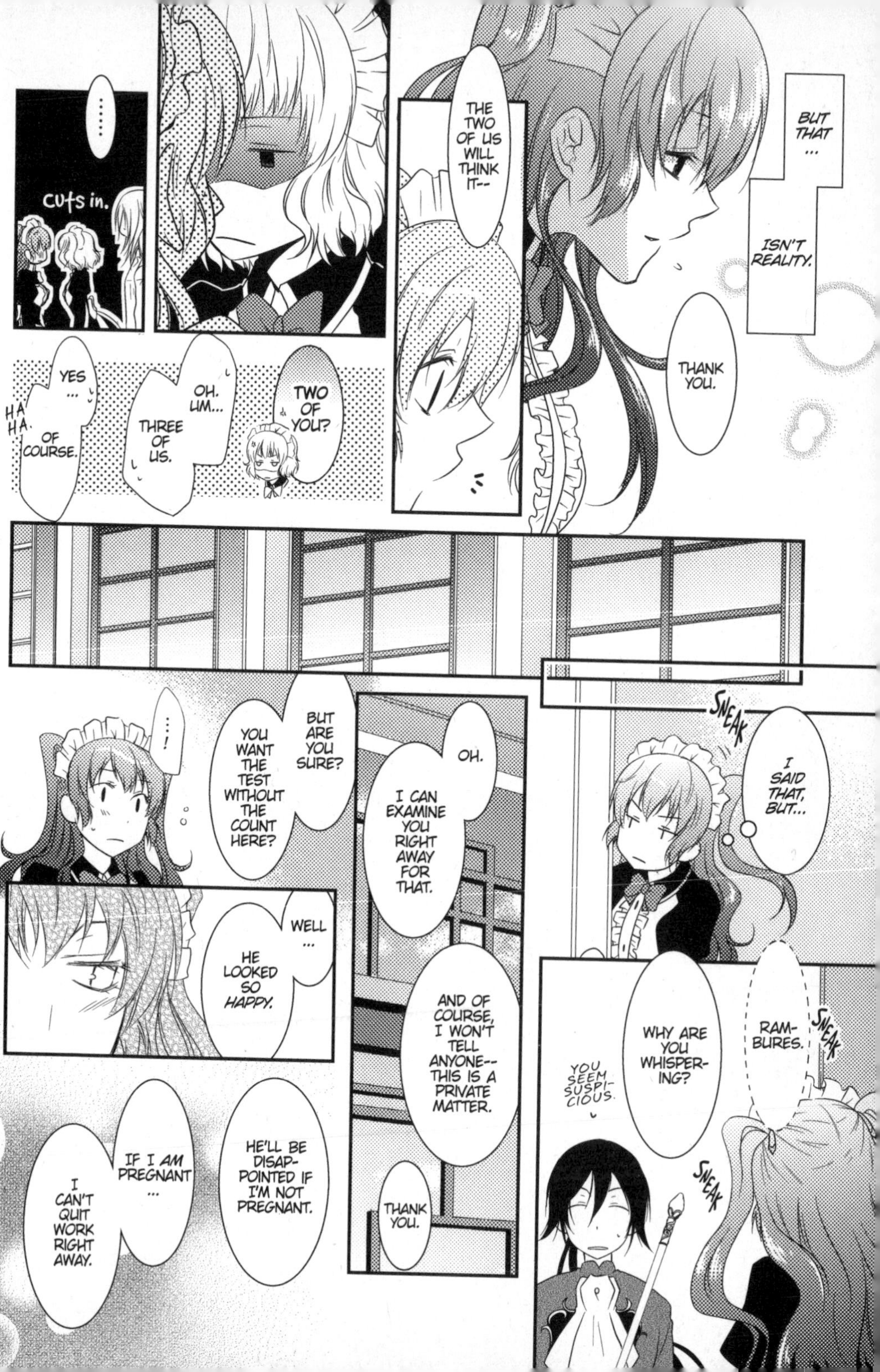
BUT THAT ...
ISN'T REALITY.
THANK YOU.
THE TWO OF US WILL THINK IT--
......
cuts in.
TWO OF YOU?
OH. UM... THREE OF US.
YES ... OF COURSE.
HA HA.
SNEAK
I SAID THAT, BUT...
RAMBURES.
SNEAK
WHY ARE YOU WHISPERING?
YOU SEEM SUSPICIOUS.
SNEAK
OH.
I CAN EXAMINE YOU RIGHT AWAY FOR THAT.
BUT ARE YOU SURE? YOU WANT THE TEST WITHOUT THE COUNT HERE?
...!
WELL ...
HE LOOKED SO HAPPY.
AND OF COURSE, I WON'T TELL ANYONE-- THIS IS A PRIVATE MATTER.
THANK YOU.
HE'LL BE DISAPPOINTED IF I'M NOT PREGNANT.
IF I AM PREGNANT ...
I CAN'T QUIT WORK RIGHT AWAY.

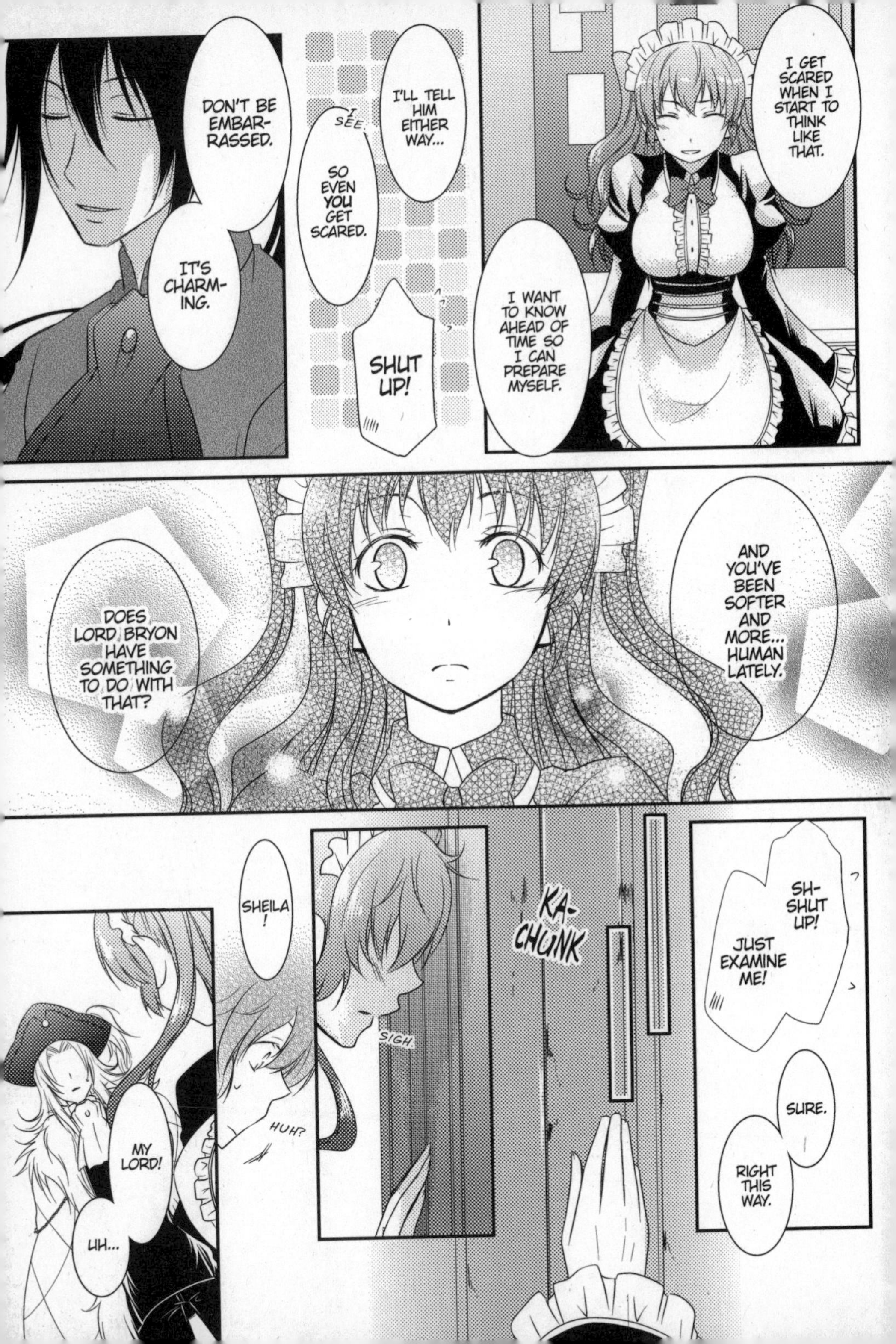
I GET SCARED WHEN I START TO THINK LIKE THAT.
I WANT TO KNOW AHEAD OF TIME SO I CAN PREPARE MYSELF.
I'LL TELL HIM EITHER WAY...
I SEE.
SO EVEN YOU GET SCARED.
SHUT UP!
DON'T BE EMBAR-RASSED.
IT'S CHARM-ING.
AND YOU'VE BEEN SOFTER AND MORE... HUMAN LATELY.
DOES LORD BRYON HAVE SOMETHING TO DO WITH THAT?
SH-SHUT UP! JUST EXAMINE ME!
SURE.
RIGHT THIS WAY.
KA-CHUNK
SHEILA!
SIGH.
HUH?
MY LORD!
UH...

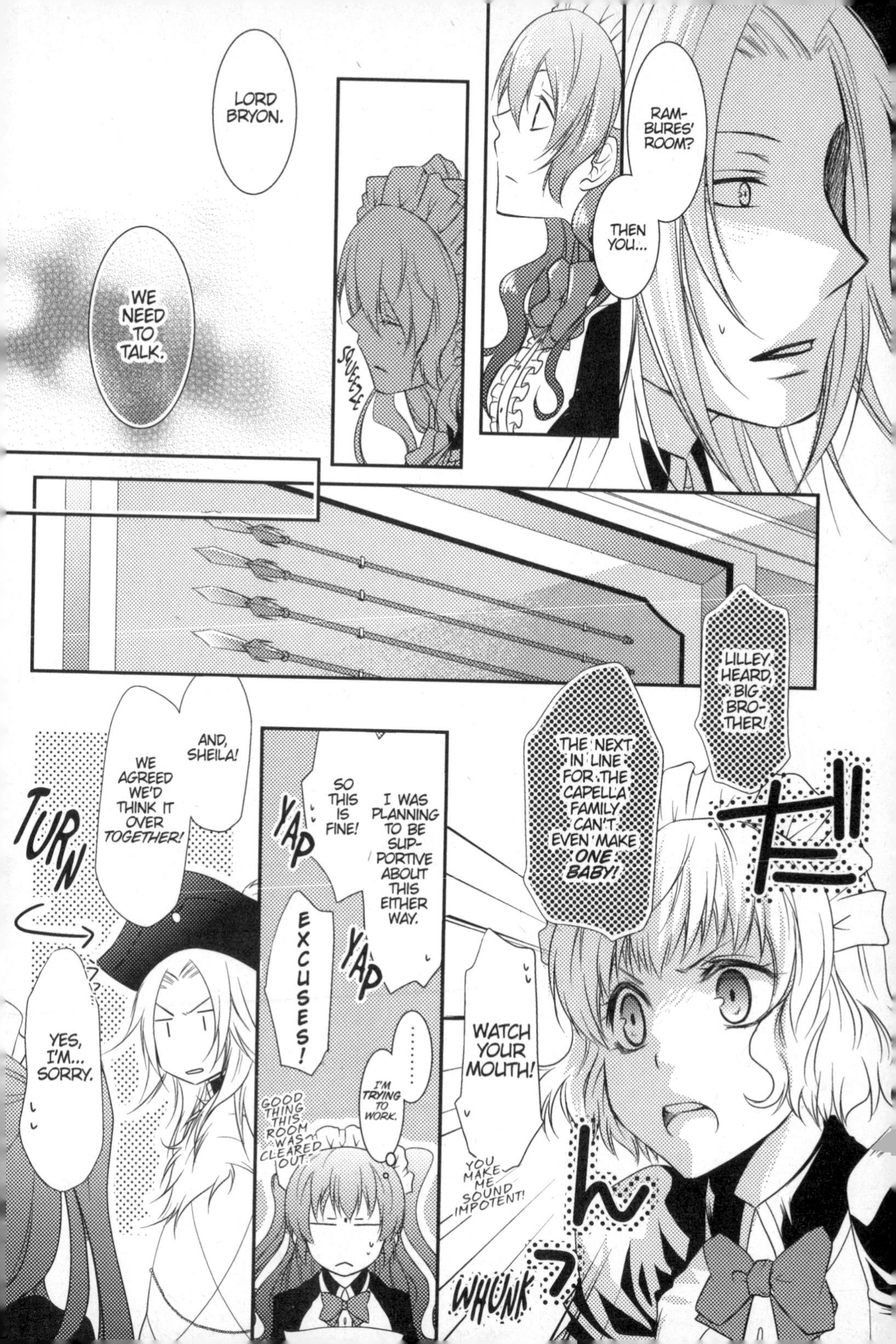
RAM-BURES' ROOM?
THEN YOU...
SQUEEZE
LORD BRYON.
WE NEED TO TALK.
LILLEY HEARD, BIG BROTHER!
THE NEXT IN LINE FOR THE CAPELLA FAMILY CAN'T EVEN MAKE ONE BABY!
WATCH YOUR MOUTH!
YOU MAKE ME SOUND IMPOTENT!
WHUNK
I WAS PLANNING TO BE SUP-PORTIVE ABOUT THIS EITHER WAY.
SO THIS IS FINE!
YAP
YAP
EXCUSES!
......
I'M TRYING TO WORK.
GOOD THING THIS ROOM WAS CLEARED OUT.
AND, SHEILA!
WE AGREED WE'D THINK IT OVER TOGETHER!
TURN
YES, I'M... SORRY.

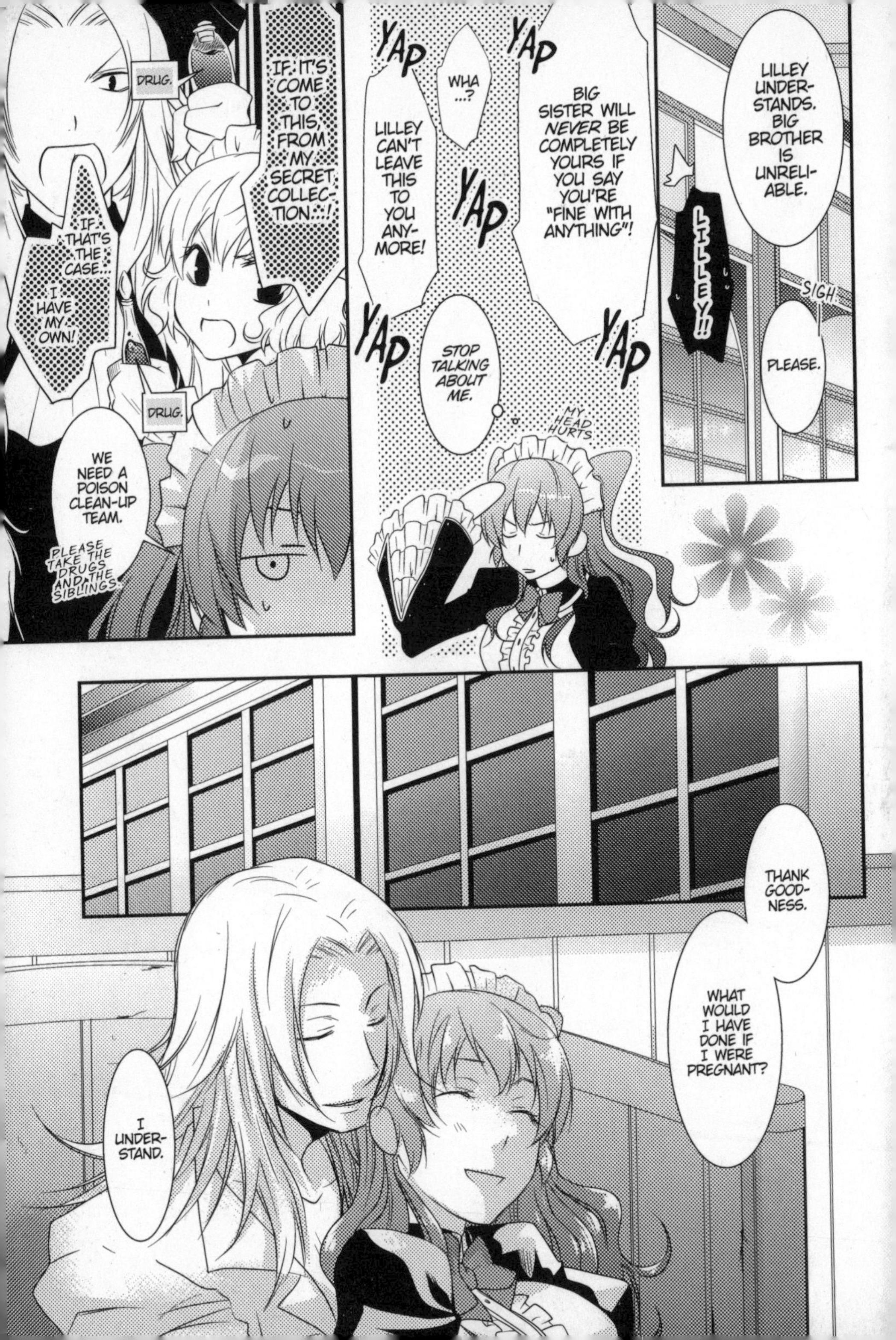
LILLEY UNDER-STANDS. BIG BROTHER IS UNRELI-ABLE.
LILLEY!!
SIGH.
PLEASE.
YAP
YAP
BIG SISTER WILL NEVER BE COMPLETELY YOURS IF YOU SAY YOU'RE "FINE WITH ANYTHING"!
WHA ...?
LILLEY CAN'T LEAVE THIS TO YOU ANYMORE!
YAP
YAP
YAP
STOP TALKING ABOUT ME.
MY HEAD HURTS
IF IT'S COME TO THIS, FROM MY SECRET COLLECTION...!
DRUG.
IF THAT'S THE CASE... I HAVE MY OWN!
DRUG.
WE NEED A POISON CLEAN-UP TEAM.
PLEASE TAKE THE DRUGS AND THE SIBLINGS.
THANK GOOD-NESS.
WHAT WOULD I HAVE DONE IF I WERE PREGNANT?
I UNDER-STAND.

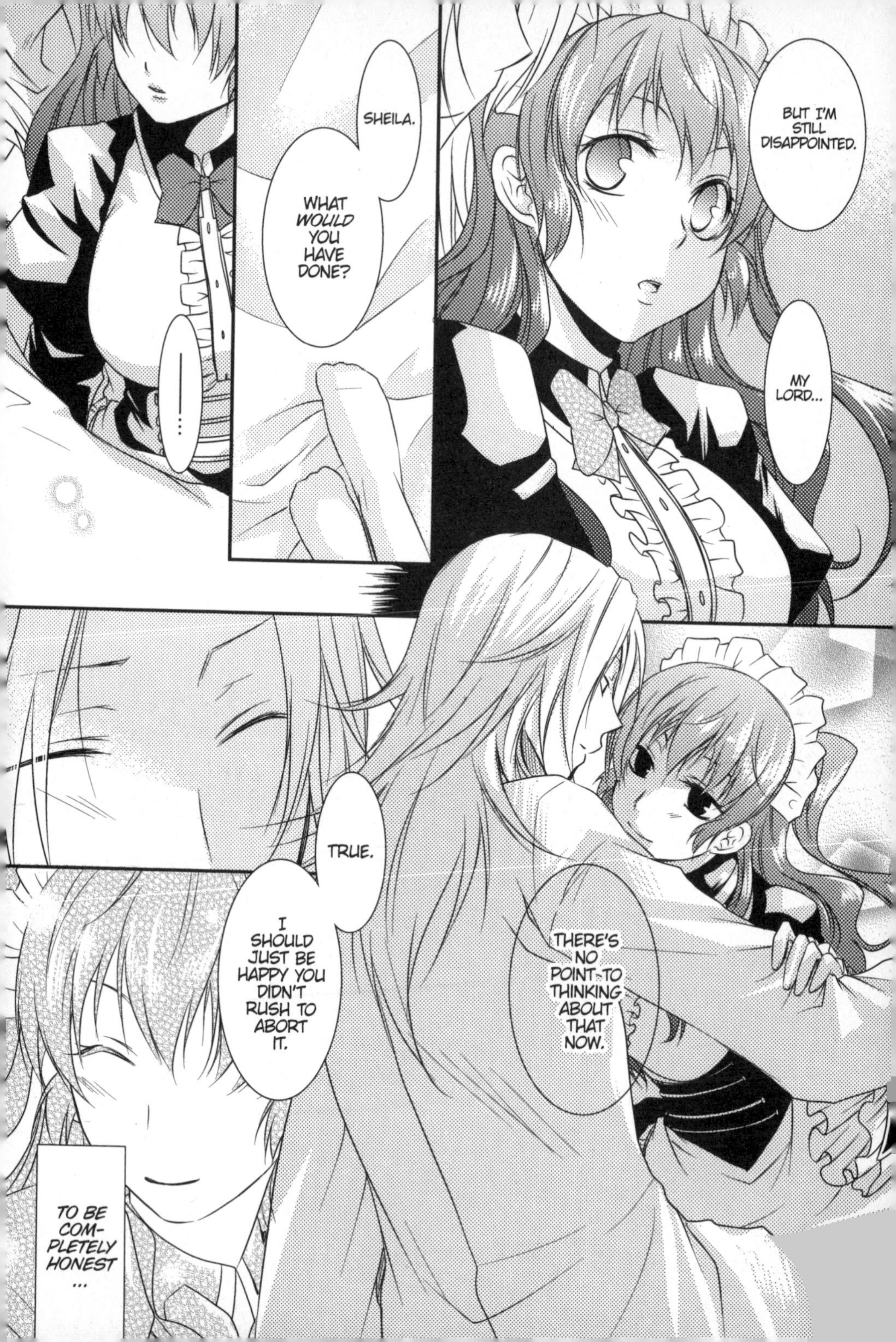
BUT I'M STILL DISAPPOINTED.
MY LORD...
SHEILA.
WHAT WOULD YOU HAVE DONE?
......
THERE'S NO POINT TO THINKING ABOUT THAT NOW.
TRUE.
I SHOULD JUST BE HAPPY YOU DIDN'T RUSH TO ABORT IT.
TO BE COMPLETELY HONEST ...

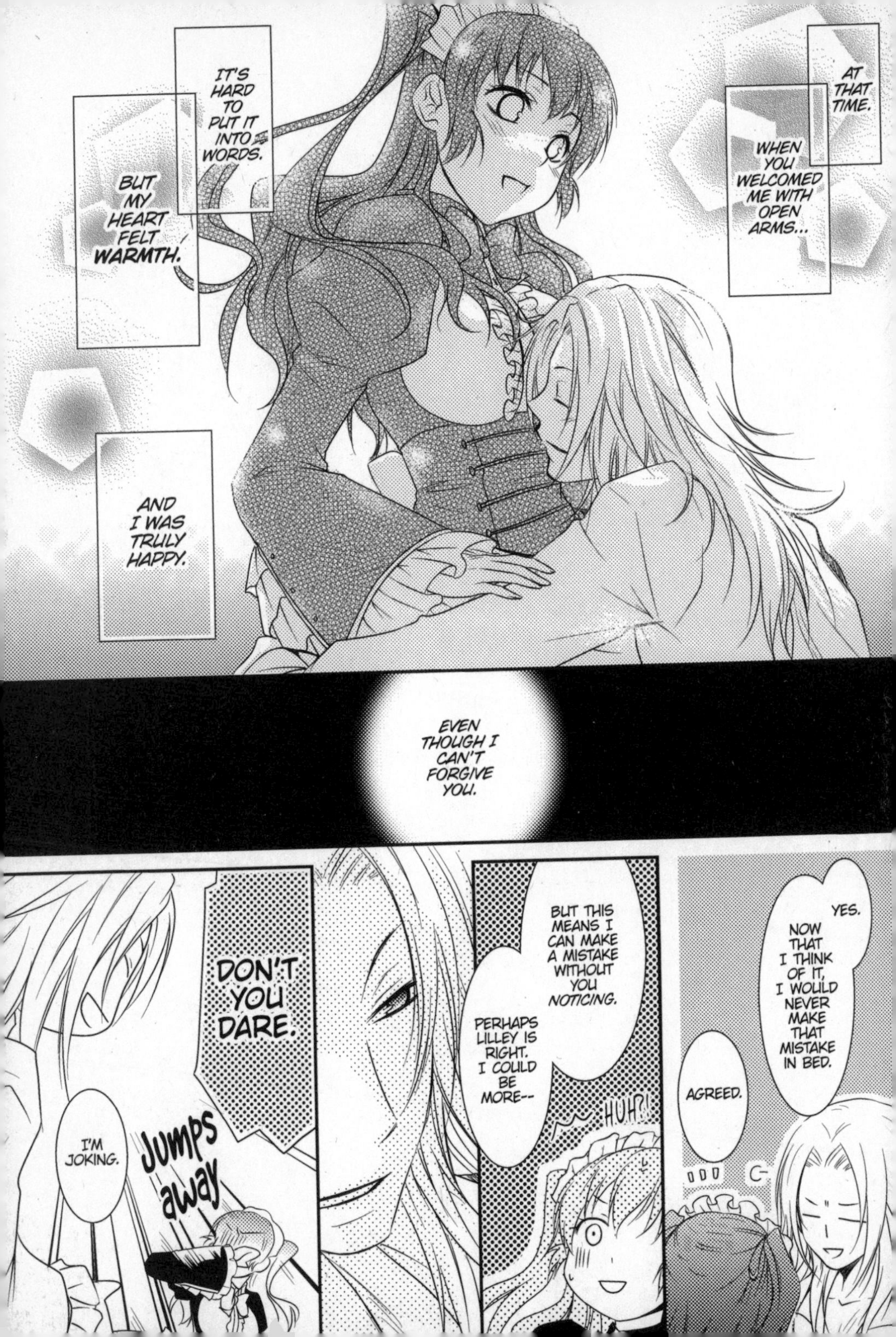

AT THAT TIME.
WHEN YOU WELCOMED ME WITH OPEN ARMS...
IT'S HARD TO PUT IT INTO WORDS.
BUT MY HEART FELT WARMTH.
AND I WAS TRULY HAPPY.
EVEN THOUGH I CAN'T FORGIVE YOU.
YES. NOW THAT I THINK OF IT, I WOULD NEVER MAKE THAT MISTAKE IN BED.
AGREED.
BUT THIS MEANS I CAN MAKE A MISTAKE WITHOUT YOU NOTICING.
PERHAPS LILLEY IS RIGHT. I COULD BE MORE--
HUH?!
DON'T YOU DARE.
Jumps away
I'M JOKING.

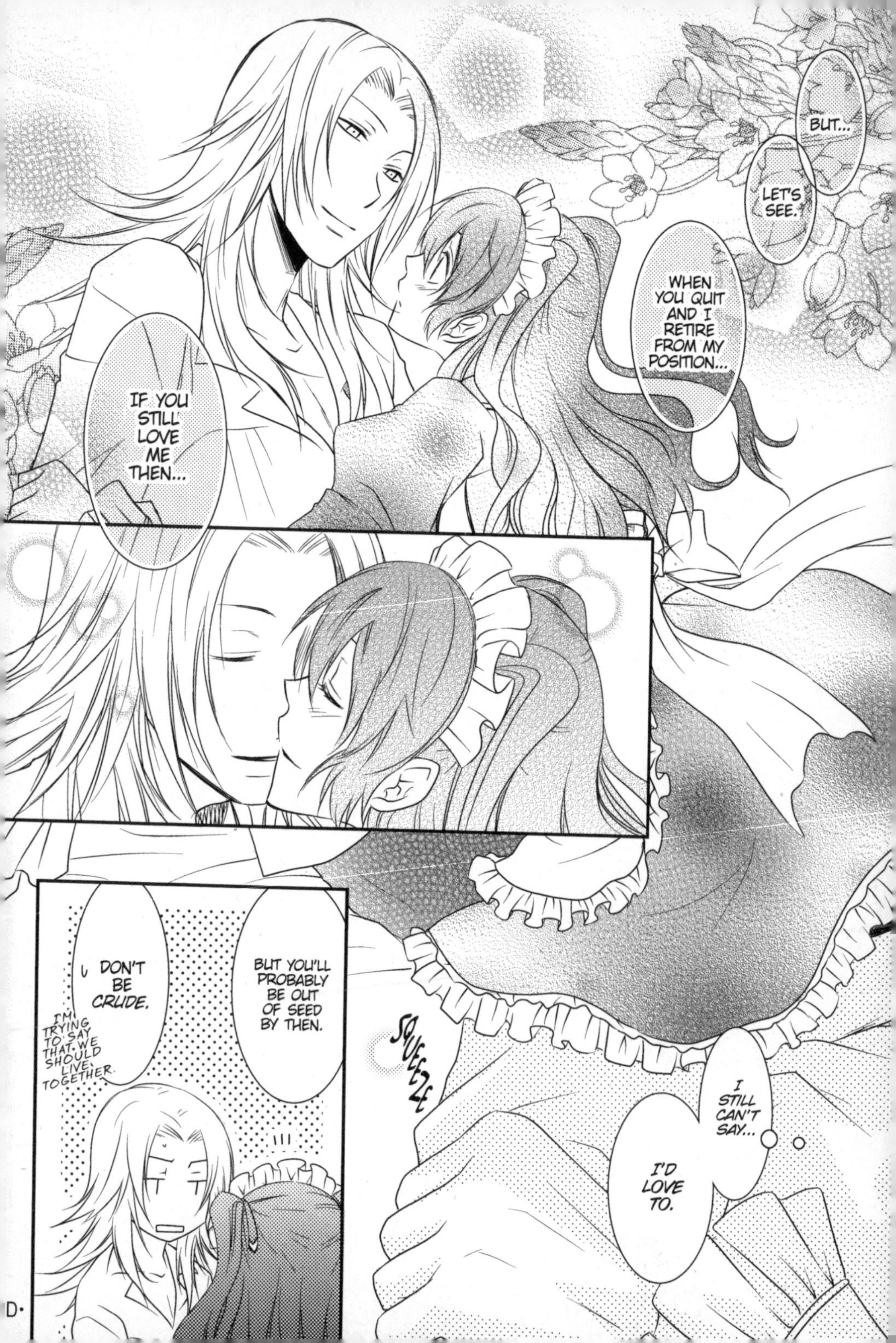
BUT...
LET'S SEE.
WHEN YOU QUIT AND I RETIRE FROM MY POSITION...
IF YOU STILL LOVE ME THEN...
I STILL CAN'T SAY...
I'D LOVE TO.
SQUEEZE
BUT YOU'LL PROBABLY BE OUT OF SEED BY THEN.
DON'T BE CRUDE.
I'M TRYING TO SAY THAT WE SHOULD LIVE TOGETHER.
!!!

A Small Conflict in Love Simulation Games That Use Affection Points.

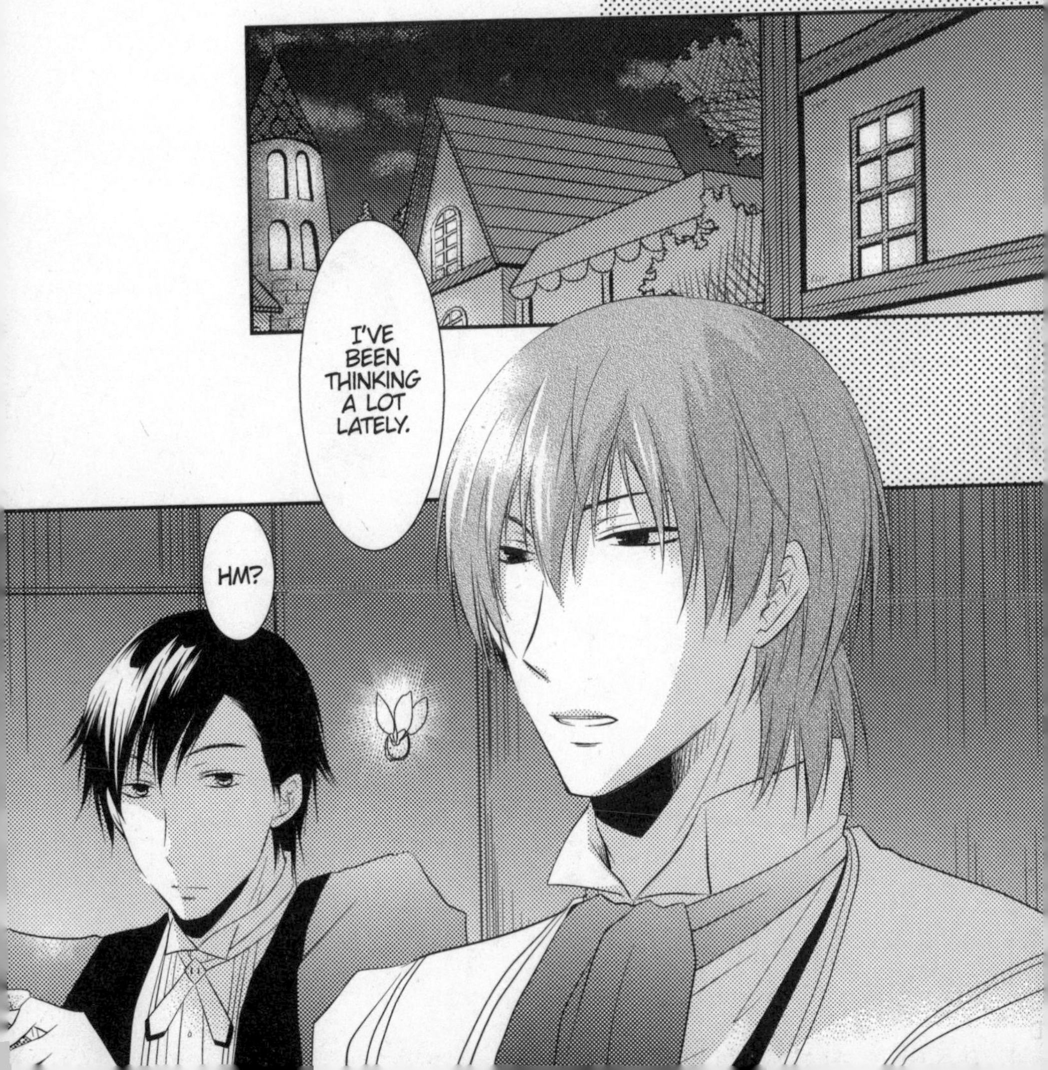
I'VE BEEN THINKING A LOT LATELY.
HM?

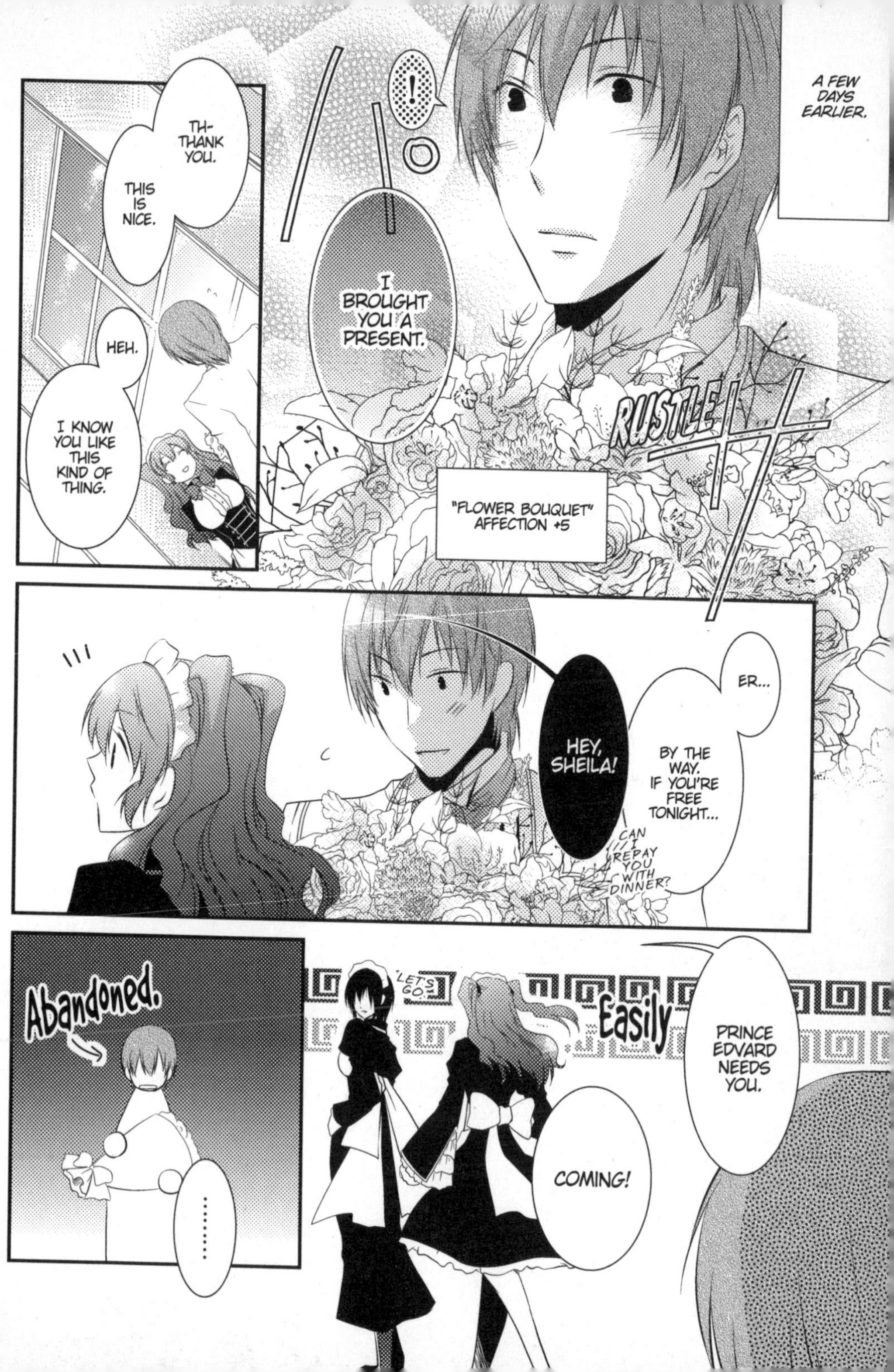
A FEW DAYS EARLIER.
!
I BROUGHT YOU A PRESENT.
RUSTLE
"FLOWER BOUQUET" AFFECTION +5
TH-THANK YOU.
THIS IS NICE.
HEH.
I KNOW YOU LIKE THIS KIND OF THING.
ER...
BY THE WAY. IF YOU'RE FREE TONIGHT...
CAN I REPAY YOU WITH DINNER?
HEY, SHEILA!
PRINCE EDVARD NEEDS YOU.
Easily
LET'S GO.
COMING!
Abandoned.
......

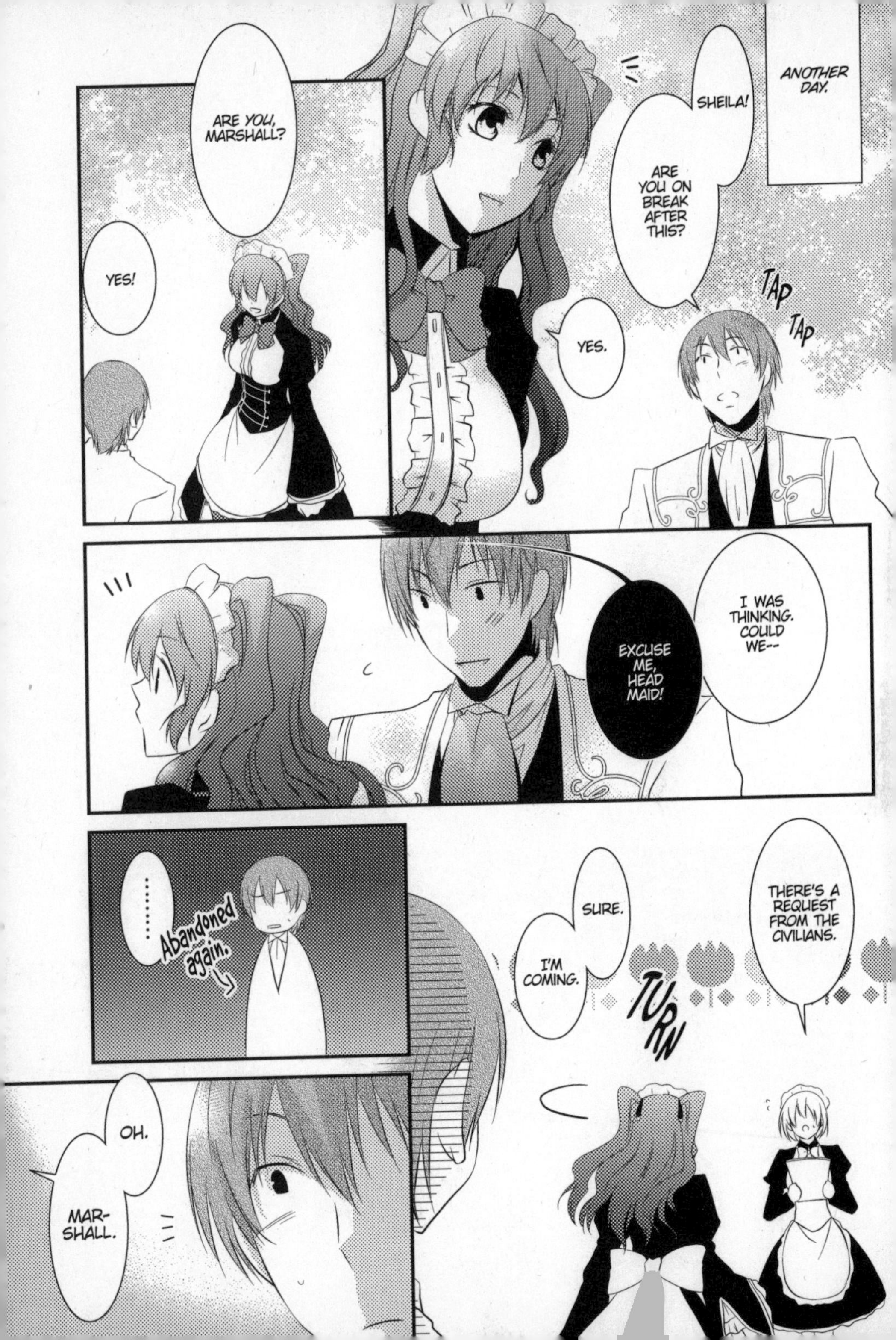
ANOTHER DAY.
SHEILA!
ARE YOU ON BREAK AFTER THIS?
TAP TAP
YES.
ARE YOU, MARSHALL?
YES!
I WAS THINKING. COULD WE--
EXCUSE ME, HEAD MAID!
THERE'S A REQUEST FROM THE CIVILIANS.
SURE.
I'M COMING.
TURN
....
Abandoned again.
OH.
MAR-SHALL.

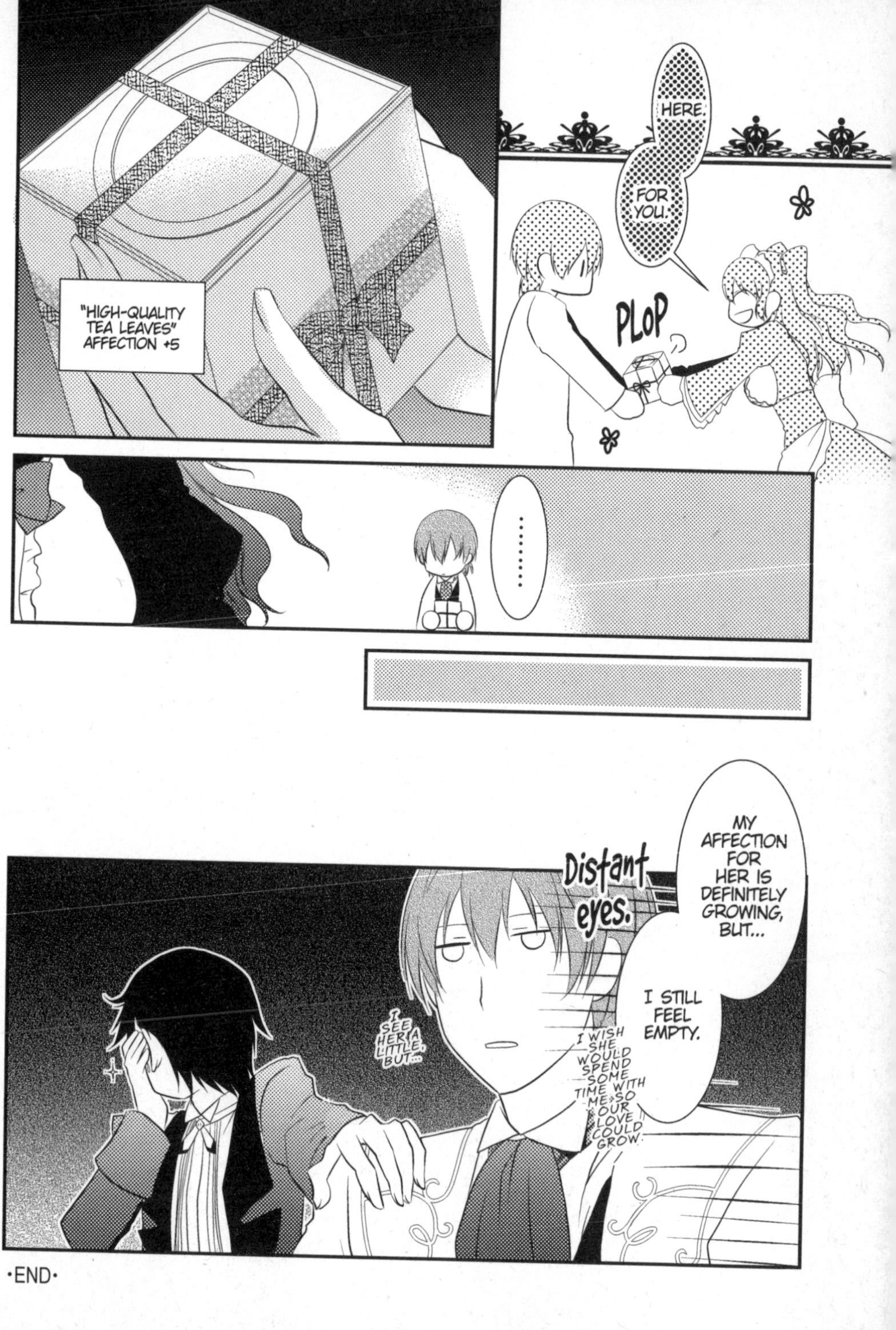
HERE.
FOR YOU.
PLOP
"HIGH-QUALITY TEA LEAVES" AFFECTION +5
....
MY AFFECTION FOR HER IS DEFINITELY GROWING, BUT...
I STILL FEEL EMPTY.
Distant eyes.
I WISH SHE WOULD SPEND SOME TIME WITH ME SO OUR LOVE COULD GROW.
I SEE HER A LITTLE, BUT...

•END•

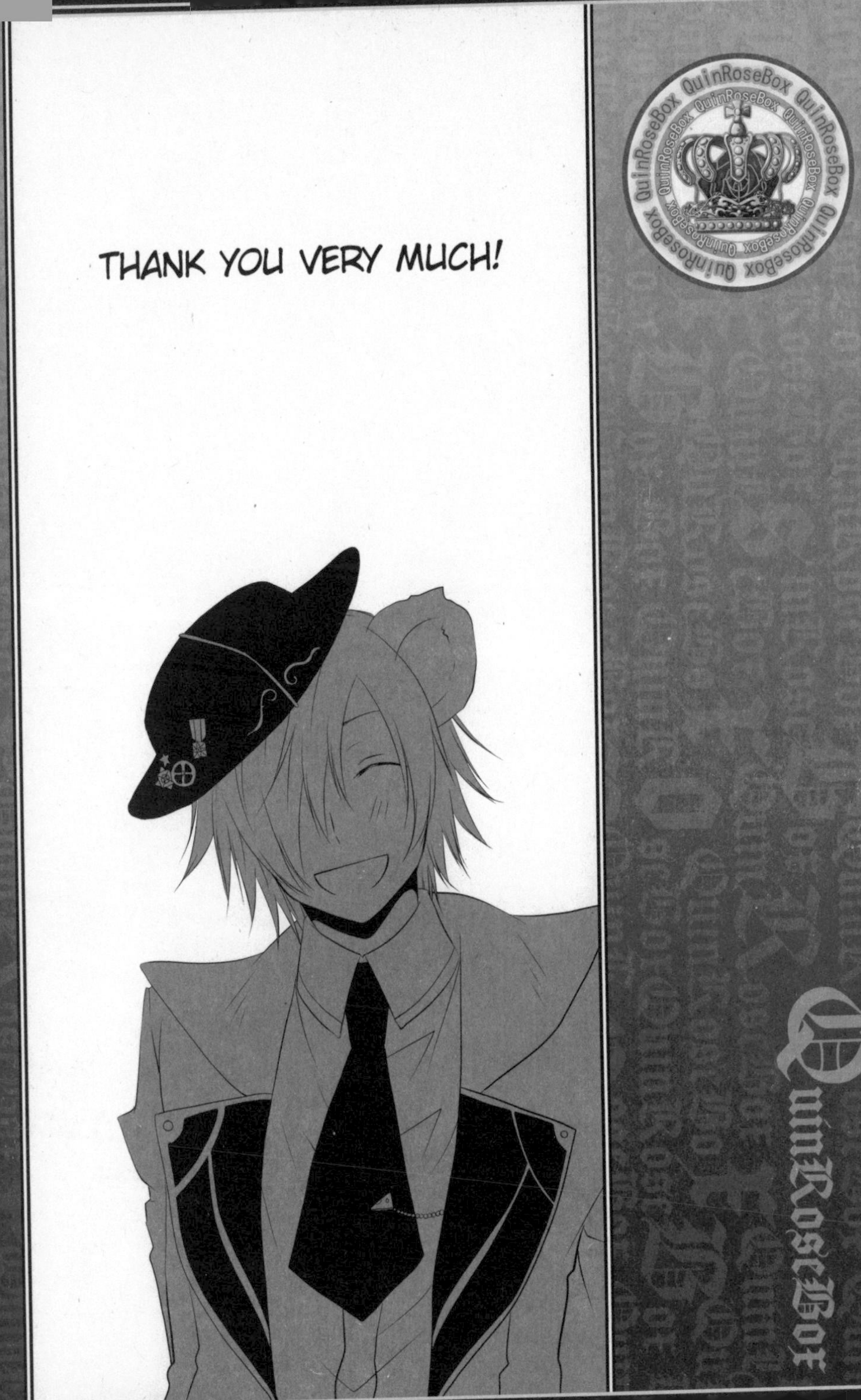
THANK YOU VERY MUCH!
QuinRoseBox

AND NOW FOR AN *ACE OF HEARTS* OUTTAKE...

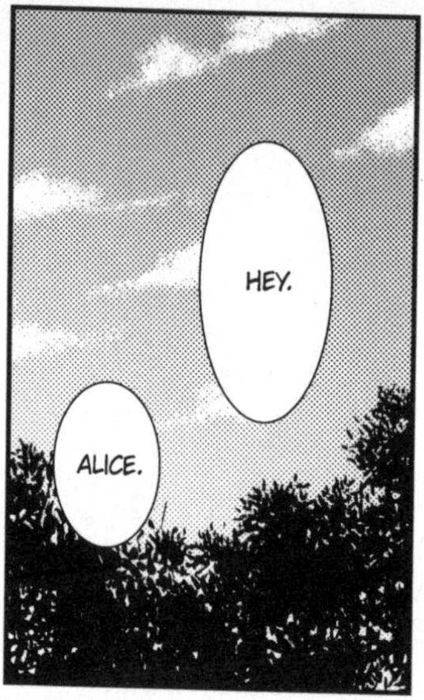
HEY.
ALICE.

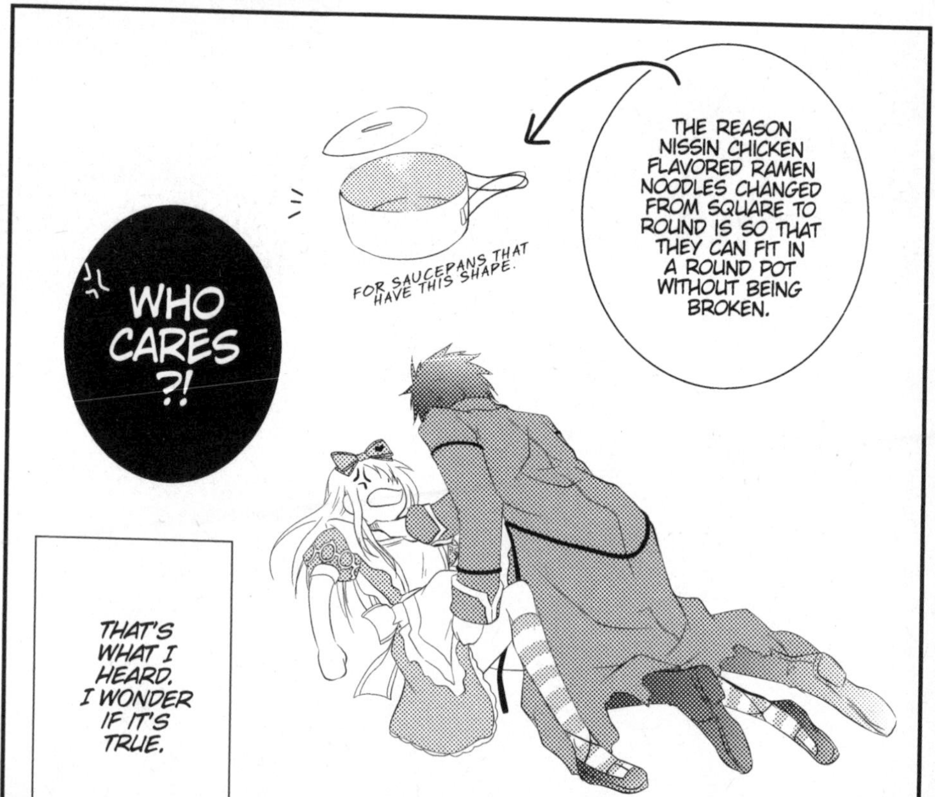
THE REASON NISSIN CHICKEN FLAVORED RAMEN NOODLES CHANGED FROM SQUARE TO ROUND IS SO THAT THEY CAN FIT IN A ROUND POT WITHOUT BEING BROKEN.
FOR SAUCEPANS THAT HAVE THIS SHAPE.
WHO CARES ?!
THAT'S WHAT I HEARD. I WONDER IF IT'S TRUE.

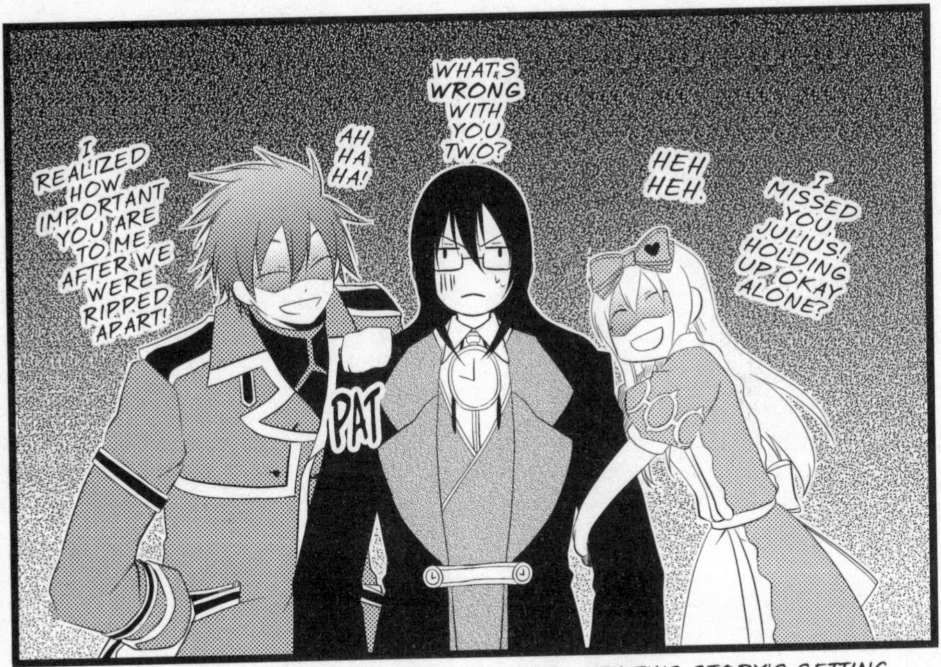
I MISSED YOU, JULIUS! HOLDING UP OKAY ALONE?
HEH HEH.
WHAT'S WRONG WITH YOU TWO?
AH HA HA!
I REALIZED HOW IMPORTANT YOU ARE TO ME AFTER WE WERE RIPPED APART!
PAT

IF THEY WENT TO THE COUNTRY OF JOKER WITH THIS STORY'S SETTING, THINGS WOULD GET DANGEROUS (FOR JULIUS).

Thank you to so many people!

You've really taken care of me.
QuinRose-sama

Thank you for your help!
Assistant-sama

Thank you for everything.
Friends and Acquaintances

And most importantly,
everyone who picks up this
book is supporting me.
The Readers

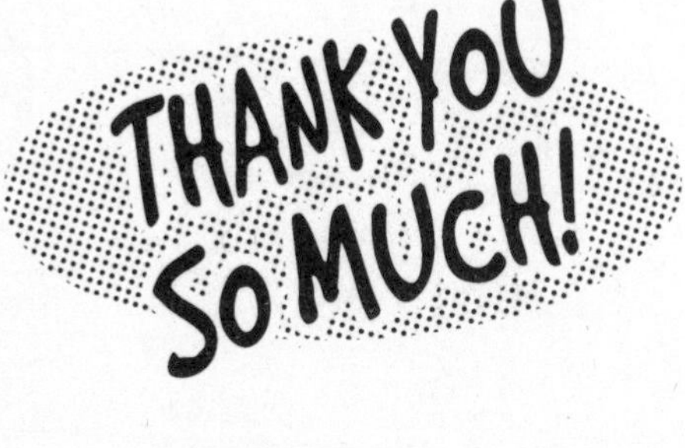
THANK YOU SO MUCH!

COMING SOON

JULY 2013

Alice in the Country of Clover:
Cheshire Cat Waltz Vol. 5

AUGUST 2013

Alice in the Country of Clover:
The Clockmaker's Story

Crimson Empire Vol. 2

SEPTEMBER 2013

Alice in the Country of Clover:
Cheshire Cat Waltz Vol. 6

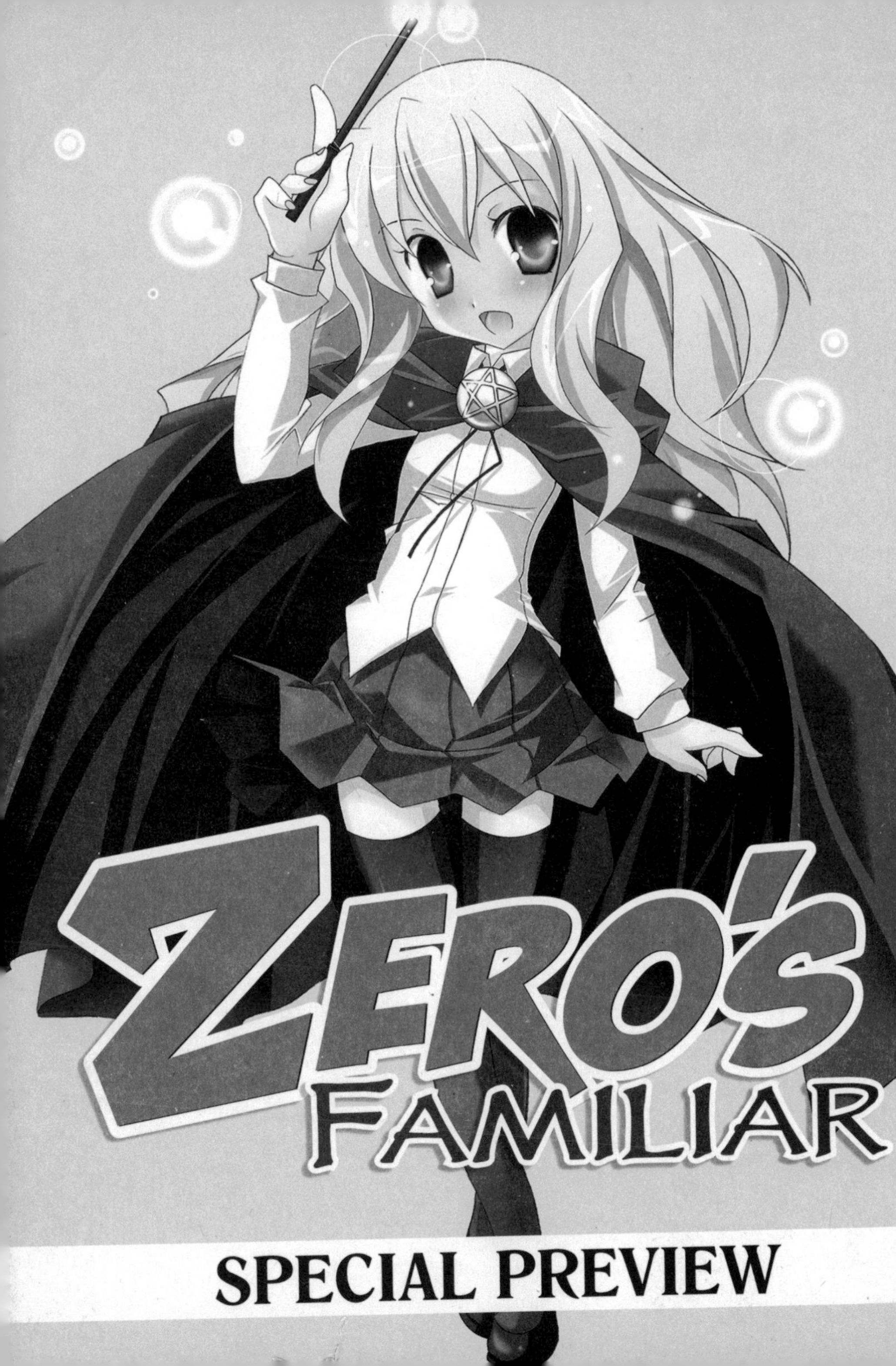
ZERO'S
FAMILIAR
SPECIAL PREVIEW

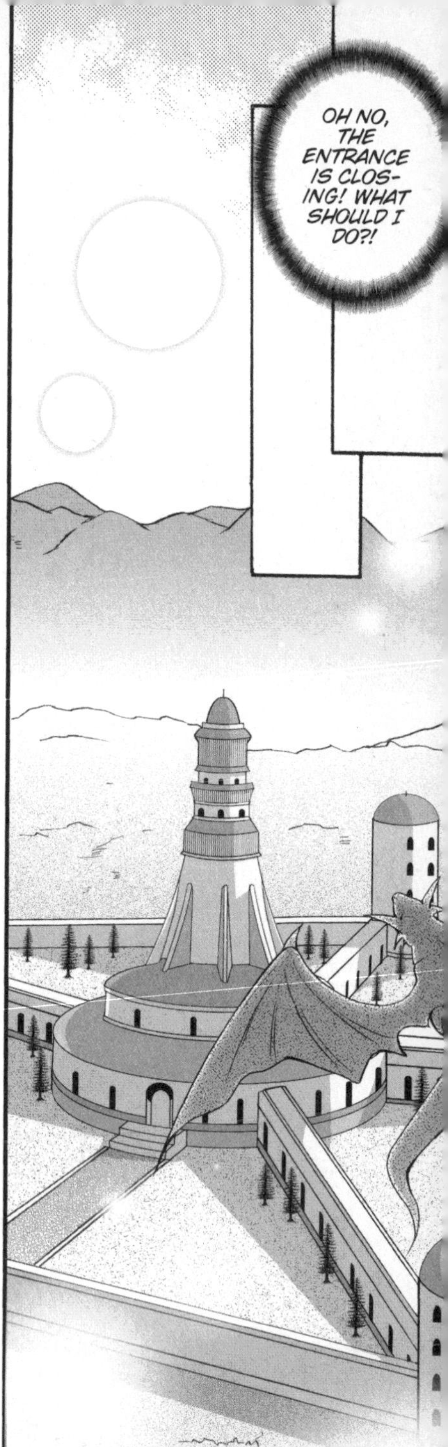
OH NO, THE ENTRANCE IS CLOSING! WHAT SHOULD I DO?!
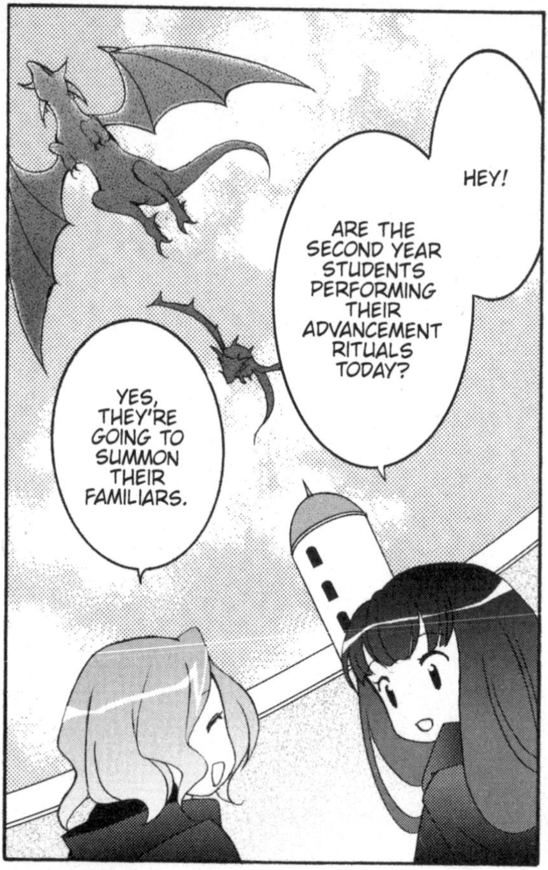
HEY!
ARE THE SECOND YEAR STUDENTS PERFORMING THEIR ADVANCEMENT RITUALS TODAY?
YES, THEY'RE GOING TO SUMMON THEIR FAMILIARS.
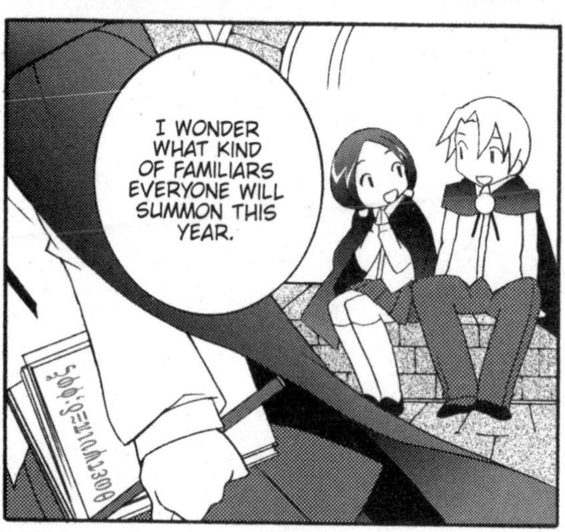
I WONDER WHAT KIND OF FAMILIARS EVERYONE WILL SUMMON THIS YEAR.

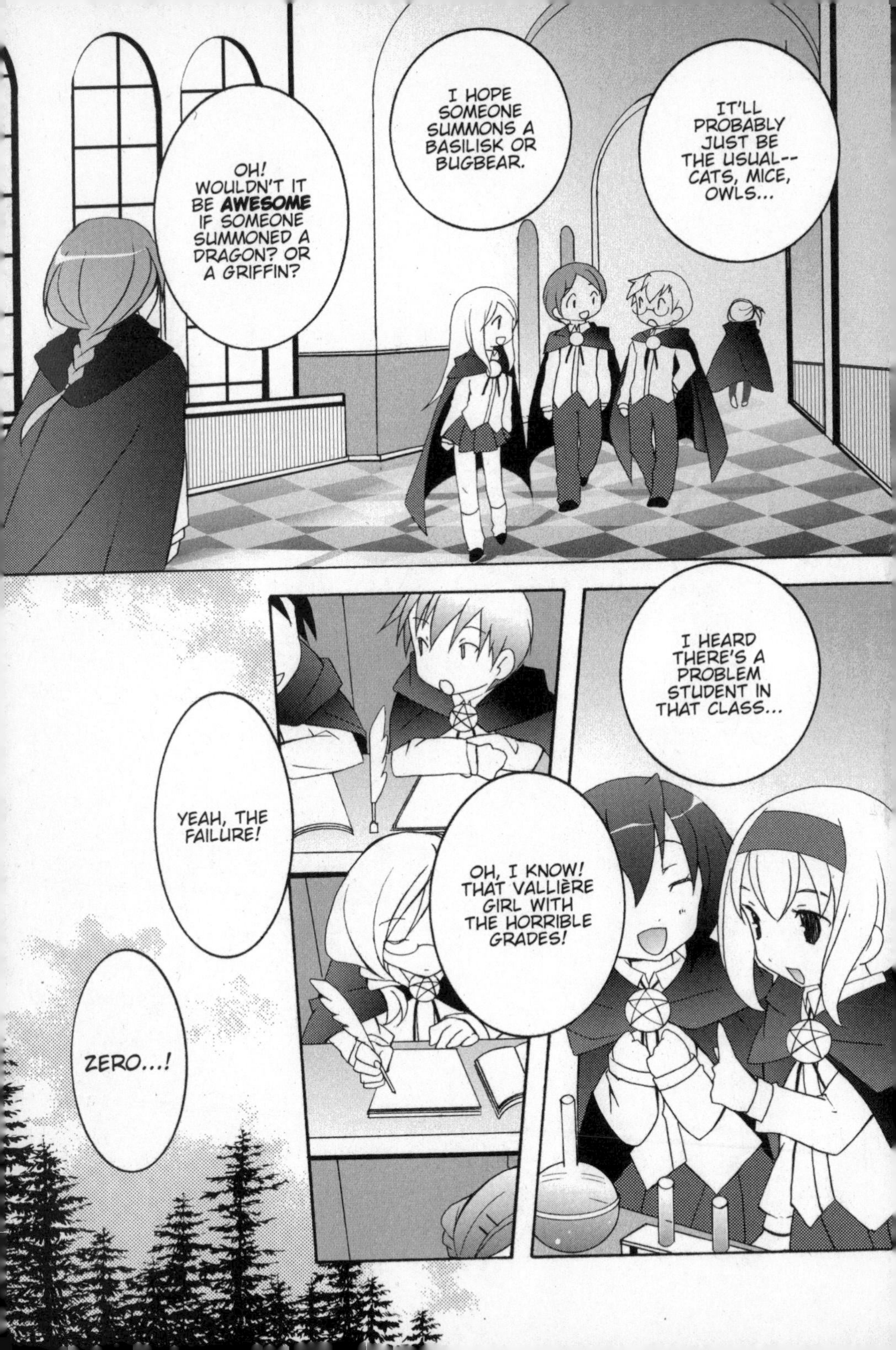
IT'LL PROBABLY JUST BE THE USUAL-- CATS, MICE, OWLS...
I HOPE SOMEONE SUMMONS A BASILISK OR BUGBEAR.
OH! WOULDN'T IT BE **AWESOME** IF SOMEONE SUMMONED A DRAGON? OR A GRIFFIN?
I HEARD THERE'S A PROBLEM STUDENT IN THAT CLASS...
OH, I KNOW! THAT VALLIÈRE GIRL WITH THE HORRIBLE GRADES!
YEAH, THE FAILURE!
ZERO...!

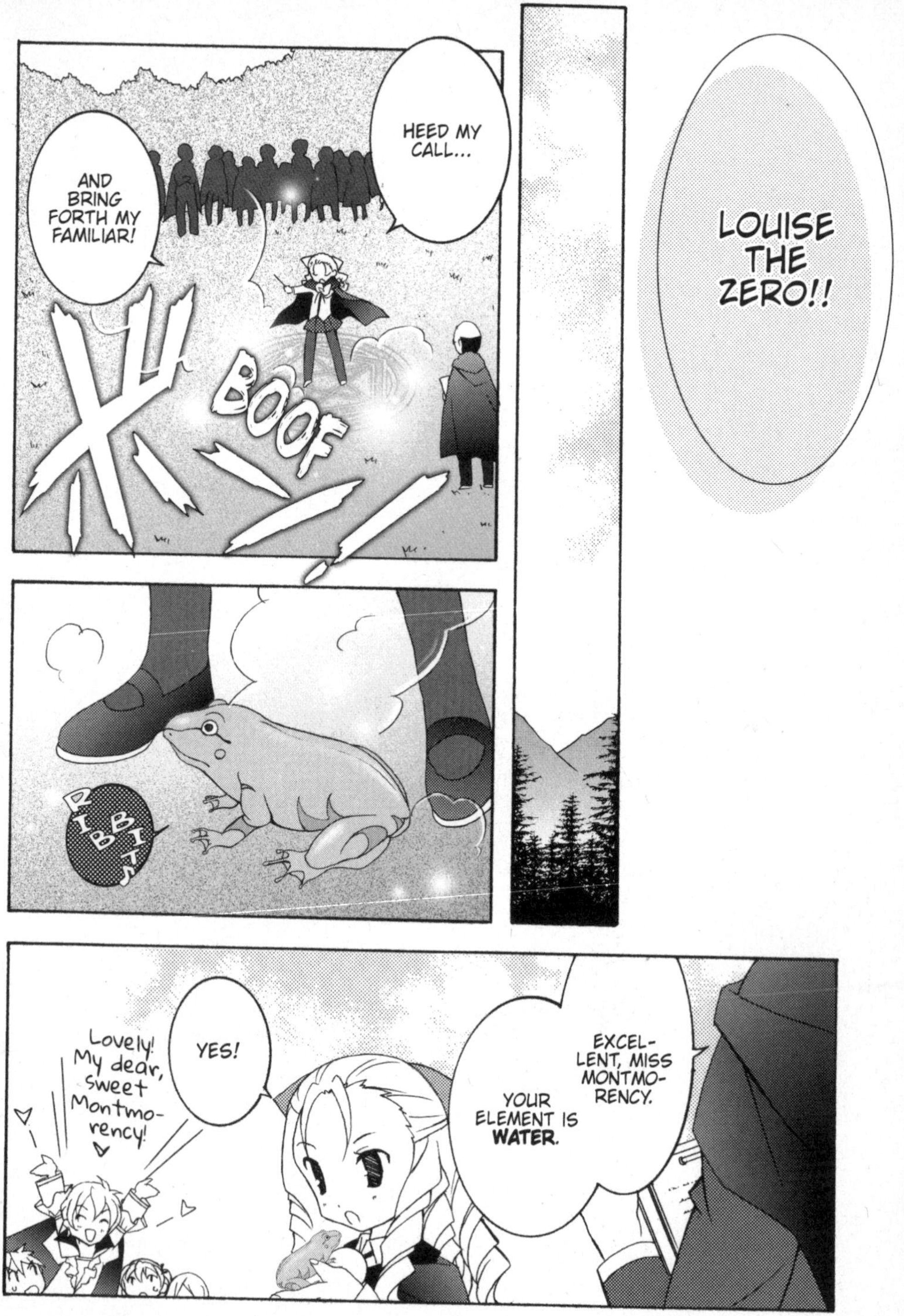
LOUISE THE ZERO!!
HEED MY CALL...
AND BRING FORTH MY FAMILIAR!
BOOF
RIBBIT♪
EXCEL-LENT, MISS MONTMO-RENCY.
YOUR ELEMENT IS **WATER**.
YES!
Lovely! My dear, sweet Montmo-rency!

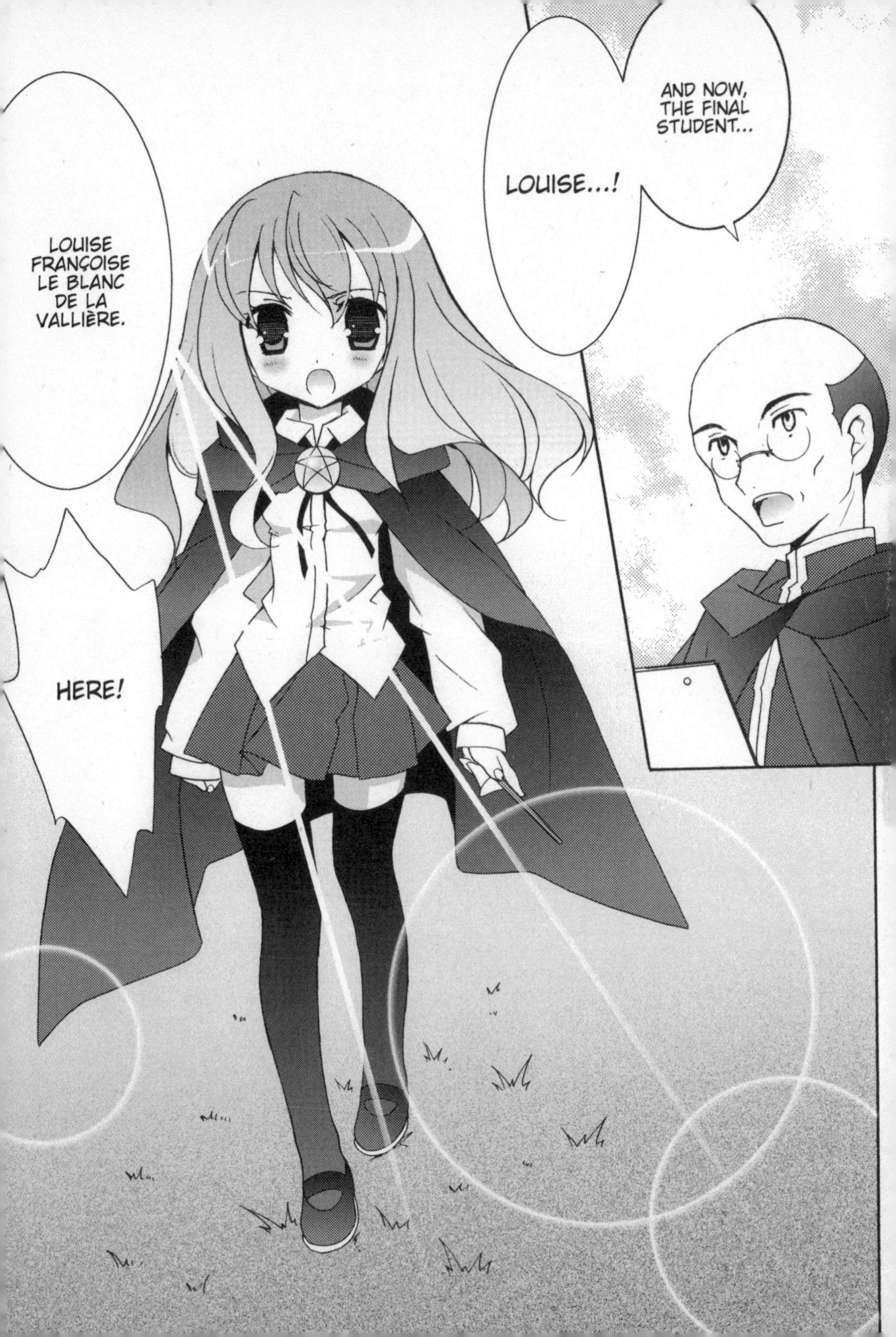
AND NOW, THE FINAL STUDENT...
LOUISE...!
LOUISE FRANÇOISE LE BLANC DE LA VALLIÈRE.
HERE!

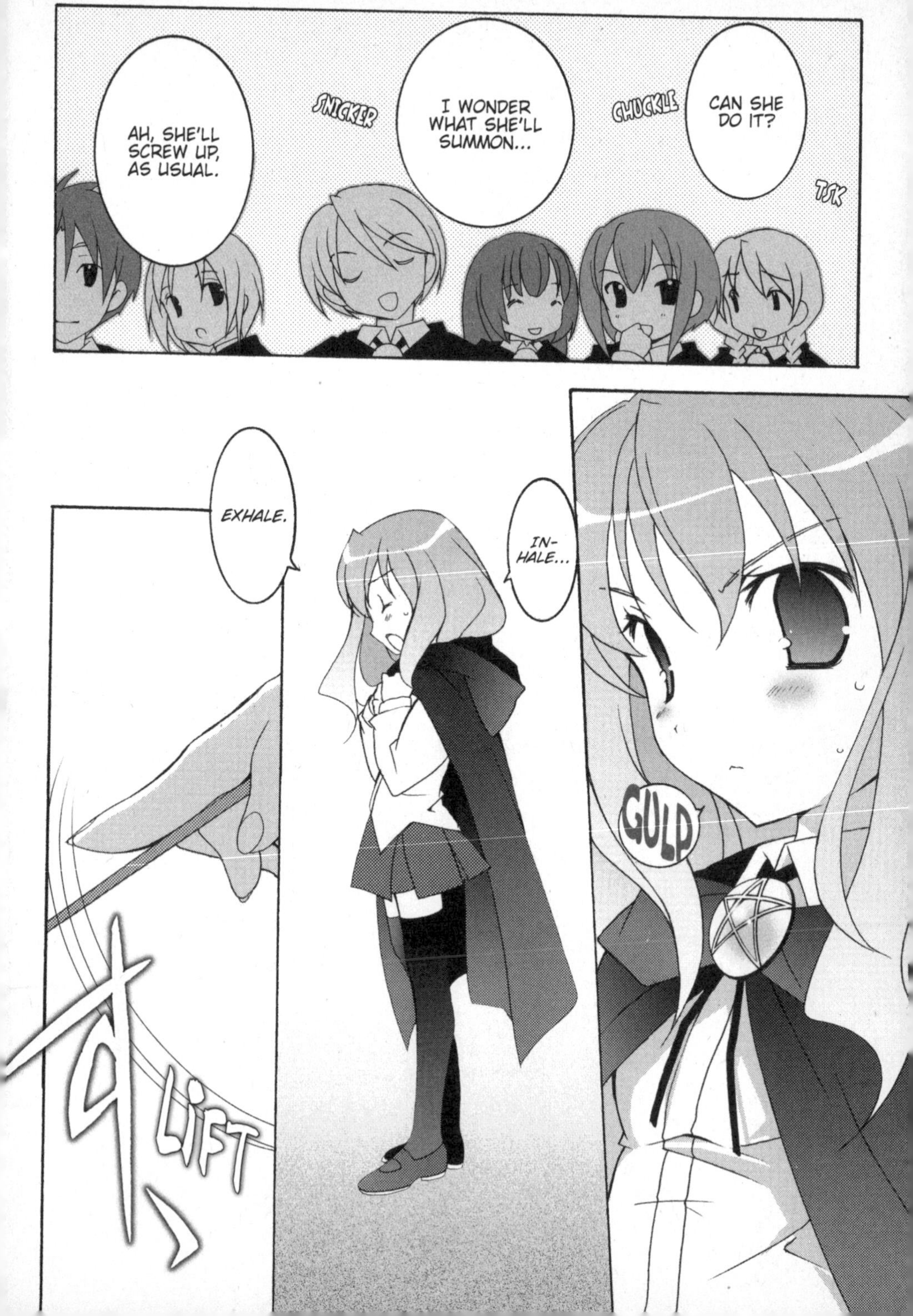
CAN SHE DO IT?
TSK
CHUCKLE
I WONDER WHAT SHE'LL SUMMON...
SNICKER
AH, SHE'LL SCREW UP, AS USUAL.
GULP
IN-HALE...
EXHALE.
LIFT

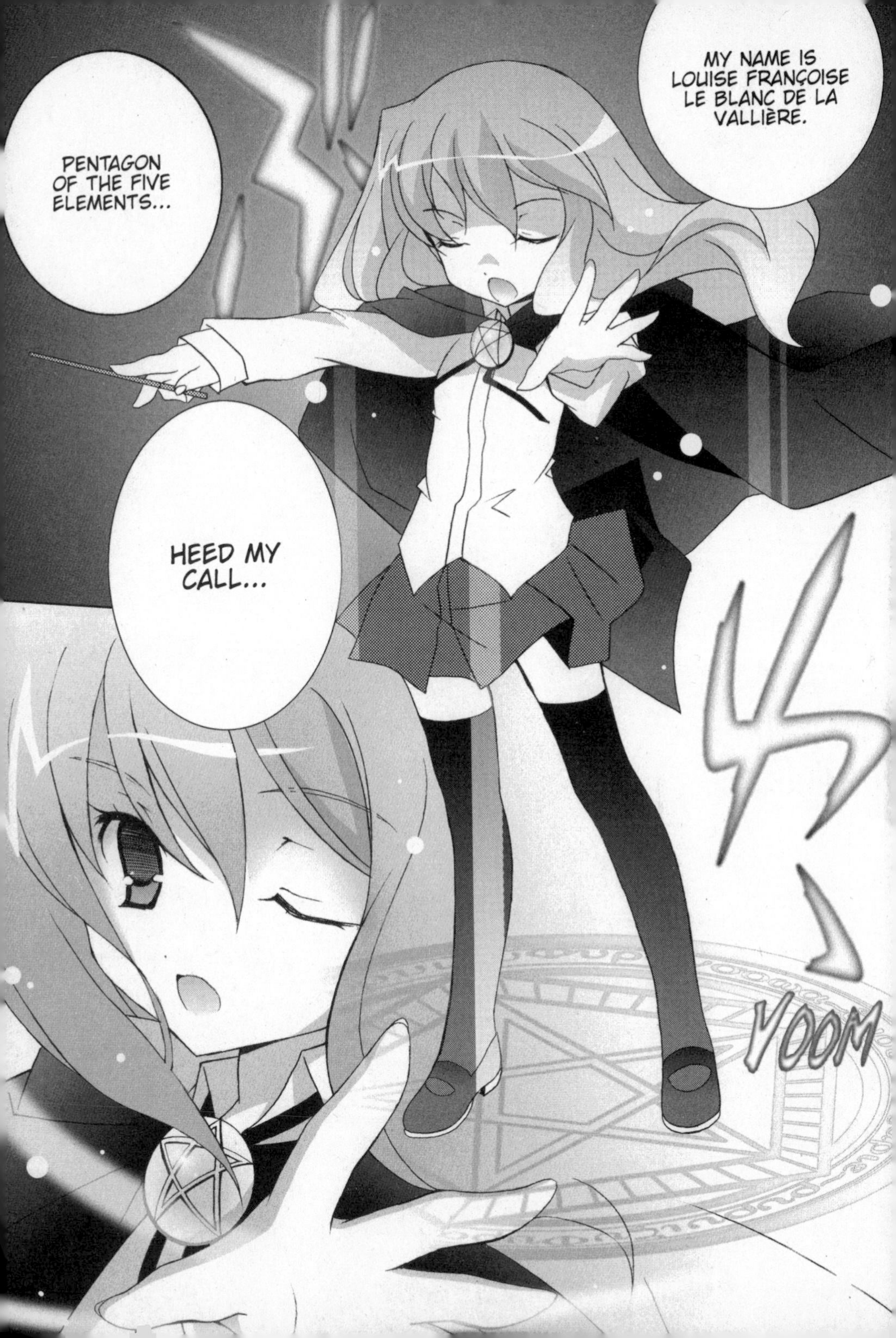
MY NAME IS LOUISE FRANÇOISE LE BLANC DE LA VALLIÈRE.
PENTAGON OF THE FIVE ELEMENTS...
HEED MY CALL...
VOOM

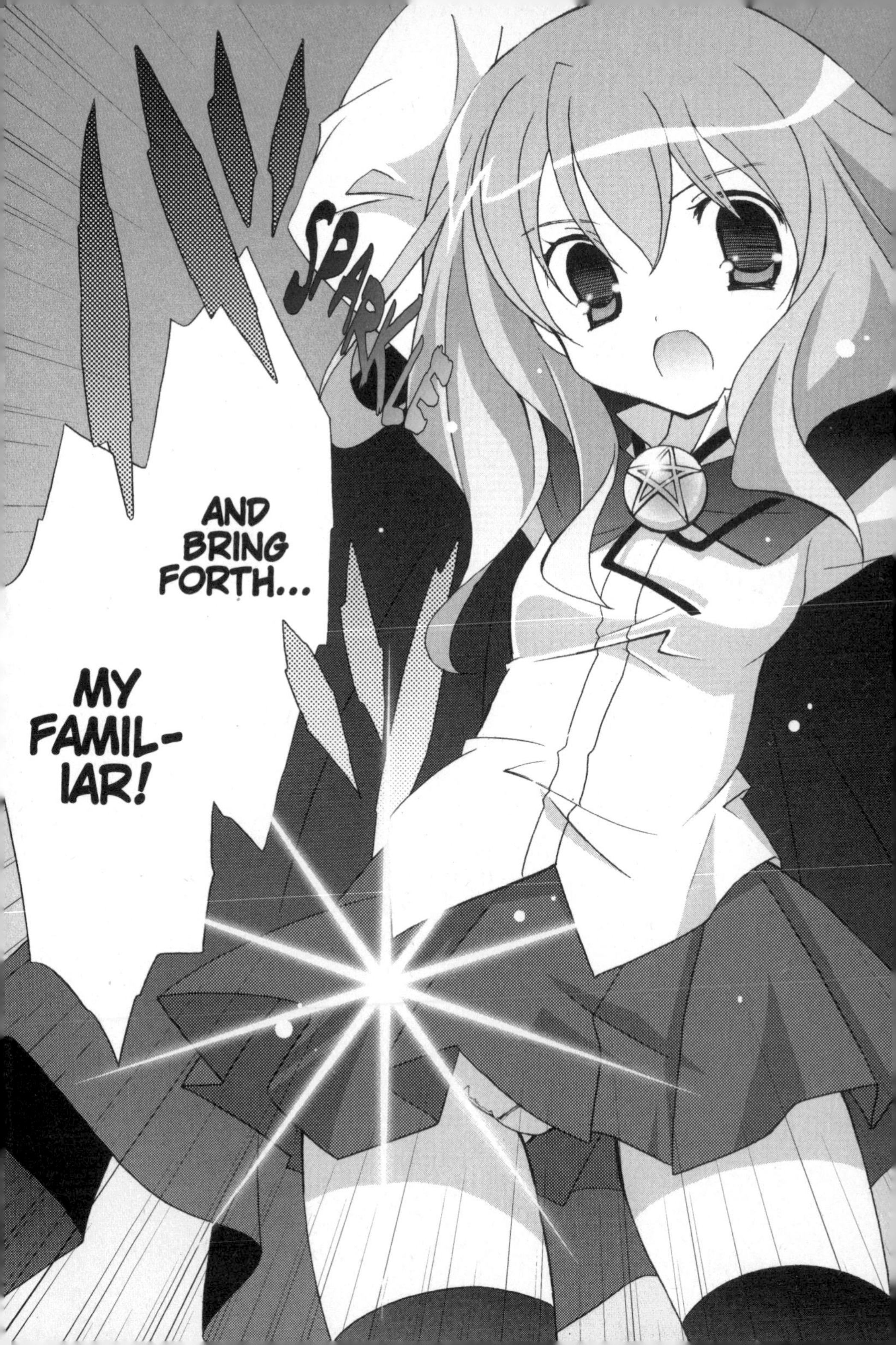
SPARKLE
AND BRING FORTH...
MY FAMIL-IAR!

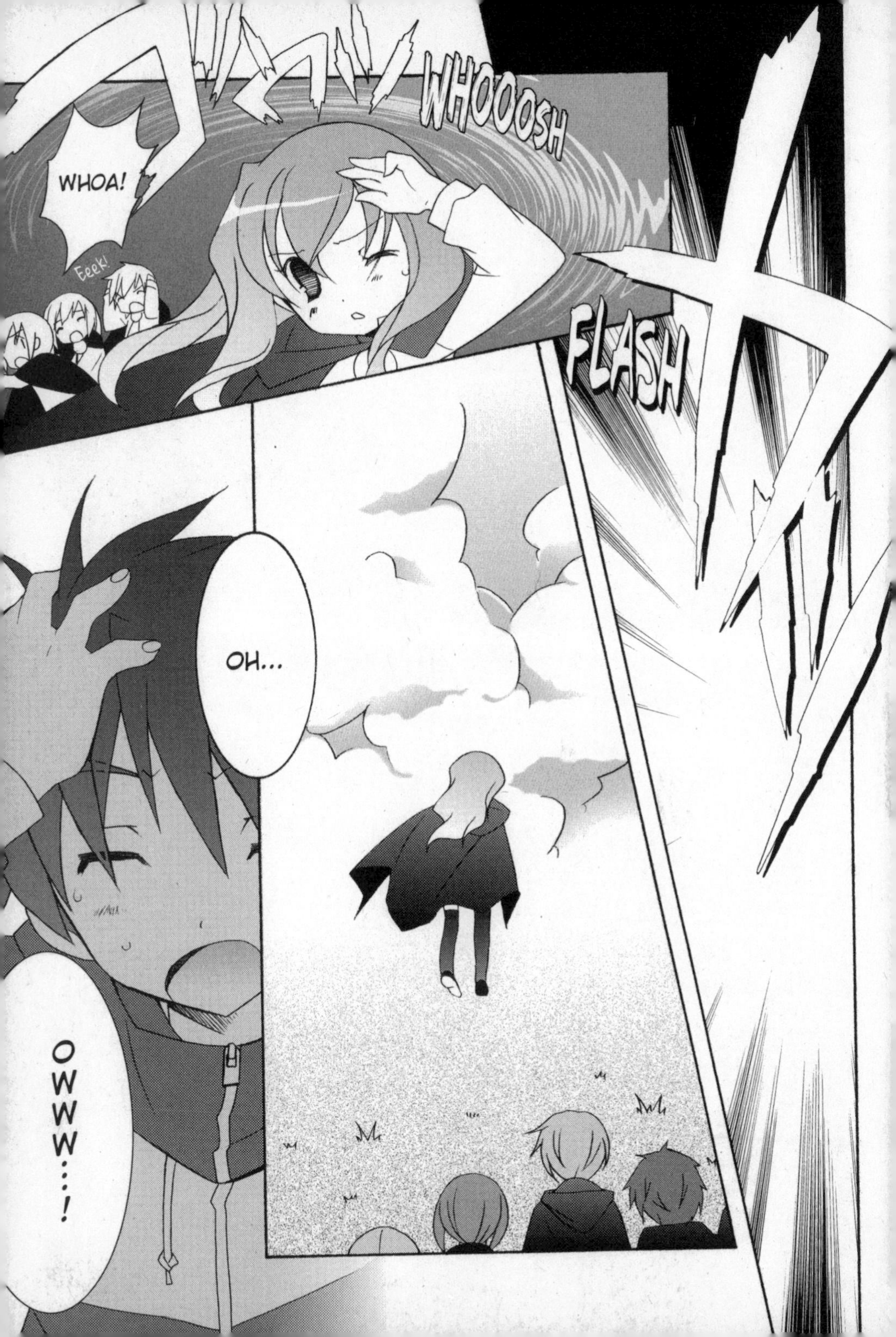
WHOOOSH
WHOA!
Eeek!
FLASH
OH...
OWWW...!

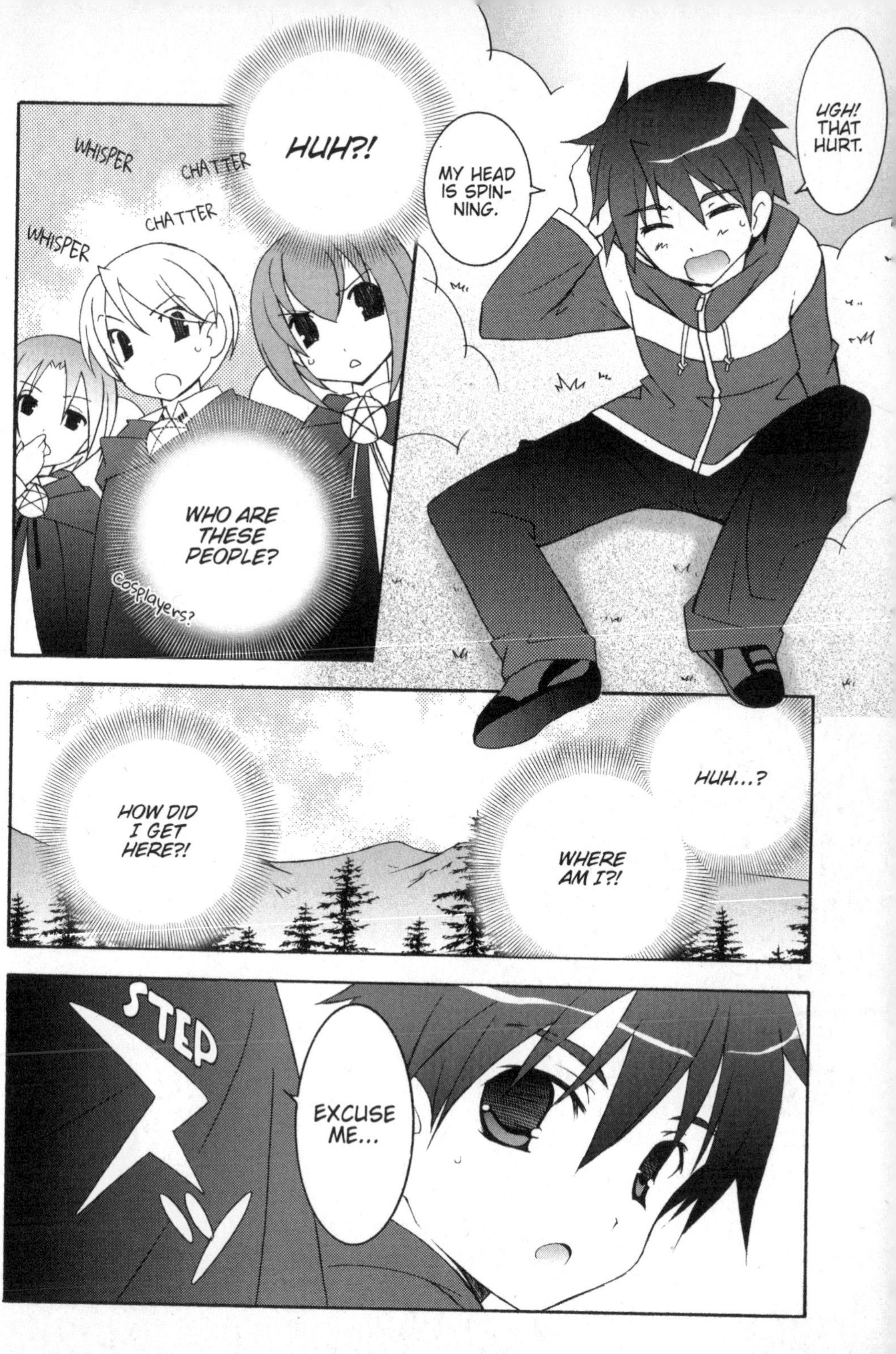
UGH! THAT HURT.
MY HEAD IS SPIN-NING.
HUH?!
CHATTER
WHISPER
CHATTER
WHISPER
WHO ARE THESE PEOPLE?
cosplayers?
HUH...?
WHERE AM I?!
HOW DID I GET HERE?!
STEP
EXCUSE ME...

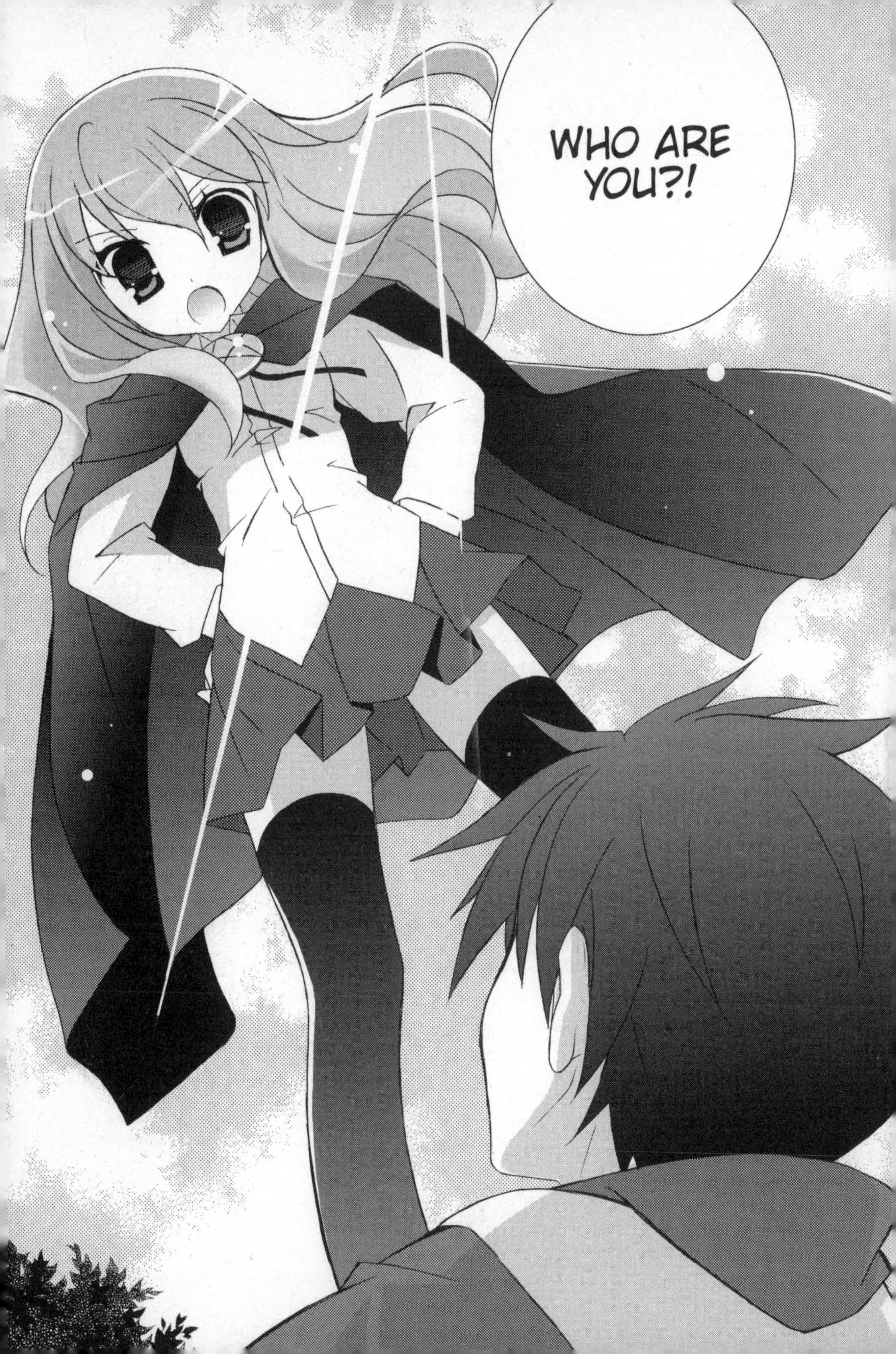
WHO ARE YOU?!

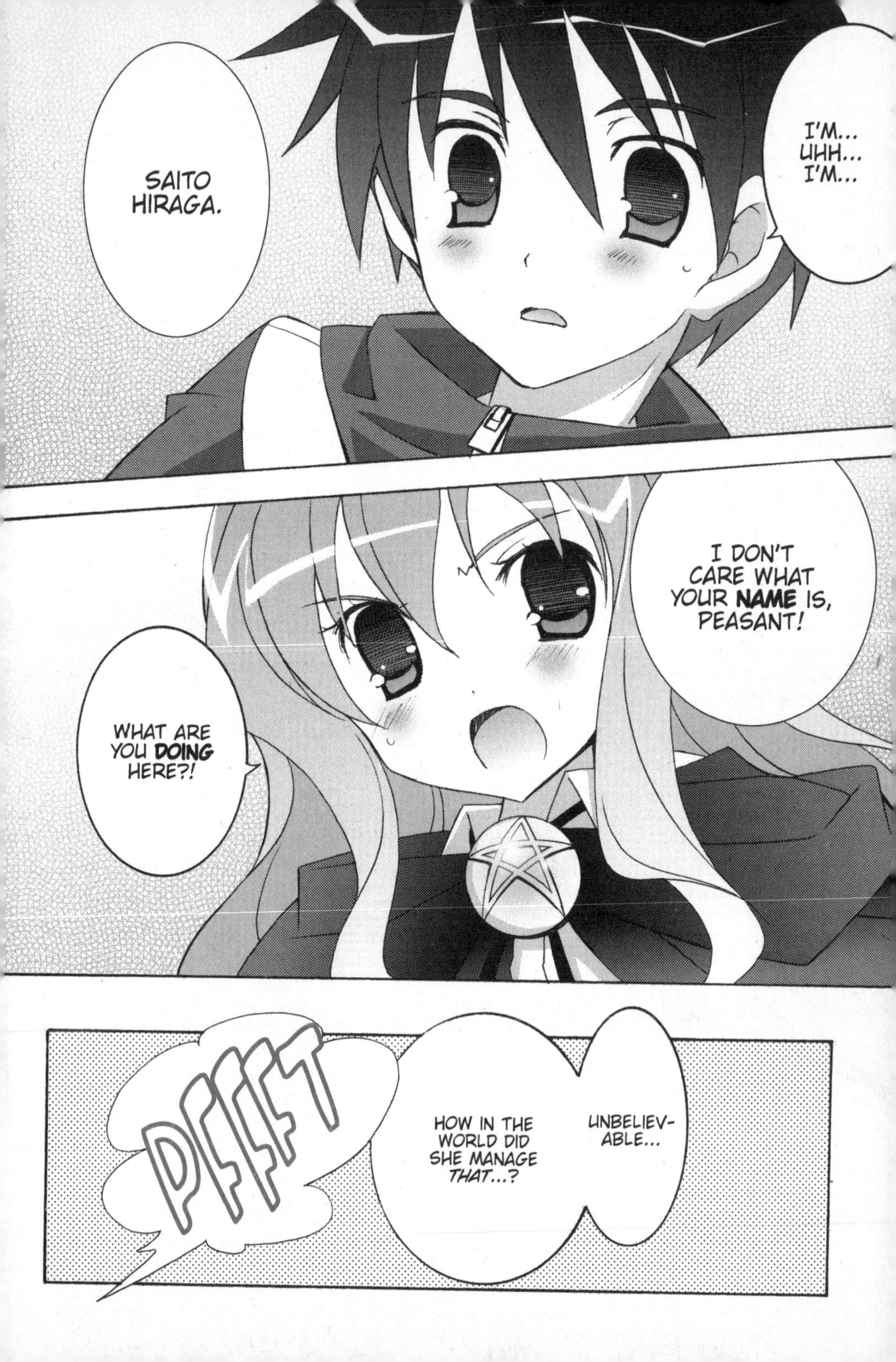
I'M... UHH... I'M...
SAITO HIRAGA.
I DON'T CARE WHAT YOUR **NAME** IS, PEASANT!
WHAT ARE YOU **DOING** HERE?!
UNBELIEV-ABLE...
HOW IN THE WORLD DID SHE MANAGE *THAT*...?
PFFFT

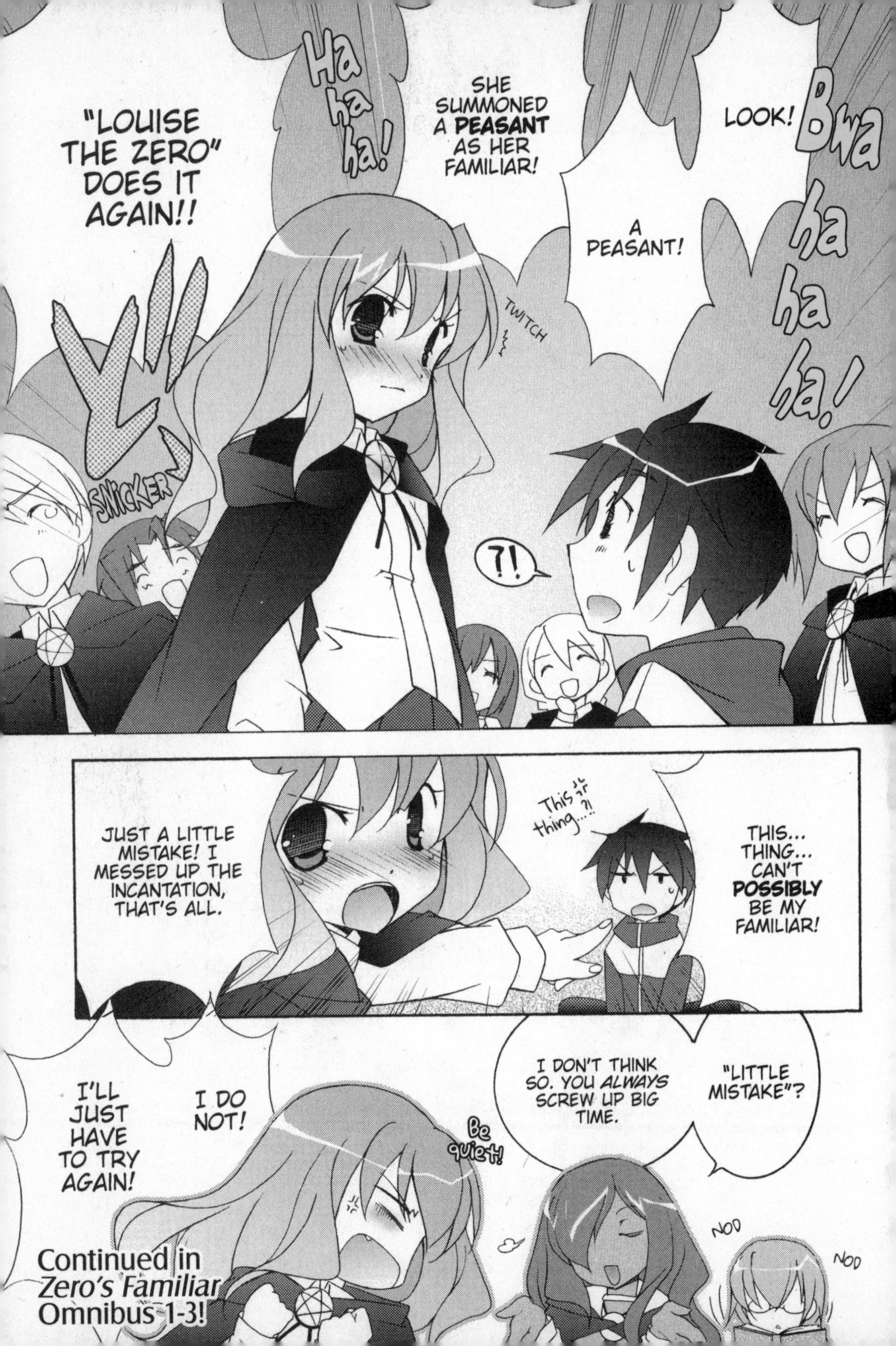
Bwa ha ha ha ha!
LOOK!
A PEASANT!
SHE SUMMONED A **PEASANT** AS HER FAMILIAR!
Ha ha ha!
"LOUISE THE ZERO" DOES IT AGAIN!!
TWITCH
SNICKER
?!
THIS... THING... CAN'T **POSSIBLY** BE MY FAMILIAR!
This thing...?!
JUST A LITTLE MISTAKE! I MESSED UP THE INCANTATION, THAT'S ALL.
"LITTLE MISTAKE"?
I DON'T THINK SO. YOU *ALWAYS* SCREW UP BIG TIME.
Be quiet!
I DO NOT!
I'LL JUST HAVE TO TRY AGAIN!
NOD
NOD

Continued in *Zero's Familiar Omnibus 1-3!*

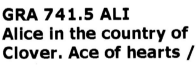